THE
LEGAL SECRETARY'S
GUIDE

THE LEGAL SECRETARY'S GUIDE

THIRD EDITION

Ann Cheyne

First published in Great Britain 1991 by Blackstone Press Limited, Aldine Place,
London W12 8AA. Telephone (020) 8740 2277
www.blackstonepress.com

First edition 1991
Second edition 1996
Reprinted 1997
Third edition 1999

ISBN: 1 85431 897 7

British Library Cataloguing in Publication Data
A CIP catalogue record for this book is available from the British Library

Typeset by Montage Studios Limited, Horsmonden, Kent
Printed by Livesey Limited, Shrewsbury, Shropshire

CONTENTS

PREFACE

This book is intended for those who can already type and who wish to break into the more lucrative and interesting field of legal secretarial work. It is aimed at those who wish to be good legal secretaries and who wish to become involved in their work. Legal secretarial work is not only very interesting, it is fun! The more you are able to put into your job, the more you will get out of it and I have therefore endeavoured to explain not only how to do things, but also why they must be done. However, it is a guide only and not meant to be a legal textbook. It relates only to the law practised in England and Wales.

Unless I produce a series of books of encyclopaedic proportions, I cannot hope to cover everything you will come across. I have therefore covered the most-used basic forms and aspects of law and have, of necessity, generalised matters. To assist you until you become familiar with legal work, I have made many cross-references throughout the book. You will see also that I repeat certain important points. After the introductory chapter, there is a glossary which includes some expressions and terms commonly used in lawyers' offices.

You may find that you will never need to refer to some parts of the book, depending on what aspect of law your firm specialises in. In the smaller firms, your duties will probably be more diverse and you may be working in many different areas of law doing everything from making the tea and ordering stationery to meeting clients and attending court.

At the end of each section there are some questions for you to test yourself on. If you find that you cannot answer them, read the section again until you are happy with your answers. Please also make sure that you read and understand all the example forms and documents shown. In some of the examples of forms and documents you will come across a space that only has an asterisk (*) typed in it. This is there to indicate that you must leave a space for something to be typed in later — often a date.

Throughout the book, where persons are referred to in the masculine this includes persons in the feminine and, similarly, persons referred to in the feminine include the masculine. All names given in the examples are purely fictitious.

This third edition has been generally revised to bring the book up to date with changes in the law which affect a legal secretary's work. In particular, the Civil Litigation chapter has been completely re-written to take into account the changes brought about by the new Civil Procedure Rules. Additionally, I am very pleased to include a new chapter called 'Quick Introduction to the Internet', written mainly by Delia Venables, who is a computer consultant specialising in the legal area.

PREFACE

The law is constantly changing and the text of this book is up to date as at June 1999.

By the time you finish this book you should have sufficient knowledge to enable you to find out for yourself anything which may not be covered. I am sure you will enjoy my book and find it of assistance to you throughout your career as a legal secretary.

Ann Cheyne

ACKNOWLEDGMENTS

The author and publishers would like to acknowledge permission to reproduce the following copyright material:

Reproduced by kind permission of the Solicitors' Law Stationery Society Ltd for educational purposes only: Civil Litigation Forms: N1, N9, N9B, N20, N150, N170, N215, N225, N244, N252, N265, N279, N434, High Court A1 (pre-CPR form), County Court N201 (pre-CPR form), Landlord and Tenant 61; Divorce Forms 4W, 7, 8, 51A, 89 and 100; Legal Aid Form 6; Companies Form 10; Probate Form 4; Conveyancing Forms Con 28B, 29 (short), Conveyancing 29 (1994), LLC1, Agreement (Incorporating the Standard Conditions of Sale (3rd edn)), Seller's Property Information Form Part II, Land Registry Forms 94A, 96, 109, AP1, CS, DL, DS1, FR1, K15, TR1.

Reproduced by kind permission of The Law Society: Conveyancing 29 (1994); Agreement (Incorporating the Standard Conditions of Sale (3rd edition)); Seller's Property Information Form Part II.

Reproduced by kind permission of the Legal Aid Board: Form APP1.

The material in the following forms is subject to Crown copyright: Land Registry forms 94A, 96, 109, AP1, CS, DL, DS1, FR1, K15, TR1; Inland Revenue form L(A) 451. Crown copyright is reproduced with the permission of the Controller of Her Majesty's Stationery Office.

Reproduced by kind permission of the Court Service: Civil Litigation Forms: N1, N9, N9A, N211, N215, N227, N242A and N243.

With thanks to Delia Venables, computer consultant, for her work on Chapter 2 about the Internet.

EXAMPLE DOCUMENTS

TABLE OF FORMS

TABLE OF FORMS

INTRODUCTION

The Lawyer's Office

The term 'lawyer' is used here because, as you will discover when you become a legal secretary, you will encounter various people for whom you may work, and they may not all be solicitors. In solicitors' offices persons who handle cases and earn money for the firm are known as 'fee earners' or 'case handlers'.

The Solicitor

The function of a solicitor is to conduct the legal affairs of his clients, give them legal advice and represent them in various matters, perhaps at court or at a tribunal. He deals direct with his clients who may come into the office to discuss matters.

The conduct of a solicitor is governed by the Law Society and only those admitted to the Roll of Solicitors can practise as solicitors. They are also officers of the Supreme Court of Judicature, i.e., the High Court, the Crown Court and Court of Appeal and, as such, come under the jurisdiction of the court.

Solicitors may practise on their own or with other solicitors as partnerships and, as a partnership, cannot limit their liability to the public, but do insure against claims. However, it is now possible, in certain circumstances, for a firm of solicitors to become a limited company, which some have done. There are also proposals to extend the ways in which solicitors might develop their businesses by forming multidisciplinary partnerships and limited liability partnerships. Partners of a firm may be responsible not only for their own actions and those of their partners, but also for the actions of their employees. Partners have ultimate responsibility for everything the firm does and they share in the profits of the firm. A firm of solicitors may employ other solicitors who are not partners (known as 'assistant solicitors') and may also employ barristers, legal executives, clerks and paralegals.

Some solicitors specialise in one field of law and this mainly applies to those in large practices. There are large firms of solicitors in London and throughout the country that consist of 50 or more partners employing 100 or more solicitors and other fee earners. There are firms even larger than this. Most of these large firms are divided into specialist departments. At the other end of the scale, particularly outside London, in rural areas, there are some very small firms with only one or two solicitors who deal with everything that comes their way. Often, a solicitor in a large city will have country solicitors as his clients, either because of his particular expertise or because the country practitioner requires the city practitioner to deliver papers, or attend court as his agent, within that city.

INTRODUCTION

As well as their ordinary work, some solicitors do voluntary work for a law centre. There are law centres throughout England and Wales offering a free service to people who are unable to see a solicitor privately, perhaps because they cannot afford it. Law centres are supported by public funds and they usually deal with problems that might be associated with underprivileged areas, such as welfare, housing and juvenile crime.

Regulation of solicitors' practices is the responsibility of the Law Society who lay down rules for conduct, ability and the regulation of client monies. If, for example, the solicitor sells a client's house, he must put that client's money into a specified account for client monies. He may, in fact, have different sums for different clients in hand at any one time but he must always maintain accurate records of all monies held. There are various organisations and committees within the Law Society that supervise matters relating to solicitors, e.g., the Office for Supervision of Solicitors is responsible for regulating the profession and investigates complaints about solicitors.

Until fairly recently, solicitors could appear only before county courts and magistrates' courts, and had a limited right of audience in the High Court and Crown Court. However, the Courts and Legal Services Act 1990 gave them a more extensive right of audience. Solicitors in private practice now have further rights of audience, but only if they are eligible to take, or are exempted from, the course and examination leading to the Higher Courts Advocacy Qualification. They are eligible only if they already have significant experience of advocacy in the lower courts.

The Legal Executive

In previous days, solicitors employed clerks to assist with their work. These clerks carried out many different functions and gradually some clerks became very involved in carrying out legal work even though they were without formal legal qualifications. As their numbers grew and they became fairly senior members of staff, they were called managing clerks. In 1892 the Solicitors' Managing Clerks' Association was formed to represent the interests of these clerks. Examinations were introduced and various attempts were made by the Association to have a recognised status for their members.

In 1963 the Institute of Legal Executives was formed. This body governs the examination standards of those who wish to become legal executives. A Fellow of the Institute has had to pass examinations of a high standard and must have completed a certain number of years' employment with a solicitor. Fellows of the Institute can, after certain conditions have been met, set up on their own account as licensed conveyancers, dealing in property transactions. Fellows of the Institute have only a very limited right of audience in the county court and, in certain circumstances, in magistrates' courts, coroner's courts and tribunals.

The Licensed Conveyancer

Licensed conveyancers are persons who are not solicitors but have passed certain examinations and are registered with the Council for Licensed Conveyancers. As the name suggests, they deal with conveyancing matters (see Chapter 12) and can set up in business on their own account to deal with these matters.

The Trainee Solicitor

Training for the solicitors' profession is in two parts — an academic part at university, polytechnic and/or College of Law and an in-service training. This in-service training in a solicitor's office or 'training contract', as it is now called, lasts for two years. In the past, it was known as 'Articles of Clerkship' and instead of being called a 'trainee solicitor', the trainee was known as an 'articled clerk'. During the training contract, the trainee must complete a Professional Skills Course, validated by the Law Society.

During the two-year period the trainee has to undergo further courses as laid down by Law Society guidelines. He will work for fixed periods in different departments of a firm or other legal establishment (a minimum of three specific areas of law).

The Barrister

Barristers (also referred to as 'counsel') do not normally take instructions direct from clients. The practice has developed that barristers have always received instructions only through a solicitor acting for a lay client or from a patent agent, trade mark agent or parliamentary agent. Now, if they are properly indemnified, barristers may take direct instructions on appropriate matters from a wider, specified range of professional people. However, they are restricted in taking direct instructions where intervention would normally be required by a solicitor, e.g., to appear before the county court, High Court or House of Lords. This does not affect their ability to take direct instructions to appear before certain tribunals on behalf of certain professional clients. Most barristers specialise in a particular field of law and their work involves basically giving advice and opinions on matters of law, and advocacy in the courts. They have a right of audience in all the courts of the land.

A large number of barristers have their 'chambers' or offices in London near the Royal Courts of Justice. They generally form a 'set' and share expenses with other barristers. There are also many barristers who have their chambers outside London. Many others work for organisations, such as in the legal department of a company, or in a firm of solicitors.

You have probably heard of Queen's Counsel (QC) but perhaps do not know quite what this is. Barristers of some standing and seniority may apply to the Lord Chancellor to become a QC and the decision is entirely in the hands of the Lord Chancellor. Once a barrister becomes a QC he is entitled to wear a silk gown, and thus the expression 'taking silk' has evolved. When a QC appears in court he usually has with him another barrister who is not a QC and who is known as a 'junior' barrister, the QC being known as the 'leader'.

Conduct of barristers is governed by the Bar Council.

The Barrister's Clerk

As barristers usually share the expenses of running a set of chambers, the administration of the set of chambers is also shared and this includes sharing clerks, secretaries and other staff. Because of this sharing, a secretary may find she is typing work for two opposing sides and must be very careful not to get their work mixed up. There are normally two or three clerks, headed by a senior clerk. They deal with the administrative paperwork of the chambers, keep the barristers' diaries and negotiate fees on their behalf, ensure that barristers new to the chambers receive work, advise solicitors which barristers would be most suitable for a particular matter, and perform many other functions. They also usually have responsibility for secretarial staff employed by their chambers.

Barristers' clerks do not generally have specific formal qualifications for the job, and they are represented by the Institute of Barristers' Clerks.

Lawyers not in Private Practice

There are many solicitors and barristers who are not in private practice. The only real difference is that those not in private practice act for one client only, that being their employer.

Many large organisations employ lawyers, either to advise generally or specifically. Among the number of such organisations are British Telecom, local authorities, banks, insurance companies and the Civil Service.

The Client

The 'product' of a lawyer is advice and representation and the person who buys that product is like any other customer — he expects good quality and value, so lawyers are anxious to serve their customers (their clients) well. An essential part of this is that the client must be able to place absolute trust and confidence in the lawyer. Hence it is all-important that the client's details are *never* discussed outside the firm. In fact, solicitors can be reprimanded by the Law Society for doing so or if their employees do so. This kind of 'discretion' can be as simple as not saying to a telephone caller 'Yes, we act for X'. It is of fundamental importance that you may divulge information only with the *express authority of the client*.

The clients must always be the most important element of the work, no matter how difficult, slow or unresponsive they may be and this must be borne in mind at all times.

Categories of Law

Civil Law

Civil law regulates relations and activities of private citizens and/or organisations between one another. This may involve purchase of property, disputes, performance and non-performance of contracts, Wills, and so on. In fact, matters which generally are of interest only to the parties involved.

In civil law it is generally a claimant who sues or brings an action against a defendant. If the defendant is found to be liable, then judgment may be entered against him and he may be ordered to, for example, pay damages to the claimant.

Criminal Law

Criminal law can be said to consist of offences committed against the State (the Crown) and action against the offender in these cases is normally taken by the Crown (usually through the police in the first instance). Private prosecutions are possible in certain circumstances.

In criminal law a prosecutor prosecutes a defendant for a criminal offence. If the defendant is found guilty, he is convicted and may be punished.

Other Categories

There are other important areas of law which are not strictly either civil or criminal. These include social security, tax and family law.

GLOSSARY

Listed below are some of the words and terms you may encounter. You will find in law that many Latin words are used. Although you may not appreciate it at the moment, this usage is very helpful because it can eliminate the need for long definitions and explanations. If you wish to have a more comprehensive list or more detailed definitions, there are legal dictionaries available. Latin or foreign words which have not been brought into common usage in the English language are usually written in italics.

Ab initio   From the beginning. If something is void *ab initio* it means void from the beginning.

Abjuration   The renunciation by oath of a legal right or privilege.

Absolute   Final, complete, without conditions.

Act of God   An unforeseen event of natural causes, such as a flood or earthquake.

Actus reus   A guilty act.

Ad diem   To the appointed day.

Address for service   The address that a party in a civil action nominates as the address where he may be served with documents relating to the action. It does not need to be that person's own address — it is often the address of a solicitor.

Ad hoc   For a specific purpose.

Ad idem   This indicates that two or more persons are in agreement.

Ad infinitum   Endless or for ever.

Adjourned *sine die*   The adjournment of legal proceedings without fixing a date on which the proceedings will be recommenced.

Administration of estates   The management and distribution of a deceased person's estate.

Ad valorem   According to the value.

Affidavit   A written statement sworn under oath or affirmed before a solicitor or other person who is empowered to administer oaths. An affidavit may be used, in some cases, as evidence in court proceedings.

Alias   An assumed name by which a person is known.

Alibi   A defence given by a person that he was elsewhere at the time an offence was committed.

Alibi Warning/Notice   A warning given to the defendant on a trial on indictment informing him that if he intends to put forward an alibi at the trial as a defence, he should give notice of the alibi to the prosecution within the prescribed time.

Ancillary   Additional and incidental to something.

Annul   To make void or invalid.

Antecedents   A person's past history.

Anton Piller **Order**   Prior to the Civil Procedure Rules (see p. 49), this was an order issued by the High Court whereby the claimant must be permitted to enter the defendant's premises to inspect, copy or remove any documents belonging to the claimant or relating to his property. It is now called a search order.

Apportionment To share or divide benefits or monies which more than one person either has the benefit of or must pay.

Attest To bear witness to or affirm that something is true.

Attestation clause This is a clause at the end of a document, and usually in a specific form, showing that the signature of a party to the document has been witnessed by another person.

Bench The judges or magistrates sitting at a court of law.

Bench warrant An order issued by the court for the immediate arrest of someone.

Beneficiary A person who is to benefit by receiving something under a will, or for whose benefit property is being held on trust.

Bequeath To dispose of personal property under a will.

Bequest Something that is bequeathed.

Bill of lading A document of title to cargo giving details of the consignor and consignee and signed by the captain or agent of a ship or aircraft.

Breach of contract The failure by one party to keep to his part of a contract.

Canon law The ecclesiastical laws governing the Church of England.

Cause list A list of cases which are to be heard in the Supreme Court.

Caveat This means 'let him beware'. A *caveat* is a notice often placed with a registry, such as the Probate Registry (see Chapter 11), which prevents any action being taken on the matter without notice first being given to the person lodging the *caveat*.

Certiorari An order issued by a higher court quashing a decision of an inferior court.

Charterparty An agreement for hire of a ship/aircraft.

Chattel Property other than freehold land (see Chapter 12). There are chattels real which are interests in land and chattels personal, which is other property either tangible or intangible.

Chose in action Something which can be owned but is intangible, such as the goodwill of a business or a copyright.

Chose in possession Personal property.

Circumstantial evidence Evidence which is not actually seen by a witness but strongly suggests that a fact is so because of circumstances.

Codicil A document which alters or adds to a will and which has been executed in the same manner as a will.

Commissioner for Oaths A person who may administer oaths (see also page 121).

Committal The sending of a person to prison for a short period or on a temporary basis. Committal for sentence or for trial is the procedure whereby a magistrates' court sends a person to the Crown Court for sentence or for trial (see also page 206).

Compos mentis Of sound mind.

Conditional fees/contingency fees See page 33.

Conduct money Money paid to a witness to cover his expenses in attending court.

Consideration If someone is making a legal agreement with another, each party must give something to the other. This is known as the 'consideration'. It does not have to be money, it can be action taken, or a promise to pay or act. Consideration cannot be something that has already been done in the past or something that one of the parties to the agreement is already bound to do in any event.

Consolidation of actions Court actions having certain similarities being tried together.

Contributory negligence Where a person has contributed by their own negligence to, for example, an accident which caused them injury.

Conveyance A legal document transferring ownership of freehold property when it is sold. It is used only for unregistered land.

Copyright   The exclusive right to publish, perform, etc. the work of someone.

Coram   In the presence of.

Counsel   A barrister.

Counterpart   A document signed by a party to a deed, quite often a lease, which is identical to the original. Each party keeps the copy signed by the other.

Court of Protection   This administers the property of persons suffering from mental disorders.

Covenant   An agreement in a deed whereby one party is obliged to do something which is for the benefit of the other party.

Cross-examination   This is where a person giving evidence in court is examined by the legal representative of another party.

Damages   Money paid by one party to another by way of compensation.

Debenture   A type of charge or mortgage given by a limited company.

Decree absolute   A court order which shows that a divorce is final.

Decree *nisi*   A court order granted mainly in divorce proceedings. It is granted six weeks before the decree absolute. This gives a period of time in which it may be shown that the divorce should not be granted for some reason (see Chapter 5).

Deed   A document which must be prepared for certain transactions, frequently used in conveyancing matters to transfer property. It must comply with certain formalities. (See also page 271.)

De facto   In fact.

De minimis   A small matter.

Demise   To grant land to another, e.g., by way of a lease.

Demurrage   Payment of damages for time used in excess of laytime for loading/unloading.

Deponent   A person who gives evidence by deposition.

Deposition   Evidence, either verbal or taken down in writing, given under oath.

Derogate   To detract from, e.g., limit a right.

Devise   To give land under a will.

Dictum   An opinion given by a judge during the hearing of a case.

Disbursement   Out of pocket expenses, e.g., for travel, postage, etc.

Distrain   To seize goods in satisfaction of a debt.

Distress Warrant   A written notice held by the court bailiff authorising him to seize or distrain the goods of a debtor.

Domicile   The country where a person has his permanent residence.

Dying declaration   A verbal statement made by someone immediately before his death in the knowledge that he is about to die.

E. & O.E.   This means 'errors and omissions excepted'. In effect, this means that no liability is accepted for minor errors, etc.

Easement   An easement is a right enjoyed by an owner of land over another piece of land which he does not own, e.g., rights of way, rights of light, etc.

Empanel   To form a jury.

Encumbrance   A right over land which is held by someone who does not own the land, e.g., a mortgage.

Equity   Very simply, this is a system of rules which when applied by the courts means that fairness will prevail.

Escrow   A document which will come into effect when a certain condition is met.

Estoppel   A rule which provides that a person is barred from denying something which he has previously asserted or which has been decided on by a court case to which he was a party.

Et seq   Abbreviation for *et sequentes* meaning 'and what follows'.

Executor/executrix   A person appointed by a will to deal with the affairs in the will according to the terms of the will. Also known as a personal representative.

Ex gratia   As a favour, not legally obliged.

Ex parte   An application made either by an interested person who is not a party to an action, or by one party in the absence of the other. Since the Civil Procedure Rules came into effect, this is now referred to as 'without notice' (see page 117).

Expert witness   A person who is an expert in a particular field, such as a surgeon or engineer, who is called to give evidence.

Fee simple   This is a term which refers to freehold property (see Chapter 12).

Fiduciary   A relationship involving trust on one person's behalf where the other is legally obliged to act in his best interests.

Fixed charge   A mortgage over a particular property.

Freezing injunction   See under *Mareva* injunction.

Garnishee order   When one party has been found to owe another money, a court order may be made so that someone who owes the debtor money pays it to the creditor.

General damages   A payment intended to compensate for a wrongful act.

Guardian *ad litem*   Before the Civil Procedure Rules came into effect (see page 49) this was a term applied to a person who defends proceedings in a court action on behalf of another who is unable to do so, such as a child or a person suffering from a mental illness. Such a person is now called a 'litigation friend'.

Habendum   A term referring to a particular type of clause in a deed.

Hereditament   Land and property which passes on the death of an intestate owner to his heir.

Immemorial   See Time immemorial.

In camera   This means in private, to which the public do not have access.

Incorporation   A process whereby something becomes a legal personality, such as a company being started.

Indemnify   To promise to compensate someone against any loss or damage they may incur.

Indenture   This is a type of deed made between parties.

Injunction   A court order which restrains or compels someone to do a particular act.

In loco parentis   Temporarily in place of a parent.

In personam   An action at court against a person.

In rem   An action against a thing, e.g., a ship or other property. A ship may be arrested through this type of action as security for a claim brought against the owner.

In situ   On the original site.

Insolvency   Being unable to pay debts. An insolvent person may become bankrupt. An insolvent company may go into liquidation or be wound up.

Intellectual property   This relates to intangible property, such as an idea or a design.

Inter alia   Among others.

Interim payment   In a court case where liability has already been determined, the party who is liable makes a payment to the other party before the final amount of damages is calculated.

Interlocutory   A proceeding which is issued before the final case is decided at court.

Interpleader   A process settling a dispute of ownership where one independent person is holding property which is claimed by other parties as being theirs.

Interrogatories   Written relevant questions asked of one party to proceedings by another party to those proceedings.

Inter vivos   Among living persons.

Intestacy   This occurs where a person dies without having made a valid will. He is said to have died intestate.

Joint and several   This is an expression used where two or more people may become liable. They are liable both individually and jointly together.

Judgment   The final decision of a court.

Judicial precedent   A previous binding decision of a court.

Jurat   A memorandum at the end of an affidavit which shows details of how the affidavit was sworn, i.e., before whom, when and where.

Knock for knock agreement   An agreement between insurance companies in which each company agrees to pay for the damage to its own insured's vehicles.

Land charges   Rights and interests in land which must be registered with the Land Registry if they are to have any legal effect. In the case of unregistered land these are registered with the Land Charges Registry. (See Chapter 12.)

Laytime   Time allowed in a charterparty to load and unload cargo.

Legacy   A gift of personal property under a will.

Legatee   A person to whom a legacy is left.

Lessor   A person who grants a lease to another. That other person is called the lessee.

Licensing justices   Magistrates who consider whether to grant or renew licences, e.g., for the sale of intoxicating liquor.

Lien   A right to hold property until a debt is paid off.

Limitation of actions   This is a legal rule whereby different types of actions must be brought before the court within a certain time.

Liquidated damages   A fixed sum of damages.

Liquidation   This is a process whereby a company is wound up.

Litigation friend   This is a term given to a person who conducts proceedings in a court action on behalf of someone who is unable to do so themselves, e.g., a child or someone suffering from mental illness. Before the Civil Procedure Rules came into effect (see page 49), a litigation friend was known as either a 'next friend' or *'guardian ad litem'*, depending on the circumstances.

Locus   The place.

Locus in quo   The place where, i.e., where the accident happened or where the crime was committed.

Locus sigilli   The place of the seal. If a document has been sealed by the court and you are sending a copy which does not show the seal you can write on the copy 'L/S' inside a circle and this indicates where the seal is placed on the original document. The date of the seal should also be given under the letters L/S.

Locus standi   A right to take part in court proceedings.

Mandamus   An order from the High Court ordering a public duty to be carried out.

Mareva **injunction**   Prior to the Civil Procedure Rules (see page 49) this was the name given to a court order which freezes the assets of a person or company so that they cannot dispose of them or take them out of the country. This is now called a freezing injunction.

Mens rea   A guilty mind. With the intention of committing a guilty act.

Mesne   This means average or intermediate. In landlord and tenant disputes you may find that a landlord claims '*mesne* profits' rather than rent in cases where a tenant remains on the premises after the tenancy has been terminated.

Messuage   A dwellinghouse and any buildings or land attached to it.

Mitigation   A person whose responsibility or guilt is not disputed may make a plea in mitigation, i.e., a statement which tries to reduce the penalty he must pay. This would normally take the form of a statement showing that he has never done anything like that before and giving reasons as to why this particular offence has occurred.

Mortgage   The use of land or other property as security for a loan. The person lending the money is the mortgagee and the person borrowing the money, and thus mortgaging his property, is the mortgagor.

Muniments   Title deeds and other documents proving ownership of land.

Next friend Before the Civil Procedure Rules came into effect, this was a term applied to a person who brings court proceedings on behalf of one who cannot, such as a child. Such a person is now called a 'litigation friend'.

Nisi This relates to a court order which will become effective at a certain time unless cause is shown within a certain period why it should not become effective.

Nominal damages These are given where someone wins the case but has not actually suffered any damage. A nominal sum is awarded just to show that the case has actually been won.

Non sequitur It does not follow.

Notice to admit A notice by one party to another in civil proceedings that they wish to bring a particular item or document into the evidence without having to prove it.

Notice to quit A notice given by a landlord to a tenant that the tenancy is to end.

Notice to treat This is a notice which must be given to a party when it is desired to exercise powers of compulsory purchase over that party's land.

Official Receiver An officer of the court who is appointed to manage the affairs of a person declared bankrupt or a company that has gone into liquidation.

Official Solicitor An official of the Supreme Court who may, in certain circumstances, be called upon to act in his capacity as a solicitor, e.g., he will quite often act as next friend to a person under a disability.

Office copies Official copies of a document or record that has been issued by a public office, such as the Land Registry or a court. An office copy normally will bear the watermark of the issuing organisation. The term is frequently used when referring to entries on the register held by the Land Registry.

Ombudsman An official who investigates complaints made against the administrative procedures of government departments and other bodies (see also page 164).

Parcels Clauses in deeds describing property. A piece of property is often described as a 'parcel of land'.

Passing off One business trying to pass itself off as another, e.g., using a trademark similar to that of a well-known company in the hope that people will believe they are dealing with the well-known company.

Peppercorn rent A nominal sum stated in a lease for which rent will not actually be collected.

Per se By itself.

Plaintiff Before the Civil Procedure Rules came into effect, the person who brought an action in civil court proceedings was called the plaintiff. Such a person is now known as the claimant.

Power of attorney The giving of authority by one person to another to act on his behalf. It can relate to general matters or a specific matter. Often given if a person is going to be out of the country. It can be revoked at any time. There is also an enduring Power of Attorney which cannot be revoked which has effect when the person giving it is no longer capable of managing their own affairs.

Praecipe A written request to the court asking it to prepare a document. A term not used much nowadays.

Preliminary act In admiralty actions, a document which gives details of a collision between ships.

Prima facie At first sight, on first impression.

Product liability The liability of a manufacturer of goods to the purchaser or consumer of those goods.

Prohibition An order from the High Court directing a lower court or body not to take a particular course of action.

Pro rata In proportion.

GLOSSARY

Provisional damages Awarded in personal injury cases if there is a chance that the claimant may, in the future, severely deteriorate due to the injury which caused the condition from which he is suffering and which is the subject of the claim.

Puisne Junior — in particular, most High Court judges are called puisne judges. It also means younger or later, e.g., a second mortgage is a puisne mortgage.

Quantum Meaning how much, i.e., the amount of damages.

Quarter days 25 March, 24 June, 29 September and 25 December. Often the days on which rent may be due under the terms of a lease.

Rack rent Rent at full market value.

Recitals Clauses at the beginning of a deed and which usually begin with the word 'WHEREAS'.

Recognisance A sum or bond pledged to the court in return for bail being granted.

Reddendum A clause in a lease giving details of the rent.

Res ipsa loquitur The thing speaks for itself — a term used in negligence actions to state that by the very fact that an accident happened, negligence must have been the cause of it.

Search order See under Anton Piller Order.

Security for costs Security deposited with the court in a civil action which guarantees that if that party loses the action there will be money available to pay the costs.

Seisin Occupation of freehold land.

Sine die This means without a day. Used in the adjournment of legal proceedings without fixing a date on which the proceedings will be recommenced.

Special damages A payment which is not intended to compensate for the wrongful act but which is reimbursement for a particular loss such as travel expenses or loss of wages.

Spent conviction A previous conviction which no longer forms part of a person's criminal record because a certain period of time has elapsed since the time of the conviction.

Stakeholder An independent person holding deposit money for the purchase of property who is obliged to hand it over to the vendor on completion.

Statutory declaration A statement solemnly declared before a person empowered to administer oaths.

Stay A postponement, e.g., of proceedings.

Structured settlement A way of paying damages to a claimant by way of instalments for the rest of his life.

Sub judice Under trial. If a matter is *sub judice* it may not be publicly discussed.

Tenure The legally recognised holding of land or of office for a certain period of time or under certain conditions.

Testator/testatrix A person who makes a will.

Testatum A clause in a deed which usually begins 'NOW THIS DEED WITNESSETH' and sets out certain details.

Testimonium A statement at the end of a deed or Will that the parties have signed it.

Time immemorial If something is said to have existed since time immemorial, it is taken to have existed as long as anyone can remember, and in fact is presumed to have existed since 1189.

Tort A wrongful act in civil law.

Tortfeasor A person who commits a tort.

Unliquidated damages Damages claimed where the sum is not known and will be determined by the court or by the parties concerned.

Vendor The seller (of property).

Venue The place at which an event, e.g., a trial, is to take place.

Vicarious liability The liability of one person for the act of another, most often the liability of an employer for acts committed by an employee in the course of employment.

Volenti non fit injuria   Used as a defence in actions claiming damages for personal injury and means that if a person consents to an act, then no injury is done. For example, in a boxing match one of the boxers cannot claim against the other for punching him on the nose!

Notes

GLOSSARY

Notes

14

1 GENERAL PROCEDURES

Letters and Post

Each firm has its own style of setting out letters, e.g., some like typing blocked and some like each paragraph indented. Various firms have their own 'house style' for letters and documents, including using a particular typeface on correspondence and documents.

Always ensure that you have the other person's reference and your own firm's reference on the letter. Usually letters are headed with the name of the matter to which they refer. Most firms keep at least one copy of any letter sent out, but always check in case more are required.

If there are enclosures, ensure you have these clipped to the letter and if you do not, it is a good idea to put a note with the letter when it goes to be signed, to show the fee earner there is an enclosure missing. Also ensure that you use the correct size envelope and enclose stamped addressed envelopes where necessary. Before letters are posted they must always be checked and signed by a responsible person.

Letters going to counsels' chambers are usually addressed to the barrister's clerk, e.g., 'Clerk to Mr D. Smith, 25 Brown Buildings, Temple, London EC4 3DA'.

If something is sent out with a 'with compliments' slip only, ensure that references, etc. are on the slip. Also ensure that a copy is kept for the file or a note made on the file of what exactly has been sent out and when it went. This also applies to forms sent out without a covering letter.

You should check with your own firm as to whether post normally goes out first or second class. Post serving documents (see Chapter 3) in civil proceedings must go out first class. 'Service' of a document is the means by which one party formally serves a document on another party and there are certain rules to be complied with regarding service of certain documents (see Chapter 3). You will probably also find in your office that post must be sent out by a certain time and it is wise to check this.

Incoming post is usually dealt with by post clerks or receptionists. However, in smaller firms you may find that one of your duties is to deal with the post. Normal procedures are that ordinary post is date stamped, sorted out and given to those to whom it is addressed with any loose enclosures being clipped to the appropriate letter. If there is post for someone who is away from the office, it should normally be given to another responsible person. In some firms the time of receipt is also stamped on the letters. If post is delivered by hand, again it should be date stamped and also the time of receipt marked on it.

GENERAL PROCEDURES

Of course, post is not the only form of written communication — most firms have telex and fax machines, and many use electronic mail systems too. However, procedures should be checked with your own firm.

Using Couriers

When post is sent out by hand, most firms have a courier firm they deal with regularly and have their own system for dealing with this. However, it is normal to note on the file in some way details of the despatch including date, time, destination and the courier used. The file reference is normally given to the courier company for use in billing, so that the client can be charged later for the courier fee. It is important also to note these details in case there is a later dispute regarding receipt of the item delivered by the courier.

Postcodes

You may need to find the postcode of an address. The Royal Mail can provide assistance in the following ways:

(a) The Royal Mail Address Help Line (0345 111222) will provide you with up to three postcodes requested in one telephone call, free of charge.

(b) They publish area address books and you can order these by telephoning 0131 550 8999. They will provide a book free of charge if it includes your firm's area.

(c) Details of computer software that provide postcodes can be obtained also by telephoning 0131 550 8999.

(d) The Royal Mail website has a postcode finder and an address finder. The web address is given at the back of this book.

Document Exchange

Most solicitors' firms are members of the Document Exchange (DX). This is a private postal system approved by the Lord Chancellor. Solicitors use the DX between themselves, barristers, some building societies and banks, land registries and certain other bodies and companies. If a firm is on this system, they will have on their notepaper their 'DX' number and exchange. LDE and CDE mean London Document Exchange and City Document Exchange respectively. When sending mail through the DX system you must always ensure that the recipient's company name, DX number and exchange are clearly printed centrally on the front of all items. You can address a letter being sent via the document exchange system as follows:

Messrs. Joe Bloggs & Co.,
DX 123
Weymouth

and put it in your firm's system for handling DX mail. Do not include the recipient's postal address on the envelope and do not put these letters in the ordinary post. The envelope must also show in the top left-hand corner your firm's name, DX number and exchange. This will often be stamped onto the envelope by your firm's post room. A directory of DX numbers is available for firms subscribing to the DX system. This directory gives more detailed information about requirements for using the system. In particular, if you wish to send overseas mail through the system, you will have to refer to the requirements given in the directory.

A service called Address Plus is available to DX members. You will be provided with software to install on to your computer and then when you type in the recipient's postcode, or even their name or DX number, it takes only a few seconds to convert this information into the correct DX address. The DX should be used wherever possible as it is cheaper than ordinary post. DX post should reach its destination the next day and can be used for service of certain documents on other solicitors (see page 64). For general enquiries about the DX system, contact Hays Document Exchange Ltd on 0990 222324.

Taking Messages

You should always note the date and time of any message you take. If someone is giving you long and complicated instructions, write them down carefully and read your note back to them. It is also quite usual to note how long you were engaged in taking the message and whether it was an incoming or outgoing telephone call or whether someone called into the office. Once you have taken a message, ensure it gets to the person it is meant for straight away. If that person is out of the office and you are unsure as to whether the message is important, give it to some other responsible person. Do not leave it on an empty desk waiting for someone to come back the next day. It is preferable to type messages rather than handwrite them, especially if they are long. Always ensure that you know the name of the caller, their telephone number and the matter to which their call relates.

Attendance Notes

A fee earner may ask you to type an attendance note. He would do this after he has seen or had a telephone conversation with a client (or some other person). An attendance note is a record of what was discussed, and includes the length of time taken or 'time engaged'. The note may therefore say that the fee earner was 'attending' Mr Smith (a client or some other person) or that Mr Smith was 'attended by' the fee earner (giving the fee-earner's name or initials) and finishing with the 'time engaged'.

Forms

You will find that there are quite a lot of forms to be used in a lawyer's office. Many forms are bought from specialist stationers, some are printed specially for a law firm and some are generated by authorised software on firms' computers. Where a form would normally have information or guidance notes for the person who will be receiving the form, these notes should not be changed in any way. Printed forms can, in fact, be very helpful because they usually have margin notes or guidance notes which aid in their completion. Some specialist law stationers provide catalogues listing all the forms they print. These catalogues can be quite useful to refer to if you are not sure which form to use. Printed forms should usually be typed or clearly hand-written in black ink.

Precedent forms are also commonly used in lawyers' offices. This is a form or document which has been drafted for use as a guide, e.g., for use as a particular type of agreement. It will have blank spaces in it for names, etc. to be inserted and will give alternative wording that can be used. It is very useful for someone wishing to draft a document because the precedent already contains most of the wording and layout they need.

GENERAL PROCEDURES

There are many more forms in use in a legal office than can be shown here and to save space backsheets (see page 61) are not always illustrated. For the same reason, not every page of all forms given in this book are shown. It is always a good idea if, when you complete a form for the first time at work, you keep a spare copy of it so you will know the next time exactly how it should be done. Keep all such copies together and make up your own 'precedent file'.

Printed forms are constantly updated and those used in this book as examples are as up to date as possible at the time of printing.

Copying Documents

It is also important, in most offices, to keep a note of how much photocopying you do on a file. This is charged either to the client or sometimes to another firm of solicitors if they have requested copies of documents.

When photocopying, check whether there is something to be copied on both sides of the paper as, if you are in a hurry, this can sometimes be missed. If there is something such as a plan or an amendment to a document which is coloured, ensure you colour it correctly after copying it, or have it colour copied. If something on a plan is referred to as being 'hatched in red' or 'red hatching' it means that it is coloured in by using red parallel lines to do so. If it states 'coloured red' then it is coloured in red and if it is 'edged in red' it is simply that. Copies of plans or part of a plan should be marked at the top right-hand corner with an arrow showing the direction of north.

You may see 'T' marks on a plan showing land. These are sometimes used on plans to indicate ownership of a boundary or liability to maintain and repair it, and the marks would be mentioned in any deed relating to the land. If there are any 'T' marks on a plan you are copying, make sure that they are clear on any photocopies.

It may be that a photocopy has to be certified as being a true copy. The following is usually typed on any such document:

We certify this to be a true copy of the original.
. . . .
Joe Bloggs & Co.
[date]

When something has been photocopied always make sure that the copy is legible before sending it out.

Layout of Documents

Most documents and statements are typed on A4 size paper. Although each type of document differs, the layout for those in each section of law is generally the same. You will find in most cases that documents are typed in draft first, i.e., a preliminary first copy which can be amended. Drafts are typed on ordinary A4 paper in double spacing on one side of the paper only. If a document or letter is a draft, it should be marked as such at the top and the pages should be numbered. If the document has a frontsheet or a backsheet (see pages 20 and 61) this should also be marked to show it is a draft.

Other draft documents that you may come across are those which might have been amended by another firm and then passed to your firm for agreement on the amendments. Your firm could then make more amendments to the draft before returning it to the other firm or even pass it on to yet another firm that is involved. This type of draft is often referred to as a travelling draft. When a travelling draft is being amended to go to another firm, different colours should be used for each set of amendments. For instance, the first time amendments are made, these would be written in red, the next person making amendments will usually use green, the next blue or violet and so on. When such an amendment is made, it is normal to note this on the top of the first page of the draft document in the same colour as the amendments, e.g., 'Amended in red [*or whatever colour is used*] by John Smith & Co. on [*whatever date the amendments are made*]'. If the draft is being photocopied, make sure it is colour copied or mark the coloured amendments on the copy by hand.

Example frontsheet

DATED   *   *   2000
_____

ALBERT FRANCIS BROWN

and

ELIZABETH MARY GREEN

_____

AGREEMENT FOR SALE

of freehold property known as
76 Burnt Oak Road, Moreland,
Hertfordshire EN6 8LB

_____

Angel Gabriel & Co.,
2 Milky Way,
Barnet, Herts.
tel: 01638 1234
ref: ABC/123

After a draft document has been approved, it is typed onto good quality paper or 'engrossed'. The engrossment is the final or 'good' copy of a document, which is usually signed by the parties concerned. Some documents are typed onto a very thick paper known as judicature paper or 'judi' for short. In fact, most people now simply refer to all thick 'legal' paper as engrossment paper. Important drafts and engrossments which have been re-typed should be proofread, i.e., read over aloud with someone else checking to see if any errors have been made. See the section on Tips for Proofreading. If there are any mistakes or alterations made to a document, you must point these out to the fee earner because, in most cases, where such an alteration is made, the person signing the document must also initial the alteration. If you find a comment in the body of the document, perhaps in brackets such as '[check this]' and it does not make sense, bring it to the notice of the person you are typing for. It may be he has missed something and will not want that actually typed into the final document. You should also check as to whether the engrossment should have its pages numbered.

Until recently most engrossed documents had to be typed on both sides of the paper, known as 'back to back' or bookwise order so that it read like a book without any missing pages. However, in these days of word processors and laser printers, it is not always possible to have something typed on both sides. In some cases this is acceptable. Sometimes a blank page is left and perhaps scored through, and some firms merely photocopy the document onto two sides of paper. It is best to check individually with your firm what is required and you will learn by experience.

You may find that you have to type something, very unusually, on 'brief paper'. This is very large paper (A3 size) and if you need to do this you will be specifically asked. In the past, it was customary for brief paper to be used for Instructions and Briefs to Counsel (see page 82) but it is hard to imagine anyone using this now. However, it may still be possible for you to come across this.

Full details on typing Instructions and Briefs to Counsel are given on page 79. Papers going to counsel must always be dated. They are bundled up and tied with pink ribbon before being sent, as shown.

GENERAL PROCEDURES

Papers to go to counsel: tying up with pink ribbon

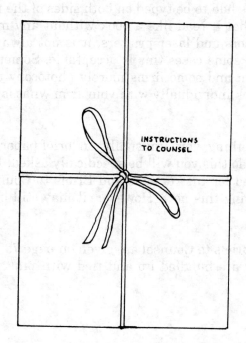

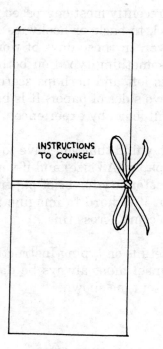

(1) Papers tied up to go to counsel when they are bulky or should not be folded. The name and address of counsel is shown on the outside.

(2) Papers which are not bulky and can be folded in half. (Do not fold photographs.) Again, counsel's name and address are shown on the outside.

You will find that nearly all documents and court forms require a backsheet. This is typed on the right-hand side of the page only and contains details of what the matter is about, the firm's name, address, reference and telephone number and the date, if appropriate (see the example on page 61). A backsheet to a document has the writing facing outwards like a book cover.

Some firms like a frontsheet to be typed for certain agreements. This contains the same type of information as a backsheet but is set out in a different manner (see the example on page 20) and is placed at the beginning of the document.

There are certain rules which must be adhered to with regard to amending court documents and those relating to civil litigation procedures are shown on page 114.

In typing both letters and documents you will sometimes come acrosss a heading, written, for example, as 'Smith –v– Jones' or 'Smith v. Jones'. The 'v' represents the Latin word *versus* which means 'against'. The person who commenced the action comes first. However, in correspondence headings some firms like to put the name of their client first even if he is not the person who commenced the action. They may then write 'Jones ats Smith', 'ats' being an abbreviated form of 'at the suit of' meaning Jones is being sued by Smith.

In text, when setting out a case name, the names of the parties to the case should either be in italics or underlined, but not both. Strictly speaking, the 'v' should not be in italics or underlined (except if this is part of a heading such as at the top of a letter), e.g.:

Smith v. *Jones*; or
Smith v. Jones

Whichever style you use, ensure that you use the same style throughout your text — you must always be consistent. The names of the parties in the title of an action on a document are not set out in this manner but should be as shown below. On the heading of court documents the words stating the role or status of the parties, e.g., claimant or defendant, not their names, should be underlined.

IN THE HIGH COURT OF JUSTICE   HQ 1999 No. 1234
QUEEN'S BENCH DIVISION
ROYAL COURTS OF JUSTICE

BETWEEN:

JOHN GREEN   Claimant

–and–

JOHN JONES   Defendant

You will see here that the words 'Claimant' and 'Defendant' have been underlined but not their names, which are in capital letters.

A further point — legal documents are quite lengthy and paragraphs often have sub-divisions. It is essential that if you are listening to dictation, you are sure of what is being dictated. For example, someone may say 'paragraph 22'. This could mean paragraph 22, or paragraph 20(2), i.e., paragraph 20, sub-paragraph 2. If the person who is dictating does not make this clear then always ask. You can then devise a system between you whereby you will always know exactly what is meant.

There are various requirements for typing different deeds and other documents, and you will need to check with the person you are working for as to what is required in your organisation. Some of these requirements are given below. They apply mainly to conveyancing matters and Wills.

Punctuation

It is not unusual for some legal documents and deeds to have no punctuation in them, especially, for example, in Wills and conveyancing deeds. This is to ensure that there is no ambiguity in the document. If punctuation is not to be used, you would normally include an extra space in the place where you would have typed a full stop or comma:

76 Burnt Oak Road   Moreland   Hertfordshire

Space at the End of a Paragraph

At the end of a paragraph, in some documents, if typing does not reach the end of a line, it is preferred to score through the rest of the line:

everything is left to the Dog's Home---

Dates

Some documents should not be dated with the date you are typing them — they have to be prepared in advance and then dated on a particular day. Therefore, you must leave enough space for the date to be inserted:

this   day of   2000

Dates are sometimes written in words instead of figures, e.g., 10 September 1999 might be written as 'the tenth day of September One thousand nine hundred and ninety-nine'.

Sums of Money

In many conveyancing documents and Wills, when typing sums of money, the amount should be in words first and then in figures in brackets:

Three hundred and fifty pounds (£350).

Some firms prefer the words to be in capital letters.

Capitals

Words in some clauses are typed in spaced capitals, e.g., 'T H I S L E A S E', 'I N W I T N E S S', 'S I G N E D by the said ...'. This is more common in older documents but many lawyers still like to use this layout.

In longer documents, each numbered paragraph often has the first word of each paragraph and certain other key words typed in capitals (see example of Lease on page 318). Some firms also like the paragraph number and the first word of the paragraph to be underlined, e.g.,

1.   <u>THE</u> Lessor hereby demises unto ...

If you are unsure as to what is the correct format or what is preferred in your office, check first before typing the document.

Concluding Words and Attestation Clauses

Some documents, e.g., Wills and most deeds transferring property, are finished at the end in a certain way. At the end of such documents there is often a clause known as the 'testimonium' or 'concluding words'. This clause usually gives the date the document is to take effect but if it does not, then the date is shown at the beginning of the document.

IN WITNESS whereof I have hereunto set my hand this   *   day of   *   2000

or

IN WITNESS whereof I have hereunto set my hand the day and year first before written

This old fashioned wording has now been modernised to a certain extent and the following wording is also acceptable, although you will, no doubt, come across both formats:

IN WITNESS of which I have hereunto set my hand the first date before written

If the document is a deed (see page 271) these words may include the fact that the document is a deed, e.g.:

IN WITNESS of which this deed has been executed on the first date before written

The attestation clause follows these words, and this gives the names of the parties to the document and details of the witnesses. This is set out as follows. The word 'SIGNED' and the names of the parties are often in capital letters.

SIGNED by the said   )
JOHN BLOGGS in the   )
presence of:)

SIGNED by the said   )
JOSEPH SMITH in the   )
presence of:)

If the document is a deed (see page 271) the attestation clause will be set out in the same manner but the wording usually includes the fact that the document is a deed, e.g.:

GENERAL PROCEDURES

Signed as a deed by   )
JOHN BLOGGS in the   )
presence of:)

Signature of witness ....
Name (in BLOCK CAPITALS) ....
Address ....
....

There are different preferences as to whether the attestation clause should be typed in single or double spacing, and which words, if any, will be in capital letters.

The wording of these clauses will differ according to the circumstances, e.g., whether an individual is signing the document or if it is being signed on behalf of a company. The clause is typed only on the left-hand side of the paper in the manner shown above and the person signing will sign on the right-hand side of the page. If possible, these clauses should be on the same page as the last part of the text of the document, i.e., they should not be started on a completely new page. Also, do not split the clause, i.e., do not have 'SIGNED by the said' on the last line of one page and then start the next page 'JOHN BLOGGS in the presence of'. Keep the whole clause together.

When sending documents to people for signature, you should indicate *in pencil* on the document with a 'X' where they should sign. The place where the witness is to sign will usually be indicated on the document (see above) but if this is not done, you can mark *in pencil* where they should sign and indicate *in pencil* that they should also print their name and give their address. Also, documents are often not dated at the same time that they are signed. A document is often signed first and then the solicitor will hold on to it and then date it on the day when the document is to take effect.

Examples of other forms of execution of deeds are:

(a)   where a company is using its seal:

The common seal of JOHN SMITH AND   )
COMPANY LIMITED was affixed in the   )
presence of:)

....
Signature of director

....
Signature of secretary

The seal of the company would be affixed on the right-hand side of the page alongside the wording.

(b)   where a company is not using a seal:

Signed as a deed by JOHN SMITH   )
AND COMPANY LIMITED acting   )   Director
by a director and its secretary   )

                                                      Secretary (or Director)

The signatures might be of a director and secretary or just two directors, depending on the rules of the company. They would normally sign on the right-hand side of the page next to the wording.

There are provisions for the signing of documents by people who cannot read or understand the document, or who are physically unable to sign.

It is best (and in some cases essential) if witnesses are independent, i.e., they are not related to the person whose signature they are witnessing or to any party to the document, neither should they benefit in any way from the document. They should normally actually witness the signature being signed and sign their own signature in the presence of the person whose signature they have witnessed.

You will also often have to indicate to the person receiving the document that they should not date it. Besides telling them not to do this in a letter the document is generally marked *in pencil* where the space has been left for the date with the words 'Do not date'. This also applies to any space left for a date on a backsheet.

Please remember, it is always important to keep a copy of everything on the file. In most cases originals are kept in the file and copies are sent out (except, of course, when the original has to be sent out for signature). Originals are, eventually, formally deposited with, for example, the court, Land Registry, Companies House, etc.

Unwanted copies of documents and letters should be disposed of in a proper manner — some offices have paper shredders or make their own arrangements in this regard.

Tips on Proofreading

You may be required to proofread a document before it is sent out. This means checking it over carefully either by yourself or reading it out loud with someone else who also has a copy. You may even sometimes be asked just to look something over for someone. If you are faced with a proofreading job, it is useful to know some of the pitfalls that are easily overlooked, as it is all too easy just to read the body of the text quickly, rather than looking for other smaller, but often important, errors.

Consistency

One of the first things to look out for is consistency throughout the document. Many organisations have their own 'house style' relating not only to the layout of the document, but also to such matters as whether or not a particular word begins with a capital letter. For example, in their documents, some firms like certain words such as Claimant or Defendant to start with a capital letter; others may like certain phrases to be in bold or italic letters. There is often no correct grammatical reason for this: it is just the house style they have adopted. When you are checking a document, you should ensure that the correct house style is adhered to throughout. Inconsistency is especially likely to occur where parts of a particularly large document are being typed by different people who may all type something in a slightly different style; when the variously typed parts are brought together to make one large document, the inconsistencies will be easily spotted. It does not give a very good impression if the style used is inconsistent throughout a document.

GENERAL PROCEDURES

Make it Easy to Read

When checking a document, try to do so from a paper copy, rather than reading it from a computer screen. If the document has particularly small type for some reason, it is helpful to enlarge it by photocopying it so that it is then easier to read.

Easy Omissions

(a)   Check for mechanical errors, e.g., a margin or tab may not be in the correct place.

(b)   If a few words have been typed in bold or italics, make sure that the typing goes back to normal type where it is supposed to.

(c)   Numbering: ensure that numbers are in the correct order and correspond to the relevant text. Footnotes, endnotes, etc. should be numbered correctly to correspond with what they relate to in the main text.

(d)   Make sure that where brackets or inverted commas have been opened, they are then closed.

(e)   Check that any mathematics are correct and that names, addresses and dates are correct. If you are typing large figures with lots of noughts, make sure you have typed in the right number.

(f)   Ensure there are no large gaps at the bottom of pages and that you do not have headings at the bottom of a page with no text under them.

Confusing Words

(a)   There are many words which sound the same but mean something different, e.g., affect/effect; principal/principle.

(b)   There are some words which we can never quite get the hang of when it comes to spelling them and it is only one letter that makes the difference, e.g., supercede or supersede; defendant or defendent?

If you are proofreading, one of the best things to have at your side is a dictionary. Also, if you are in doubt, you should always ask — it is better to check whether something is correct, than to produce a document which is full of avoidable mistakes.

Checking for Someone Else

If you are checking a document that someone else will be amending, make sure that any alterations you write on to the document are clearly written (perhaps using a red pen) and can be easily seen so that the person who will type them knows straight away to which part of the document your comments refer. You should mark not only the text you wish to be amended, but also indicate in the margin alongside that there is an amendment, for example, by making a tick or a cross in the margin next to the text. If you are writing a comment on the document, rather than an amendment to be typed, it is a good idea to draw a circle around the comment so that the person making the amendment will see that they do not actually have to type the comment. For example, if you want someone to check an address in the document, you might write against the address 'please check'. You would not want them to type that comment, so if you draw a circle around it, they will notice that it is something different from a straightforward amendment.

If amendments you are making are too long to fit in clearly, put them on another sheet of paper (called a 'rider'). Riders are normally numbered according to the page number to which they refer. If there is more than one rider for a page, the riders should also be given a letter, e.g., two different riders to be inserted on page 6 of a document would be called rider 6A and rider 6B, etc. Ensure that reference to the rider is marked on the main text where it is to be inserted. Do not write too close to the edge of a page, because often when pages are photocopied, writing at the edges will not be clear.

Sewing Up Documents

You may need to learn the very simple art of sewing up documents. Some documents have to be sewn up with green tape as shown, rather than stapled. Some may be bound by the use of a binding machine or simply put in ring binders. Again, you should check with your firm for the preferred method for each type of document. Green ribbon or tape is used for sewing up documents but occasionally black ribbon is used for Wills.

Documents are sewn up as follows (also see the diagrams on page 31):

(a) Neatly clip or pin together the sheets of paper to be sewn together (except when it is a Will — see page 260), so that they do not move around. A backsheet will have the writing facing outwards like a cover.

(b) Make holes in the left-hand margin (Figure 1) of the document about half an inch in from the edge. A bodger or awl (a sharp pointed instrument) is normally used for this. Most people make five holes but some like only three. If making only three holes you would leave out the holes marked (1) and (5) in the diagram and put (2) and (4) slightly further apart. The holes should be evenly spaced with hole No. (3) in the middle.

(c) Measure the amount of green ribbon needed — just over two and a half times the length of the document will be sufficient. Cut this from the roll of ribbon and thread the needle. A special large needle is used for this. Do not double the ribbon over too much.

(d) Starting at the front of the document at hole No. (3) in the diagram (the middle one) insert the needle and pull it through to the other side leaving about two and a half inches of green ribbon loose at the front.

(e) The needle and the rest of the ribbon will now be at the back of the document. Take it back round over the left-hand margin and back again through hole No. (3) (Figure 2). Make sure the needle does not go through the green ribbon already in place and keep the ribbon flat on the document. Do not let it twist or tangle. Keep the ribbon tight and flat but not too tight so as to pull the paper.

(f) The needle will again now be at the back of hole No. (3). Take it up along the back of the document to hole No. (2) (Figure 3). Bring it through hole No. (2) out to the front of the document.

(g) Take the needle over the left-hand margin (as at (e) above), back through the back of hole No. (2) and through to the front of hole No. (2).

(h) Take the needle up to hole No. (1), through to the back, around the left-hand margin and back through hole No. (1).

(i) You will now be at the back of the document. Take the ribbon (now at the back of hole No. (1)) down to hole No. (2) and through to the front.

(j) You will now be at the front of hole No. (2). Take the ribbon down the document and through hole No. (3), to the back. You will now have sewn the top part of the document.

(k) Take the ribbon down to hole No. (4) and through this hole to the front of the document. Take it around the left-hand margin over to the back and then again through hole No. (4).

(l) Take the ribbon down to hole No. (5) and through to the back of the hole. Bring the needle over the margin so that it comes to the front of hole No. (5) again. Take the needle through the hole. You will now be at the back of the document. Go up to hole No. (4) and through the hole to the front of the document.

(m) Now take the needle up to the green ribbon which goes across the margin at hole No. (3). Slide the needle under that ribbon and under the ribbon leading from holes (3) to (2).

(n) Cut the ribbon off now so that the last bit is the same length as the original bit of ribbon left at the front of the document. Tie a firm knot or two with the two ends of ribbon.

Your finished document should be like Figure 4 on both sides and tied off at the front. Remember, while sewing, if you keep the ribbon flat while you work, do not allow it to get twisted, and put the needle cleanly through the holes you should not have too much trouble.

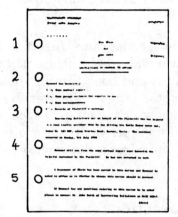

FIG. 1

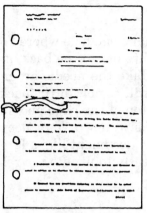

FIG. 2

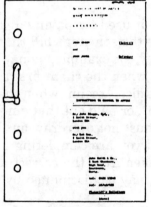

FIG. 3

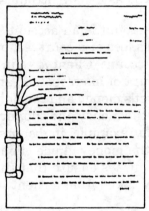

FIG. 4

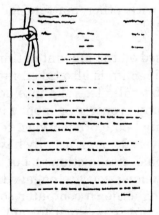

FIG. 5

Sewing Up in One Corner Only

Some documents, such as exhibits to affidavits (see page 127) may be sewn up only in one corner. This method is often preferred for Wills. You will need only about 9 inches of ribbon for this.

Just make one hole where hole No. (1) is shown on the diagrams. Insert the needle from the front through to the back, again leaving about two and a half inches of ribbon loose at the front. Take the needle around the left-hand margin and back through hole No. (1) so that the needle is now at the back of hole No. (1). Then take the needle over the left-hand corner at the top of the page and slide it under the ribbon which is already secure. Then tie off as previously shown. Your document should look like Figure 5. If you are sewing something into the document like a large plan, sew it along the edge in the usual way and then fold it over neatly to fit into the rest of the document.

Financial Transactions

Most firms have forms to be completed requisitioning monies, i.e., for petty cash, cheques, etc. A copy is usually given to the accounts department and a copy kept on the file. Solicitors have two basic main accounts — Office Account and Client Account.

Office Account is an account which has money in it used for paying disbursements such as counsel's fees or a court fee, or when a client pays the solicitor's bill that money is paid into Office Account. Client Account holds clients' money, for example, money paid to the solicitor on account of his costs (i.e., an advance payment) when the client first consults him. This is the client's money and can only be transferred to Office Account when the solicitor has either earned the money and submitted a bill to the client, or paid out that amount on behalf of the client, for example, in disbursements. Solicitors must not overdraw on their Client Account or use the money of one client to fund another. If you are completing a form to requisition money always ensure that the money is being taken from the correct account. If money is wrongly taken from a client's account, a solicitor may be disciplined by the Law Society.

Billing Clients

Some large firms have a costs department to do this. Some employ costs draftsmen who are persons specialising in drafting bills, and deal with other matters for the firm such as drawing bills for assessment of costs (see page 142).

Charges for work carried out by a solicitor are based on the amount of time which he spends on a particular matter. The time of anyone assisting him is also taken into consideration. A solicitor's charges must be fair and reasonable and will also take into account such things as the complexity of the matter and the value of any property or money involved. Everyone concerned with a matter must try to keep a detailed note of meetings, telephone calls and, indeed, time spent on every file. Secretaries, however, do not normally have to note how long they spend typing something except in exceptional circumstances but if you go out, for example, to court, you should make a note of how long you are engaged. In many firms, a formal time recording system is used incorporating either a computer software package or pre-printed time sheets. However, even where there is no such formal system, you must remember the importance of detailed notes.

You may have heard of 'no win-no fee' agreements. In certain cases, solicitors and clients may agree upon this method of charging. There are two types of fees which fall into this category — contingency fees and conditional fees. A contingency fee is one which depends on the final outcome of the case, e.g., the solicitor may charge a percentage of a sum of money the client receives. A conditional fee applies where the solicitor and client agree that if the case is lost, no solicitor's charges will be payable, but if it is won, the solicitor's charges may be increased by up to 100%. If a solicitor enters into an agreement for payment of his fees in this manner, he will often have back-up from insurance cover. However, there are rules and regulations governing these types of fees and it is not possible to apply them in all cases.

In many firms you will find that you will have to type the bill (or VAT invoice). Bills should bear the fee earner's reference and the number of the file or matter, the name of the client and a note of which of his matters or files it refers to. They are usually typed in triplicate — the top copy for the client, a copy for the file and one for the accounts department. Solicitors' bills must be signed by a solicitor before they are sent out, otherwise he may not be able to sue for his money if the bill is not paid.

You will find that some items bear Value Added Tax ('VAT' — current standard rate 17½%). Solicitors' costs and some expenses or disbursements such as counsels' fees bear VAT. Court fees do not bear VAT. If you are not sure, then you must check with the fee earner. Some bills include VAT charged at zero rate which effectively means that no VAT is charged. This usually applies to persons, businesses and lands outside the United Kingdom.

Payment of Fees

Throughout this book mention is made of 'fees' to be paid, for example, when issuing certain court proceedings or making enquiries of a local authority. There are many different types of fees payable and these are often amended by the various bodies imposing them. It is therefore not practical to show fees in this book because they could well be amended at any time.

Most legal offices keep an up-to-date note of any relevant fees and it is always a good idea to keep a copy of these at your desk. Often books which are relevant to a particular matter will list fees, as do some relevant websites. Many legal diaries also have in them some of the commonly used fees. There are also booklets available listing fees.

If you cannot find out how much a particular fee is, you can always telephone the organisation to whom you will be paying the fee and make a note of it for later use.

Files

All firms have their own system of numbering or labelling files and of storing them when they are finished with. Lots of firms refer to a case or file as a 'matter'.

It is essential in all legal offices to keep filing up to date and neat and tidy. Make sure you always keep a copy of everything sent out on the file and in its correct place.

Some solicitors' offices keep separate files for correspondence and documents. Some also divide the filing into different bundles with correspondence between the solicitor and his client in one bundle, and correspondence between the solicitor and the other party on another bundle. In any event, whichever way the filing is done, it must be kept in date order.

Reminder Systems

When working in law, dates are all important. Most documents have to be completed or served at a certain stage during proceedings or within a certain time. Most lawyers therefore keep notes in their diaries for useful time limits and dates of importance and these are usually on the following lines:

(a) The last day on which something has to be done.
(b) A note two or three days before the final date.
(c) A note a week or two before the event, depending on what it is.

You may find that you are frequently asked to make a diary note regarding some event or time limit and mentioned later in various sections are certain time limits that you may wish to make a diary note about. It is this type of diary note which is being referred to. It is best, of course, to check with your fee earner exactly how he wants his diary noted as it is his responsibility to ensure that time limits are adhered to and he should tell you any he wishes to be reminded of.

Some firms also have computerised reminder systems which, of course, makes life a lot easier.

Conflict of Interest

It sometimes happens that a firm is acting for one party to an action and by coincidence the other party comes along and asks the same firm to act for him. It is not normally permissible for solicitors to act for both sides and this is known as a conflict of interest. Most firms have some system of checking whether they already act for a particular party, and new clients are not taken on normally until this has been cleared.

Conflict of interest can also arise in other ways, e.g., the solicitor being consulted may be a shareholder in a company upon which the client is seeking advice and whereby, depending on the advice given, the company could stand to make a substantial sum of money. In those circumstances, the solicitor would have to inform the client of the potential conflict as soon as he became aware of it himself. He would then ask the client to instruct another firm.

The Law Library

A great deal of any lawyer's work involves research in textbooks. English law is a 'common law' system where the decision in one case may affect the reasoning of the court in later cases. Decisions of higher courts bind lower courts and law that is built up through decisions made in cases is referred to as 'case law'. A decision made in one court which will have to be followed by another court is referred to as a 'judicial precedent'. A precedent will only be binding on a lower court where the same principles of law are being considered. If a lawyer wishes to quote or 'cite' such a case, he is citing an 'authority'.

There is also a great deal of law made in Parliament, through Acts of Parliament, statutory instruments and regulations (statute law). When typing the word 'Act' in the context of an Act of Parliament, it should begin with a capital 'A'. Similarly, when referring to a Bill that is introduced into Parliament (the Bill will eventually become an Act if it passes successfully through Parliament), a capital 'B' is used. Acts of Parliament are divided into different sections, which in turn may be divided into sub-sections. When referring to a section, you would normally type, e.g., section 2 of the Data Protection Act 1998, although the house style adopted by your firm may differ slightly. An Act of Parliament will usually have a Schedule, which would be referred to as a Schedule 'to' an Act, e.g., Schedule 3 to the Data Protection Act 1998. The books most commonly used to find out about Acts of Parliament are *Halsbury's Laws of England* and *Halsbury's Statutes*.

Halsbury's Laws is set out in alphabetical order and covers practically everything in law, subject by subject. There is an index in each volume and a general index. The first and last subjects in each volume are listed on the spine cover.

Halsbury's Statutes works in the same way, but contains the text of statutes. There is an alphabetical table of statutes at the beginning of each volume. At the end of each year this book of statutes is produced as a new volume with cross-references to other volumes.

Halsbury's Statutory Instruments contains lists of statutory instruments under subject headings and includes copies of important ones. A statutory instrument is a form of delegated legislation, usually made by a Government minister under powers conferred by an Act of Parliament. A statutory instrument will normally be in the form of Regulations, Rules or Orders and a great number are passed every year. They are numbered throughout each year and are cited by their year and number, e.g., S.I. 1999 No. 123.

Copies of individual Acts of Parliament, statutory instruments, etc. can be obtained from HM Stationery Office (HMSO). Some of these are available on their website (see the section at the end of this book on Useful Web Addresses).

As well as having access to copies of statutes, etc. a solicitor needs to have access to copies of decided cases (law reports) to see what decision was made in a case which may be similar to one he is now dealing with. It is worth noting that cases are not always referred to by the names of the parties involved, e.g., in shipping, you will nearly always find that it is the name of the ship which is referred to, rather than the parties involved.

Certain reference books containing reported cases are widely used by lawyers, e.g., All England Law Reports (All ER), Weekly Law Reports (WLR) and the Law Reports. Law Reports are divided into sub-sections: Appeal Cases (AC), Chancery Division (Ch), Queen's (or King's) Bench Division (QB or KB), Probate Division (P) and Family Division (Fam). A reference to a case in one of these books would be something like '*Smith* v *Brown* [1976] 1 QB 201'. The case of *Smith* v *Brown* would be found in Queen's Bench series, and would be in volume 1 of those marked 1976, and here the report will be on page 201. When quoting a case or 'citing' it, the name of the parties to the case is usually written in italics, e.g., *Smith* v *Brown*, and the reference to that case would be in ordinary type, e.g., [1976] 1 QB 201. There are different law reports covering different aspects of law, for example, 'Tax Cases' or 'Lloyd's Law Reports'. There are many other books which contain case references and details of decided cases but it is not really appropriate to go into further detail here.

You will come across some references to cases which have the year of the case report in square brackets as shown above, and some which have the year of the report inside ordinary round brackets. Square brackets are used when the date is an essential part of the reference and the case cannot be found without knowing the date, e.g., [1976] 1 QB 201. Round brackets are used when the date is not an essential part of the reference, when the case can be found whether or not the date is given (it will usually have a volume number) e.g., (1886) 5 App Cas 316.

There are also books of forms and precedents — *The Encyclopaedia of Forms and Precedents* and *Atkin's Court Forms,* which show how certain documents might be set out. Many books have an annual service system to keep them up to date. When there is a change in the law or procedures, publishers of the relevant books, if they have a service to which the owner of the book has subscribed, will send him new pages to be inserted into the book. These books are in ring binder form and the old page is removed whilst inserting the new one. It is very important that books having this facility are kept up to date and this is often a task given to secretaries.

An increasing number of reference books, e.g., rule books and certain law reports, are available on CD-Rom. There are also legal computer database systems which some lawyers' offices use to gain information. Another source of valuable up-to-date information is the Internet (see Chapter 2).

Going to Court

You may find that at some stage you will be asked to go to court, perhaps with a solicitor or with a barrister. If it is a trial at court, you should check beforehand with the clerk to the barrister attending as to which court you will be in and what time the barrister is to be met. You may find that you will have to do this for the fee earner in any event if he is attending court. It is also important that witnesses, etc. are told where to go and what time to be there. The fee earner will normally tell you who to inform.

If you go to court it will be to assist, e.g., ensuring that witnesses are there and letting them know where to go, perhaps making telephone calls and also to take notes of what is happening. If you do not do shorthand (these days a great deal of legal secretaries are audio secretaries and do not do shorthand) then take a note of as much as you can, jotting down important points. You will find with experience that you know what to note and until then, the person you go to court with will tell you what to note. Some of the important points which may be mentioned at court and which must be noted are those relating to liability (whether one party admits or is found to have responsibility in the case), quantum (amounts of money), any time limits imposed, any adjournments made and any orders made or judgment given.

If you are asked how a judge should be addressed during a court hearing, a High Court judge is called 'My Lord' or 'My Lady', a circuit judge is 'Your Honour', and a District judge is 'Sir' or 'Madam'.

Where a hearing takes place in a courtroom, this is called 'open court' and the judge wears robes and a wig. Hearings other than trials may also take place in the judge's room (this used to be referred to as 'in chambers' and you may still hear the expression). A hearing other than a trial could be, for example, an application to a judge to resolve a particular issue in proceedings relating to a forthcoming trial (see page 116 regarding applications). The judge does not wear robes and wig for a hearing in his room.

The cases to be heard in court on a particular day will usually be listed, and the list will normally be displayed in the court building where it can be easily seen. It will tell you which courtroom the case will be heard in. You will find that if you do attend a court hearing or trial, you may well have to wait for some time before your case comes on. The first hearing of the day will normally start at 10.00 am.

When going to court, ensure you have with you any documents relating to the matter, names of anyone you have to meet, a notepad, pen or pencil and some change for the telephone. Also ensure that you are smartly dressed — remember you are representing your firm when you are out. If you get to court and are not sure about something, you can ask the court usher, if it is appropriate to do so, or telephone back to your office. Always give yourself plenty of time to get where you are going.

It is essential to remember that you must never talk to a witness in the witness box (and this also means if he is out of the witness box but still under oath, e.g., during a break). Similarly, you must never talk to a juror. This is very important and can amount to contempt of court if you do talk to these people. You should also not approach a witness who is to give evidence for the other party in the case.

Always remember that you must never commit your firm to doing or saying anything unless you have been expressly told to do so by a fee earner. If you are not sure about something — ask. It is always best to keep a record of transactions, conversations, etc. If you are taking a message from a client or other solicitor, you should note the time and date of the conversation and what has been said.

Confidentiality

You may find sometimes that the Press will telephone, especially if your firm is dealing with someone famous or a particularly important or newsworthy matter. You should *never*, without a fee earner's permission, give any information whatsoever to the Press or anyone else. Do not even admit that you are acting for a certain client or dealing with a particular matter.

If people from outside the firm have access to your office or you can be overheard on the telephone, you must similarly remember the importance of confidentiality. Do not leave papers lying around on your desk for all to see and be discreet when talking on the telephone. Confidentiality is of the utmost importance. You must *never* discuss anything that you find out at work with anyone outside the office.

Common Sense

There are some further useful points to remember.

If the person you are working for leaves something for you to do and goes out and you think you will not finish it by the time he wanted it, or before you go home — never just leave it — always ask a responsible person what should be done.

If someone calls in to the office or is at the other end of the telephone and the person dealing with the matter is not available, do not make decisions yourself about legal matters. You must always refer them to a responsible person in the firm. You must *never* commit the firm to anything.

The golden rule is — if you are in any doubt about anything — ask.

GENERAL PROCEDURES

Test Yourself on Chapter 1

Test your knowledge by completing this assignment. If you find that you have difficulty with anything, read the chapter again until you are happy with your answers.

1. What is the DX? How would you find another firm's DX number? How would you address an envelope to a DX address?
2. If you cannot contact someone to find out their postcode and the information is not on the file, how might you be able to obtain this information?
3. What is meant by 'engrossing' a document?
4. If something is referred to on a plan as being 'hatched in red', what does this mean? What are 'T' marks on a plan?
5. If you are certifying a document as being a true copy of an original, what should be written on the copy document?
6. What is the 'testimonium' and an 'attestation clause'? If an individual has to sign a deed, give an example of how you would write the clause where he must place his signature.
7. If you are sending Instructions to Counsel, how will these be tied up?
8. Practise sewing up a document.
9. If you are going to court to assist a solicitor or barrister, what sort of things would you take with you?
10. *Ashton* v *Turner* [1980] 3 All ER 870. If you saw this written down, what would it mean to you? If you have access to Law Reports, see if you can find this particular case.
11. Now go through the chapter and if there are any words that are unfamiliar to you or that you cannot spell, write or type them correctly several times until you feel you know them.

2 QUICK INTRODUCTION TO THE INTERNET

The text for this chapter has been written by Delia Venables with some additions by me. Delia Venables is a computer consultant specialising in the legal area. As well as advising firms individually, she writes extensively on the Internet, producing Information Technology articles which she calls *'Nuggets'* on topics like case management, voice recognition, the integrated system, obtaining computer skills, networks, Year 2000 issues and similar topics. She is the author of the book, *Guide to the Internet for Lawyers*, regularly writes and produces the *Internet Newsletter for Lawyers* and has co-written with Nick Holmes *Researching the Legal Web* (Butterworths, 1997) (2nd edition to be published at the end of 1999). She will be pleased to send details of the services and products offered on request. Delia Venables' contact details and Web address are in the address section of this book.

What is the Internet?

The Internet is the totality of all the computers and networks around the world 'talking' to each other. Thus, you can be sitting at a computer in your office and you can be looking at information which has come from New York, Tokyo or Sydney.

The world's telephone system, including satellites, is used as infrastructure for the Internet, supplemented by special 'backbones' added specifically for Internet traffic. However, you do not really need to know about the infrastructure. For around £15 or less a month (assuming you already have a Windows-based computer and modem) you can just use it.

Estimates of how many people are using the Internet around the world vary widely, but 100 million is probably not a bad guess. This figure is doubling every year. At any one time, probably half the users are in the USA, since it was their Government (as part of the Cold War effort) that invented the Internet, their Universities (as part of their scientific research) which developed it further and their entrepreneurs (more recently) who have dominated the field. All the big names, like Microsoft, Netscape, Sun, Oracle, IBM and Novell, are based in the USA.

The Internet is not controlled by any one country or group of companies or government. Even the USA could not shut down the Internet now, since it has rooted itself just about everywhere. Given the fact that information made available in one place can then be viewed around the world, it is not possible for any one country to control the content, although governments do try to do this on occasions.

The Internet has all the characteristics of human life and communication, good and bad. You will find some parts of it useful, some fascinating, some abhorrent and much of it just useless.

QUICK INTRODUCTION TO THE INTERNET

Jargon

The World Wide Web (or Web for short) is the set of information-handling protocols which make it easy to access information on the Internet in a visual way, using Windows and a mouse.

A Web Page is the unit of information which is accessed by the user. Groups of pages together are referred to as a Site. When you look at a page of information on the screen, you see a number of key words underlined in blue. These are called Hyperlinks and clicking on any of these takes you to the document referred to in the link and brings that up on the screen. That page may well be on a quite different computer in a different country or it may be just down the road. You may also notice that where text or graphics link to another document, when you move your mouse pointer over that text or graphic on the screen, the mouse pointer will change to a hand symbol.

Each page has an address called a Uniform Resource Locator (URL). These are the rather ugly sets of characters usually starting in http://www which you now often see in newspaper articles. If you know the Web address of a particular site that you wish to visit, you can simply type the address in the appropriate place on your browser and press the Enter key on your keyboard.

A Web Browser is the software which enables the user to access the information available on the Web. The two big names in this field are Netscape, with its 'Navigator' software, and Microsoft, which offers 'Internet Explorer'. Browsing is what you do when you use a browser to access the Web, follow leads and collect information. The various buttons shown at the top of the page (Back, Forward, Home, Reload, etc.) are options specific to browser software.

It may be worth mentioning the use of a couple of these buttons, especially the Favorites (American spelling!) or Bookmark button. By using this button, you can 'bookmark' pages that you think you may wish to return to frequently, which means that you can go straight to that page in future by just clicking on the name in your Favorites or Bookmark list.

When you view a Web page on your computer, it is in fact downloaded on to the computer. When you next visit that page, your computer remembers that you have been there before and in fact, for the sake of speed, shows you the page it already has. This can cause a problem if the person whose page it is has changed it since you last viewed it. If you use your Refresh or Reload button, your browser will re-visit that Web page and load a fresh copy on to your screen. You can change the settings in your browser so that they will display a fresh page whenever you wish.

Surfing is really the same thing as browsing but the word offers a connotation of fast and vigorous activity with the emphasis on pleasure rather than need.

A Web Server is a computer which hosts a site (or many sites) and is permanently online to the Internet. Special software is needed to manage the site, called Web server software.

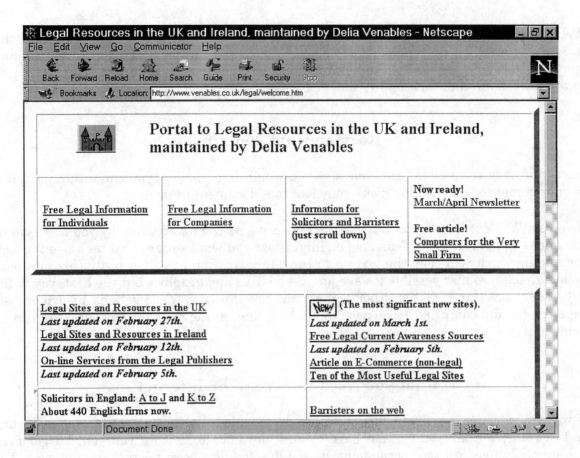

Delia Venables' website

Searching the Internet

If you know the address of the site you want, all well and good — you can just type in the address. If you do not know the address or are just looking for information on a particular subject, then you will have to make a search. There is a Search button on the browser which will take you to a search page. Alternatively, if you know it, you can type in the Web address of a particular search engine. A search engine will search a whole database of Web pages and try to give you results (often far too many) containing the words you searched for. To make a search, type in the appropriate box on the Web page a key word or words and click the Search button or press the Enter key on your keyboard. When you make a search, you will more than likely get a very large number of results. It is best to use as many relevant search terms or phrases that you can and your search can include or exclude certain words. Searches can be made in various ways, perhaps by typing in a string of words enclosed in inverted commas, and/or using the plus and minus signs. The methods of refining a search differs between search engines and the best way to find out about these is to locate the 'help' or 'tips' document for each search engine on its home page. There are many search engines that you can choose from — a few are listed in the Web address section of this book, as are some of the sites that will give you help on searching.

There are also directories on search sites. A directory categorises Web sites by subject matter. You can click on the name of the relevant category on the Web page, which will usually then give you a sub-category, and so on until you find what you are looking for.

Web pages can be very lengthy so it is useful to know that you can use the Find command to locate something on a particular Web page once you are on that page. This command works in the same way as the Find command on word processing software, usually by going to the Edit menu and then on to Find, or by using a shortcut.

Keeping what you Find

Once you have reached information that you would like to keep, you can either save it on to your computer (or a floppy disk), copy it into a document or print it.

To save a Web document, you can use the File, Save As command whereby you can save the document as plain text. You can also highlight text you want to copy and then use the Copy command, which will copy the text on to the clipboard. You can then paste this into other applications. It is also possible to save and copy URLs and graphics but the best way to find out about these and all the other things you can do with Web pages is to explore and experiment. You can print a web page by clicking first on the relevant page and then on the Print button.

What you Need to Access the Internet

If you are working in a firm which has already provided Internet access for its fee earners and secretaries, then you will not have to work out how to do it for yourself. Larger firms will probably need a fixed (permanent) leased line to allow access across the network. This is more complicated to set up than a simple dial-up line and should only be done by the computer supplier or network manager.

However, this section could be of use if you are setting up basic Internet access for your firm, or are doing it for yourself, at home.

To get connected, you need the following:

(a) A good Personal Computer, typically costing, these days, under £1,000.
(b) A printer. Although you do not, strictly speaking, need a printer to use the Internet, it would be perverse to try to do without one. Printers can cost anything from £150 for a cheap ink jet printer, or £300 for a basic laser printer, and on upwards.
(c) A modem is needed to translate the information of the computer, which is digital, to the information of normal phone lines, which is analogue — and then back again at the other end. The current generation of modems run at '56K'. Modems cost around £100, with prices still falling. The same modems, once installed, can be used for any other dial-up service. The modem may come already installed in the PC if you buy it in the initial purchase; this makes the overall configuration smaller and neater, since no extra 'box' is required and no extra power supply. However, external modems work just as well and the costs are the same. External modems are easier to install or return to the supplier, if something goes wrong.
(d) A telephone line. It is best to use a separate phone line rather than attempt to use a switchboard system (unless you have a very recent telephone switchboard system). It is also possible to have an ISDN line (Integrated Services Digital Network), which transfers information around twice as fast as ordinary lines with normal modems, although these are still relatively expensive.

(e)   Basic computer experience is desirable and, in particular, familiarity with Windows 95 or 98. Using the Internet is not for the computer novice. Loading software, using menus and the mouse, running multiple applications, minimising, maximising and switching applications, and similar activities are all standard Windows techniques which are needed during any meaningful Internet access.

(f)   The right software. You need software to dial up and make a connection, browser software and e-mail software. The easiest way to get all this is from your Internet Service Provider.

(g)   An Internet Service Provider. This is a company which has set up one or more large and powerful computers and large banks of modems to make a connection to the Internet 'backbone' and which provide the link to the Internet for the users. Well known names here include Demon, MSN, BTInternet, Pipex Dial, CompuServe and AOL.

E-mail

E-mails are really just small text files stored on a computer somewhere. Here are some e-mail addresses:

delia@venables.co.uk
sales@blackstone.demon.co.uk
aclegalsec@yahoo.com

When you have an e-mail address, you have a little piece of disk storage reserved for you on your Internet Service Provider's computer (ISP) to receive those e-mails addressed to you. To look at your e-mail, you dial up the service and download (transfer) your e-mails to your own computer. You can then disconnect (thereby keeping phone charges to a minimum) and read and consider your e-mails at leisure. If you have e-mail access set up on the firm's network, the e-mails will come direct to the e-mail system on the network and be sent on to your PC without you, as an individual, having to do anything. In particular, you will not have to worry about whether you are 'online' or not — that will be the concern of your system administrator.

You can send an e-mail from your computer wherever you are, as long as you have a computer and modem available; you can be at work or at home or on a train (using a portable computer and mobile phone connection) or in a foreign hotel. Your e-mail address can move around the world with you and the person to whom you are sending it can also be anywhere.

The e-mail goes virtually instantly and is extremely cheap. You can prepare long and complicated documents off line (i.e., without being online) and then make your connection when you are ready. You will only pay for the few seconds that it takes the computer to send your e-mail — generally at a local phone call rate. This is because you will be dialling in to your ISP on a local phone call rate even if you are sending your e-mail to Hong Kong. Used carefully, almost any group of e-mails can be sent (and your own mail collected) within the minimum call charge of around 5p.

You can attach documents to a simple message and the document can then be read into the word processing program of the person who is receiving it. This is a major advantage over fax, to add to the advantages of speed and cheapness.

Many firms, these days, have a policy about e-mails, called an Acceptable E-mail Use Policy. There will be particular sections added to the 'e-mail template' covering the name and address of the firm and confidentiality aspects, and it is important not to send any e-mail, even internally, which contains a potentially libellous message, or anything which could be interpreted as 'harassment' — sexual or otherwise. Bear in mind also that the firm is entitled to look at your e-mails, even if you think they are personal — and it can be sued on the basis of their content.

In Summary — Why the Internet is Important for Lawyers

The Internet is important for the following reasons:

(a)   For communication with clients, official bodies, and others in the legal profession, as already explained.

(b)   It is now possible to keep up to date, on a day-by-day basis, with legal issues, Bills, Acts, statutory instruments, cases in progress and judgments. Many legal publishers now have extensive online versions of their publications and access via the Internet can be a great deal quicker (although not necessarily cheaper) than traditional means.

(c)   It is very useful to be able to access other information sources around the world (not specifically legal), for example, information on medical, scientific, economic, commercial, environmental and social topics.

(d)   Many areas of law now have a substantial Internet component, for example, electronic commerce, international taxation, defamation, communications, entertainment, liability for content, copyright, trademarks and intellectual property. It would be very difficult to give good advice in any of these areas without understanding a bit about the Internet and how it works.

(e)   The Internet can be a medium for attracting new clients, and quite a number of firms are now doing this. Their Internet 'pages' can include articles and publications which attract their chosen audience and which would be much too expensive to distribute by conventional means.

3 CIVIL LITIGATION

If you are working in the civil litigation department, this means that you are dealing with matters which involve two or more parties arguing over something which could end up in a court case. This could be a claim for a debt or for damages, e.g., compensation for personal injury resulting from an accident, defamation (slander or libel), breach of contract, or even simply a dispute with a neighbour. Not all such matters end up in court as the great majority are often settled before court proceedings are even started, or during the proceedings.

Proceedings in the courts are known as actions or matters. Generally, an action is a dispute between parties and a matter is a question to be resolved by the court. In the type of actions described in this chapter, the party commencing the action is known as the claimant and the party against whom the action is brought is known as the defendant. The parties are described differently in some other matters and these are dealt with later in their own sections. Most actions or matters have a time limit within which the proceedings may be commenced. For instance, if a person is injured in an accident he must commence court proceedings within three years of the date of the accident, or an action founded on contract must be brought within six years of the date on which the cause of action arose. There is more to this and there are exceptions to these, but the point is that by statute most actions have a set time limit within which proceedings must be brought. This limitation of actions is governed by the Limitation Act 1980.

Once the client consults a solicitor, the solicitor will normally send a 'letter before action' to the other party involved. This contains details of what his client's grievances are and asks the other party to reply within a certain time with his proposals for settlement. The solicitor must also sort out such matters as arranging legal aid (see Chapter 7) if necessary, collecting evidence, preliminary negotiations with a view to settlement, making enquiries about the other party, etc. and ultimately, if all else fails, he must prepare the matter for trial.

As a result of the new Civil Procedure Rules (CPR) that took effect from April 1999, most civil litigation forms and documents are now the same, whether the court involved is the High Court or the county court. Prior to the introduction of the CPR, there were many differences between High Court and county court forms and procedures. Litigation can last a long time and, therefore, because the CPR are new, you will still come across some of the old style forms and documents — some of these are discussed on page 144.

Since the CPR came into effect, court cases are allocated to 'tracks', generally depending on the value of the claim. The tracks are:

(a)   the small claims track;
(b)   the fast track;
(c)   the multi-track.

Further details of these are given on page 89. However, secretaries will not need to worry about which track a case will be allocated to, as this is a decision that will be made by the fee earner.

Throughout this chapter you will see how a fairly typical claim for money progresses. It is fair to say, however, that many cases will be very different, involving injunctions, orders for performance, winding up of companies, arrests of ships and so on. The areas of law you work in will differ greatly because of the particular area of practice of the firm you work for, e.g., personal injury, commercial, entertainment, marine, etc. Each type of specialist litigation has its own special systems and terms, and you can only learn these with experience. Some specialist procedures are still governed by rules which existed before the CPR.

There are many more forms in use than are shown in this book. Even where forms are illustrated, not every page of every form is always given. However, once you are familiar with those shown, others will be easy to complete. Not all firms use all the printed forms — some use their own precedents and in fact if you find you do not have room on a printed form, it can often all be typed onto a plain sheet of A4 paper, but you should always follow the layout of the form and include all the relevant details, including any guidance notes. However, you should check first with the person you are working for that it is permissible not to use the official form. It is worth noting that on the Court Service website (http://www.courtservice.gov.uk) there are many of the new CPR forms that can be down-loaded to your pc and then completed on your own computer.

Once you have grasped the essentials of an ordinary, straightforward case, you will not go far wrong on other matters.

The Civil Courts

In the structure of the courts, the High Court is a superior court to the county courts. As mentioned on page 34, the English legal system has evolved mainly through case law. This means that inferior courts (county courts, magistrates' courts and certain tribunals) are bound by the decisions made by the High Court. Similarly, the High Court is generally bound by decisions made by the Court of Appeal and the House of Lords. The first time a case is dealt with in court (as opposed to going on to another court by way of appeal) the court is known as the court of first instance.

The High Court

The Royal Courts of Justice are based in the Strand in London, with other branches of the High Court, known as District Registries, being in larger towns throughout England and Wales.

The High Court consists of three divisions:

(a) Chancery Division, which deals with matters such as trusts, contentious (i.e., disputed) probate (see Chapter 11), revenue cases and disputes about ownership of land, and also includes the Companies Court and the Patents Court.

(b)   Family Division which, as its name implies, deals with family matters such as some defended divorce cases, legitimacy, custody and wardship and adoption (see also Chapter 5). All non-contentious (i.e., undisputed) probate is the responsibility of this division.

(c)   The Queen's Bench Division, which is the most used division of the High Court as it deals with all matters which are not specifically allocated to the other divisions (e.g., contract and tort). It also deals with other important matters and includes the Admiralty Court and the Commercial Court.

In certain circumstances, where a division of the High Court sits as an appeal court (see also page 241 regarding judicial review and case stated), it is referred to as a Divisional Court of the High Court.

Apart from the three main divisions of the High Court, there is the Technology and Construction Court (formerly known as the Official Referees' Courts) — the name may be abbreviated to TCC. This is not a formal division of the High Court, but proceedings may be commenced in the TCC or may be transferred to it from the Chancery or Queen's Bench Division. Cases that existed before the change of name will keep their claim numbers (see page 53) which incorporated 'ORB' but new cases will have claim numbers 'TCC'. The judges used to be known as Official Referees but are now known as judges of the Technology and Construction Court. This court deals mainly with matters relating to the construction industry, civil or mechanical engineering, computer related claims and various other specific matters. The TCC is based at St. Dunstan's House, 133–137 Fetter Lane, London EC4V 1BT, which is just around the corner from the Central Office of the Royal Courts of Justice in the Strand.

Appeals against decisions made in the High Court can, of course, be made to the Court of Appeal (see Chapter 9).

High Court judges are appointed from the ranks of barristers and solicitors. They hear cases and may be promoted to the Court of Appeal or even to the House of Lords. They also hear some legal matters which may be heard in private and do not have to be heard in open court. These may be heard in a different room within the court or even in a different building. These rooms are known as the judge's room or chambers. As with everything relating to your work, you must not discuss with anyone outside the firm matters which are dealt with in the judge's room.

In the High Court a judge has a clerk to assist him. There is also present during each trial an officer of the court called an associate. The associate records, among other things, any orders made by the judge during the trial, the judgment given and the time occupied by the trial. There are various other court officers but it is not necessary to describe them all in this book.

For the correct ways of referring to judges in a document, see Chapter 13.

In the Royal Courts of Justice in London, interlocutory matters, i.e., those matters which must be dealt with by the court before and after the final trial (but not the trial itself, which is dealt with by a judge), are normally heard by a Master, except where it is requested that a judge be allocated. In the Family Division these matters are dealt with by a District judge of the Principal Registry of the Family Division, in the Commercial Court, a judge, and in the TCC, a judge. In District Registries these matters are dealt with by District judges. All these people have considerable judicial powers.

CIVIL LITIGATION

The County Court

There are many county courts throughout England and Wales. Each district has its own county court and a District judge is responsible for his own court. Some of the larger courts in urban areas have more than one District judge, while in some of the smaller areas, courts are grouped together, having just one District judge between them. A District judge is appointed by the Lord Chancellor and is a solicitor or barrister of some years standing. Circuit judges, who travel from one court to another within a particular circuit, also hear cases in the county courts.

The District judge is assisted by clerical staff, who deal with issuing proceedings, keeping the court diaries and records and a whole range of administrative work. The clerical staff come under the supervision of the Court Manager. There is then another department consisting of the court bailiffs who are officers of the court who perform various functions, including personal service of documents and enforcing judgments.

Besides hearing civil litigation cases, some county courts, but not all, may deal with certain divorce cases, probate (see Chapter 11), admiralty, bankruptcy and race relations matters. Certain types of proceedings relating to copyright, designs and patents may also be heard in county courts, but an even wider range may be heard in the Patents County Court. Just as a point of interest, in addition to others who have rights of audience at court, registered patent agents have the right to conduct litigation before The Patents County Court. At the Central London County Court, there is also what is known as the Central London County Court Business List. Certain actions may be commenced at that court for inclusion in the business list if they are business actions (there are certain criteria to be fulfilled).

For the correct ways of referring to judges, see Chapter 13.

Sittings, Vacations and Court Office Hours

The High Court has four sittings or terms a year. These are known as the Michaelmas, Hilary, Easter and Trinity sittings. When there is no court term or sitting (except for certain matters) these periods are known as vacations. There is one Long Vacation which lasts from the beginning of August to the end of September. There are shorter vacations — the Christmas, Easter and Whitsun vacations.

Terms and vacations are as follows:

  (a) Michaelmas Term is from 1 October to 21 December and is followed by the Christmas Vacation.

  (b) Hilary Term is from 11 January to the Wednesday before Easter Sunday and is followed by the Easter Vacation.

  (c) Easter Term is from the second Tuesday after Easter Sunday to the Friday before the Spring Holiday and is followed by the Whitsun Vacation.

  (d) Trinity Term is from the second Tuesday after the Spring Holiday to the last Friday in July and is followed by the Long Vacation.

Some business is carried on in the courts during the vacations but the court office hours are shorter than during term time. In county courts, business is as usual during vacation times but the court office may close earlier in the afternoons and there will normally be a reduction in numbers of the judiciary (judges, etc.) in attendance.

The courts are normally not open at weekends or bank holidays. Generally, office hours are 10 am to 4.30 pm for the High Court and 10 am to 4 pm for the county courts.

Civil Procedure Rules

The Civil Procedure Rules (CPR) are a very recent introduction and it is hoped that they will enable the courts to deal with cases in a more time-saving way and with less expense.

Generally, the CPR apply to all proceedings commenced since the Rules came into force on 26 April 1999, except some existing cases and those with their own specialist rules, such as insolvency proceedings, some probate, family proceedings and a few other matters. In most cases, where proceedings had already been started before the CPR came into effect, and where those proceedings have not come before a judge within a year of the CPR coming into effect, the proceedings will be stayed, i.e., they will be halted (there are exceptions to this). If proceedings have been stayed, a party may apply for the stay to be lifted.

Because the CPR are so new, it may be that some of the procedures outlined here will change.

Before Commencing Court Proceedings

When solicitors are first consulted in a potential litigation case, they will try to resolve the matter without having to go to court. The solicitor acting for the aggrieved party will write to the other party or his solicitor, and they will then try to reach an amicable settlement. The aggrieved party's solicitor will write first, setting out what it is that his client is claiming, and will say in the letter that if no satisfactory reply is received within a certain time, he will commence court proceedings. This type of letter is referred to as a 'letter before action'. In some instances, there are now specific guidelines which apply to letters before action and the preliminary information to be exchanged between solicitors. These guidelines are known as pre-action protocols.

Pre-Action Protocols

As at April 1999, there are pre-action protocols relating only to personal injury and clinical negligence claims, but it is envisaged that this will extend to some other types of actions.

A protocol sets out what should be done at what stage by the solicitors before any court proceedings are issued, with the aim of getting the parties involved in the dispute to reach agreement regarding the information they will exchange between themselves, and to do this within set timescales. This should improve communication between the parties, which will hopefully lead to more cases being settled without having to go to court. If a party does not comply with the protocols, they may be penalised by the court.

Personal Injury Protocol

The Personal Injury Protocol is intended to be used mainly in fast track cases (see page 98) where the value is less than £15,000, although it is hoped that its guidelines will be followed in higher value cases.

In a personal injury claim, the protocol suggests that the letter before action (see above) should be in a certain format containing specific information laid down in the protocol and it should normally be sent to the defendant's insurers as well as the defendant. This is because in many claims relating to accidents where personal injury has occurred, it is the insurers who will be dealing with the claim, rather than the defendant. Therefore, it is best if the insurers know of the claim at the outset. The protocol guidelines give a specimen letter of claim showing what information should be included in the letter. There are other matters laid down in the protocol, but it is not appropriate to go into further detail here.

Some terms you will come across regarding damages in personal injury cases are general damages, special damages, provisional damages and structured settlements. General damages means the claim for actual compensation, e.g., for the injuries sustained. Special damages relate to the amount being claimed for particular losses such as repairs to a car, loss of wages, etc. Provisional damages are sought where it is thought that the claimant's medical condition which is due to the accident which is the subject of the claim will not get any worse, but if he does deteriorate, he will be able to apply for further compensation. A structured settlement is a way of paying money to a claimant in settlement of his claim by way of instalments for the rest of his life, such payments often being funded by an annuity from an insurance company.

Settling a Case Without Going to Court

Over the last few years, methods of settling disputes without going to court have been actively encouraged. Since the introduction of the CPR, in many cases, there is provision that the parties must try to settle before issuing court proceedings, court being a last resort. The court will allow time for attempts to be made to settle the case. See Chapter 4 for information on arbitration and mediation.

Commencing Proceedings

High Court proceedings will be issued, i.e., the action will be commenced, in either the Central Office of the Royal Courts of Justice in London or in one of the District Registries of the High Court in England and Wales. Because procedures can vary in the High Court depending on which Division the proceedings are commenced in, where this chapter mentions High Court procedures, it will refer to an ordinary action for a claim for damages in the Queen's Bench Division unless otherwise stated.

The courts which are designated to hear multi-track trials and some fast track trials are known as Civil Trial Centres. There are over 50 civil trial centres throughout the country and a case which has not been started in one of them, or has been started in the Royal Courts of Justice in London, will normally be transferred to a civil trial centre if it is appropriate to do so.

County court proceedings are usually commenced in the court most convenient to the claimant or his solicitors, but may be transferred at a later stage to a court that suits the defendant if the case is defended.

The Civil Procedure Rules are the rules now governing most claims in the High Court and the county court. However, certain procedures will still be governed by old rules, namely the Rules of the Supreme Court for some High Court procedures and the County Court Rules for some county court procedures. The Rules of the Supreme Court are often referred to and abbreviated as 'RSC'. You may come across a reference such as 'RSC O. 14 r.1' which means 'Rules of the Supreme Court, Order 14, rule 1'. County Court Rules are usually abbreviated to 'CCR'. The new Civil Procedure Rules are abbreviated to 'CPR', e.g., 'CPR 20' or 'Part 20 CPR'. The books containing the Rules of the Supreme Court and the County Court Rules are *The Supreme Court Practice* known as the 'White Book', and *The Civil Court Practice* known as the 'Green Book' because of the colour of their covers. Both books contain or have supplements referring to the Civil Procedure Rules, which are also published separately in various formats. The CPR do not apply to matters such as insolvency proceedings, some probate, family proceedings and certain other matters which all have their own rules and regulations. In any event, the rule books will not be something that you, as a secretary, will particularly need to worry about.

If the solicitor has written his letter before action and no satisfactory reply has been received, or it has not been possible to settle the case, then it is time to commence proceedings. The first step is to complete a Claim Form (see below).

Regarding financial value, currently, a claim may be started in the High Court where:

(a) The claimant expects to recover more than £15,000 (or, for a personal injury claim, he must expect to recover more than £50,000 in respect of pain, suffering and loss of amenity).

(b) It is a specific type of claim governed by a statute which states that claims of that type must be commenced in the High Court.

(c) It is a claim which needs to be in a specialist High Court list.

Claims must be started in a county court if the claimant expects to receive:

(a) not more than £15,000 or;

(b) less than £50,000 in respect of pain, suffering and loss of amenity in a personal injury claim.

Where a claim has no financial value, it will be allocated to the track (see page 89) which the court considers to be the most appropriate for it, taking into consideration such factors as the nature of the remedy sought and the complexity of the case.

We are going to deal here mainly with an action for a claim for money. For example purposes, most of the completed forms and documents shown here are for a claim in the county court but High Court forms and documents are in the same format.

Payment of Court Fees

Fees are payable to the court at various stages of the proceedings when certain documents are to be issued by the court. Your office will undoubtedly have a list of these fees but if you are not sure, you can telephone the relevant court to confirm whether a fee is payable and how much it is. There are different fees for the High Court and the county court and for different types of proceedings, such as family proceedings.

Cheques for court fees should normally be made payable to HM Paymaster General. When posting a document to the court to be issued, you should always include a stamped, addressed envelope so that the court can return the relevant papers.

The Claim Form and Particulars of Claim

To issue court proceedings for a claim for money or damages, a Claim Form (Form N1) must be completed.

The Claim Form should be typed, but if it is being completed by hand, it should be in black ink and written in capital letters. With the claim form there are notes for the defendant on replying to the claim form. Once the Claim Form is complete, you should photocopy it, together with the notes for the defendant. The number of copies required are one copy for your firm's file, one copy for the court and one copy for each defendant. The forms will then be sent or taken to the court office, together with the appropriate fee. One Claim Form may be used to start more than one claim, if it is appropriate to do so. Correspondence to a court should be addressed to the Court Manager.

The Claim Form must have with it (either typed on to the Form itself or attached to it) concise details of the claim. These details are called the Particulars of Claim (see below).

As a general guide, the Claim Form will normally expire after four months, i.e., it must be served (see page 63) within four months of being issued by the court, or six months where it is to be served outside England and Wales — otherwise it may become invalid. There are exceptions to this and extensions of time may be applied for but it is not necessary to go into detail here.

The Claim Form must contain the following information:

The Heading

The heading of the Claim Form must indicate the name of the court and the division of the court (see page 46) in which the claim is to be started. This information will be inserted into the box at the top right-hand corner of the front page of the claim form and will be in one of the following formats:

(a) For a claim in a county court:

'In the *Southtown* County Court'. (You must insert the correct name of the court.)

(b) For a claim in a District registry of the High Court:

'In the High Court of Justice *Queen's Bench* Division' (inserting the correct division of the court) and directly beneath that:

'*Southtown* District Registry' (inserting the name of the District Registry)

(c) For a claim in the Royal Courts of Justice in London:

'In the High Court of Justice *Queen's Bench* Division' (insert the correct division of the court) and directly beneath that:

'Royal Courts of Justice'.

See also the example forms and documents in this book for layout.

Where an action has been included in a specialist court, e.g., Central London County Court Business List, Patents Court, etc., all documents relating to the action must be marked at the top (right-hand corner on court forms) beneath the name of the court, with words indicating the specialist court, e.g., 'Business List'; 'Patents Court'. Where a claim relates to Chancery business and it is issued in the High Court, it should be marked in the appropriate place, as shown above, 'Chancery Division' and if it is issued in the county court, it should be marked 'Chancery Business'.

The court will allocate a number to the claim. Under the old system, claim numbers in the High Court were allocated according to the year of issue and the first letter in the claimant's (then called the plaintiff) surname. It is anticipated that a new system of numbering will come into effect at the same time as the Civil Procedure Rules. The claim number will be something like HQ 1999 No.1234. The 'H' is for High Court, and the 'Q' shows that it has been issued in the Queen's Bench Division. A claim issued in the Chancery Division will commence 'HC'. This will be followed by the year of issue and then the actual number allocated by the court. Numbering in the county court may vary according to which county court issues the claim.

All this information, i.e., the court or division where the action is proceeding; the claim number (once a number has been allocated by the court); the name of each party and the status of each party, e.g., claimant or defendant, is known as the 'title' of the action and all court documents should include this information at the top of the document.

There are special procedures for some other types of claim, but these need not be dealt with here.

Claimant and Defendant Details

Where a party to an action is an individual, all known forenames and surname must be included, stating whether Mr, Mrs, Miss, Ms, or any other title, such as Dr. The residential address must be given, including postcode and telephone number (if known) in England and Wales.

Other information describing parties to the proceedings must be included on the Claim Form, where appropriate. When completing the form with any of the details given below, you should type the relevant party's name where italics are shown here, but do not type in italics.

A party may be trading under a name that is not his own, e.g., he may be the proprietor of a small business. Add after his name the words 'trading as', e.g., '*Mr Bill Green* trading as *Green's Grocers*'. The address for service (see page 63) should be either the residential address of the party or the principal or last known place of business.

Where one of the parties is a firm, the name of the firm should be stated, followed by the words 'a firm', e.g., '*Smith and Associates* — a firm'. The address for service should be either the residential address of a partner in the firm or the principal or last known place of business.

Where a party is suing or being sued in the name of a club or other unincorporated association use: '*Joe Bloggs* suing [or sued on behalf of] *The Local Tennis Club*'.

Where a party is a company registered in England and Wales (see Chapter 10 on companies and businesses), the name of the company must be given, e.g., 'ABC Limited'. The address must be either the company's registered office (see page 247) or any place of business that has a real, or the most, connection with the claim, e.g., the branch or office of the company that the claimant has been dealing with.

A corporation (other than a company): the name of the corporation must be stated, e.g., 'The Utopia Urban District Council'. The address must be either the corporation's principal office or any other place where the corporation carries on activities and which has a real connection with the claim.

Where the party is an overseas company, give the name of the company. The address will be either that which is registered under the Companies Act 1985 or the address of the place of business having a real, or the most, connection with the claim.

Where a party is suing or being sued in a representative capacity, use the form of words: 'Mrs Jane Bloggs as the representative of Mr Joe Bloggs (deceased)'.

If either party is under 18 years of age (unless exception is granted by the court) or is a patient within the meaning of the Mental Health Act 1983, they must conduct proceedings through an adult, who is called a litigation friend, and this must be shown on the Claim Form. The person who is the litigation friend used to be called 'next friend' or 'guardian ad litem' and you may still come across these terms. The description for such a party in this instance could be:

Under 18 years old: after the child's name type, e.g., 'a child by Mr John Smith his litigation friend'.

A child conducting his own proceedings: type after his name 'a child'.

A patient within the meaning of the Mental Health Act as mentioned above. Type after his name, e.g., 'by Mr John Smith his litigation friend'.

You will not need to worry about most of these details, such as whether a company is registered overseas or in England and Wales — the fee earner will know this. However, it will be useful for you to know how the names and details should be set out. Full details are also set out in the court form, Notes for Claimant (Form N1A).

Where there is more than one claimant or more than one defendant, they should be numbered in the title, e.g:

1. John Bloggs
2. Peter Brown
3. Annabel Green

Claimants [Defendants]
(whichever is applicable)

Brief Details of Claim

This must contain a concise statement setting out the nature of the claim and state the remedy sought, e.g., payment of money; damages for personal injury; return of goods. The full details of the claim should be set out in a Particulars of Claim (see below), which is a statement of case (see page 79).

Value

This will assist the court in deciding which track (see page 89) the case will be allocated to.

If the claim is for a known, specified amount of money, type that sum in the box next to 'Amount claimed' in the box at the bottom right-hand corner of the front page.

If the value of the claim is not known, type in the space under 'Value':

'The Claimant expects to recover' (followed by whichever of the following applies to the claim):

'not more than £5,000', or
'more than £5,000 but not more than £15,000', or
'more than £15,000' (or 'more than £50,000' if it is a claim for personal injuries to be issued in the High Court).

If the claim includes a personal injury claim for 'not more than £5,000', the form must also state here:

'The Claimant's claim includes a claim for personal injuries and the amount he expects to recover as damages for pain, suffering and loss of amenity is'. These words are then followed by either:

'not more than £1,000'; or
'more than £1,000'.

If the claim is for housing disrepair relating to residential premises, similar details concerning the value of the claim must be inserted. The wording can be found on the court form Notes for Claimant on completing a claim form (N1A).

If it is not possible to put a value on the claim, this must be stated on the Claim Form by typing in 'The Claimant cannot say how much he expects to recover'.

Proceedings may be issued in the High Court only if they fulfil specified criteria. If the claim is one that may be started in the High Court, this must be stated on the Claim Form, e.g., 'The Claimant wishes to issue his claim in the High Court because he expects to recover more than £15,000', or whichever reason applies for issuing in the High Court.

Defendant's Name and Address

The box at the bottom left-hand corner of the first page of the Claim Form must be completed, giving the full name and address of the defendant who is receiving the Claim Form. If there is more than one defendant, a separate Claim Form should be completed for each individual defendant, giving that defendant's details in the box on the relevant Claim Form. If it is anticipated that the proceedings will be served on the defendant outside England and Wales, it may be necessary to obtain the court's permission, but this is something that the fee earner will deal with.

Until you become used to dealing with court forms, read any printed notes for guidance that are with the form. These will nearly always tell you where something has to be inserted or deleted on the form and will usually tell you exactly the sort of information needed to complete it.

CIVIL LITIGATION

Claim Form

SPECIMEN

In the SOUTHTOWN COUNTY COURT

Claim No.

SEAL

Claimant

Mr Paul Xavier
4 Millionaire's Row
Southtown
Herts
ES3 4PL

Tel: 0181 333 9999

Defendant(s)

Mr John Jones
1 Breakneck Drive
Southtown
Herts
EN7 6LP

Tel: 0181 222 8888

Brief details of claim

Payment of money as reimbursement for damage caused to the
Claimant's Rolls Royce motor car, registration No. 123 ABC,
arising out of a road traffic accident on 5th July 1999 which
was due to the negligent driving of the defendant.

Value

[Note: see the main text of this book for more information
on when to include something under this heading]

Defendant's name and address

Mr John Jones
1 Breakneck Drive
Southtown
Herts
EN7 6LP

	£
Amount claimed	7000.00
Court fee	*
Solicitor's costs	*
Total amount	*
Issue date	

The court office at

is open between 10 am and 4 pm (4.30 pm in High Court) Monday to Friday. When corresponding with the court, please address forms or letters to the Court Manager and quote the case number.

N1 Claim Form (CPR Part 7) (4.99)

Oyez 7 Spa Road, London SE16 3QQ

4.99 F35986

N1 (and Notes N1A, N1C, N1(FD))

5093000
★ ★ ★ ★ ★

SPECIMEN

Claim No.	

Particulars of Claim (attached) (to follow)

Statement of Truth

* (I believe) (The Claimant believes) that the facts stated in these particulars of claim are true.

* I am duly authorised by the Claimant to sign this statement.

Full name   Paul Xavier

Name of Claimant's solicitor's firm   John Smith & Co.

Signed   position or office held

* (Claimant)/(Litigation friend)/(Claimant's solicitor)   (if signing on behalf of firm or company)

*delete as appropriate

John Smith & Co.,   (ref: XAV/789)
2 Bank Chambers,
High Road,
Southtown, Herts
EN5 6AX

DX 1234 Southtown
Claimant's solicitors.

Claimant's or Claimant's solicitor's address to which documents or payments should be sent if different from overleaf including (if appropriate) details of DX, fax or e-mail.

Particulars of Claim

This sets out full details of the claim. If there is room, details should be typed on to the Claim Form but if not, they may be typed on to separate sheets of paper and attached to the Claim Form. Where the Particulars of Claim are on a separate sheet of paper, they should include details of the court where the proceedings are being issued; the claim number, where this has been allocated; the title, i.e., the names of the parties, stating who they are, i.e., claimant or defendant; and should have a heading stating 'Particulars of Claim'. The address for service (usually the solicitor's office) must also be included, as well as a Statement of Truth (see below).

Where a party to the proceedings has a lengthy name, it must appear correctly in the title, but any further reference to that person in that document may be abbreviated, such as by initials or an identified shortened name.

Where the full Particulars of Claim are not served with the Claim Form, the Claim Form must contain a statement that Particulars of Claim will follow.

The fee earner will deal with the details in the Particulars of Claim which must include a concise statement of the facts relied upon; details of any interest that is being claimed; and any other matters that may be relevant. If the claim is a personal injury claim, the Particulars must also contain the claimant's date of birth and brief details of his injuries. In this case, a schedule of any past and future expenses and losses that are being claimed must be attached to the Particulars of Claim. If the claimant is relying on medical evidence to support his claim, he must provide his medical report with the Particulars of Claim. If the claimant is seeking provisional damages (see page 12) this must be stated in the Particulars together with certain other information. Similarly, a copy of any document that the claimant considers to be necessary to his claim may be attached to or served with the Particulars of Claim.

The Particulars will usually state at the end exactly what it is that the claimant claims, e.g., damages and interest. If the Particulars have been settled by counsel, i.e., drawn up by a barrister, the document must give his name at the end. The document will also show the date it has been served, the name of the solicitors serving it and stating for which party they act. In personal injury claims, as mentioned above, a copy of any medical report to be relied on, together with a note of special damages claimed, should be included. 'Special damages' is the amount being claimed for particular losses such as repairs to a car, loss of wages, etc. The term 'general damages' refers to the claim for damages for compensation, e.g., compensation for injuries.

Where the claim is for a sum of money expressed in a foreign currency, it must expressly state on the form:

(a) that the claim is for payment in a specified foreign currency;
(b) why it is for payment in that currency;
(c) the sterling equivalent of the sum at the date of the claim; and
(d) the source of the exchange rate relied on to calculate the sterling equivalent.

There are various other matters to be included in certain types of claim and the fee earner will provide you with the information whenever this is necessary.

The Particulars of Claim may be served separately on the defendant up to 14 days after the date on which the Claim Form is served on him. If this is done, the forms for the defendant to reply to the claim (see below) must be served with the Particulars of Claim (rather than with a Claim Form on its own not accompanied by the Particulars of Claim). When the Particulars of Claim document has been served separately, it must be filed with the court within seven days of it being served on the defendant, together with a Certificate of Service (see page 67).

When a Particulars of Claim is served, whether or not it is included in the Claim Form, it must be accompanied by the Response Pack (Form N9) (see page 69). This includes:

(a) a form for defending the claim and/or making a counterclaim (see page 85),
(b) a form for admitting the claim (see page 70),
(c) a form for acknowledging service (see page 71), and
(d) notes for the defendant on replying to the Claim Form.

There are some exceptions to this under Part 8 CPR, when only the Acknowledgment of Service has to be served with the Claim Form, but this procedure will not be dealt with here.

The Particulars of Claim is a statement of case (see page 79). As with the Claim Form, the appropriate number of copies must be made. There will always be at least three copies required: one for the file, one for the court; and one for each defendant. Remember, if the Particulars of Claim are being served separately, the defendant's notes for replying to the Claim Form should accompany them and copies should be made accordingly. The copies should always be good typed copies or photocopies, not carbon copies. Whether or not the Particulars are included in the Claim Form, they must be verified by a Statement of Truth.

An example Particulars of Claim is shown below. Most statements of case will follow a similar format. However, under the new Civil Procedure Rules, this may well be simplified and, therefore, could change.

The spaces at the bottom of the document where the date should be are often left blank at the time of typing and will be dated the day it is actually served on or posted to the other party. The date can be either typed or handwritten and must be inserted before the document is served. The original is served and a dated copy must be kept in the file. A backsheet will normally also be typed as shown on the example Particulars of Claim.

CIVIL LITIGATION

Example Particulars of Claim (as a separate document from the Claim Form)

IN THE SOUTHTOWN COUNTY COURT   Claim No. 00.12345

BETWEEN:

PAUL XAVIER   Claimant

and

JOHN JONES   Defendant

PARTICULARS OF CLAIM

1. The Claimant was the owner and driver of a Rolls Royce motor car, registration number 123 ABC.

2. On 5th July 1999 the Claimant was driving his said motor car along Mulberry Close, New Barnet, Hertfordshire.

3. The Defendant failed to keep any or any proper lookout and drove his car across the road and into the Claimant's car, causing £7,000 worth of damage to the car as shown in the attached schedule.

The Claimant therefore claims:

(i)   damages in the sum of £7,000;

(ii)   interest thereon pursuant to section 69 of the County Courts Act 1984

ROB ROY

Statement of Truth

The Claimant believes that the facts stated in these Particulars of Claim are true. I am duly authorised by the Claimant to sign this statement.

Full name: John Smith

Name of Claimant's solicitor's firm: John Smith & Co.

Signed

(Claimant's solicitor)

DATED this   *   day of   *   2000 by John Smith and Co., of 2 Bank Chambers, High Road, Southtown, Herts. EN5 6AX. Solicitors for the Claimant.

Example backsheet for Particulars of Claim (or other statement of case) where required

<u>Claim No. 00.12345</u>

IN THE <u>SOUTHTOWN</u>
<u>COUNTY COURT</u>

BETWEEN:

PAUL XAVIER   Claimant

and

JOHN JONES   <u>Defendant</u>

<u>PARTICULARS OF CLAIM</u>

John Smith & Co.,
2 Bank Chambers,
High Road,
Southtown,
Herts. EN5 6AX

tel: 01438 12345

ref: AB/cd/123

Solicitors for the Claimant

Statement of Truth

A Statement of Truth must be included in the Claim Form as well as certain other documents. It is, in fact, already printed at the end of the Claim Form. It must be included in the Particulars of Claim if they are served separately from the Claim Form. The format for a Statement of Truth in a Claim Form and/or Particulars of Claim is shown below but this will obviously be changed accordingly for other documents.

[I believe] [*or the party on whose behalf the document is being signed believes*] that the facts stated in this [Claim Form] [*or whatever document the statement of truth relates to*] are true.

A Statement of Truth may sometimes be in a separate document, which must contain the heading and title of the action and the claim number, and must identify the document being verified, e.g., '... the facts stated in the Claim Form issued on [*date*] are true'; or '... the facts stated in the [*Particulars of Claim*] served on the [*Defendant*] on [*date*] are true'.

A Statement of Truth must be signed by either the relevant party, his litigation friend or the solicitor acting for that party on his authority. If the party is a company or other corporation or a partnership, there are formalities regarding who should sign on behalf of the company or other organisation. A legal representative signing on behalf of a party must state that he is authorised by that party to sign the statement and must also state the capacity in which he signs and the name of his firm, if appropriate. As a secretary, you should not sign the Statement of Truth yourself.

Address for Documents

The box at the bottom left-hand corner of the second page should be completed to show the address of the claimant or the claimant's solicitor to which documents and/or payments should be sent, if it is different from the address already given under the heading 'Claimant'. If your firm is prepared to accept service (see page 63) by DX (see page 16), fax or e-mail, the relevant details should be included here.

Getting the Claim Form Issued by the Court

Once the Claim Form has been completed and signed either by the claimant or by the solicitor acting for him, it should be taken or sent, together with the Particulars of Claim, if appropriate, to the court so that it can be issued by the court. It must be accompanied by the correct number of copies (one for your file, one for the court and one for each defendant), plus a stamped and addressed envelope if sent by post. The appropriate number of copies of the Notes for the Defendant (N1C) must also go with the Claim Form. The fee for issuing the proceedings will also have to be paid to the court. Fees to issue a claim are determined according to the value of the claim and you can obtain this information from the court. In reality, your office will no doubt have an up-to-date list of court fees showing when fees are payable and how much they are. Cheques should be made payable to HM Paymaster General (HMPG). Any other documents, such as a legal aid certificate, which need to be filed with the court at this time should also accompany the Claim Form. Correspondence to the court should be addressed to the Court Manager.

Many firms have an outdoor clerk, who deals with, amongst other things, taking documents to court. If your firm has such a person, the signed Claim Form and any other relevant documents, together with the correct number of copies and the fee, should be passed to him.

Once the court is satisfied that the Claim Form and any other documents are in order, they will complete their own paperwork to issue the proceedings. They will stamp all the documents to show that they have been issued by the court and give the claim a Claim Number. The court may serve the Claim Form or the claimant's solicitors can request to serve it. If the claimant's solicitors are going to serve it, the court will return to them a sealed copy of the Claim Form for service. The court 'seals' a document by imprinting on it an official stamp which shows that the court has issued that document.

When the court has allocated a claim number, this should always be included on any documents relevant to the proceedings, as well as the court details and the names and status of the parties (see also page 53 regarding title of the action).

Issuing Proceedings by Fax in the Admiralty and Commercial Court Registry

Proceedings may be issued by fax out of the Admiralty and Commercial Court Registry in London when the court office is closed to the public. This facility is for this court only and is not for any other type of matter or application. The form must be transmitted to the court office on fax number 0171-936 6667 and must bear a specially worded endorsement. This number is not for general correspondence. The issuing solicitor must sign a certificate confirming date and time of transmission. The transmitted document and the signed certificate must then be taken to the court office, when it is next open to the public, to be sealed by the court or, if it has already been served, a copy endorsed to the effect that it is a true copy must be taken to the court, with the appropriate number of copies, together with the signed certificate and the transmission report. The fee for issuing the proceedings must also be paid at this time. As soon as possible after the form has been sealed by the court, any person with an unsealed copy must be informed of the claim number. Proceedings requiring permission of the court to be issued cannot be issued in this way.

Issuing in Bulk

Where county court claims are to be issued in bulk, e.g., in their hundreds or thousands, usually by organisations such as debt collection agencies or mail order companies, this would put a great strain on the local court. Therefore, provided certain criteria are fulfilled, application may be made to commence proceedings through the Claim Production Centre in Northampton (the full address is given in the address section at the back of this book). The Claim Production Centre will prepare and issue the claim forms from information in a particular format which has been provided by the organisation wishing to issue the claims. The documents are sent direct to the defendants by the Centre on behalf of the court in whose name the claims are issued, i.e., the court where the claimant wishes the proceedings to be commenced.

It is also possible to have further steps in the proceedings, e.g., entering judgment (see page 72), dealt with at the Claim Production Centre if the Claim Forms are issued in the name of the Northampton County Court.

Service

'Service' is a term used to express the fact that a document has been delivered to another party in accordance with any specific rules that must be adhered to, e.g., the rules of the court. Generally, a document may be served only within the court's jurisdiction, i.e., within England and Wales, but permission may be granted by the court for service outside the jurisdiction.

Once the Claim Form and any other relevant documents have been issued by the court, the documents must be served on the defendant. There are several ways in which service may be effected and this may sometimes depend on exactly which document is going to be served.

Postal

Postal service should be by first class post. Registered post or recorded delivery should not be used for normal postal service of documents in civil litigation matters. Service on a limited company must be on its registered office (see Chapter 10). Service on an individual is to his last or usual known address. More information on permitted addresses for service is given on Form N1A, Notes for Claimant (see under claimant and defendant details on page 53 and also address for service on page 66). Once the Claim Form has been posted by first class post, it is deemed by the court to have been served the second day after it was posted.

If you are posting documents for service yourself, you may have to make a note in the file about what time you posted it and from which post box or, if your firm is large and has a post room, what time it went to the post room. Check with the fee earner if this is required and what the practice of the firm is.

As mentioned on page 34 with regard to diary notes, you may be asked to make a diary note for 14 days after deemed service of the Claim Form and/or Particulars of Claim. This will be the date by which the court should have heard from the defendant regarding how he intends to proceed with the claim, often by receiving back from the defendant a completed Acknowledgment of Service (see page 71). If the defendant has done nothing by this time, it may be possible to enter judgment against the defendant (see page 72).

Service using the DX

The Document Exchange (see page 16) may be used for serving documents only if:

    (a)   the party's address for service includes a DX number; or
    (b)   the notepaper of the party who is to be served or the notepaper of his solicitor who is authorised to accept service includes a DX number.

As well as one of the two above conditions being satisfied, the party who is to be served or his solicitor must not have indicated in writing that they are unwilling to accept service by DX.

Service by DX is deemed to be effected the second day after it was left at the Document Exchange.

Service by Fax

Before a document can be served by fax, the party who is to be served or his solicitor must previously have indicated in writing to the party serving the document that he is willing to accept service by fax and must have provided the fax number to which the documents should be sent. Where it is being served on a solicitor, the fax number should always be that of the solicitor's office address. If the solicitor's notepaper has on it a fax number or he includes the fax number on the Claim Form or any response to a claim filed at court, this is usually taken as an indication that he is willing to accept service by fax.

If a document to be served by fax is transmitted on a business day before 4.00 pm, it is deemed to have been served on that same day. Otherwise, it is deemed to have been served on the day after it has been transmitted.

When a document is served by fax or other electronic means, it is not essential to follow it up with a hard copy but if this is not done and the documents have not been received, the court may take into consideration the fact that a hard copy was not sent.

Service by other Electronic Means

Service by e-mail or other electronic means is acceptable only where both parties are legally represented and the legal representative has previously expressly indicated in writing that he will accept service in this way and has provided the e-mail address or other identification which may be used for service. Again, this must be to the firm's business address. If a document is served in this way, it is deemed to have been served on the second day after the day on which it is transmitted.

Leaving a Document at an Address

Service may also be effected by delivering a document or leaving it at a permitted address as laid down by the rules of the court. In these circumstances, it is deemed to have been served the day after it is delivered to or left at the permitted address.

Personal Service

This is where the documents are simply handed to the defendant personally. (There are specific rules to deal with service in this manner upon a company or partnership.) It is highly unlikely that a secretary will be asked to do this but if you are, make sure that you note the date, time and method of service, i.e., exactly how you handed over the documents, when and where. There are various rules relating to personal service and these should be checked beforehand if the need arises. However, personal service is normally effected by enquiry agents or process servers.

Delivering or Leaving the Document at an Address

If the document is left at a permitted address (see Address for Service, below), it is deemed to have been served the day after it was delivered to or left at that address.

Other Methods of Service

Where it is desired to effect service in another way, e.g., by placing advertisements in newspapers, an application must be made to the court. Similarly, the court has power to dispense with service of a document.

If a document is to be served on a child or patient within the meaning of the Mental Health Act 1983, service will usually be on a parent or guardian or a litigation friend. However, there are various rules to be followed in these cases.

There are also steps to be taken if serving a document on a member of HM Forces or on a member of the US Air Force. Details are given in the CPR, including addresses to write to for making enquiries as to the address of that person.

Address for Service

The address to which a document may be delivered, i.e., the address for service, must be in England and Wales but, as stated previously, there are exceptions to this. The address for service is normally somewhere where it is logical to assume that the defendant will receive the documents, such as a usual or last known residence or place of business. The court rules specify which sort of places are permitted, e.g., home address, business address of a firm, registered office of a company. Where someone has instructed a solicitor, the solicitor's business address is usually his client's address for service (but see below regarding service of the Claim Form).

Who May Serve the Documents

If the document is one which has been issued or prepared by the court, it may be served by the court. However, there are exceptions to this, one of these being where the solicitors notify the court that they wish to serve the document themselves.

A Claim Form may only be served on the defendant's solicitors if the defendant has in fact authorised those solicitors to accept service of documents on his behalf and, in that case, all documents should normally then be served on the solicitors.

Calculating a Specified Number of Days

Under the Rules, periods of time are usually calculated in 'clear days'. This means that the first day when the period begins and the last day when it ends, are not included in the calculation. If the specified period is five days or less and includes a Saturday, Sunday, Christmas Day, Good Friday or Bank Holiday, that day is not counted.

If the court imposes a time limit, the date for complying should include the time of day by when any act should be done. If a month is indicated by the court, this will mean a calendar month.

Service of the Claim Form

Generally, the Claim Form must be served on the defendant within four months after it has been issued by the court.

If the court is to serve the Claim Form, the form must always include the defendant's address for service and this may be the defendant's solicitors only if they are authorised by the defendant to accept service on his behalf. When the Claim Form is served by the court, the court will send a notice to the claimant informing him of the date when the Claim Form is deemed to have been served.

Where the claimant or his solicitors are serving the Claim Form themselves, they must include with it the Response Pack (Form N9) which includes an Acknowledgment of Service and the forms for defence and/or counterclaim and admission forms (see page 69). A Certificate of Service (see below) must then be filed with the court.

In certain circumstances, a Claim Form may be served in a manner which has been specified in a contract, e.g., a contract may state how any disputes relating to it are dealt with. The Claim Form may also be served, with the permission of the court, on an agent of someone who is overseas.

Certificate of Service

Some documents, such as the Claim Form, require a Certificate of Service (Form N215) to be completed and filed with the court, stating that the document has not been returned undelivered and giving details of the date of service (and the time if service is by fax or other electronic means), together with details of how service was effected, e.g., whether it was by post and, if so, the date of posting; if it was by using the DX, the date of delivery to the document exchange.

Notice of Non-service

If a document was going to be served by the court and the court was unable to serve it, the court will complete a Notice of Non-service stating how they attempted to effect service and send this to the party who requested service. The court is then no longer under any further duty to try to effect service — it is up to the party wishing to serve the document.

Certificate of Service

SPECIMEN

In the	
SOUTHTOWN COUNTY COURT	
Claim No.	00.12345
Claimant	PAUL XAVIER
Defendant	JOHN JONES

On the   *   *(insert date)*

the   Claim Form   *(insert title or description of documents served)*

a copy of which is attached to this notice was served on *(insert name of person served, including position i.e. partner, director if appropriate)*

Tick as appropriate

- ☑ by first class post
- ☐ by delivering to or leaving
- ☐ by fax machine (.................time sent)
  (you may want to enclose a copy of the transmission sheet)
- ☐ by other means *(please specify)*

- ☐ by Document Exchange
- ☐ by handing it to or leaving it with

- ☐ by e-mail

at *(insert address where service effected, include fax or DX number or e-mail address)*

```
1 Breakneck Drive
Southtown
Herts
EN7 6LP
```

being the Defendant's:

- ☑ residence
- ☐ place of business
- ☐ registered office
- ☐ other *(please specify)*

The date of service is therefore deemed to be   *   *(insert date – see over for guidance)*

I confirm that at the time of signing this Certificate the document has not been returned to me as undelivered.

Signed
     (Claimant)(~~Defendant~~)('s Solicitor)(~~'s Litigation friend~~)

Position or office held
(if signing on behalf of firm or company)

Date

N215 Certificate of Service (4.99)

[P.T.O.

Defendant's Response to the Claim Form

When the defendant receives the Claim Form and/or Particulars of Claim, he will receive other documents too.

Notes for Defendant on Replying to the Claim Form

These Notes (Form N1C) accompany the Claim Form (or the Particulars of Claim if served separately from the Claim Form (see page 58)). When you are making copies of the Claim Form or Particulars of Claim for service on each defendant, you should ensure that every defendant has a copy of these Notes. They set out the choices open to the defendant which are to:

   (a) pay the amount claimed; or
   (b) admit that he owes all or part of the claim and ask for time to pay; or
   (c) dispute the claim.

If the Particulars of Claim were received by the defendant at the same time as the Claim Form, he must reply within 14 days of the date it was served on him. If the Claim Form states that the Particulars of Claim will follow, he should not reply until he has received the Particulars of Claim (which should arrive no more than 14 days after he receives the Claim Form).

If the defendant simply does not reply at all, judgment may be entered against him (see page 72).

The Notes will then set out how the defendant should pay if he wishes to do so, and also tell him what he should do if he wishes to admit or dispute the claim. He will be sent with the Claim Form or Particulars of Claim a Response Pack (see below) which includes the forms he will need to complete, depending on what he decides to do.

Response Pack

The Response Pack (Form N9) includes forms on which the Defendant may:

   (a) admit all or part of the claim where the claim is for a specified amount (Form N9A);
   (b) admit all or part of the claim where the claim is for an unspecified amount of money or is not a claim for money (Form N9C);
   (c) submit a Defence and/or Counterclaim where the claim is for a specified amount (Form N9B);
   (d) submit a Defence and/or Counterclaim where the claim is for an unspecified amount or is not a claim for money (Form N9D).

The Response Pack Form also comprises an Acknowledgment of Service form which will be completed, signed and returned to the court by the defendant or his solicitors, if necessary (see page 71).

The defendant has a specified time from the date of service of the Claim Form to file his Admission form or Defence and Counterclaim Form. An extension of time up to 28 days may be agreed between the parties. If such an extension is agreed, the defendant must notify the court in writing. If the defendant's solicitors are serving the Defence on the other parties, they must ensure that every party to the claim is served with a copy, as well as filing a copy with the court. Remember to keep a copy for your file.

Admitting All or Part of the Claim

If the defendant admits the claim in full and it is for a specified amount of money, he should take or send the money, together with any interest and costs claimed, to the claimant at the address given for payment on the Claim Form. He must do this within 14 days. When making the payment, the defendant should ensure that he quotes the Claim Number and obtains a receipt. Payment in this instance will not be accepted by the court.

If the defendant admits the claim in full and it is for a specified amount, but he wants time to pay the money, he must complete Form N9A and send it to the claimant at the address given for payment on the Claim Form within 14 days. The claimant will decide whether or not to accept the proposal for payment. If he accepts, he may ask the court to enter judgment (see page 72) against the defendant and the court will then send the defendant a court order telling him how the payments should be made. If the proposal is not accepted, the court will decide on the rate of payment to be made.

Where the claim is for an unspecified amount and the defendant admits that he is liable for the whole claim, he may make an offer to the claimant to settle the claim. He must do this by completing Form N9C and sending it to the court within 14 days. The court will send a copy to the claimant, who will then tell the court whether the offer is acceptable. The claimant must send his reply to the court, sending a copy of his reply to the defendant, within 14 days. If the claimant does not reply in this way, the claim will be stayed, i.e., it will not proceed any further. Once the claimant accepts the defendant's offer, the claimant may request the court to enter judgment against the defendant for the amount due or whatever other remedy is being sought. The request for judgment will be made on the appropriate form.

If an offer made by the defendant is not acceptable to the claimant, the claimant may request the court to enter judgment against the defendant for an amount or remedy that will be decided on by the court, together with any costs. The court will enter judgment and refer its file to a judge for directions for management of the case. The claimant and the defendant will be sent a copy of the order made by the court.

Where the defendant admits that he is liable for the claim but does not make any offer to settle, he should complete Form N9C and send it to the court within 14 days. The court will send a copy to the claimant who may request the court to enter judgment against the defendant for an amount which will be decided by the court, together with costs. The court will then enter judgment and the file will be sent to a judge for directions for management of the case. Both the claimant and the defendant will be sent a copy of the order made by the court.

If the defendant admits part of the claim, but not all of it, he should complete both a form for admission and a form for defence and send them to the court within 14 days. The claimant will then decide whether to accept this part admission. If he does accept, he may request the court to enter judgment against the defendant and the court will then send a court order to the defendant telling him to pay. If the claimant does not accept the part admission, the case will proceed as a defended claim (see below).

When your firm is acting for any party and you are completing the forms, always ensure that you have kept a copy on the file, and remember that a copy of the forms must be served on all parties to the claim.

Disputing/Defending the Claim

If the claim is for a specified amount of money and the defendant is an individual, i.e., not a company or some other organisation, and he wishes to dispute or defend the claim, the claim may be transferred to the court nearest his home or nearest to his solicitor's office. The court which is the nearest court is often referred to as the home court.

If the defendant needs more than 14 days to reply to the claim, he must complete the Acknowledgment of Service and send it to the court within 14 days (see below).

The defendant must also complete the appropriate form for admitting/defending the claim, depending on whether the claim is for a specified amount or for an unspecified amount or non-money claim and depending on what it is exactly that he wishes to do regarding the claim. He could:

(a)   dispute all of the claim (this might be because he has already paid it or that he simply disagrees with the claim);

(b)   admit part of the claim and dispute part of it;

(c)   make a claim of his own against the claimant (a counterclaim) or bring someone else into the proceedings (see page 85 regarding Part 20 claims);

If the claim is for damages for personal injuries and the claimant has attached a medical report and/or schedule of expenses and losses (e.g., earnings), the defendant must say whether he agrees or not with the contents of these documents. The defendant may also have obtained a medical report on the claimant's injuries and if he has, he should attach it to his Defence (see page 85).

In the Defence, the defendant must reply specifically to the allegations contained in the Particulars of Claim, e.g., he must state which allegations he denies, giving his reasons; which he admits, as well as other detailed information regarding the claim.

A Statement of Truth should also be signed by the defendant as for the Claim Form (see above). If the Defence is a separate document, it will have the same type of layout as the Particulars of Claim.

All the forms are very clear and have notes on them to help in their completion. There are boxes on the forms which should either be filled in or ticked.

Acknowledgment of Service

This is on Form N9 (Response Pack). Where the defendant intends to defend the claim and he needs more time to file his Defence or if he is disputing the court's jurisdiction, he should complete the Acknowledgment of Service and return it to the court. It should be filed with the court within 14 days of service of the Claim Form. However, if the Claim Form stated that the Particulars of Claim were to follow, the defendant has 14 days after service of the Particulars of Claim in which to file the Acknowledgment of Service. The court will inform the claimant in writing that the defendant has lodged the Acknowledgment of Service. He is then allowed 28 days from the date of service of the Particulars of Claim to file his Defence (or to make an application to the court if he disputes the fact that the court has jurisdiction to try the claim).

Where the defendant has instructed a solicitor, the solicitor's address will usually be inserted in the box where it asks for the address to which documents about the claim should be sent. Do not forget to include your firm's correct reference. The form will now be signed by the solicitor acting for the defendant, or by the defendant himself.

If the defendant has been named incorrectly or not in full on the Claim Form, his correct name should be inserted on the Acknowledgment of Service in the appropriate box. The correct name should be followed by the words 'described as' and then the incorrect name.

Where the defendant does not file either an Acknowledgment of Service or a Defence (or an Admission) within the specified time, judgment in default of filing one of these documents may be entered against him for the full amount of the claim (called 'default judgment').

Always remember to keep a copy of the Acknowledgment of Service for your file.

Entering Default Judgment

In most cases, if the defendant fails to file the Acknowledgment of Service or Defence or Admission within the specified time, judgment in default of doing so may be entered against him. This means that the claimant may file a request with the court for an order stating that the defendant must comply with whatever the claimant sought in his Claim Form, for example, pay the money claimed plus any interest accrued, plus costs. A form for Request for Judgment will be completed: which form to be used depends on what type of claim it is and whether the court will decide on the amount to be paid). In some cases, an application (see page 116) will have to be made to the court to allow judgment to be entered. Even when judgment has been entered, the defendant may, under certain circumstances, ask for it to be set aside, i.e., made ineffective, or to be varied.

A request for Judgment and Reply to Admission form will be completed if the Defendant admits the claim but asks for time to pay.

Response Pack

You should read the "notes for Defendant" attached to the claim form which will tell you when and where to send the forms.

Included in this pack are:

- either **Admission Form N9A** (if the claim is for a specified amount) or **Admission Form N9C** (if the claim is for an unspecified amount or is not a claim for money)

- either **Defence and Counterclaim Form N9B** (if the claim is for a specified amount) or **Defence and Counterclaim Form N9D** (if the claim is for an unspecified amount or is not a claim for money)

- **Acknowledgment of service** (see below)

SPECIMEN

Complete

If you admit the claim or the amount claimed and/or you want time to pay	▶ the admission form
If you admit part of the claim	▶ the admission form and the defence form
If you dispute the whole claim or wish to make a claim (a counterclaim) against the Claimant	▶ the defence form
If you need 28 days (rather than 14) from the date of service to prepare your defence, or wish to contest the court's jurisdiction	▶ the acknowledgment of service
If you do nothing, judgment may be entered against you	

Acknowledgment of Service

Defendant's full name if different from the name given on the claim form

In the	SOUTHTOWN COUNTY COURT
Claim No.	00.12345
Claimant (including ref.)	PAUL XAVIER (ref: XAV/789)
Defendant	JOHN JONES

Address to which documents about this claim should be sent (including reference if appropriate)

Joe Bloggs & Co 1 Broad Walk Southtown Herts		if applicable	
		fax no.	0181 444 2323
		DX no.	DX 56 Southtown
Tel. no. 0181 444 7777 Postcode EN4 9PP		e-mail	

Tick the appropriate box

1. I intend to defend all of this claim ☐

2. I intend to defend part of this claim ☑

3. I intend to contest jurisdiction ☐

If you file an acknowledgment of service but do not file a defence within 28 days of the date of service of the claim form, or particulars of claim if served separately, judgment may be entered against you.

If you do not file an application within 28 days of the date of service of the claim form, or particulars of claim if served separately, it will be assumed that you accept the court's jurisdiction and judgment may be entered against you.

Signed

(Defendant)(Defendant's solicitor)
(Litigation friend)

Position or office held
(if signing on behalf of firm or company)

Date

The court office at

is open between 10 am and 4 pm (4.30 pm in High Court) Monday to Friday. When corresponding with the court, please address forms or letters to the Court Manager and quote the claim number.

N9 Response Pack (4.99)

Oyez 7 Spa Road, London SE16 3QQ

N9

4.99 F36015
5093018
★ ★ ★ ★ ★

Admission (specified amount)

I	You have a limited number of days to complete and return this form
I	Before completing this form, please read the notes for guidance attached to the claim form

When to fill in this form

I Only fill in this form if you are admitting all or some of the claim **and** you are asking for time to pay

How to fill in this form

I Tick the correct boxes and give as much information as you can. **Then sign and date the form.** If necessary provide details on a separate sheet, add the claim number and attach it to this form.

I Make your offer of payment in box 11 on the back of this form. **If you make no offer the claimant will decide how much and when you should pay.**

I If you are not an individual, you should ensure that you provide sufficient details about the assets and liabilities of your firm, company or corporation to support any offer of payment made in box 11.

I You can get help to complete this form at **any** county court office or Citizens Advice Bureau.

Where to send this form

I **If you admit the claim in full**
Send the completed form to the address shown on the claim form as one to which documents should be sent.

I **If you admit only part of the claim**
Send the form **to the court** at the address given on the claim form, together with the defence form (N9B).

How much of the claim do you admit?

☐ I admit the full amount claimed as shown on the claim form **or**

☐ I admit the amount of ☐ £

1 Personal details

Surname	JONES
Forename	JOHN

☐ Mr ☐ Mrs ☐ Miss ☐ Ms

☐ Married ☐ Single ☐ Other *(specify)*

Age 36

Address
1 Breakneck Drive
Southtown
Herts

Postcode EN7 6LP

Tel. no. 0181 222 8888

In the	SOUTHTOWN COUNTY COURT
Claim No.	00.12345
Claimant (including ref.)	PAUL XAVIER (XAV/789)
Defendant	JOHN JONES

2 Dependants *(people you look after financially)*

Number of children in each age group

under 11 ☐   11-15 ☐   16-17 ☐   18 & over ☐

Other dependants
(give details)

3 Employment

☐ **I am employed as a**
My employer is

Jobs other than
main job *(give details)*

☐ **I am self employed as a**
Annual turnover is........................... £

☐ **I am not** in arrears with my national insurance contributions, income tax and VAT

☐ **I am** in arrears and I owe........... £

Give details of:
(a) contracts and other work in hand
(b) any sums due for work done

☐ **I have been unemployed for** years months

☐ **I am a pensioner**

4 Bank account and savings

☐ **I have a bank account**

☐ The account is in credit by........ £

☐ The account is overdrawn by.... £

☐ **I have a savings or building society account**

The amount in the account is.......... £

5 Residence

I live in ☐ my own house   ☐ lodgings

☐ my jointly owned house   ☐ council accommodation

☐ rented accommodation

6 Income

SPECIMEN

My usual take home pay *(including overtime, commission, bonuses etc)*	£	per
Income support	£	per
Child benefit(s)	£	per
Other state benefit(s)	£	per
My pension(s)	£	per
Others living in my home give me	£	per
Other income *(give details below)*		
	£	per
	£	per
	£	per
Total income	**£**	**per**

7 Expenses

(Do not include any payments made by other members of the household out of their own income)

I have regular expenses as follows:

Mortgage *(including second mortgage)*	£	per
Rent	£	per
Council tax	£	per
Gas	£	per
Electricity	£	per
Water charges	£	per
TV rental and licence	£	per
HP repayments	£	per
Mail order	£	per
Housekeeping, food, school meals	£	per
Travelling expenses	£	per
Children's clothing	£	per
Maintenance payments	£	per
Others *(not court orders or credit debts listed in boxes 9 and 10)*		
	£	per
	£	per
	£	per
Total expenses	**£**	**per**

8 Priority debts

(This section is for arrears only. Do not include regular expenses listed in box 7.)

Rent arrears	£	per
Mortgage arrears	£	per
Council tax/Community Charge arrears	£	per
Water charges arrears	£	per
Fuel debts: Gas	£	per
Electricity	£	per
Other	£	per
Maintenance arrears	£	per
Others *(give details below)*		
	£	per
	£	per
Total priority debts	**£**	**per**

9 Court orders

Court	Claim No.	£	per

Total court order instalments	**£**	**per**

Of the payments above, I am behind with payments to *(please list)*

10 Credit debts

Loans and credit card debts *(please list)*

	£	per
	£	per
	£	per

Of the payments above, I am behind with payments to *(please list)*

11 Offer of payment

☐ I can pay the amount admitted on

or

☐ I can pay by monthly instalments of £

If you cannot pay immediately, please give brief reasons below

12 Declaration   I declare that the details I have given above are true to the best of my knowledge

Signed

Date

Position or office held *(if signing on behalf of firm or company)*

Defence and Counterclaim (specified amount)

- Fill in this form if you wish to dispute all or part of the claim and/or make a claim against the Claimant (counterclaim).
- You have a limited number of days to complete and return this form to the court.
- Before completing this from, please read the notes for guidance attached to the claim form.
- Please ensure that all boxes at the top right of this form are completed. You can obtain the correct names and number from the claim form. The court cannot trace your case without this information.

How to fill in this form

- Complete sections 1 and 2. Tick the correct boxes and give the other details asked for.
- Set out your defence in section 3. If necessary continue on a separate piece of paper making sure that the claim number is clearly shown on it. In your defence you must state which allegations in the particulars of claim you deny and your reasons for doing so. **If you fail to deny an allegation it may be taken that you admit it.**
- If you dispute only some of the allegations you must
  - specify which you admit and which you deny; and
  - give your own version of events if different from the Claimant's.

In the	SOUTHTOWN COUNTY COURT
Claim No.	00.12345
Claimant (including ref.)	PAUL XAVIER (ref: XAV/789)
Defendant	JOHN JONES

- If you wish to make a claim against the Claimant (a counterclaim) complete section 4.
- Complete and sign section 5 before sending this form to the court. Keep a copy of the claim form and this form.

Legal Aid

- You may be entitled to legal aid. Ask about the legal aid scheme at any county court office, Citizens Advice Bureau, legal advice centre or firm of solicitors displaying the legal aid sign.

1. How much of the claim do you dispute?

☐ I dispute the full amount claimed as shown on the claim form

or

☐ I admit the amount of £ [   ]

If you dispute only part of the claim you must **either**:

- pay the amount admitted to the person named at the address for payment on the claim form (see How to Pay in the notes on the back of, or attached to, the claim form). Then send this defence to the court

or

- complete the blue admission form **and** this defence form and send them to the court.

☐ I paid the amount admitted on *(date)* [   ]

or

☐ I enlose the completed form of admission

(go to section 2)

2. Do you dispute this claim because you have already paid it? *Tick whichever applies*

☐ **No** *(go to section 3)*

☐ **Yes**   I paid £ [   ] to the Claimant

on [   ] *(before the claim form was issued)*

Give details of where and how you paid it in the box below *(then go to section 5)*

[   ]

3. Defence

SPECIMEN

N9B Defence and Counterclaim (specified amount) (4.99)

Defence (continued)

| Claim No. | 00.12345 |

SPECIMEN

4. If you wish to make a claim against the Claimant (a counterclaim)

If your claim is for a specific sum of money, how much are you claiming? £

- To start your counterclaim, you will have to pay a fee. Court staff will tell you how much you have to pay.

My claim is for *(please specify nature of claim)*

- You may not be able to make a counterclaim where the Claimant is the Crown (e.g. a Government Department). Ask at your local county court office for further information.

What are your reasons for making the counterclaim?
If you need to continue on a separate sheet put the claim number in the top right hand corner

5. Signed

(To be signed by you or by your solicitor or litigation friend)

*(I believe)(The Defendant believes) that the facts stated in this form are true. *I am duly authorised by the Defendant to sign this statement

*delete as appropriate

Position or office held
(if signing on behalf of firm or company)

-

Date

Give an address to which notices about this case can be sent to you.

Joe Bloggs & Co
1 Broad Walk
Southtown
Herts

Postcode EN4 9PP

Tel. no.   0181 444 7777

if applicable

fax no.	0181 444 2323
DX no.	DX 56 Southtown
e-mail	

Oyez   7 Spa Road, London SE16 3QQ

N9B

4.99 F36013
5093034
★ ★ ★ ★ ★

SPECIMEN

Request for Judgment and reply to Admission (specified amount)

In the	
SOUTHTOWN COUNTY COURT	
Claim No.	00.12345
Claimant (including ref)	PAUL XAVIER (ref: XAV/789)
Defendant (including ref)	JOHN JONES (ref: JON/cd)

- Tick box A or B. If you tick box B you must complete the details in that part and in part C. Make sure that all the case details are given. Remember to sign and date the form. Your signature certifies that the information you have given is correct.

- If the Defendant has given an address on the form of admission to which correspondence should be sent, which is different from the address shown on the claim form, you must tell the court.

- Return the completed form to the court.

A ☑ **The Defendant has not filed an admission or defence to my claim.**

Complete all the judgment details at C. Decide how and when you want the Defendant to pay. You can ask for the judgment to be paid by instalments or in one payment.

B ☐ **The Defendant admits that all the money is owed.**

Tick only **one** box below and complete all the judgment details at C.

☐ **I accept the Defendant's proposal for payment.**

Say how the Defendant intends to pay. The court will send the Defendant an order to pay. You will also be sent a copy.

☐ **The Defendant has not made any proposal for payment.**

Say how you want the Defendant to pay. You can ask for the judgment to be paid by instalments or in one payment. The court will send the Defendant an order to pay. You will also be sent a copy.

☐ **I do NOT accept the Defendant's proposal for payment.**

Say how you want the Defendant to pay. Give your reasons for objecting to the Defendant's offer of payment in the space opposite. (Continue on the back of this form if necessary.) Send this form to the court **with Defendant's admission N9A**. The court will fix a rate of payment and send the Defendant an order to pay. You will also be sent a copy.

C Judgment details.

I would like the judgment to be paid

☑ (immediately)

☐ (by instalments of £ _____ per month)

☐ (in full by _____)

Amount of claim as admitted (including interest at date of issue)................

Interest since date of claim (if any)................

Period from .... to ....

Rate ....%

Court fees shown on claim

Solicitor's costs (if any) on issuing claim

Sub Total

Solicitor's costs (if any) on entering judgment

Sub Total

Deduct amount (if any) paid since issue

Amount payable by Defendant

I certify that the information given is correct

Signed

~~(Claimant)~~(Claimant's Solicitor)~~(Litigation friend)~~

Position or office held

(if signing on behalf of firm or company)

Date

The court office at

is open between 10 am and 4 pm (4.30 pm in High Court) Monday to Friday. When corresponding with the court, please address forms or letters to the Court Manager and quote the Claim number.

N225 Request for Judgment and reply to Admission (specified amount) (4.99)

Oyez   7 Spa Road, London SE16 3QQ

4.99 F36061

5093204

★ ★ ★ ★ ★

Statements of Case

As you have seen, there are many forms to complete. However, they do not all need to be completed at the same time nor, indeed, is every single form needed for every case. These forms are necessary so that everyone knows exactly what the other parties involved are saying and so that everyone knows what the next step is that they should take, and when they should take it. Besides completing forms, documents such as the Particulars of Claim and Defence will often need to be drawn up. These documents, and others, the purpose of which is to set out the facts relied upon in the action, are called statements of case. Before the introduction of the Civil Procedure Rules, these documents were known as pleadings.

The first statement of case is the Claim Form and/or Particulars of Claim (if not included in the Claim Form); followed by the Defence and/or Counterclaim under Part 20 CPR (see page 85). The claimant may then serve a Reply to the Defence and/or Defence to the Counterclaim. Permission must be obtained from the court before any other statement of case may be served.

When typing a statement of case, always remember to include the title of the action, i.e., the court or division in which the action is proceeding; the claim number; the names and status of the parties; and also state which document it is that is being typed, e.g. Particulars of Claim or Defence. The words stating what the document is, e.g., Particulars of Claim, will usually be typed in capital letters and centred and then perhaps either underlined (see the example Particulars of Claim) or this heading will be between two parallel lines (see heading for Brief to Counsel below). Your organisation will have its own style. Whatever format is used should be followed through to the backsheet (see page 61), if there is one.

Generally, all statements of case should have the pages numbered and each paragraph in the body of the document numbered. They must be verified by a Statement of Truth (see page 62). If the document has been settled by counsel (see below), it must bear his name at the end. A statement of case must show the date it has been served, the name of the solicitors serving it and the party for whom they act. The date of service will often be left blank when you type it so that this can be written in later. A backsheet will usually be typed. Remember to proofread documents (see page 27) that have been copy typed and also to keep a dated copy on your file. (For an example layout of these documents, see the example Particulars of Claim on page 60.) However, under the CPR, it is envisaged that these documents may be simplified and, therefore, the format may change.

Instructing Counsel

Barristers (called 'counsel') are often asked to give advice on a particular matter or to draft a statement of case. When a solicitor wishes to ask counsel to draft a statement of case, or to advise in writing or in a conference, he has to set out exactly what he requires counsel to do. He should state the relevant details of his case and instruct counsel, for example, to settle a Particulars of Claim, or to advise on liability, etc. These instructions being sent to the barrister are called Instructions to Counsel. Incidentally, a meeting with junior counsel is called a conference and a meeting with a QC is called a consultation.

If the solicitor wishes counsel to appear at a trial or hearing of some sort, counsel is instructed in exactly the same way and is briefed to appear at the hearing. Instructions asking counsel to appear in this manner are called Brief to Counsel.

Instructions and Briefs to Counsel are typed on A4 size paper. At one time, they were typed on A3 size paper (brief paper), but it is highly unlikely that you will encounter this any more.

Instructions and Briefs to Counsel start off with the heading and title of the action, including the claim number, if known (same format as statements of case). Of course, if proceedings have not been issued, it will not yet have a claim number. After the title is a description of what is required of counsel, e.g., Instructions to Counsel to Settle Particulars of Claim, and this is typed at the top, after the names of the parties, in the centre of the page. This is usually typed in capital letters and may be underlined or between two parallel lines (as shown), but your own organisation will more than likely have its own style:

BRIEF TO COUNSEL TO APPEAR ON BEHALF OF
THE CLAIMANT AT SOUTHTOWN COUNTY
COURT ON TUESDAY, 21st DECEMBER 1999 at 2.00 P.M.

The fee earner will then list any enclosures with the Instructions or Brief and set out details of the case.

When the Instructions are completed, a backsheet should also be typed. Backsheets are typed on the right-hand side of the page as shown on page 61 because the Instructions are folded over that way. The backsheet must contain the heading and title of the action, as well as any claim number, what the Instructions are about (centred as above, if appropriate), the name, address, reference and telephone number of the instructing solicitors and the date the Instructions are sent. If the matter is urgent, the backsheet should be marked accordingly. If it is a legal aid case, the legal aid reference number must also be marked on the backsheet.

You must always keep a copy of the Instructions or Brief in the file. If Instructions in the same matter are being sent to more than one counsel, a separate backsheet is typed for each of them. In this event, where counsel's name appears on the backsheet, the name and address of the barrister to whom that particular set of papers is being sent must be put first. If this is junior counsel appearing with leading counsel (a QC), then after junior counsel's name type 'you with' and then put the name of leading counsel.

Where the set of papers is going to leading counsel, put his name and address first on the backsheet. Under that type 'with you' and then put the name of junior counsel. See the example backsheet for Instructions to Counsel. Do not forget to include your firm's name, address and reference, and the date. Instructions are normally typed on one side of the paper only, i.e., not back to back.

There are often enclosures, e.g., copies of relevant documents, to go with Instructions to Counsel, and these should have a frontsheet (see page 84) for each enclosure. Each enclosure has its frontsheet numbered to correspond with the number it is given in the Instructions.

Once the fee earner is happy that everything is in order, any enclosures to go with the Instructions or Brief are put with it and they are all tied together in a bundle with pink tape showing the backsheet only. If the bundle is thin enough to be folded over showing only the typed part of the backsheet, then this is the preferred method (see page 22). Do not fold X-rays or photographs.

The Instructions are then either taken down by hand to the barrister's chambers if they are near enough or are sent in the post or through the DX. If you are asked to write a letter sending Instructions, you would address it to the barrister's clerk, i.e., Clerk to Mr Rob Roy, then his address, and simply say 'We enclose Instructions to Counsel, which kindly place before Mr Roy.' If the matter is urgent, this should be mentioned in the letter. In some cases, it is also wise to telephone the barrister's clerk and advise him of the urgency of the papers.

You may have to find the barrister's full address or telephone number. Addresses and telephone numbers of barristers and solicitors can be found in a law directory (there are quite a few), such as *Butterworth's Law Directory*.

When the barrister has drafted a document or 'settled' it, it is returned in draft form to the instructing solicitor. When it has been approved by the solicitor (or other fee earner), it must be typed on to good quality A4 size paper and typed in the correct layout, with a backsheet if appropriate. If a barrister has settled a statement of case or other document, his name must be typed at the end of that document. If there is anything in a draft document which does not seem to make sense or you are not sure about, then clarify it with the fee earner before typing it, or type it but make a note about it for the fee earner on a separate piece of paper. See also the section 'Layout of Documents' in Chapter 1. The CPR intend to simplify document layout and, therefore, the format shown here for documents may change.

CIVIL LITIGATION

Example Instructions to Counsel

<u>IN THE SOUTHTOWN COUNTY COURT</u>   <u>Claim No. 00.12345</u>

BETWEEN:

PAUL XAVIER   <u>Claimant</u>

and

JOHN JONES   <u>Defendant</u>

<u>INSTRUCTIONS TO COUNSEL TO ADVISE</u>

Counsel has herewith:

1. Copy garage estimate for repairs to car.
2. Copy correspondence.

Instructing Solicitors act on behalf of the Claimant who was involved in a road traffic accident when he was driving his Rolls Royce motor car, index No. 123 DEF, along Station Road, Barnet, Herts. The accident occurred on Monday, 5th July 1999.

Counsel will see from the copy of the garage estimate enclosed the extent of the damage to the Claimant's car.

Particulars of Claim have been served in this matter and Counsel is asked to advise as to whether he thinks this matter should be pursued.

If Counsel has any queries relating to this matter, he is asked please to contact Mr. John Smith of Instructing Solicitors on 01438 12345.

[date]

Example backsheet for Instructions to Counsel

Claim No. 00.12345

IN THE SOUTHTOWN
COUNTY COURT

BETWEEN:

PAUL XAVIER   Claimant

and

JOHN JONES   Defendant

INSTRUCTIONS TO COUNSEL TO
ADVISE

Mr John Bloggs, QC,
1 Smith Street,
London EC4

with you

Mr Rob Roy,
2 Smith Street,
London EC4

John Smith & Co.,
2 Bank Chambers,
High Road,
Southtown,
Herts. EN5 6AX

tel: 01438 12345

ref: AB/cd/123
Solicitors for the Claimant
[*date*]

CIVIL LITIGATION

Example frontsheet for an enclosure

<u>IN THE SOUTHTOWN COUNTY COURT</u>   <u>Claim No. 00.12345</u>

BETWEEN:

PAUL XAVIER   <u>Claimant</u>

and

JOHN JONES   <u>Defendant</u>

Bundle 1 — Copy Garage Estimate

Defence

When the defendant has received the Claim Form and Particulars of Claim, one of the courses of action open to him is to file a Defence. He may also wish to file a Counterclaim against the defendant and/or some other person (see Part 20 Claims below). A Counterclaim is a claim by the defendant made in response to the claimant's claim and which is included in the same proceedings, for example, if the claimant states that there was a car accident and the defendant damaged his car, the defendant might want to make a counterclaim against the claimant for damage to his own car.

The Defence should be made on the correct form, depending on whether the claim is for a specified amount (Form N9B) or an unspecified amount or non-money claim (Form N9D). If there is not enough room on the form, the Defence should be continued on separate sheets of paper. Each paragraph of the Defence should be numbered and each page numbered, and if the Defence is settled by counsel, his name should appear at the end. Remember to include the details in the box at the top right-hand of the form, i.e., the name of the court, the claim number and names of the claimant and defendant. This information should always be included on any separate sheets of paper.

If the defendant wishes to make a counterclaim against the claimant at the same time as filing his Defence, he may include this on the form for Defence and Counterclaim.

The Defence and/or Counterclaim must contain a Statement of Truth (see page 62) which will be signed by the defendant or his solicitors. Do not, as a secretary, sign this yourself. You should type on the form your firm's name, address and other details, including your reference. Keep a copy of the completed Defence on your file.

If the court is going to serve the Defence, it should be filed at court within 14 days after service of the Particulars of Claim. If the defendant has filed an Acknowledgment of Service, more time may be allowed for him to serve his Defence. The defendant and claimant can agree that the time limit for filing the Defence may be further extended by up to 28 days. If they do agree to such an extension of time, the defendant must notify the court in writing. As well as there being a copy for the court, there should be a copy for the claimant and for every other party that is involved in the action.

If the solicitors are serving the Defence, they must file a copy with the court, and serve a copy on all other parties to the proceedings within the specified time limit. Always keep a copy of the Defence on your file.

If a period of six months has expired since the end of the time for filing a Defence and the defendant has not filed an admission, defence or counterclaim, or if he has admitted the claim and the claimant has not applied to enter judgment in that time, the claim will be stayed, i.e., nothing further will happen unless one of the parties applies for the stay to be lifted.

Part 20 Claim

On receiving the Claim Form and Particulars of Claim, the defendant may wish to make a claim of his own against the claimant or against someone who is not already a party to the proceedings. These claims are dealt with under Part 20 CPR. Sometimes, permission is needed from the court to file a Part 20 claim.

A fee is payable to the court on filing a Part 20 Claim Form (Form N211). As with the ordinary Claim Form (N1) discussed on page 52, the Part 20 Claim Form has with it explanatory notes for the Part 20 claimant (Form N211A) and notes for the Part 20 defendant (Form N211C).

Where a Counterclaim under Part 20 is being served at the same time as the Defence, the Defence and Counterclaim should form one document, with the Defence first, followed by the Counterclaim.

If the claimant serves a Reply and a Defence to the Counterclaim, the Reply and Defence to Counterclaim should form one document, with the Reply going first, followed by the Defence to Counterclaim.

If the defendant makes a Part 20 claim, the title to the action (see also page 53) must show clearly that the parties are now involved in a Part 20 claim. Examples of how this is done are shown below.

PAUL XAVIER	claimant
JOHN JONES	defendant/Part 20 claimant
ANN BLOGGS	Part 20 defendant

This shows that Paul Xavier is the original claimant, having made a claim against John Jones. This made John Jones the defendant in the original action. John Jones, the defendant, then decided that he would issue a Part 20 claim against Ann Bloggs, making him a Part 20 claimant as well as a defendant to Paul Xavier's action. Because John Jones has now issued his Part 20 claim against Ann Bloggs, she is now a Part 20 defendant. If John Jones had decided to bring his Part 20 claim against Paul Xavier too, then Paul Xavier, besides being the claimant, would also be a Part 20 defendant.

Unfortunately, it does not get any easier — there can be more than one Part 20 claim, in which case, the parties to the first Part 20 claim would be described as, e.g., 'Part 20 claimant (1st claim)'; the parties to the second Part 20 claim would be described as 'Part 20 claimant (2nd claim)', and so on. However, where it does get complicated (e.g., if a party is a claimant and Part 20 defendant (1st claim)), rather than referring to him like that throughout the proceedings, as long as he is referred to correctly in the title of the proceedings, he may then be referred to by his name, e.g., 'Mr Xavier'.

Where the Part 20 Claim is served on someone who is not already a party to the proceedings, it must be accompanied by a form for defending the claim; a form for admitting the claim; an Acknowledgment of Service form; together with a copy of every Statement of Case which has already been served in the proceedings and any other document the court may direct that they should have. A copy of the Part 20 Claim Form must be served on everyone that is already a party to the proceedings.

Claim Form
(Additional claims- CPR Part 20)

SPECIMEN

In the	
SOUTHTOWN COUNTY COURT	
Claim No.	00.12345

Claimant(s)   PAUL XAVIER

SEAL

Defendant(s)   JOHN JONES

Part 20 Claimant(s)   JOHN JONES

Part 20 Defendant(s)   ANN BLOGGS

Brief details of claim

Value

Defendant's name and address

	£
Amount claimed	
Court fee	
Solicitors costs	
Total amount	
Issue date	

The court office at

is open between 10 am and 4 pm Monday to Friday. When corresponding with the court, please address forms or letters to the Court Manager and quote the claim number.

N211 - w3 Claim Form (CPR Part 20 - additional claims)(4.99)   *Printed on behalf of The Court Service*

CIVIL LITIGATION

Particulars of Claim (attached)

SPECIMEN

Statement of Truth

*(I believe)(The Part 20 Claimant believes) that the facts stated in these particulars of claim are true.

* I am duly authorised by the Part 20 claimant to sign this statement

Full name _____

Name of Part 20 claimant's solicitor's firm _____

signed_____ position or office held_____

*(Part 20 Claimant)('s solicitor)(Litigation friend)   (if signing on behalf of firm or company)

*delete as appropriate

Part 20 Claimant ('s solicitor's) address to which documents or payments should be sent if different from overleaf. If you are prepared to accept service by DX, fax or e-mail, please add details.

Reply

Having received the Defence, the claimant may reply to it. A Reply will be set out in the same manner as the Particulars of Claim and must include the heading, the claim number and the names and status of the parties to the claim. If the claimant is serving a Reply and Defence to Counterclaim, these should normally be together in one document, with the Reply going first, followed by the Defence. It will also contain a Statement of Truth.

A Reply to a Defence will normally be filed with the court when the claimant files his Allocation Questionnaire (see below). At the same time, all parties to the claim must be served with a copy of the Reply and, of course, you must keep a copy on your file.

Where the claim is for a sum of money and the Defence is simply that the money has been paid, the court will send a notice to the claimant asking him to state in writing whether he wants the claim to continue. If the claimant does wish the case to continue, he must serve a copy of his response on the defendant.

Allocation Questionnaire

Once a Defence has been filed, the court will serve an Allocation Questionnaire (Form N150) on each party. The details given on the Questionnaire will assist the court in deciding how the case will be managed and which track it will be allocated to (see below). Each party must complete the Allocation Questionnaire and file it with the court no later than the date specified on it by the court. However, the parties concerned should consult each other when completing the Questionnaire so that they can provide the court with mutually agreed information wherever possible.

If any party wishes to make an application to the court relating to the claim, for example, they may wish to apply for summary judgment (see page 96) or for some special directions regarding the claim, they should send their application to the court at the same time as they file the Allocation Questionnaire. A fee may be payable to the court for certain applications.

Where a party wishes any documents to be taken into account by the judge, he should also file these documents with the court at the same time as the completed Allocation Questionnaire, confirming that the other parties have been sent these documents and stating when they would have received them, and whether any other party has agreed the contents of the documents.

The sections of the Allocation Questionnaire are dealt with as follows.

Settlement

If any party to the claim wishes to have the court proceedings stayed because they think there is a chance that the claim could be settled, they can include this on the Allocation Questionnaire. If a settlement is reached, the claimant must notify the court.

Track

Claims are allocated to tracks, depending on the value of the claim and certain other factors such as the nature of the claim, the complexity of the case, the importance of the claim, the amount of oral evidence that may be required or the number of parties involved. Allocating a case to a particular track will determine the way in which the case will be managed. The tracks are:

(a)   The small claims track. This is the normal track for a claim which has a financial value of not more than £5,000. However, there are exceptions to this amount where the claim is for damages for personal injuries or the claim is by a tenant of residential premises claiming against his landlord to carry out repairs to the premises. See also page 96.

(b)   The fast track. This is the normal track for claims where the value of the claim is not more than £15,000 and where the claim is not one which would be dealt with in the small claims track. Again, exceptions may be made in allocating a case to this track. See also page 98.

(c)   The multi-track. This is the normal track for any claim which does not come into the small claims or fast track categories. See also page 102.

Pre-action Protocols

These are mentioned on page 49. If a protocol applies to the claim, details must be given on the Questionnaire in the boxes provided.

Applications

Details must be given here of any applications to be made to the court, such as an application for summary judgment (see page 96).

Witnesses of Fact

If it is known what witnesses of fact will be called at the hearing, the name of the witnesses together with details of which facts they are witnesses to must be given.

Experts' Evidence

Details of any experts to be relied upon must be given. An expert could be someone like a doctor giving evidence in a personal injury claim, or a surveyor giving evidence about the value of property, etc.

Any party wishing to call an expert to give evidence or put forward an expert's report as evidence must first obtain the court's permission. Normally, expert evidence will be given as a written report unless the court has directed otherwise. See also page 131 regarding expert evidence.

Location of Trial

This part of the Questionnaire asks for any reasons why a case may need to be heard at a particular court, e.g., one of the parties might be disabled and a particular court might have better facilities or be more convenient for him. The trial will normally take place at the court where the case is being managed but it is possible for it to be transferred to another court for hearing if there is sufficient reason for this.

If a party wishes the case to be heard in the Royal Courts of Justice in London, his reasons should be given on the Allocation Questionnaire.

Representation and Estimate of Hearing/Trial Time

The fee earner will have decided whether he is going to represent the client at court or whether a barrister will be instructed. Any relevant details must be given, together with a note on how long it is anticipated that the hearing of an application or the trial is likely to take. Details of dates which are not convenient should also be given.

Costs

This part of the Questionnaire relates only to costs incurred by legal representatives.

Other Information

This is the place on the Questionnaire to include any other facts relevant to the timetable that will be set by the court.

Once the Questionnaire is complete, it must be signed as appropriate and dated. It should be returned by the specified date to the court named on the form. A fee is payable to the court on returning the Questionnaire (or, if allocation takes place without a Questionnaire, the fee is payable within 21 days of allocation). Make sure that you note which court it should go to because the case may already have been transferred to another court. Keep a copy of the Questionnaire on your file.

CIVIL LITIGATION

Allocation Questionnaire

SPECIMEN

In the	SOUTHTOWN COUNTY COURT
Claim No.	00.12345
Last date for filing with court office	

To

SEAL

Please read the notes on page five before completing the questionnaire.

Please note the date by which it must be returned and the name of the court it should be returned to since this may be different from the court where proceedings were issued.

If you have settled this case (or if you settle it on a future date) and do not need to have it heard or tried, you must let the court know immediately.

A Settlement

Do you wish there to be a one month stay to attempt to settle the case?

☐ Yes ☐ No

B Track

Which track do you consider is most suitable for your case? *(Tick one box)*

☐ small claims ☐ fast track ☐ multi-track

If you think your case is suitable for a specialist list, say which:

If you have indicated a track which would not be the normal track for the case, please give brief reasons for your choice:

1

C Pre-Action protocols

Have you complied with any pre-action protocol
applicable to your claim?

☐ None
applicable
to this claim
☐ Yes ☐ No

If Yes, please say which protocol:

SPECIMEN

If No, please explain to what extent and for what
reason it has not been complied with:

D Applications

If you have not already sent the court an application
for summary judgment, do you intend to do so?

☐ Yes ☐ No

If you have not already issued a claim in the case
against someone not yet a party, do you intend to
apply for the court's permission to do so?

☐ Yes ☐ No

In either case, if Yes, please give details:

E Witnesses of fact

So far as you know at this stage, what witness of
fact do you intend to call at the hearing?

Witness name	Witness to which facts

2

F Experts' evidence

SPECIMEN

Do you wish to use expert evidence at the hearing? ☑ Yes ☐ No

Have you already copied any experts' report(s) to the other party(ies)? ☐ None obtained as yet ☐ Yes ☐ No

Please list the experts whose evidence you think you will use:

Expert's Name	Field of expertise (eg. orthopaedic surgeon, mechanical engineer)

Will you and the other party(ies) use the same expert(s)? ☐ Yes ☐ No

If No, please explain why not:

Do you want your expert(s) to give evidence orally at the hearing or trial? ☐ Yes ☐ No

If Yes, give the reasons why you think oral evidence is necessary:

G Location of trial

Is there any reason why your case needs to be heard at a particular court? ☐ Yes ☐ No

If Yes, give reasons (eg. particular facilities required, convenience of witnesses, etc.)

and specify the court:

3

[P.T.O.

H Representation and estimate of hearing/trial time

Do you expect to be represented by a solicitor or counsel at the hearing/trial?

☐ No ☐ Solicitor ☐ Counsel

How long do you estimate it will take to put your case to the court at the hearing/trial?

days	hours	minutes

SPECIMEN

If there are days when you, your representative, expert or an essential witness will not be able to attend court, give details:

Name	Dates not available

I Costs (only relates to costs incurred by legal representatives)

What is your estimate of costs incurred to date, excluding disbursements, VAT and court fees?

£

What do you estimate the overall costs are likely to be, excluding disbursements, VAT and court fees?

£

J Other Information

Have you attached documents you wish the judge to take into account when allocating the case?

☐ Yes ☐ No

Have they been served on the other parties?

☐ Yes ☐ No

If Yes, say when

Have the other parties agreed their content?

☐ Yes ☐ No

Have you attached a list of the directions you think appropriate for the management of your case?

☐ Yes ☐ No

Are they agreed with the other parties?

☐ Yes ☐ No

Are there any other facts which might affect the timetable the court will set? If so, please state

Signed   Date

[Counsel][Solicitor][for the][Claimant][Defendant]

Oyez   7 Spa Road, London SE16 3QQ

4.99 F35984

5093123
★ ★ ★ ★ ★

N150 – Allocation Questionnaire

Allocation to a Track

The court will allocate the claim to a track (see page 89) when it receives all the Allocation Questionnaires or when the period for filing the Questionnaires has expired or, if it has stayed the proceedings, at the end of the period of the stay. The case will be allocated to a procedural judge who will deal with the management of the case and allocate it to a track. Before deciding on the most suitable track for the case, the court may hold an allocation hearing if it is thought necessary.

Once the court has allocated a case to a track, it will serve a Notice of Allocation on every party (a different form will be used by the court for the Notice of Allocation, depending on the track to which the case has been allocated). At the same time, the court will serve on every party a copy of the Allocation Questionnaires completed by the other parties and a copy of any further information provided by another party. Before it allocates a case to a track, the court may order a party to provide further information about his case. Having allocated a case to a particular track, the court may re-allocate a claim to a different track if it considers it appropriate to do so.

Transferring a Case to Another Court

If the claim is for a specified amount of money and the defendant is an individual (not a company or some other organisation), the court will normally automatically transfer the proceedings to the court which is nearest to the address for service given by the defendant in his Defence (the defendant's 'home court'). This will usually apply unless the case is one which must be heard in a specialist list in the High Court. If the claim is against more than one defendant with different home courts, the proceedings will be transferred to the home court of the defendant who filed his Defence first.

Before allocating a claim to a particular track, the court may, if it feels it appropriate to do so, transfer a case to another court in any event.

Summary Judgment

In many cases (but not those in the small claims track) a party may apply to the court to decide the claim or an issue without a trial, by way of summary judgment. The court may also, of its own initiative, give summary judgment, although in this instance, it must give the parties an opportunity to be heard. Summary judgment is a way of deciding a claim without trial and may be given against either party on all or part of the claim if it is considered that either party has no real prospect of success.

The Small Claims Track

The small claims track is for straightforward claims which have a financial value of not more than £5,000 (subject to the exceptions relating to claims for damages for personal injuries or housing disrepair where there is a £1,000 limit). If a claim of a higher value is suitable for the small claims track, it may be allocated to the small claims track if the parties agree. Claims in the small claims track are heard in a county court, usually by a District judge.

The small claims track aims to avoid large amounts of work before trial and hearings for cases on this track are more informal than for claims on the other tracks. Some parts of the CPR which apply to fast track and/or multi-track cases do not apply to small claims procedures, e.g., offers and payments under Part 36 CPR (see page 132) are not part of the small claims procedure.

When a case has been allocated to the small claims track, the court will manage the case by setting dates and time limits for various things which must be done by the parties. This is called giving 'directions'. The court will also encourage the parties to use an alternative dispute resolution procedure (see Chapter 4) where it considers this to be appropriate. It is possible for someone to conduct his own case in the small claims track without instructing a solicitor. See also page 89 regarding the allocation of claims to a track.

Preparing for the Hearing

One of the things the court will do is to give 'directions', i.e., instruct the parties on what they should do to prepare their case for a hearing or for trial. Directions will usually have to be carried out within a certain time limit, e.g., each party must, at least 14 days before the date of the final hearing, file and serve on every other party copies of all documents on which he intends to rely at the hearing. The court may give any other directions that may be laid down, and may also give any special or further directions it considers to be appropriate.

The court will fix a date for a preliminary hearing (see below) if it is considered that this will be helpful, otherwise a date may be fixed for the final hearing. The court must normally give the parties at least 21 days' notice of the final hearing date, and inform them how much time will be allowed for the hearing. It may even be considered by the court that a hearing is not necessary at all, in which case, it must ask the parties whether they agree to this. If the judge decides a case without a hearing, he will prepare a note of the reasons for his judgment and the court will send a copy to each party.

Preliminary Hearing

The court may hold a preliminary hearing for various reasons. These include:

(a) it feels that special directions are needed to ensure a fair hearing and also thinks that one of the parties should attend court so that they fully understand the special directions that are to be given;

(b) one of the parties may have no real prospect of success at a final hearing and the court may be able to dispose of the claim at a preliminary hearing before anything further is done;

(c) where the court considers that the claim is not suitable for the small claims track.

If the court does decide to hold a preliminary hearing, it must give the parties at least 14 days' notice. If all parties agree, the court may treat the preliminary hearing as the final hearing of the claim.

At or after the preliminary hearing, the court will give any appropriate directions and will fix the date of the final hearing if this has not already been done, also informing the parties of the time allowed for the final hearing.

The Final Hearing

A small claims hearing is a public hearing before a District judge or Circuit judge. The judge may decide to hold the hearing in private if the parties agree or if there are other reasons which are permitted. The small claims hearing will usually take place in the judge's room but could take place in a courtroom. It will be more informal than trials on the other tracks, e.g., the court may decide that evidence need not be given on oath. A small claims hearing should normally be disposed of within one day.

If one of the parties does not attend the final hearing and has not given the court written notice at least seven days before the hearing date that he will be unable to attend, the court may strike out that party's Claim or Defence and/or Counterclaim. A party may ask the court to decide the case in his absence but this request must be made to the court in the notice informing the court that he will be unable to attend. As with a case decided without a hearing, if it is heard in the absence of a party who has given suitable notice, the court will send to the parties a copy of the judge's notes giving reasons for his judgment.

If the defendant does not attend the final hearing but the claimant does, the court may proceed with the hearing on the basis of the evidence given by the claimant.

The Fast Track

The fast track is the normal track for claims where the value of the claim is not more than £15,000 and where the claim is not one which would be dealt with in the small claims track. Exceptions may be made in allocating a case to this track.

When a case is allocated to the fast track, the court will give directions for the management of the case by setting dates and time limits for various things which must be done by the parties. The court will either fix the trial date or fix a specific period of time (not covering more than four weeks) — a 'window' — during which the trial will take place. The Notice of Allocation sent by the court to the parties will specify the date of trial or the period of time in which the trial will take place. The CPR provide that the trial should take place in 30 weeks or less from the time that the directions were given. A case in the fast track should not normally last more than one day which, of course, may depend on the number of witnesses to be called, the number of experts that may be required, and the complexity of the issues involved.

The court will send the parties a Listing Questionnaire (see page 103) which they must complete and return by the date specified in the Notice of Allocation. Once the date for filing the completed Listing Questionnaire has passed, the court will fix the date for trial or, if it has already done this, it will confirm the date. It will also give any directions for the trial, including a trial timetable and specify any further steps that need to be taken before trial. At least three weeks' notice of the date of trial will usually be given.

The timetable for the trial may be agreed by the parties, subject to approval of the trial judge. The timetable will specify the time allowed for both the claimant and defendant's evidence and the time allowed for the submissions to be made to the court on behalf of each party.

Request for Further Information

In fast track and multi-track cases (see page 102), if one party wishes to request further information from another party, based on that party's statement of case, he can make a Request for Further Information under Part 18 CPR.

The party seeking further information (the first party) should serve on the party from whom he is seeking the information (the second party) a written Request, giving a date by which a Response should be served, and stating that the Request is made under Part 18 CPR. If a Request for Information is very brief and it is likely that the response will be brief, this may be done in a letter, otherwise a Request should be in a separate document. If the Request is made in a letter, it must state that it is a Request under Part 18 CPR and the letter should not contain anything other than the Request. Before the CPR came into effect, a Request for Information was known as a Request for Further and Better Particulars.

All requests for further information, whether in a letter or a separate document, should be headed with the title of the action; identify the first and second parties; give the claim number; and state in its heading that it is a Request made under Part 18 CPR, giving the date when the Request is made. The pages and paragraphs should be numbered and where the Request relates to another document, e.g., it may be a request for further information about something mentioned in the Particulars of Claim, that other document must be referred to and the paragraph or words to which the Request relates should be clearly identified (see the example Request for Further Information). The date by which the Response is expected must also be given.

If the Request is in document format, rather than a letter, it may have the numbered paragraphs of the Request on the left-hand side of the paper, so that the second party can reply on the same document opposite each numbered paragraph on the right-hand side of the paper. If the Request is prepared in this way, an extra copy should be prepared for the second party to keep.

The Response to a Request must be in writing and dated and signed by the responding party or his legal representative. The Response will have the same type of layout as the Request. If it is in a separate document (and not one where the answers can be given on the right-hand side of the page of the Request), the text of each paragraph of the Request must be set out and then the Response will be given below that (see example). It may also have a backsheet.

A Response should also be verified by a Statement of Truth (see page 62). When one party serves his Response on another party, he must also serve a copy on any other party to the proceedings and file a copy with the court, as well as keeping a copy on his own file.

Example Request for Further Information

IN THE SOUTHTOWN COUNTY COURT   Claim No. 00.12345

BETWEEN:

PAUL XAVIER   Claimant

and

JOHN JONES   Defendant

REQUEST FOR FURTHER INFORMATION

UNDER PART 18 CPR

DATED 9th APRIL 2000

1. Of paragraph 1 in the Particulars of Claim dated ****, 'the claimant was the owner and driver of a Rolls Royce motor car registration number 123 ABC.' State how long he had owned this car.

2. Of paragraph 3 in the Particulars of Claim dated ****, '... failed to keep any or any proper lookout.' State exactly how the defendant failed to keep any or any proper lookout.

JOHN BROWN

[*counsel's name, if appropriate*]

Dated the 9th day of April 2000.

Joe Bloggs & Co., of 1 Broad Walk, Southtown, Herts. EN4 9PP. Solicitors for the defendant.

[*The Request would also identify the party seeking the information (the first party) and the party who is to provide the information (the second party). Additionally, it must contain a date specifying by when the first party expects to receive a Response to the Request. As mentioned previously, it may also be set out in a different format with the questions on the left-hand side of the paper, leaving room on the right-hand side for the other party's Response.*]

Example Response to Request for Further Information

IN THE SOUTHTOWN COUNTY COURT   Claim No. 00.12345

BETWEEN:

PAUL XAVIER   Claimant

and

JOHN JONES   Defendant

RESPONSE TO REQUEST FOR FURTHER
INFORMATION UNDER PART 18 CPR
DATED 9th APRIL 2000

1.   Of paragraph 1 in the Particulars of Claim dated ****, 'the claimant was the owner and driver of a Rolls Royce motor car registration number 123 ABC.' State how long he had owned this car..

ANSWER

The claimant had owned this car for 2 years.

2.   Of paragraph 3 in the Particulars of Claim dated ****, '... failed to keep any or any proper lookout.' State exactly how the defendant failed to keep any or any proper lookout.

ANSWER

The defendant failed to keep any or any proper lookout because he had his eyes closed at the time.

I believe that the facts stated in this Response to Request for Further Information are true. [*Note: the wording of this Statement of Truth will vary according to who is signing it*]

Signed ....

[*The status of the person signing the Statement of Truth will be inserted, e.g., defendant, defendant's solicitors, and if the solicitors are signing it they will also state that they are authorised by their client to do so*]

DATED this 19th day of April 2000.

John Smith & Co., of 2 Bank Chambers, High Road, Southtown, Herts. Solicitors for the Claimant.

Disclosure and Inspection of Documents

One of the directions given for fast track and multi-track cases may be about disclosure and inspection of documents. This is described on page 109.

Expert Evidence

The parties may obtain reports from experts, for example, medical reports in a claim for personal injuries, or surveyors' reports in cases relating to property, or any other type of expert evidence that may be appropriate for the claim. Often each party will wish to obtain its own expert evidence but it is preferred, where possible, for a single joint expert to be agreed. If a single joint expert cannot be agreed, then expert evidence should be exchanged between the parties. The directions will specify the time by which any such reports must be served on or exchanged with the other parties involved.

The parties should also try to agree their reports if possible, usually no later than 14 days after they have been served on the other party. If the reports cannot be agreed, the directions may provide for the experts to discuss their reports in an attempt to reach agreement. If the experts cannot reach agreement, they must prepare a statement setting out the issues on which they agree and disagree and their reasons, and this statement must be filed with the court.

If one party wishes to address any questions to the other party's expert, the directions deal with how this will be done. See also page 131 regarding experts' evidence.

Witnesses of Fact

In a similar way to experts' reports being exchanged, if any party intends to rely on the statements of any witnesses of fact, he should exchange or serve these on the other parties. The directions deal with the timing of this.

In fast track cases, the court will also give directions as to when the Listing Questionnaire (see page 103) must be completed and filed. Once the Listing Questionnaire has been completed, the court may give further directions.

The Multi-Track

The multi-track is the normal track for any claim which does not come into the small claims or fast track categories. A multi-track claim will normally be heard in a Civil Trial Centre or may be heard in the Royal Courts of Justice in London (RCJ), although there are special provisions for RCJ cases. In multi-track cases, the court has more flexibility in managing the case than the courts have in small claims track and fast track cases.

As with cases in the other tracks, when a case is allocated to the multi-track, the court will give directions for the management of the case and set a timetable for the steps to be taken between the giving of directions and the trial. In multi-track cases, the court may also hold case management conferences (see below) and may give any other directions it considers to be appropriate.

Case Management Conferences and Pre-Trial Review

Once a Defence has been filed, the court may fix a case management conference if the case is allocated to the multi-track. This will usually be conducted by the procedural judge, i.e., the judge allocated to deal with the management of the case prior to trial. The party's legal representative must attend the case management conference. The legal representative must be someone who is fully involved in the case and who can deal with any matters that may arise during the conference. If appropriate, the parties to the claim will attend the conference. The fee earner attending the conference may wish to prepare a case summary to assist the court at the conference. If he does, the case summary will set out brief details of the claim in chronological order, together with the issues of fact which are agreed or in dispute and the evidence needed to decide them. The summary should, if possible, be agreed with the other parties and should not normally be longer than 500 words.

Various matters will be discussed at the case management conference, such as proposals for the management of the proceedings, including a proposed trial date or period in which the trial should take place. The parties will normally have to state whether they have discussed the question of Alternative Dispute Resolution (see Chapter 4) and if not, why not.

The case management conference will review the steps which have been taken by the parties to prepare the case, in particular their compliance with any directions that may have been given by the court. Any further directions that may be necessary to progress the claim may also be decided at the conference, as well as trying to ensure that the parties reach agreement on any matters where at all possible.

The court may hold another case conference or a pre-trial review if it is estimated that the case will last for more than 10 days. A pre-trial review will be held between four and eight weeks before the trial date, after the Listing Questionnaires (see below) have been filed with the court. The purpose of the pre-trial review is to decide on a timetable for the trial, and this will include such things as the evidence that will be allowed, an estimate of how long the trial will last, and various other matters. The pre-trial review will normally be conducted by the trial judge and it should be attended by the legal representatives who will be representing the parties at the trial.

Listing Questionnaire

In fast track and multi-track cases, the court will send each party a Listing Questionnaire (Form N170) which they must complete and return to the court by the date specified in the Notice of Allocation (which the court sent to the parties to notify them which track the case will be allocated to). The date specified for filing the Listing Questionnaire will not be more than eight weeks before the trial date or the beginning of the trial period.

The court will use the information provided by the parties in their Listing Questionnaires to fix the date for trial (or confirm the date if it has already been fixed) and to confirm the estimated length of trial. It will also set a timetable for the trial itself. In multi-track cases, the court will also decide whether to hold case management conferences (see above).

If any party does not return the Listing Questionnaire or does not provide other information required by the court, or if the court considers it necessary, the court may fix a listing hearing or give any other directions it may consider appropriate.

The Listing Questionnaire is self-explanatory, dealing with matters such as whether or not any directions have been complied with, experts and other witnesses, estimation of length of trial, estimated number of pages of evidence in the trial bundle (see below). It also asks those whose case has been allocated to the fast track whether they would accept less than three weeks' notice of the trial date.

Although it is not necessary for the parties to exchange copies of the Questionnaires before they are filed with the court, it is desirable that they do so to avoid the court being given conflicting or incomplete information.

The Questionnaire must be signed and dated, with a copy being kept on the file, and then returned to the court, together with the appropriate fee. If listing for trial takes place without a Questionnaire, the fee is payable within a specified time after the case is listed.

Listing Questionnaire

SPECIMEN

In the	SOUTHTOWN COUNTY COURT
Claim No.	00.12345
Last date for filing with court office	

To

- The court will use the information which you and the other party(ies) provide to fix a date for trial (or to confirm the date and time if one has already been fixed), to confirm the estimated length of trial and to set a timetable for the trial itself. In multi-track cases the court will also decide whether to hold a pre-trial review.

- If you do not complete and return the questionnaire the procedural judge may

  - make an order which leads to your statement of case (claim or defence) being struck out.

  - decide to hold a listing hearing. You may be ordered to pay (immediately) the other parties' costs of attending.

  - if there is sufficient information, list the case for trial and give any appropriate directions.

A Directions complied with

1. Have you complied with all the previous directions given by the court? ☐ **Yes** ☐ **No**

2. If no please explain which directions are outstanding and why.

Directions outstanding	Reasons directions outstanding

3. Are any further directions required to prepare the case for trial? ☐ **Yes** ☐ **No**
(If no go to section B)

4. If yes, please explain directions required and give reasons.

Directions required	Reasons required

N170 Listing Questionnaire (4.99)   [P.T.O.

B Experts

SPECIMEN

1. Has the court already given permission for you to use written expert evidence?
☐ Yes ☐ No
(If no go to section B6)

2. If yes, please give name and field of expertise.

Name of expert	Whether joint expert *(please tick, if appropriate)*	Field of expertise

3. Have the expert(s') report(s) been agreed with the other parties?
☐ Yes ☐ No

4. Have the experts met to discuss their reports?
☐ Yes ☐ No

5. Has the court already given permission for the expert(s) to give oral evidence at the trial?
(If yes go to Q7) ☐ Yes ☐ No

6. If no are you seeking that permission?
☐ Yes ☐ No
(If no go to section C)

7. If yes, give your reasons for seeking permission.

8. If yes, what are the names, addresses and fields of expertise of your experts?

Expert 1	Expert 2	Expert 3	Expert 4

9. Please give details of any dates within the trial period when your expert(s) will not be available.

Name of expert	Dates not available

SPECIMEN

C Other witnesses

(If you are not calling other witnesses go to section D)

1. **How many other witnesses (including yourself) will be giving evidence on your behalf at the trial?** *(do not include experts – see section B above)*

☐ *(Give number)*

2. **What are the names and addresses of your witnesses?**

Witness 1	Witness 2	Witness 3	Witness 4

3. **Please give details of any dates within the trial period when you or your witnesses will not be available.**

Name of witness	Dates not available

4. **Are any of the witness statements agreed?**   ☐ Yes   ☐ No

(If no go to question C6)

5. **If yes, give the name of the witness and the date of his or her statement.**

Name of witness	Date of statement

6. **Do you or any of your witnesses need any special facilities?**   ☐ Yes   ☐ No

(If no go to question C8)

7. **If yes, what are they?**

8. **Will any of your witnesses be provided with an interpreter?**   ☐ Yes   ☐ No

(If no go to section D)

9. **If yes, say what type of interpreter e.g. language (stating which), deaf/blind etc.**

[P.T.O.

D Legal representation   *SPECIMEN*

1. Who will be presenting your case at the hearing or trial? ☐ You ☐ Solicitor ☐ Counsel

2. Please give details of any dates within the trial period when the person presenting your case will not be available.

Name	Dates not available

E Other matters

1. How long do you estimate the trial will take, including cross-examination and closing arguments?

Minutes	Hours	Days

If your case is allocated to the fast track the maximum time allowed for the whole case will be no more than one day.

2. What is the estimated number of pages of evidence to be included in the trial bundle?

(please give number)

Fast track cases only

3. The court will normally give you 3 weeks notice in the fast track of the date fixed for a fast track trial unless, in exceptional circumstances, the court directs that shorter notice will be given. Would you be prepared to accept shorter notice of the date fixed for trial?   ☐ Yes   ☐ No

Signed

Claimant/Defendant or Counsel/Solicitor for the Claimant/Defendant

Date

Oyez   7 Spa Road, London SE16 3QQ

4.99 F35985
5093131
★ ★ ★ ★ ★

N170 – Listing Questionnaire

108

The Trial Bundle

The trial bundle is an indexed bundle of documents contained in a ring binder with each page clearly numbered consecutively. It must be lodged at the court within a specified time before the hearing. The judge will normally read these papers before the trial takes place. The bundle will usually include copies of some or all of the following:

(a) the Claim Form and all statements of case;

(b) a case summary (this should be no more than 250 words outlining the matters still in issue). This will assist the judge in reading the papers before trial and, if possible, the parties should try to agree the case summary.

(c) any requests for further information and responses to the requests;

(d) any witness statements that it is intended to rely on as evidence;

(e) any witness summaries (see page 128);

(f) any notices of intention to rely on hearsay evidence (see page 131);

(g) any notices of intention to rely on evidence that is not being given verbally at court or is not in a witness statement, affidavit or expert's report, or is not hearsay evidence. This could be something like a plan or a photograph.

(h) medical reports and responses to them;

(i) experts' reports and responses to them;

(j) any order giving directions regarding the way the trial is to be conducted; and

(k) any other documents which are necessary.

Of course, all these documents will not be required at every trial. It will depend on the circumstances of the individual case. The original documents, together with copies of any other court orders, should be available at the trial.

If at all possible, the parties should try to agree the contents of the trial bundle.

If there is more than 100 pages in the bundle, numbered dividers should be placed between different groups of documents. If more than one bundle is going to the court, they should each be distinguished, perhaps by using different colours. The party filing the trial bundle must supply identical bundles to all other parties to the proceedings and for the use of the witnesses.

Disclosure and Inspection of Documents

Where a case is allocated to the fast track or the multi-track, the parties should disclose to the other parties in the case details of documents upon which they rely or which materially undermine their own case or support the other party's case. This is termed as 'standard disclosure'. Any further disclosure will be determined by the procedural judge. Where a party has or knows of documents that he should disclose, he must provide a list of those documents to the other party, unless the parties have agreed that there will be no list (or this has been dispensed with by the court), stating that the document exists or has existed. This is referred to as disclosure of documents. Before the Civil Procedure Rules, this was known as 'discovery'.

Once a document has been disclosed in this way, the party to whom it has been disclosed has a right to inspect it unless the document is no longer in the control of the party who disclosed it or the party disclosing it has a right or duty to withhold inspection of it.

The documents which are to be disclosed should be listed on Form N265. They should be listed in chronological or some other convenient order and should be numbered consecutively. Each document should have a brief description, e.g., letter to claimant's employer; brief to counsel. If there is bulky correspondence between the same people, instead of itemising each letter, they can be listed as a bundle with an appropriate description, e.g., letters between Joe Bloggs and John Smith between 1 November 1998 and 8 July 1999. The list must indicate which documents are no longer in that party's control and state what has happened to them.

The list is divided into sections showing:

(a) documents to which there is no objection to them being inspected or copied;
(b) those where there is an objection to them being inspected (giving reasons);
(c) those which the disclosing party has had, but no longer has.

The list must also include a disclosure statement (unless the parties have agreed that there will be no disclosure statement) which gives details of the extent of any search made to locate relevant documents. The disclosure statement must also certify that the party disclosing understands the duty to disclose documents and that he has carried out that duty to the best of his knowledge. The wording of the disclosure statement is shown on the first page of the list of documents (Form N265).

If, after a list of documents has been served, further documents come to light, a supplemental list of documents must be prepared.

If a party wishes to inspect a document, he must give the disclosing party written notice that he wishes to inspect it and the disclosing party must allow inspection within seven days of receiving that notice. The party inspecting may ask for a copy of the document if he agrees to pay reasonable copying charges. The copy should be supplied within seven days.

If it is desired that a document in the list should not be inspected by the other party, e.g., it may be a privileged document, the disclosure statement must summarise the reasons for this. If a document is privileged, this means that the party whose document it is has a right not to disclose or produce it. Examples of such documents are correspondence between the solicitor and his client, Instructions to Counsel, Counsel's Opinion, and 'without prejudice' documents. 'Without prejudice' is written on correspondence between solicitors usually when a settlement of the case is being sought. Such correspondence is not produced at any later court proceedings. You may find that you often have to type the words 'Without Prejudice' at the top of a letter. If it is considered that disclosure of a document may damage the public interest, the relevant party may apply to the court for permission not to disclose that document.

If disclosure is required by someone who is not a party to the proceedings, application must be made to the court.

SPECIMEN

List of Documents: Standard Disclosure

Notes:
- The rules relating to standard disclosure are contained in Part 31 of the Civil Procedure Rules.
- Documents to be included under standard disclosure are contained in Rule 31.6.
- A document has or will have been in your control if you have or have had possession, or a right of possession, of it **or** a right to inspect or take copies of it.

In the	SOUTHTOWN COUNTY COURT
Claim No.	00.12345
Claimant (including ref)	PAUL XAVIER (XAV/789)
Defendant (including ref)	JOHN JONES (JON/cd)

Disclosure Statement

(1) Insert date

I state that I have carried out a reasonable and proportionate search to locate all the documents which I am required to disclose under the order made by the court on(')   [19][20].

(I did not search for documents –

1. pre-dating

2. located elsewhere than

3. in categories other than

)

I certify that I understand the duty of disclosure and to the best of my knowledge I have carried out that duty. I further certify that the list of documents set out in or attached to this form, is a complete list of all documents which are or have been in my control and which I am obliged under the order to disclose.

I understand that I must inform the court and the other parties immediately if any further document required to be disclosed by Rule 31.6 comes into my control at any time before the conclusion of the case.

(I have not permitted inspection of documents within the category or class of documents (as set out below) required to be disclosed under Rule 31(6)(b) or (c) on the grounds that to do so would be disproportionate to the issues in the case.)

Signed   **Date**

(Claimant)(Defendant)('s Litigation friend)

Position or office held *(if signing on behalf of firm or company)*
Please state why you are the appropriate person to make the disclosure statement.

N265 List of Documents: Standard Disclosure

P.T.O.

111

List and number here, in a convenient order, the documents (or bundles of documents if of the same nature, e.g. invoices) in your control, which you do not object to being inspected. Give a short description of each document or bundle so that it can be identified, and say if it is kept elsewhere i.e. with a bank or solicitor.

I have control of the documents numbered and listed here. I do not object to you inspecting them/producing copies:

1. Estimate - Speed & Co. dated 20 July 1999
2. Car hire account -
    Smith & Co.   dated 1 August 1999

SPECIMEN

List and number here, as above, the documents in your control which you object to being inspected.
(Rule 31.19).

I have control of the documents numbered and listed here, but I object to you inspecting them:

Say what your objections are.

I object to you inspecting these documents because:

| List and number here, the documents you once had in your control, but which you no longer have. For each document listed, say when it was last in your control and where it is now. *(Continue overleaf if necessary).* | I have had the documents numbered and listed below, but they are no longer in my control: |

Interrogatories

Interrogatories are formal questions asked of one party by the other which they feel have relevance to the case in hand. Their format is the same as for other documents, i.e., they must include the title of the action (see page 53). The Response to the Interrogatories will be in question and answer form — setting out the question and then giving below it the answer (the same way as a response to the more common Request for Further Information — see page 99). Interrogatories are normally only permitted in multi-track cases and then only with the court's permission. Paragraphs should be numbered.

Amending a Statement of Case

A statement of case (formerly known as a pleading) may be amended at any time before it is served on another party. If it has already been served, it may be amended only with the written consent of all the other parties involved or with the permission of the court.

If making an application to the court to amend a statement of case, a copy of the statement of case showing the proposed amendments should be filed with the application. Once permission to amend has been given, the amended statement of case should be filed with the court, usually within 14 days. A copy of the amended statement of case should be served on all parties to the proceedings. Depending on the amendments made, it may be necessary to re-verify the statement of case by a Statement of Truth.

An amended statement of case and the court copy of it, if permission was needed from the court, should include the following endorsement:

> Amended [Particulars of Claim *or whatever is the document*] by Order of [Master *Bloggs*] [District Judge *Bloggs*] (*or whoever made the Order*) dated ....

If the court's permission was not required to make the amendment, the statement of case should be endorsed as follows:

> Amended [Particulars of Claim *or whatever is the document*] under CPR [17.1(1)] [17.1(2)(a)] dated ....

Rule 17.1(1) would be inserted in the endorsement above if the statement of case has not yet been served on another party. Rule 17.1(2)(a) applies where the written consent of all the other parties has been obtained.

The amended statement of case does not have to show the original text (which may have been deleted) unless the court thinks this is necessary. Where this is the case, both the original text and the amendments would have to be shown. This may be done in one of two ways.

    (a)   by coloured amendments, either made by hand or computer generated; or
    (b)   by numbering the amendments in superscript (this may only be done in a computer generated document — the numbers should not be inserted by hand — and colours should not be used in this instance). Where this method is adopted, insertions should be underlined and numbered; and deletions should be struck through and numbered.

Where colour is used to make the amendments, the text to be deleted is struck through in colour and any text replacing it or additional text should be written in the same colour, or written in black and underlined in that colour. Red should be used the first time that any document is amended. If, however, at another time, it is desired to amend the already amended statement of case, a different colour must be used for the amendments to show that it is an entirely different set of amendments. This time, the colour should be green. After green, the next colour is violet and then yellow. It is not, however, very common to go past the green amendment stage.

In the example below showing how coloured amendments would be made, the line striking through the text would be in red and where the text is underlined, either the text would be in red or it would be underlined in red. Therefore, all amendments would be clearly shown in red. Thus:

1. The Claimant was the owner and driver of a Rolls Royce motor car, registration number 123 ~~ABC~~ <u>DEF</u>.
2. On 5 July 1999 the Claimant was driving his said motor car along <u>Station Road,</u> ~~Mulberry Close,~~ Barnet, Hertfordshire.

If the amendments are made by numbering them, you would strike through text to be deleted, following this with the appropriate number in superscript, e.g., ~~the car veered off the road~~[1]. Text to be added will be typed in and underlined, with the superscript number next to it, e.g., <u>the car veered off the road</u>[1].

The number will relate to the stage the amendments have reached, i.e., the first time amendments are made, all the amendments made at that time will be numbered 1 (in relation to the scheme using colours, this would be the red amendment stage); on the next occasion when amendments are made to the document (the green amendment stage if using colours), all the amendments at that stage will be numbered 2, and so on.

If the amendments to the statement of case have been settled by counsel, then as with other documents settled by counsel, it must show his name. If the amended document is one where both the amendments and the original text have to be shown, counsel's name will be typed at the end either in the appropriate colour or with the appropriate numbering. This will be typed beneath where counsel's name is shown on the original text, if applicable. In a similar manner, where amendments have to be shown, if the document had been previously served on another party, once it has been amended, it will have to be re-served on the other party and this will have to be shown on the new document as an amendment.

Thus, if the document has to show all the amendments made, it will contain details of both the date of service of the original document and details of service of the amended document. Remember to amend the backsheet as well to show that the new document is an amended one. For example, if the old document was a Particulars of Claim, you would add in red the word 'Amended' before 'Particulars of Claim' (which would stay in black).

Photocopies of documents which have to show the amendments that have been made must also be clear. Therefore, if colour has been used for making the amendments, this must be shown on the copy, either by colour copying or by underlining and/or striking through the amendments in the appropriate colour so that the copy is the same as the original. However, as stated earlier, not all amended statements of case will require the amendments to be shown.

Applications for Court Orders

A court order may be required by a party either before issuing proceedings or at some time before the trial date. To obtain a court order, an application must be made to the court by way of an Application Notice. Before the CPR, an application to the court for an order was made by way of summons (indeed, some still are). An application made to the court after proceedings have been issued, but before the trial date, may be termed an 'interlocutory' application. There are many reasons for making an application to the court, such as asking for more time to file a statement of case or perhaps one party will not comply with the request of another and the only way to resolve this would be for the court to make a decision on the matter.

The person making the application is called the Applicant and the person against whom the order is sought is the Respondent. If proceedings have already been started or have been transferred to another court, the application must be made to the court where the proceedings are being dealt with. If the claim has already been listed for trial, the application must be made to the court where the trial will take place. If proceedings have not yet been started, an application must be made to the court where proceedings would normally be started.

Applications to the court must normally be made by filing with the court an Application Notice (Form N244). It must state what order is being sought by the Applicant and why he is seeking the order. As well as all the usual details, such as name of the court, claim number, names of the parties to the action, the Notice must also include:

   (a)   a request for a hearing, giving an estimate of the time the hearing will take; or a request that the application is dealt with without a hearing;

   (b)   the full name of the Applicant or his solicitor;

   (c)   details of the order sought (sometimes a draft order should be attached);

   (d)   the reasons for making the application;

   (e)   if the Applicant is not already a party to the proceedings, his address for service;

   (f)   in some cases, the Application Notice will have to be verified by a Statement of Truth (see below and also see page 62);

   (g)   it must be signed by the Applicant or his solicitor.

If the application is being verified by a Statement of Truth, it would state 'I believe [or the Applicant believes] that the facts stated in this application notice are true.' If the Statement of Truth is in a separate document, it would say 'I believe [or the Applicant believes] that the facts stated in the application notice issued on [date] for [whatever remedy is being sought] are true.' Do not, as a secretary, sign the Statement of Truth yourself.

If an application is supported by a witness statement, a copy of any such statement should be included for service on the Respondent. Similarly, if the application is asking that the Respondent provides further information relating to a statement of case, a copy of the Request for Further Information should be attached to the application.

Two copies of the Application Notice must be prepared, and should then be given to whoever in your firm will go to court to have it issued (the outdoor clerk, or it can be sent to the court by post). There is a box on the form to complete giving an estimate of how long the hearing will take (the fee earner will deal with this aspect). The appropriate fee must be paid to the court to issue the Application Notice. If you are posting the Application Notice to the court, you must also send a stamped and self-addressed envelope. The court will notify the Applicant of the date and time of the hearing (known as the 'return date'). The fee earner may ask you to note in his diary the date and time of the application and inform whoever will be attending.

The court may serve (see page 63) the Application Notice on the Respondent, or the Applicant's solicitors may wish to serve it. The original sealed Application Notice should be kept in the file and a copy will be served on the other party. It must be served at least three days before the date when the court will be dealing with it. Copies of any witness statements in support of the application must be served at the same time. If there is not enough time to serve the Application Notice, e.g., the matter may be extremely urgent, informal notification must be given to the other parties unless it is a case where the application is being made without notice (see below).

If you are asked to write a letter serving an Application Notice, it will be on the following lines:

Dear Sirs,

Xavier v Jones

We enclose, by way of service, Application Notice returnable before Master Bloggs at 11 a.m. on Tuesday, 10th February, 2000. Kindly acknowledge receipt.

Yours faithfully,

Once the Respondent has received the notification of the hearing time and date, he or his solicitors will be able to arrange to attend court and make representations. However, in some instances, applications may be made to the court without giving notice to the Respondent. Before the CPR came into effect, this type of application was known as an *ex parte* application. Without notice applications may also be made by an interested person who is not a party to the action. The rules of the court set out which applications may be heard with or without notice. In practice, most are with notice.

An application will be heard by a Master (at the Royal Courts of Justice in London), or a judge, usually in the rooms of the Master or judge, rather than in a courtroom. If something is heard in the rooms of the Master or judge, it may be referred to as being heard 'in chambers' although this term is not used now under the new Civil Procedure Rules. Alternatively, the court may, if it considers it appropriate, conduct an application hearing over the telephone or by video conferencing and, in these cases, certain rules and procedures apply. Where it is possible to do so, all applications relating to a particular case should be dealt with by the same Master or judge.

Normally, the Applicant's solicitors should take with them to any hearing a draft of the order they are seeking. If the case is one that is being heard in the Royal Courts of Justice in London and the order sought is particularly long or complicated, the solicitors should also provide the draft of the order to the court on disk in a specified word processing format.

An application may be dealt with by the court without a hearing if the parties agree to the terms of the order sought, or the parties agree that the court should dispose of the application without a hearing, or the court does not consider that a hearing will be appropriate.

The court may issue an Application Notice of its own motion, for example, if it is felt that some issue needs to be resolved between the parties. If a hearing date for an application has been arranged and is then cancelled, this is known as 'vacating' it.

CIVIL LITIGATION

Application Notice *SPECIMEN*

- You must complete Parts A **and** B, **and** Part C if applicable.
- Send any relevant fee and the completed application to the court with any draft order, witness statement or other evidence; and sufficient copies of these for service on each Respondent.

In the	
SOUTHTOWN COUNTY COURT	
Claim No.	00.12345
Warrant No. (if applicable)	
Claimant (including ref)	PAUL XAVIER (XAV/789)
Defendant(s) (including ref)	JOHN JONES (JON/cd)
Date	

You should provide this information for listing the application

1. Do you wish to have your application dealt with at a hearing?

Yes ☐　　No ☐　　If Yes, please complete 2

2. Time estimate　　(hours)　　(mins)

Is this agreed by all parties?　　Yes ☐　　No ☐

Level of judge

3. Parties to be served:

Part A

1. Enter your full name, or name of solicitor.

☑ [We](¹)　　John Smith & Co　　[on behalf of] [the Claimant] [~~the Defendant~~]

2. State clearly what order you are seeking and if possible attach a draft.

intend to apply for an order (a draft of which is attached) that(²)

3. Briefly set out why you are seeking the order. Include the material facts on which you rely, identifying any rule or statutory provision.

because(³)

Part B

[I] [We] wish to rely on: *tick one box*

the attached [witness statement] [affidavit] ☐　　my statement of case ☐

evidence in Part C overleaf in support of my application ☐

4. If you are not already a party to the proceedings, you must provide an address for service of documents.

Signed

(Applicant)('s Solicitor)('s Litigation friend)

Position or office held (if signing on behalf of firm or company)

Address to which documents about this claim should be sent (including reference if appropriate)(⁴)

John Smith & Co 2 Bank Chambers High Road Southtown Herts (ref: XAV/789) Tel. no.　01438 12345　　Postcode　EN5 6AX	if applicable	
	fax no.	01438 98765
	DX no.	DX 1234 Southtown
	e-mail	

The court office at

is open between 10 am and 4 pm (4.30 pm in High Court) Monday to Friday. When corresponding with the court, please address forms or letters to the Court Manager and quote the claim number.

N244 Application Notice (4.99)

[P.T.O.

118

Part C

SPECIMEN

Claim No.	

[I] [We] wish to rely on the following evidence in support of this application:

Statement of Truth

*[I believe][The Applicant believes] that the facts stated in this application are true.

Signed

(Applicant)('s Solicitor)('s Litigation friend)

Position or office held
(if signing on behalf of firm or company)

Date

*delete as appropriate

Oyez   7 Spa Road, London SE16 3QQ

4.99   F36081

5093238

★ ★ ★ ★ ★

N244

Orders

After the application has been heard, an order is made by the court, i.e., a decision on that particular matter, and this must be adhered to by the parties unless a successful appeal is made against the decision. The order will normally be drawn up and served either by the court or by one of the parties' solicitors with the court's permission. Alternatively, the court may dispense with the need to draw up an order.

If the terms of the application have been agreed by the parties and there is no need for a hearing, the order must be drawn up in the agreed terms and it must state on it that it is 'By Consent'. This can only be done where the parties are legally represented. The consent order must be signed by the solicitors or counsel for all relevant parties. It must be taken or sent to the court office to be sealed and a copy lodged with the court.

An order must normally state on it the name and judicial title of the person who made it, e.g., 'District Judge Bloggs' (the exceptions to this are stated in the Rules). If the hearing was in private, when the order is drawn up, the fact that it was heard in private must be clearly marked in the title, e.g., 'Before [*title and name of judge*] sitting in private.' The order must be dated the date the order was actually made (not necessarily the date it is typed) and must be sealed by the court.

The layout of an order is fairly simple. It is headed, as are all court documents, with the title of the action. The person who made the order, e.g., the judge, will be inserted as mentioned above, and the body of the order will be something like:

Upon hearing solicitors for both parties [*or whoever attended the hearing*]

IT IS ORDERED that [*details of the order are given here*]

And that costs of this application be [*details of how the costs for this application are awarded are inserted here*]

DATED the   *   day of   *   2000
[*The date the order is actually made is inserted here*]

If an order is drawn up by a party to the proceedings but is to be served by the court, that party must provide the court with sufficient copies for a copy to be retained by the court and a copy to be served on him and all the other parties.

If you have to serve an order on another party, you would send a copy of the sealed order (not the original) and your letter would be along the following lines:

Dear Sirs

Xavier v Jones

We enclose, by way of service, copy order in this matter. Kindly acknowledge receipt.

Yours faithfully,

Consolidation

You may sometimes have to type an application for consolidation of actions. Consolidating two or more actions means that for certain reasons, the actions would be joined together so that they are heard all at the same time.

Notice to Admit Facts/Documents

A party may serve a notice on another party requiring him to admit certain facts which he specifies in the notice. This Notice to Admit Facts must be served no later than 21 days before the trial.

Similarly, where a document has been disclosed (see page 109) to a party, he may serve notice on the disclosing party requiring him to prove at trial the authenticity of any document that he specifies in the notice. A notice to prove documents must be served no later than seven days before the trial, or by the latest date for serving witness statements (see page 128).

Affidavits

An affidavit is a written statement of evidence sworn on oath or affirmed to be true. It is often used in court proceedings. In some proceedings, an affidavit is used as evidence instead of witness statements (see page 128) or statements of case. The person who makes the affidavit and signs it is called the deponent.

An affidavit may be sworn in the presence of a practising solicitor, notary public or barrister, and when they do this, it is known as administering an oath. They have the powers of a Commissioner for Oaths, and this is a term you may come across. A Commissioner for Oaths is appointed by the Lord Chancellor but everyone who can administer oaths is not necessarily a Commissioner for Oaths. Certain other people are also authorised to administer oaths, e.g., a Circuit judge, District judge, Justice of the Peace, or an authorised officer of the court. A fee is normally payable for swearing an affidavit, as well as a smaller fee for each exhibit sworn, to the person who administers the oath. An affidavit relating to a particular matter cannot be sworn before a solicitor whose firm is involved in that matter and must be before someone who is independent of the person swearing it or any of the parties' solicitors. There are rules to be followed where a person making an affidavit cannot read or sign it.

An outline of the procedures involved in the actual swearing of the oath is that the person swearing the affidavit (the deponent) will sign the affidavit and any exhibit sheets (see below for information on exhibits). The person who is administering the oath will give the deponent to hold in a specific manner the New Testament, the Old Testament or the Koran (or whatever is appropriate to that person's religious beliefs). The person administering the oath will hold the signed affidavit and any exhibits and ask: 'Is this your name and handwriting?'. When the deponent answers that it is, he will be asked to repeat words swearing that the contents of the affidavit are true. The person administering the oath will then complete the jurat (see below). If the deponent is under 17, instead of being asked to say that he 'swears' the oath, he will say 'I promise'.

If the deponent does not wish to swear as above, he will be asked what would be binding on his conscience. If the deponent objects altogether to being sworn, he may affirm that the contents are true. If he is swearing a statutory declaration, he will 'declare' that the contents are true.

The affidavit should be typed on good quality A4 size paper and should have a 3.5 cm margin. It should normally be typed only on one side of the paper. The pages must be numbered consecutively. It must always give the title of the action, which means the court or division in which the claim is proceeding; the claim number; and the names and status (claimant, defendant, etc.) of the parties or the name of the matter to which it refers. Where there are several parties with the same status, e.g., several claimants or several defendants, etc., the name of one of the parties may be given followed by '(and others)', e.g.,

John Bloggs (and others) claimants

The following information must always be typed on each affidavit and any exhibit to that affidavit in the top right-hand corner before the title of the action:

(a) on which party's behalf the affidavit is sworn;
(b) the initials and surname of the person who has sworn it (the deponent);
(c) the number of that person's affidavit, i.e., if it is his first affidavit in that action, you would write '1st';
(d) if the affidavit refers to any exhibits (see below), the identifying initials and number of all exhibits referred to; and
(e) the date it has been sworn.

This information must also be given on any backsheet (see page 61). All numbers, including dates, should be in figures, e.g., '7th July 1999'. If reference is made in the affidavit to any documents, there should be a note in the margin of the affidavit giving the reference of any such document. The body of the affidavit generally begins with the following words:

I, (*name of deponent in capital letters*) of (*address and occupation of deponent*) state on oath:

The paragraphs are then numbered.

If the affidavit is being given in a business or professional capacity, the address should be that of the deponent's employment, rather than his home address, and it should state the position he holds, together with the name of his employer. It should also be stated whether the deponent is a party to the proceedings.

At the very end, where details are given of the swearing, i.e., where and when sworn and in whose presence, this is called the jurat. The jurat should follow immediately after the end of the text and must not be by itself on a separate page — the text of the affidavit should never end on one page with the jurat following on the next. It is typed on the left-hand side of the page in the following manner, and the signature of the deponent should be written opposite the text.

```
SWORN at          *                    )
in the County of        *              )
this        *       day of       *     )
2000                                   )
```

Before me,

A Solicitor
[*or whoever else the affidavit has been sworn before*]

The jurat must be signed by everyone swearing the affidavit. There are provisions in the rules for making affidavits by people who cannot read or are unable to sign. The person before whom an affidavit is sworn must sign it, and his name and qualification must be printed beneath his signature. His address must also be given.

The affidavit should have a backsheet (see example). Any alterations made to an affidavit must be initialled by the person swearing it at the time of swearing. Therefore, if you have made any errors or changes to the affidavit, you must draw these to the attention of the fee earner.

If there is more than one page to the affidavit, it must be bound securely in such a way that it will not hinder the court when they are filing it away. Commonly, affidavits are sewn up (see page 29) with green tape along the left-hand margin. However, you should check the method used in your own firm. If it is not possible to bind the affidavit, each page should be identified with the case number and the initials of the deponent and of the person before whom it was sworn.

An affidavit may have an exhibit, e.g. a document referred to in the affidavit which is part of the affidavit evidence. An exhibit is not bound in with the affidavit itself, but must be kept separate from it. When an exhibit is referred to in an affidavit, it is referred to by the initials of the person swearing the affidavit and includes the number of the exhibit. For example, if the affidavit is sworn by Marmaduke Smith, his first exhibit would be 'MS1', the second would be 'MS2' and so on. (See the example exhibit sheet.) These initials and numbers are also included on the first page and backsheet of the affidavit in the top right-hand corner. Each exhibit should then have a frontsheet which includes everything shown on the front of the affidavit down to and including the names of the parties. It would be set out as shown in the example. The exhibit frontsheet is placed on top of the exhibit and they are bound together (often sewn with green tape). If it is sewn, this is usually done only in the top left-hand corner. The exhibit sheet also has to be sworn. Once sworn, keep the original affidavit and exhibits as these will be filed with the court later, and serve photocopies. The pages of the photocopies which are to be served on other parties or kept on your file can simply be stapled together.

If there are several letters to be referred to as exhibits to an affidavit, they should be put together as a bundle. They should be arranged in chronological order with the earliest on the top and secured firmly. If there is a mix of original and copy letters exhibited as one bundle, the front page of the exhibit should state that the bundle consists of so many original letters and so many copies. Bundles should not be stapled but should be securely fastened in a way that does not interfere with the reading of the documents, e.g., sewn, or whatever method is used in your firm. The pages should be numbered consecutively at the bottom.

If an exhibit contains more than one document, the front page should set out a list of the documents giving the dates of the documents.

If an exhibit is something other than a document, it should be clearly marked with an exhibit number or letter in a way that it cannot become detached from the exhibit. A small item can be placed in a container marked appropriately.

Affirmations/Statutory Declarations

Instead of making an affidavit in which he swears on oath that what he has said is true, a person may 'affirm' the truth instead. The affirmation takes the same format as an affidavit but, at the beginning, instead of saying 'I ... state on oath', he says 'I ... do solemnly and sincerely affirm ...' and in the jurat the word 'sworn' is replaced by the word 'affirmed'. Similarly, someone may swear a document called a statutory declaration. Again the same rules apply, but he will be asked to 'declare' that the contents of his declaration are true.

Example Affidavit

Filed on behalf of: claimant
Name of deponent: J. Bloggs
No. of Affidavit: 1st
[Initials and number of any exhibits]
Date Affidavit Sworn: ****

IN THE SOUTHTOWN COUNTY COURT

Claim No. 00.12345

BETWEEN:

PAUL XAVIER

Claimant

and

JOHN JONES

Defendant

AFFIDAVIT

I, JOSEPH BLOGGS of 26 Southtown Road, Northtown, Essex, IG5 3TR mechanic, MAKE OATH and say as follows:

1.   At 6.35 p.m. on the 5th July 1999, I was walking down Mulberry Close, New Barnet, Hertfordshire when I saw a blue Volvo drive straight into a Rolls Royce. The driver of the Volvo appeared to have his eyes closed instead of looking where he was going.

2.   The Rolls Royce had no chance stop in time to avoid the accident.

SWORN at   *   )
in the County of   *   )
this   *   day of   *   )
2000   )

Before me,

A Solicitor

Example backsheet for Affidavit

<u>Claim No. 00.12345</u>

<u>IN THE SOUTHTOWN</u>

<u>COUNTY COURT</u>

BETWEEN:

Filed on behalf of: Claimant
Name of deponent: J. Bloggs
No. of Affidavit: 1st
[Initials and number of any exhibits]
Date Affidavit Sworn: ****

PAUL XAVIER   <u>Claimant</u>

and

JOHN JONES   <u>Defendant</u>

AFFIDAVIT

of

<u>JOSEPH BLOGGS</u>

John Smith and Co.,
2 Bank Chambers,
High Road,
Southtown,
Herts. EN5 6AX.

tel: 01438 12345

ref: AB/cd/123

Solicitors for the claimant

Example exhibit sheet

Filed on behalf of: Claimants
Name of deponent: M. Smith
No. of Affidavit: 1st
[Initials and number of any exhibits]
Date Affidavit Sworn: ****

IN THE HIGH COURT OF JUSTICE

QUEEN'S BENCH DIVISION

ROYAL COURTS OF JUSTICE   HQ 1999 1234

BETWEEN:

PETER BROWN (and others)   <u>Claimants</u>

and

BEATRICE GREEN (and others)   <u>Defendants</u>

This is the exhibit referred to in the affidavit of Marmaduke Smith and marked 'MS1'.

SWORN at   *   )
in the County of   *   )
this   *   day of   *   )
2000   )

Before me,

A Solicitor

Witnesses

At trial, a witness must attend court and give his evidence orally in public. However, the party relying on that witness must usually serve on the other party a statement by that witness containing the evidence he will be giving orally. At other hearings, witness evidence may be in statement form. The court may make exceptions to this and may also allow a witness to give evidence through video link or some other means.

Witness Statements

A witness statement is the equivalent of the evidence that the witness would or will give if he is called to court to give his evidence verbally. The layout is similar to that of an Affidavit (see above). It should show the title of the action and should contain the same type of details at the top right-hand corner of the first page as are on an Affidavit. Therefore, at the top right-hand corner of the first page, it will state the party on whose behalf it is made, e.g., claimant; the initials and surname of the witness; the number of the statement, e.g., if it is the witness's second statement in this action, you would type '2nd'; the identifying initials and number of any exhibits referred to and the date the statement was made. See the example Affidavit, which is similar. The paragraphs should be numbered, but it does not have the jurat at the end. It should be signed by the person who makes the statement and must be verified by a Statement of Truth (see page 62), the wording of which is as follows:

I believe that the facts stated in this witness statement are true.

If the Statement of Truth for the witness statement is in a separate document, that document should contain the title of the action, the claim number and it should identify the document being verified:

I believe that the facts stated in the witness statement filed on [date] or served on [whichever party] on [date] are true.

In some circumstances, a witness summary may be used rather than a statement. A witness summary is a summary of the evidence, if known, which would otherwise have been included in a witness statement or, if the evidence is not known, the matters about which the party serving the witness summary will question the witness. The summary should normally include the name and address of the witness. Witness summaries and/or statements are usually exchanged between parties before trial.

Witness Summons

A witness summons is a document issued by the court requiring a witness to attend court to give evidence and/or to produce documents to the court.

There must be a separate summons for each witness. It will be issued and dated by the court office where the case is proceeding or where a particular hearing will be held. Two copies of the witness summons (Form N20) must be filed with the court, which will keep one and return a sealed copy to the party applying for the summons, if they wish to serve it themselves. The witness summons will be served by the court unless the party issuing it informs the court at the time of issue that they wish to serve the summons themselves. If the court is serving the summons, they will keep one copy and serve the other by post on the witness. The court will keep a copy of the summons they have served and complete a certificate of service which is on the reverse of the copy summons.

If the court is going to serve the summons, money known as 'conduct money' must be deposited with the court. This money will be offered to the witness and should cover his reasonable travelling expenses to get to and from court and a sum to compensate him for loss of his time. Similarly, if your firm is serving the summons, this money must be offered or paid to the witness.

It is sometimes necessary to obtain permission from the court to issue a witness summons, particularly if it is required to issue the summons less than seven days before the date of trial.

As soon as the court date is known, all witnesses should be informed as they may have made other arrangements. You may find that some witnesses, such as police officers or Armed Forces personnel, have a certain way in which they like a witness summons to be served, e.g., through a senior officer, so it is best to check.

CIVIL LITIGATION

SPECIMEN
Witness Summons

In the	SOUTHTOWN COUNTY COURT
Claim No.	00.12345
Claimant (including ref.)	PAUL XAVIER (XAV/789)
Defendant (including ref.)	JOHN JONES (JON/cd)
Issued on	

To

Joseph Bloggs
26 Southtown Road
Northtown
Essex
IG5 3TR

You are summoned to attend at *(court address)*

                    (am)(pm) on   of

at

(and each following day of the hearing until the court tells you that you are no longer required).

☐ to give evidence in respect of the above claim

☐ to produce the following document(s) *(give details)*

The sum of £   is paid or offered to you with this summons. This is to cover your travelling expenses to and from court and includes an amount by way of compensation for loss of time.

This summons was issued on the application of the Claimant (Defendant) or the Claimant's (Defendant's) solicitor whose name, address and reference number is:

Do not ignore this summons
If you were offered money for travel expenses and compensation for loss of time, at the time it was served on you, and you

- fail to attend or produce documents as required by the summons; or
- refuse to take an oath or affirm for the purpose of answering questions about your evidence or the documents you have been asked to produce

you may be liable to a fine or imprisonment and may in addition be ordered to pay any costs resulting from your failure to attend or refusal to take an oath or affirm.

The court office at

is open between 10 am and 4 pm (4.30 pm in High Court) Monday to Friday. When corresponding with the court, please address forms or letters to the Court Manager and quote the claim number.

N20 Witness Summons (4.99)

[P.T.O.

Evidence by Deposition

It is possible for a party to a case to apply to the court for an order for someone to be questioned or 'examined' at a hearing to obtain evidence from them. They can also be required to produce any necessary documents. Evidence obtained in this way is known as a deposition. The person to be examined to give evidence is called a deponent. He will be questioned under oath before a judge, an examiner of the court or someone else who has been appointed by the court. As with a witness summons, when the order is served on the deponent, he should be offered or paid money to cover his reasonable travel expenses to and from the place where he is to be examined and a sum for compensation for loss of time.

The deponent's evidence may be electronically recorded by the court, as well as being recorded by the examiner in writing or by a shorthand writer or stenographer, so that the deponent's final written statement (the deposition) is accurate. The deposition must be signed by the examiner, who will also make a note of the time taken for the examination.

Civil Evidence Act Notice/Hearsay Evidence

If a party intends to rely on hearsay evidence at trial, either because a witness is unable to attend court or the evidence is some other form of hearsay evidence, he must, depending on the circumstances, either serve a witness statement or notice complying with the Civil Evidence Act 1995 on the other parties. The other parties must be informed if the witness will not be attending the trial to give oral evidence.

It may be that the evidence will be in the form of a document, in which case a copy of any such document must be supplied to the other parties. The witness statement or notice must contain specific details regarding the evidence and must be served within the time limits laid down by the court rules. There are further rules for cross-examining or attacking evidence given in this way.

In some circumstances, such as if the evidence relates to a hearing other than a trial, a Civil Evidence Act notice will not be necessary.

Expert Evidence

Parties may wish to obtain evidence from experts, e.g., in a personal injury case, it may be desired to obtain evidence from a doctor or specialist or, in a property matter, from someone such as a surveyor. However, expert evidence may only be given or taken into consideration with the permission of the court. There are various rules about what an expert's report must contain.

If two or more parties wish to submit expert evidence on a particular issue, it is preferred that the evidence is dealt with by one single expert only and the court may give directions to this effect. The parties wishing to submit the expert evidence are called 'the instructing parties'. If they cannot agree on who should be the expert, the court may select the expert. When one party is instructing a joint expert, he must send a copy of the instructions to the other instructing parties. If there is more than one expert, the court may direct that they discuss the issues between them and try to reach agreement if possible.

Where one party has provided expert evidence or a joint expert has been appointed by the court, another party may pose to the expert certain written questions. This must be done within a specified time. The expert's answers will be treated as part of his report.

131

Offer To Settle/Part 36 Payment

Quite often, if the defendant thinks that the claimant is likely to win all or part of the claim, the defendant will offer to settle the claim or make a payment into court to try to settle the claim. If he makes an offer or payment into court in accordance with Part 36 CPR and the claimant does not accept the offer or payment and the case proceeds to trial, and he is then awarded less money by the court than the defendant paid in to court or offered, or fails to achieve from the court what was, in effect, offered by the defendant, the claimant may have to pay the costs that the defendant incurs after the date has passed for accepting the offer or payment, including the costs of the trial. If the claimant accepts the payment into court or offer, then he will be entitled to payment of his costs up to the date of accepting the offer or payment in. (See also page 141 regarding costs.) However, if the claim is for money, a payment into court, rather than an offer, must be made in order to protect costs in this way. There are also consequences for the defendant if the claimant achieves more at court than the defendant proposed in a Part 36 offer.

Offers and payments made in this way are known as Part 36 offers or Part 36 payments and do not apply to cases on the small claims track. Part 36 offers and payments may be increased or improved upon. The offer or payment may be made with regard to part of the claim or all of it. The claimant may also make a Part 36 offer to settle the claim. Indeed, any party may make an offer to settle, but if he does not do it in accordance with the rules, he may not gain the benefits regarding costs.

A Part 36 offer or payment must not be made known to the trial judge until after the case has been decided (there are one or two exceptions). This is extremely important because if the judge knows that an offer or payment into court has been made, he will have to adjourn the trial and the solicitors responsible for letting him know may have to pay for the costs of the adjournment, which can be extremely expensive. Make sure that you *never* include in any trial bundle any notices, forms or other documents relating to such an offer or payment.

Notice of Offer/Payment Notice

If a party wishes to make a Part 36 payment or an increased Part 36 payment, he must file with the court a Part 36 Notice of Payment into Court. The Part 36 Notice of Payment into Court must include:

  (a) a statement saying that it is a Part 36 offer or payment;
  (b) the amount of the payment or increased payment;
  (c) whether it relates to the whole claim or to part of it. If it relates to part of the claim, it must be stated which part it relates to;
  (d) whether it takes any counterclaim into account.
  (e) it must be signed by the person making the offer or payment in, or by his legal representative, if he has one.

To make the Part 36 payment, the Notice of Payment into Court (Form N242A) must be taken or sent to the court together with the remittance (usually a cheque) which, if it is a District registry or county court, must be made payable to Her Majesty's Paymaster General.

If the payment is being made to the Royal Courts of Justice in London (RCJ), the cheque must be made payable to the Accountant General of the Supreme Court and must be accompanied by a sealed copy of the Claim Form together with Court Funds Office Form

100. For payment to the RCJ, these forms and cheque must be filed at the Court Funds Office at 22 Kingsway, London WC2B 6LE. A copy of the Court Funds Office receipt should be filed with the relevant court office in the RCJ, together with the Notice of Payment In.

Payments in cash should not be sent through the post. Once the payment has been made, the court will issue a receipt and will mark the Notice with the court's seal. The court will serve the Part 36 Payment Notice unless the party making the offer notifies the court at the time of paying in the money that he has served the Notice.

If the money is being paid into court under an order of the court, a sealed copy of the order should be filed with the court at the same time as paying in the money.

If the Part 36 payment or offer has been made at least 21 days before the trial date, the claimant may accept the payment or offer without the court's permission. He must, in these circumstances, give the defendant written notice of acceptance not later than 21 days after the offer or payment was made. There are other rules regarding the acceptance of Part 36 payments and offers outside this time limit or after the trial has started.

A copy of the Notice of Payment into Court must also be served on the other party and a letter sending this would be along the following lines:

Dear Sirs,

Re Xavier v Jones

We enclose Part 36 Notice of Payment into Court. Kindly acknowledge receipt.

Yours faithfully,

If the person making the offer serves the notice (rather than the court), a certificate of service must be filed at the court.

Accepting a Part 36 Offer or Payment

If a party wishes to accept a Part 36 payment or offer, he must file with the court a Notice of Acceptance of Payment into Court (Form N243) and a Request for Payment. He must also send Notice of Acceptance to the party making the payment in or offer. This must be done within specified time limits otherwise other procedures may have to be followed. In certain circumstances, the court's permission will be required before the payment in can be accepted.

The Notice of Acceptance must show on it the claim number and the title of the proceedings and must be signed by the person accepting the offer or payment, or by his solicitor if he is legally represented. If the court is the Royal Courts of Justice in London, the claimant should, at the same time, also file Court Funds Office Form 201 with the Court Funds Office.

The Request for Payment Form requires details to be completed, such as name and address of the party's legal representative and details of the bank account to which the payment will be transmitted. A party receiving a payment out of court may apply in writing for payment to be made to him by cheque. The payment will be made to a party's legal representative, where he has one.

Notice of Payment into court
(in settlement - Part 36)

SPECIMEN

To the Claimant ('s Solicitor)

In the	SOUTHTOWN COUNTY COURT
Claim No.	00.12345
Claimant (including ref)	PAUL XAVIER (ref: XAV/789)
Defendant (including ref)	JOHN JONES (ref: JON/cd)

```
John Smith & Co
2 Bank Chambers
High Road
Southtown
Herts
EN5 6AX
```

Take notice the defendant ___John Jones___ has paid £ 5000 ___ (a further amount of £ ____) into court in settlement of

(tick as appropriate)

- ✓ the whole of your claim
- ☐ part of your claim *(give details below)*
- ☐ a certain issue or issues in your claim *(give details below)*

The (part) (issue or issues) to which it relates is(are):*(give details)*

☐ It is in addition to the amount of £____already paid into court on

☐ It is not inclusive of interest and an additional amount of £____ is offered for interest *(give details of the rate(s) and period(s) for which the amount of interest is offered.)*

☐ It takes into account all(part) of the following counterclaim:*(give details of the party and the part of the counterclaim to which the payment relates)*

☐ It takes into account the interim payment(s) made in the following amount(s) on the following date(s): *(give details)*

Note: This notice will need to be modified where an offer of provisional damages is made (CPR Part 36.7) and/or where it is made in relation to a mixed (money and non-money) claim in settlement of the whole claim (CPR Part 36.4).

N242A - w3 Notice of payment into court (in settlement) (4.99)

The Court Service Publications Unit

For cases where the Social Security (Recovery of Benefits) Act 1997 applies

The gross amount of the compensation payment is £_____

The defendant has reduced this sum by £_____ in accordance with section 8 of and Schedule 2 to the Social Security (Recovery of Benefits) Act 1997, which was calculated as follows:

Type of benefit   Amount

SPECIMEN

The amount paid into court is the net amount after deduction of the amount of benefit.

Signed

Position held
(If signing on
behalf of a firm
or company)

Defendant('s solicitor)

Date

CIVIL LITIGATION

Notice of acceptance of payment into court (Part 36)

SPECIMEN

Note: to the claimant

If you wish to accept the payment made into court without needing the court's permission you should:
- send this completed notice to the defendant not more than 21 days after you received this notice
- and at the same time send a copy to the court

<table>
<tr><td colspan="2">In the SOUTHTOWN COUNTY COURT
—</td></tr>
<tr><td>**Claim No.**</td><td>00.12345</td></tr>
<tr><td>**Claimant**
(including ref.)</td><td>PAUL XAVIER
(ref: XAV/789)</td></tr>
<tr><td>**Defendant**
(including ref.)</td><td>JOHN JONES
(ref: JON/cd)</td></tr>
</table>

• Delete as appropriate I accept the payment into court in settlement of (the whole of) (part of)* (certain issue(s) in)* my claim set out in the notice of payment into court received on ☆☆☆ *(insert date)*

I declare that:-

☑ it is not more than 21 days since I received the notice of payment into court

or

☐ it is more than 21 days since I received the notice and I have agreed the following costs provisions with the other party(ies) *(give details below)*

or

☐ the defendant's payment was made less than 21 days before the start of the trial and I have agreed the following costs provisions with the other party(ies) *(give details below)*

And I request payment of the money held in court to be made to

claimant's (solicitor's) full name and address (and ref)	John Smith & Co 2 Bank Chambers High Road Southtown Herts EN5 6AX (ref: XAV/789)

name and address of bank		sort code	
title of account		account number	
Signed		Position held (If signing on behalf of a firm or company)	
	Claimant('s Solicitor)		
Date			

Interim Payments

This is a payment often applied for once liability is no longer an issue. This means that if the defendant does not dispute that he must pay the claimant something, but does not agree on the final sum, then the claimant may, in certain circumstances, ask for some money on account until the final amount is resolved. If the defendant pays this, all well and good, but if he does not, then an application for an interim payment may have to be made to the court. In any event, if it is desired to make a voluntary interim payment regarding a claim by a child or patient under the Mental Health Act, the permission of the court must first be obtained.

Any money paid by way of interim payment will be deducted from the final amount eventually recovered by the claimant. An interim payment has no connection with a Part 36 payment as mentioned above.

Notice of Discontinuance

If, after proceedings have been served, the party instigating those proceedings wishes to discontinue all or part of his action, he must serve a Notice of Discontinuance (Form N279) on the other parties and file a copy with the court. In some cases, consent of the other party or the court's permission may be required to do this. A Notice of Discontinuance will have on it the title of the action (see page 53). The Notice must state in it that all parties to the action have been served with a Notice of Discontinuance, and if there is more than one defendant to the action, it must specify against which parties the claim is discontinued.

Notice of Change of Solicitor

If, for some reason, a new firm of solicitors is to act for a party to an action, a Notice of Change of Solicitor must be completed by the new solicitor. This also applies if someone has been representing himself (a 'litigant in person') and then instructs a solicitor to act for him or, conversely, if a solicitor has been instructed but the person wishes now to represent himself. The Notice of Change of Solicitor (Form N434) should be filed with the court and sent to every other party to the action as well as to the former solicitor. The Notice must give the new address for service (see page 66).

Notice of Discontinuance

Note: Where another party must consent to the proceedings being discontinued, a copy of their consent must be attached to, and served with, this form.

In the	SOUTHTOWN COUNTY COURT
Claim No.	00.12345
Claimant (including ref)	PAUL XAVIER (XAV/789)
Defendant (including ref)	JOHN JONES (JON/cd)

To the court

The Claimant [Defendant]

(tick only one box)

☑ discontinues all of this [claim] [counterclaim]

☐ discontinues that part of this [claim] [counterclaim] relating to: *(specify which part)*

against the [Defendant] [following Defendants] [Claimant] [following Claimants]

(*(enter name of Judge)* granted permission for the Claimant to

discontinue [all] [part] of this [claim] [counterclaim] by order dated).

I certify that I have served a copy of this notice on every other party to the proceedings.

Signed

Position or office held

(Claimant)(Claimant's solicitor)(Litigation friend)   (if signing on behalf of firm or company)

Date

The court office at

is open between 10 am and 4 pm (4.30 in High Court) Monday to Friday. When corresponding with the court, please address forms or letters to the Court Manager and quote the claim number.

N279 Notice of Discontinuance (4.99)

Oyez   7 Spa Road, London SE16 3QQ

4.99 F36066

5093343

★ ★ ★ ★ ★

N279

SPECIMEN
Notice of Change of Solicitor

In the	SOUTHTOWN COUNTY COURT
Claim No.	00.12345
Claimant (including ref)	PAUL XAVIER (XAV/789)
Defendant (including ref)	JOHN JONES (JON/cd)

Note: You should tick either box A or B as appropriate **and** box C. Complete details as necessary.

[I][We] give notice that

A ☐ my solicitor *(insert name and address)*

has ceased to act for me and I shall now be acting in person.

B ☑ we *(insert name of solicitor)* Jeffrey Armstrong & Co

have been instructed to act on behalf of the Claimant (Defendant) in this claim in place of *(insert name and address of previous solicitors).*

Joe Bloggs & Co., of 1 Broad Walk, Southtown, Herts, EN4 9PP

C ☑ [I] [We] have served notice of this change on every party to claim (and on the former solicitor).

Address to which documents about this claim should be sent (including any reference)

Jeffrey Armstrong & Co 635 Poddlebank Road London ref: 2397/bn tel: 0171 444 65655 Postcode W13 7PR		if applicable	
		fax no.	0171 444 33097
		DX no.	DX 34 Poddlebank 6
		e-mail	

Signed

Position or office held

(Defendant) (Defendant's solicitor) (Litigation friend)

(if signing on behalf of firm or company)

Date

The court office at

is open between 10 am and 4 pm (4.30 pm in High Court) Monday to Friday. When corresponding with the court, please address forms or letters to the Court Manager and quote the claim number.

N434 Notice of Change of Solicitor (4.99)

Oyez 7 Spa Road, London SE16 3QQ

4.99 F36080

5093377
★★★★★

N 434

Approaching Trial

There is always a great deal of work to be done before a trial. This can include informing witnesses, and bundling up documents for court and for other parties. Bundles of documents should have their pages numbered. This is called paginating. The numbers should be put at the bottom of the document at the centre and all documents should be put in chronological order, with the earliest document first and the latest at the back of the bundle so that it can be read in order of events, like a book. Conferences and consultations are arranged with counsel and you may find yourself heavily involved at this stage.

In some cases, prior to trial, skeleton arguments are lodged with the court. A skeleton argument is a brief outline of the relevant issues and facts of law pertaining to the case which the judge can read before the hearing, thus saving time. Skeleton arguments should normally be typed in double spacing on A4 paper. A copy should be served on all other parties to the action.

Judgment

When the trial judge gives his final decision on the outcome of a case, this is known as the judgment. The judgment must be formally written down or 'drawn up'. This will normally be done by the court or one of the parties' solicitors. If it is drawn up by one of the parties and is to be served by the court, sufficient copies must be filed at the court for each of the parties plus one for the court.

Enforcing Judgment

If judgment has been entered against the defendant and he does not pay, it may be necessary to force him to pay, normally after enquiries are made about his means. The procedures in the High Court and County Court may differ. They will all involve completing the appropriate form and paying a court fee. Some of those you may encounter are:

(a) Seizing goods. Upon completing the correct form and paying a fee, an officer of the court where the judgment debtor (the person who owes the money) has any goods may seize those goods, sufficient to cover the amount owed, plus any costs. The goods are then sold at public auction. Certain goods are exempt from seizure. If someone else comes forward to say that he owns the goods rather than the debtor, this will be resolved by the court.

(b) Garnishee proceedings. This is a process whereby if someone owes money to the judgment debtor, the court can order the person who owes him money (called a 'garnishee') to pay the money to the judgment creditor (the person who is owed the money) instead. An example would be money held in a bank account and the bank being ordered to pay the money directly to the judgment creditor.

(c) Charging order. This imposes a charge on any land or interest in land or security owned by the judgment debtor.

(d) Attachment of earnings. The debtor's employer must pay out of the debtor's wages a certain sum each week or month until the debt is cleared.

(e) Committal. This is only appropriate where there is disobedience of a court order. It can only follow a hearing before a judge where the defaulter has an opportunity to explain why he has disobeyed the court order.

There are other methods of enforcing judgment, such as obtaining possession of land or an order for the return of specific goods.

Registration of Judgments

Details of county court judgments are registered with the Registry of County Court Judgments. The entry stays on the Register for six years. However, if someone pays money satisfying a judgment within a month from the date of the judgment, he may ask the court to cancel the registration of the judgment. The court will send a certificate of cancellation once they have proof that the payment has been made. If the payment was made more than one month after the day the judgment was made, the court can be asked to mark the judgment as satisfied, but the entry will remain on the Register. The court will send the applicant a certificate of satisfaction. A fee is payable to the court for these services.

The Register can be searched on payment of a fee, and this is particularly useful to organisations such as banks, building societies and credit companies to check whether someone is a good credit risk. The Register is kept by the Registry Trust Ltd, at 173/175 Cleveland Street, London W1P 5PE.

There is no register of High Court judgments.

Costs

At the end of a civil litigation case, the court will make an order regarding the costs of the case. These will usually be paid by the party losing the case. However, the court may order that one party pays only a part of the other's costs, rather than the whole amount if it considers that there are valid reasons for making such an order. Costs are commonly awarded on the following bases:

(a) Standard basis. The winner of the case will be allowed a reasonable amount in respect of all costs reasonably incurred. If there is a dispute as to what is reasonable, it is resolved in favour of the party paying the costs.

(b) Indemnity basis. All costs are allowed unless they are unreasonable. If there is a dispute as to what is reasonable, it is resolved in favour of the party receiving the costs.

There is also a provision for fixed costs in certain cases. This means that where this provision applies, the only costs recoverable are those set out in the Tables in Part 45 of the Civil Procedure Rules. When the court makes an order as to costs, if it does not specify the costs, it may order a detailed assessment of costs (see below).

Besides the court awarding costs at the end of a case, costs relating to a specific application notice may be awarded at the time of the application, rather than having to wait until the whole action is finalised. Some of the terms used by the court when costs are awarded are:

'Claimant's (or defendant's) costs' or 'costs in any event': this means that whichever party the court names can recover the costs of that particular application from the other party whatever the final outcome of the action.

'Costs reserved': the party in whose favour an order for costs is made at the end of the trial will be entitled to the costs of the application in question unless the court orders otherwise.

'Costs in the cause': the costs of a particular application will be paid by the party who is ordered to pay the costs of the trial.

'Claimant's (or defendant's) costs in the cause': the party named at an application will be entitled to recover the costs of his application provided that judgment is given in his favour at the trial. However, if judgment is not given in his favour at the trial, he will not be liable to pay the costs of the other party for the application.

'Costs thrown away': where proceedings or any part of them have been ineffective or have been subsequently set aside, the party in whose favour the order for costs is made will be entitled to recover the costs of those proceedings.

'No order as to costs': each party must bear his own costs.

Detailed Assessment of Costs

The amount of the costs to be paid by one party to another are generally currently agreed between the parties. However, if the parties cannot agree on the amount of costs or the way they have been made up, the party which is to receive payment (the receiving party) may apply for a detailed assessment of costs (or this may be ordered by the court). Before the CPR, this procedure was called 'taxation of costs' or costs would be 'taxed'. If there is to be a detailed assessment of costs, an appointment will be made to go before a costs judge or costs officer, who will make a decision on the costs to be paid. The receiving party must serve on the party who will pay the costs (the paying party) a Notice of Commencement of Assessment of Bill of Costs (Form N252), together with a copy of the bill of costs. Copies must also be served on any other relevant parties.

A bill of costs has to be drawn which itemises in chronological order all the steps taken in the action and all time spent on the case, including details of correspondence, telephone calls, witnesses involved, etc. Drawing this bill is very specialised and is usually done by a costs draftsman. The bill has to be lodged with the court within a specified time, together with the solicitor's file which must include all relevant papers, vouchers and receipts. If the parties agree on the amount of costs, either party may apply for a costs certificate.

Any party to the assessment proceedings may serve on another party Points of Dispute if he wishes to dispute any item in the bill of costs. A copy of the Points of Dispute must be served on all parties to the assessment proceedings. A Reply to the Points of Dispute may be served within a specified time.

If any party is not happy with the result of the assessment, he may appeal against this within a specified time.

Notice of commencement of assessment of bill of costs

In the	SOUTHTOWN COUNTY COURT
Claim No.	00.12345
Claimant (include Ref.)	PAUL XAVIER (XAV/cd)
Defendant (include Ref.)	JOHN JONES (JON/cd)

To the claimant(defendant)

Following an _(insert name of document eg. order, judgment)_ dated
(copy attached) I have prepared my Bill of Costs for assessment. The Bill totals £ . If you choose to dispute this bill and your objections are not upheld at the assessment hearing, the full amount payable (including the assessment fee) will be £ together with interest _(see note below)_. I shall also seek the costs of the assessment hearing

You must send me any points of dispute by _(insert date 21 days from the date of service of the certificate)_

Your points of dispute must include

- details of the items in the bill of costs which are disputed
- concise details of the nature and grounds of the dispute for each item and, if you seek a reduction in those items, suggest, where practicable, a reduced figure

You must also serve copies of your points of dispute on all other parties to the assessment identified below.

I certify that I have also served the following (persons)(person) with a copy of this certificate and my Bill of Costs

If I have not received your points of dispute by the above date, I will ask the court to issue a default costs certificate for the full amount of my bill (see above) plus fixed costs and court fee as specified in the Costs Practice Direction and Civil Courts fee order.

Signed .... **Date**

(Claimant)(Defendant)('s solicitor)

Note: Further interest may be added to all High Court judgments and certain county court judgments of £5,000 under the Judgments Act 1938, the County Courts Act 1984 and the Late Payment of Commerical Debt (Interest) Act 1998.

The court office at

is open between 10 am and 4 pm Monday to Friday. When corresponding with the court, please address forms or letters to the Court Manager and quote the claim number.

N252 -w3 Notice of commencement of assessment of bill of costs (4.99)   _Printed on behalf of The Court Service_

Forms and Documents in Older Proceedings

You will undoubtedly come across some of the older forms and documents which were in use before the CPR came into effect. There were different forms for High Court actions and county court actions.

In the High Court, an originating application such as a Writ of Summons (normally simply referred to as a Writ) would be issued. Instead of a Particulars of Claim, a Statement of Claim would set out the details of the claim if these were not included on the Writ. Once a Writ was served, the defendant had to complete an Acknowledgment of Service. An example of a Writ is shown below.

In the County Court, proceedings were commenced by requesting the court to issue a summons. The summons or a request for a summons would be prepared by the claimant's solicitors and this would then be sent to the court for issue. There were two types of summons — a default summons and a fixed date summons. The default summons was used for claiming money, whether or not it was a specific amount, but there were two types of default summons — one for a fixed amount and the other for an unspecified amount of damages. The fixed date summons was used for other types of actions, such as for the recovery of land, for the return of goods or for an injunction. An example of a Request for Issue of a Default Summons is shown below.

There were various differences between the procedures in the High Court and the county court, even where the action was for the same type of thing. Some of the previous names and terms have been changed by the CPR and you may still hear them used. A few of these are:

(a)   Discovery — now called 'disclosure'.
(b)   *Ex parte* — now 'without notice'.
(c)   Further and Better Particulars — now 'Further Information'.
(d)   *In camera* or in chambers — now 'in private'.
(e)   Leave of the court — now 'permission of the court'.
(f)   Minor or infant is now simply 'child'.
(g)   Next friend or *guardian ad litem* — now called 'litigation friend'.
(h)   Payment into court. This procedure is now called a 'Part 36 payment'.
(i)   Plaintiff — now 'claimant'.
(j)   Pleadings — now 'statements of case'.
(k)   Statement of Claim (and Points of Claim). High Court documents which were the equivalent of the Particulars of Claim in the county court. Both the High Court and county court now use only a Particulars of Claim.
(l)   Summons — now 'application'.
(m)   Subpoena. This is now a witness summons.
(n)   Taxation of costs. This referred to a procedure relating to costs (see above). It is now called 'detailed assessment of costs'.
(o)   Taxing Master is now called 'costs judge'.
(p)   Third Party proceedings — now 'Part 20 Claim'.
(q)   Writ or county court summons — now a 'Claim Form'.

COURT FEES ONLY

Writ of
Summons
[Unliquidated
Demand]
(O.6,r.1)

IN THE HIGH COURT OF JUSTICE

19 96–G .—No.

Queen's Bench Division

[~~District Registry~~]

Between

SPECIMEN

JOHN GREEN   Plaintiff

AND

JOHN JONES   Defendant

(1) Insert name.

To the Defendant ([1]**)** JOHN JONES

(2) Insert address.

of ([2]) 2 Southtown Road, Northtown, Essex

This Writ of Summons has been issued against you by the above-named Plaintiff in respect of the claim set out on the back.

Within 14 days after the service of this Writ on you, counting the day of service, you must either satisfy the claim or return to the Court Office mentioned below the accompanying **Acknowledgment of Service** stating therein whether you intend to contest these proceedings.

If you fail to satisfy the claim or to return the Acknowledgment within the time stated, or if you return the Acknowledgment without stating therein an intention to contest the proceedings, the Plaintiff may proceed with the action and judgment may be entered against you forthwith without further notice.

(3) Complete
and delete as
necessary.

Issued from the ([3]) [Central Office] [~~Admiralty and Commercial Registry~~]
[~~District Registry~~] of the High Court
this   *   day of   *   19 *

NOTE:—This Writ may not be served later than 4 calendar months (*or, if leave is required to effect service out of the jurisdiction, 6 months*) beginning with that date unless renewed by order of the Court.

IMPORTANT

Directions for Acknowledgment of Service are given with the accompanying form.

The Plaintiff's claim is for damages for personal injury and pecuniary losses incurred arising out of a road traffic accident which occurred at Mulberry Close, Barnet, Herts., on 5th July 1995 and which was caused by the negligence of the Defendant.

SPECIMEN

---

(1) If this Writ was issued out of a District Registry, this indorsement as to place where the action arose should be completed.

(2) Delete as necessary.

(3) Insert name of place.

(4) For phraseology of this indorsement where the Plaintiff sues in person, see *Supreme Court Practice*, vol. 2, para 1.

(1) [(2) [The cause] [One of the causes] of action in respect of which the Plaintiff claim relief in this action arose wholly or in part at (3) in the district of the District Registry named overleaf.]

(4)**This Writ** was issued by John Smith & Co.

of 2 Bank Chambers, High Road, Southtown, Herts.

[Agent xxxx for   ]

of x

Solicitors for the said Plaintiff whose address (2) [is] [are]

64 Railway Cuttings, Southtown, Herts.

Solicitor's Reference AB/cd/123   Tel. No: 0438-12345

OYEZ The Solicitors' Law Stationery Society Ltd., Oyez House, 7 Spa Road, London SE16 3QQ   3.95 F29285

5044019
★ ★ ★ ★

High Court A1

Request for Issue of Default Summons

● Please read the notes over the page before filling in this form.

1 Plaintiff's full name address

JOHN GREEN,
16 NORTHTOWN ROAD,
SOUTHTOWN,
HERTS.
EN4 9PP

2 Name and address for service and payment *(if not as above)* **Ref./Tel. No.**

JOHN SMITH & CO.,
2 BANK CHAMBERS, HIGH ROAD,
SOUTHTOWN, HERTS. EN6 7PP
AB/cd/123   Tel: 0438-12345

3 Defendant's full name *(eg Mr. Mrs or Miss where known)* **and address Company no.** *(where known)*

MR. JOHN JONES,
2 SOUTHTOWN ROAD,
NORTHTOWN,
HERTS.

For court use only

Case number

Summons in form: N1 ☐
                   N2 ☐

Service by: Post ☐
Plaintiff('s solr) ☐

● Please be careful when filling in the request form. Do not write outside the boxes.

● Type or write in BLOCK CAPITALS using black ink.

● If the details of the claim are on a separate sheet you must also give the court a copy for each Defendant.

● You can get help to complete this form and information about court procedures at any county court office or citizens' advice bureau.

4 What the claim is for

Give brief description of the type of claim.

Damages for personal injury and pecuniary loss incurred.

5 Particulars of the Plaintiff's claim

See separate Particulars

SPECIMEN

My claim is worth   £5,000 or less ☐   over £5,000 ☑

Total claim over £3,000 and/or damages for personal injury claims over £1,000

I would like my case decided by   trial ☑   arbitration ☐

7 Signed
Plaintiff or Plaintiff's solicitor
(or see enclosed "Particulars of claim")

6   Plaintiff's claim   ★
        Court fee   ★
        Solicitor's costs   ★
        Total Amount   ★

For court use   Issued on

How the claim will be dealt with if defended

If the total you are claiming is £3,000 or less and/or your claim for damages for personal injury is worth £1,000 or less, it will be dealt with by arbitration (small claims procedure) unless the court decides the case is too difficult to be dealt with in this informal way. Costs and the grounds for setting aside an arbitration award are strictly limited. If the claim is not dealt with by arbitration, costs, including the costs of help from a legal representative, may be allowed.

If the total you are claiming is more than £3,000 and/or you are claiming more than £1,000 for damages for personal injury, it can still be dealt with by arbitration if you or the Defendant asks for it and the court approves. If your claim is dealt with by arbitration in these circumstances, costs may be allowed.

N201   Request for default summons (Order 3, rule 3(1))

147

Landlord and Tenant

Landlord and tenant matters are a specialised subject and this section merely attempts to give you an idea of the type of work it involves. You will come across many disputes including the termination of tenancies, harassment, improvements to premises, service charges or parties to the tenancy not keeping to the terms of the tenancy.

Any statements of case or Instructions to Counsel you may have to prepare concerning landlord and tenant matters will be set out in the same way as shown earlier.

There are various types of tenancies, for example, they may be for a fixed term, i.e., for a set length of time, or perhaps on a weekly or monthly basis. The person who owns the property is the lessor or the landlord and the person taking on the tenancy is the lessee or tenant. There are also licensors and licensees of premises and lodgers. However, these people do not have the same type of legal protection as tenants.

Premises used as Dwellings

Tenants of premises used as a dwelling have certain rights and protection. In the private sector, tenancies are primarily governed by the Housing Act 1988 and tenancies which were entered into before the Housing Act 1988 came into force are governed by the Rent Act 1977. A tenancy which falls within the Rent Act is known as a protected tenancy during the term of the tenancy. When the tenancy ends, a statutory tenancy may come into effect. Such tenancies have security of tenure and rent control. Security of tenure means that the landlord cannot end the tenancy unless he obtains a court order and the court cannot make the order unless there is a good reason for so doing. The good reason must be one which is defined by statute.

Tenants who have protected or statutory tenancies, as well as some housing association tenants, can apply to a Rent Officer for the registration of a fair rent. In fact, the application for a fair rent may be made not just by the tenant, but also by the landlord, or jointly. There are certain formalities to follow in this procedure. Once the fair rent has been registered, the landlord cannot increase the rent, although there can be a review of the rent after two years. If there is any dispute regarding the fair rent which has been registered, referral may be made to a Rent Assessment Committee which, besides fixing fair rent, has a wide range of other responsibilities.

There are also tenancies known as assured tenancies and assured shorthold tenancies, which are governed by the Housing Act 1988 (as amended by the Housing Act 1996). The assured tenancy works in a similar way to protected and statutory tenancies except that there is no rent control and the landlord can give further reasons for requiring possession. The assured shorthold tenancy can be for a short fixed term with a minimum of six months and, with such a tenancy, it is easier for the landlord to recover possession. The rent for an assured shorthold tenancy can be more in keeping with the current market rate.

With regard to public sector tenancies, e.g., local authority housing, new town corporations and housing action trusts, tenants have a secure tenancy. A secure tenancy can be terminated by the landlord only if he obtains a court order, and certain conditions have to be satisfied before this is granted. However, since February 1997, local authorities and housing action trusts have had the power to operate an introductory tenancy scheme. This means that any such tenancy is not secure during a trial period of one year. During this trial period, the landlord can recover possession if it believes that the tenant has not been behaving satisfactorily. Normal grounds for possession are not necessary but, before bringing possession proceedings, the landlord must notify the tenant of its decision to seek possession, giving its reasons. Tenants have the right to have an internal administrative review of the decision but if, after the review, the authority still wishes to go ahead with the possession, the court must order possession.

Secure tenants, as well as having security of tenure, have various other statutory rights including the right to exchange tenancies, the right to have urgent repairs carried out quickly, the right to be consulted on matters of housing management and the right to buy. The right to buy for public sector housing was introduced by the Housing Act 1980 (the principal legislation now being the Housing Act 1985, as amended). Those who have been tenants for a specified period of time may have the right to buy the freehold or leasehold of their premises. A considerable percentage of the market value of the property is given as a discount, depending on the length of time the tenant has occupied public sector housing.

Business Premises

Tenancies of business premises are mainly governed by the Landlord and Tenant Act 1954.

If the tenancy is for a fixed term and the landlord wishes to terminate the tenancy, he must give notice of this to the tenant not less than six months, nor more than 12 months, before the date the tenancy is to be terminated. The tenant may, within two months, give notice to the landlord that he does not wish to leave the premises. He may then apply to the court for a new tenancy. The application to the court must be made not less than two months nor more than four months after the landlord gave his notice.

If the landlord has not served any notice on the tenant, the tenant may serve on the landlord a statutory request for a new tenancy. The landlord may then serve notice on the tenant that he is not willing to renew the tenancy. The tenant must then make an application to the court for a new tenancy. The time limits for service of these notices and for making application to the court are the same as those mentioned in the previous paragraph. If the tenant does not wish to renew his fixed term tenancy, he must give notice in writing to the landlord not later than three months before the date on which the tenancy would end.

Any claim issued in accordance with the provisions of section 25 or section 26 of the Landlord and Tenant Act 1954 is valid only for two months, i.e., it must be served within two months of being issued.

A new arbitration scheme has been introduced by the Law Society and the Royal Institution of Chartered Surveyors as an alternative to going to court to determine lease renewal terms and rent for commercial properties. This scheme is known as PACT (professional arbitration on court terms). The procedure can be used where both parties have identified the issues between them and are prepared to adopt the procedure to resolve them. Commercial landlords and tenants can have the terms and rent payable under their new lease decided by a surveyor or solicitor who has been specially trained under the scheme.

Notice to Quit

There are many ways to terminate a lease, and one of these is where the landlord serves on his tenant a Notice to Quit. The length of the notice given may depend on the length of the tenancy, e.g., a monthly tenancy will usually require a month's notice, etc., although a yearly tenancy can normally be ended on just six months' notice. However, a Notice to Quit is not, by any means, appropriate in all cases. If the tenant is unwilling to leave the premises, the landlord must apply to the court for an order of possession, which the court will grant only if certain conditions are satisfied. As with most court proceedings, a fee is payable on making such an application.

One term you may come across in landlord and tenant matters is the expression *mesne profits*. This is a term used in cases where a tenancy has been terminated but the tenant remains in the premises. It refers to the money the landlord would have received as rent had the tenancy continued.

NOTICE TO QUIT

(BY LANDLORD OF PREMISES LET AS A DWELLING)

Name and Address of Tenant

To .... JOHN GREEN .... of

.... 82 EAST AVENUE ....

.... NORTHTOWN, HERTS. EN9 7LR ....

Name and Address of Landlord

[I] [We] [as] [on behalf of] your landlord[s], ... PHILIP BROWN ....

of .... 84 EAST AVENUE ....

.... NORTHTOWN, HERTS. EN9 7LR ....

*Me/them or as appropriate

give you **NOTICE TO QUIT** and deliver up possession to*................ him ....

†Address of premises

of † .... 82 EAST AVENUE ....

.... NORTHTOWN, HERTS. EN9 7LR ....

‡Date for possession

on ‡.........................*.................. ...., or the day on which a complete period of your

tenancy expires next after the end of four weeks from the service of this notice.

Date of notice

Dated ....*...................... ....

Signed ....*..

Name and Address of Agent if Agent serves notice

John Smith & Co

....

2 Bank Chambers, High Road,

....

Southtown, Herts. EL6 3RX

....

Ref: AB/cd/123
Tel: 01438-12345

INFORMATION FOR TENANT
(See Note 2 overleaf)

1. If the tenant or licensee does not leave the dwelling, the landlord or licensor must get an order for possession from the court before the tenant or licensee can lawfully be evicted. The landlord or licensor cannot apply for such an order before the notice to quit or notice to determine has run out.

2. A tenant or licensee who does not know if he has any right to remain in possession after a notice to quit or a notice to determine runs out can obtain advice from a solicitor. Help with all or part of the cost of legal advice and assistance may be available under the Legal Aid Scheme. He should also be able to obtain information from a Citizens' Advice Bureau, a Housing Aid Centre or a Rent Officer.

[P.T.O.]

NOTES

1.   Notice to quit premises let as a dwelling must be given at least four weeks before it takes effect, and it must be in writing (Protection from Eviction Act 1977, s. 5 as amended).

2.   Where a notice to quit is given by a landlord to determine a tenancy of any premises let as a dwelling, the notice must contain this information (The Notices to Quit etc. (Prescribed Information) Regulation 1988).

3.   Some tenancies are excluded from this protection: see Protection from Eviction Act 1977, ss. 3A and 5(1B).

1.98 T01017
5059339

Landlord and Tenant 61

* * *

Children

You may come across cases involving children (persons under 18 years of age) or persons with a mental disability. As these persons cannot pursue their own litigation they have to have someone to do it for them. Someone who sues on behalf of such a person is known as a litigation friend. This could perhaps be a relative or a social worker. The claimant in such proceedings would, for example, be shown as 'John Smith (a child) by Mary Jones, his litigation friend'.

When such persons are themselves sued, they must have a responsible person to represent them. This person is also known as a litigation friend.

International Law

International law can be either public international or private international law. The former governs relations between states, for example, such things as treaties and wars — and is unlikely to concern you. The latter governs the relations between individuals and/or companies between different jurisdictions and is of importance to solicitors who practise international law.

Solicitors often keep lists of lawyers in other countries and one must always remember that laws of other countries may differ greatly from English law. In fact, even the laws of Scotland are different in many ways and permission must be obtained from the court to issue court proceedings in Scotland.

However, many judgments obtained outside England and Wales may be enforced within the jurisdiction. A judgment obtained in another part of the United Kingdom or in another EC Member State may be registered in the courts of England and Wales. Once the judgment has been registered, it may be enforced as though it were an English judgment. Money judgments obtained in certain other countries may be registered and enforced here in a similar way.

With regard to enforcing an English judgment outside England and Wales, the judgment may be registered with a court in another part of the UK and then enforced in that court as though it were a judgment of that court. Further, if a judgment has been obtained in England and Wales, application can be made for the judgment to be enforced in another EC country. For other countries, there may be a reciprocal agreement but, if not, then new proceedings may have to be commenced in that country.

The European Court of Justice

One of the main tasks of the European Court of Justice (ECJ), often referred to simply as 'the European Court' (its full title is the Court of Justice of the European Communities), is to assist national courts in interpreting and applying Community law and to ensure its uniform application. Attached to the ECJ is the Court of First Instance of the European Communities (CFI) which is, in effect, a subordinate part of the ECJ. The CFI exercises at first instance the jurisdiction of the ECJ in certain specified matters. The ECJ sits in Luxembourg and is an entirely separate body from the European Court of Human Rights which sits at Strasbourg.

Certain actions may be brought against a Member State or against a Community institution, often by the European Commission or by another Member State, Community institution or legal or natural person. Some actions are lodged with the CFI and others are lodged direct with the ECJ. There is a right of appeal on a point of law against a judgment of the CFI to the ECJ.

Both civil and criminal courts of Member States may refer a point of European law to the ECJ if they consider that guidance is necessary before they can give judgment in a case before them. The request for guidance is known as the preliminary reference, and the answer given by the ECJ is known as the preliminary ruling. Until the ECJ has ruled on the point, the national proceedings are suspended; after the ruling is made by the ECJ, the national court applies that ruling to the case and continues to judgment.

Test yourself on Chapter 3

Test your knowledge by completing this assignment. If you find that you have difficulty with anything, read the chapter again until you are happy with your answers. There are some forms for you to complete with this assignment. Use the following information to complete the forms.

James McIntyre lives at 83 Camden Hill, Northtown, Sussex S23 7AL. He is suing Amy Crashing for damage caused to his car when he was involved in a road traffic accident with the car she was driving at 3.00 pm on 10 June 1999 at Camden Hill. His car is a green Ford Fiesta, registration number P387 LUR. The damage to Mr McIntyre's car is valued at £4,000. The claim will be issued in the Northtown County Court and the claim number will be 99.3865. Nigel Parker saw the accident happen and will swear an affidavit on behalf of James McIntyre saying what he saw. There will be no exhibits to the affidavit.

The solicitors for Mr McIntyre are Poddleberry, Catt & Co., of 16 Somerset Row, Northtown, Sussex S31 8PP (tel: 01646 58733; ref: LP/McI/68).

Miss Amy Crashing lives at 48 Avon Hills, Northtown, Sussex, S44 6PQ. Her car is a black Rolls Royce, registration number AC1. Her solicitors are Peters, Gold & Barry of Fox Hill, Northtown, Sussex S27 8L (tel: 01646 643821; ref: LB/Crash/321).

1. You are asked to prepare the Claim Form ready for it to be sent to court to be issued. Do this on the appropriate form: the Particulars of Claim will be served later. Once the Claim Form is ready and has been approved by a fee earner, what else would you do before posting it to the court?
2. What is meant by 'service' of a document? Name two methods of service. Complete the Certificate of Service showing that the Particulars of Claim was served on the defendant on the day you are doing this exercise. Service was by post to the defendant's home.
3. Draft as far as you can in the correct format the Particulars of Claim, which are being served separately from the Claim Form (you can follow the example on page 60). Also draft a backsheet for the Particulars of Claim. When serving the Particulars of Claim, are any other documents required to be served at the same time?
4. Complete the Acknowledgment of Service on behalf of Amy Crashing. She intends to defend the claim. What other courses of action would be open to her?
5. If Amy had decided simply to ignore all the papers served on her, Mr McIntyre's solicitors might have decided to enter judgment by default. What does this mean? Complete the appropriate form.
6. What is meant by a 'Part 20 claim'? If a lady called Jean Armstrong had been brought into the action because Amy Crashing wished to allege that the accident was Jean's fault for some reason, how would the status of the parties be described in the title to the action in the Part 20 claim? (James McIntyre will still be described as the claimant.)
7. What are the following:

   (a) statement of case;
   (b) Allocation Questionnaire;
   (c) Listing Questionnaire.

8. Write down a list of the documents that might be included in a trial bundle.
9. What is meant by 'disclosure and inspection of documents'? What sort of information will go on to a List of Documents?

10. What information will be included on an Application Notice?
11. Write out the jurat for an affidavit that is to be sworn. Besides the names of the parties to the action and the actual content of the affidavit, what other information must be included on an affidavit, particularly at the top of the page?
12. Now go through the Chapter and if there are any words that are unfamiliar to you or that you cannot spell, write or type them correctly several times until you feel you know them.

Claim Form

SPECIMEN

In the	
Claim No.	

Claimant

SEAL

Defendant(s)

Brief details of claim

Value

Defendant's name and address

£

Amount claimed	
Court fee	
Solicitor's costs	
Total amount	
Issue date	

The court office at

is open between 10 am and 4 pm Monday to Friday. When corresponding with the court, please address forms or letters to the Court Manager and quote the claim number.

N1 - w3 General claim form(4.99)

Printed on behalf of The Court Service

SPECIMEN

Particulars of Claim (attached)(to follow)

Statement of Truth
*(I believe)(The Claimant believes) that the facts stated in these particulars of claim are true.
* I am duly authorised by the claimant to sign this statement

Full name _____

Name of claimant's solicitor's firm _____

signed_____ position or office held_____
*(Claimant)(Litigation friend)(Claimant's solicitor) (if signing on behalf of firm or company)
*delete as appropriate

Claimant's or claimant's solicitor's address to which documents or payments should be sent if different from overleaf including (if appropriate) details of DX, fax or e-mail.

Certificate of service

In the	
Claim No.	
Claimant	
Defendant	

On the ....*(insert date)*

the ....*(insert title or description of documents served)*

a copy of which is attached to this notice was served on *(insert name of person served, including position i.e. partner, director if appropriate)*

....

Tick as appropriate

☐ by first class post

☐ by delivering to or leaving

☐ by fax machine (...............time sent)
(you may want to enclose a copy of the transmission sheet)

☐ by other means *(please specify)*

☐ by Document Exchange

☐ by handing it to or leaving it with

☐ by e-mail

at *(insert address where service effected, include fax or DX number or e-mail address)*

being the defendant's:

☐ residence   ☐ registered office

☐ place of business   ☐ other *(please specify)* ....

The date of service is therefore deemed to be .... *(insert date - see over for guidance)*

I confirm that at the time of signing this Certificate the document has not been returned to me as undelivered.

Signed ....
(Claimant)(Defendant)('ssolicitor)('slitigationfriend)

Date ....

Position or ....
office held
(if signing on behalf
of firm or company)

Response Pack

SPECIMEN

You should read the 'notes for defendant' attached to the claim form which will tell you when and where to send the forms

Included in this pack are:

- either **Admission Form N9A** (if the claim is for a specified amount) or **Admission Form N9C** (if the claim is for an unspecified amount or is not a claim for money)

- either **Defence and Counterclaim Form N9B** (if the claim is for a specified amount) or **Defence and Counterclaim Form N9D** (if the claim is for an unspecified amount or is not a claim for money)

- **Acknowledgment of service** (see below)

Complete

If you admit the claim or the amount claimed and/or you want time to pay ▶	the admission form
If you admit part of the claim ▶	the admission form and the defence form
If you dispute the whole claim or wish to make a claim (a counterclaim) against the claimant ▶	the defence form
If you need 28 days (rather than 14) from the date of service to prepare your defence, or wish to contest the court's jurisdiction ▶	the acknowledgment of service
If you do nothing, judgment may be entered against you	

Acknowledgment of Service

Defendant's full name if different from the name given on the claim form

In the	
Claim No.	
Claimant (including ref.)	
Defendant	

Address to which documents about this claim should be sent (including reference if appropriate)

	if applicable	
	fax no.	
	DX no.	
Tel. no. Postcode	e-mail	

Tick the appropriate box

1. I intend to defend all of this claim ☐

2. I intend to defend part of this claim ☐

3. I intend to contest jurisdiction ☐

If you file an acknowledgment of service but do not file a defence within 28 days of the date of service of the claim form, or particulars of claim if served separately, judgment may be entered against you.

If you do not file an application within 28 days of the date of service of the claim form, or particulars of claim if served separately, it will be assumed that you accept the court's jurisdiction and judgment may be entered against you.

Signed _____

(Defendant)(Defendant's solicitor) (Litigation friend)

Position or office held (if signing on behalf of firm or company)

Date

The court office at

is open between 10 am and 4 pm Monday to Friday. When corresponding with the court, please address forms or letters to the Court Manager and quote the claim number.

N9 -w3- Response Pack (4.99)   *Produced on behalf of The Court Service*

Request for judgment by default
(amount to be decided by the court)

SPECIMEN

In the	
Claim No.	
Claimant (including ref)	
Defendant	

To the court

The defendant has not filed (an acknowledgment of service)(a defence) to my claim and the time for doing so has expired.

I request judgment to be entered against the defendant for an amount to be decided by the court and costs.

Signed [   ]

(Claimant)(Claimant's solicitor)(Litigation friend)

Position or office held [   ]
(if signing on behalf of firm or company)

Date [   ]

Note: The court will enter judgment and refer the court file to a judge who will give directions for the management of the case including its allocation to track.

The Court Manager

The court office at

is open between 10 am and 4 pm Monday to Friday. When corresponding with the court, please address forms or letters to the Court Manager and quote the claim number.

N227 - w3 Request for judgment by default (amount to be decided by the court)(4.99)

Printed on behalf of The Court Service

4 TRIBUNALS, OTHER BODIES, ARBITRATION

There are many tribunals, various other bodies and arbitral institutions which have the power of adjudication. Some tribunals you may encounter could be the Commissioners for Income Tax, Lands Tribunal, Mental Health Review Tribunal, tribunals relating to social security matters, employment tribunals and many others. You may also find that you are making an application on someone's behalf to the Criminal Injury Compensation Authority. All these hearings are usually quite informal in comparison to a court hearing. Tribunals and other such bodies have their own rules and regulations for making applications and for appeals. They also supply their own forms, which are not usually available from stationers.

Legal aid is not normally available for applications to tribunals, except for those to Employment Appeal Tribunals, the Lands Tribunal and one or two other exceptions. However, advice and assistance can be given under the Green Form Scheme (see Chapter 7).

It is not possible in this book to go into detail of all the tribunals, etc. you could encounter, but dealt with below are a few of the most common.

Employment Tribunals

There are various centres throughout England and Wales where employment tribunal (previously called industrial tribunal) hearings take place. Applications are dealt with in offices according to the postal code for the place where the applicant worked or the place where the matter complained about took place. If help is needed on this, contact the enquiry line on 0345 959775.

Employment tribunals deal with employment related matters, including unfair dismissal, redundancy, equal pay applications, sex discrimination, race relations, maternity rights and discrimination in employment against disabled people.

An application to the employment tribunal is made on Form IT1. Forms may be obtained from Job Centres, law centres and Citizens Advice Bureaux. There are notes on the form to assist with its completion. The completed form should be sent to the appropriate office within a specified time limit (usually three months from the date of the act which gave rise to the complaint).

Once the application is received and checked by the Employment Tribunal office, an acknowledgment will be sent to the applicant and the application will be given a case number. A form IT3 (Notice of Appearance), together with a copy of IT1, is sent to the

Respondent. The Respondent must set out on form IT3 his answers to the applicant's claim and send this to the Employment Tribunal office within a specified time.

When the Employment Tribunal Office receives IT3 from the Respondent, a copy of both IT1 and IT3 are sent to the Advisory, Conciliation and Arbitration Service (ACAS), who will try to help the parties to resolve the dispute. If the dispute is settled, form COT3, which records the agreement, is filed and that is the end of the matter.

If no settlement is reached, a date for a hearing before the Employment Tribunal is fixed, giving not less than 14 days' notice to each party. Up to seven days before the hearing, either party may make further written points to the tribunal, and if any party does this, they must send a copy of the further points to the other party. If the hearing goes ahead, a decision on the matter is then reached. The parties may be told of the decision at the time or they may have to wait for several weeks. Hearings are usually held in public and the press may attend.

Besides the final hearing, the tribunal might also hold an interlocutory hearing, a pre-hearing review or a preliminary hearing. An interlocutory hearing is held if the tribunal wants to clarify any issues. A pre-hearing review is held if the tribunal thinks that either of the parties are unlikely to be successful and if that party still wishes to proceed, he may be ordered to pay a deposit. If the case goes ahead, it will be heard by a different tribunal. A preliminary hearing is held where the tribunal considers that it may not be able to deal with part of the application because it is not a matter over which the tribunal has any power. An interim relief hearing may also take place, where a re-employment order or an order continuing the contract of employment might be made.

If one of the parties is unhappy with the decision reached, then, in certain specific circumstances, the employment tribunal can be asked to review its decision and if it agrees to do this, there will be a re-hearing. An appeal against the employment tribunal's decision may be made to the Employment Appeal Tribunal (EAT) on a point of law only. Appeal may be made from the EAT to the Court of Appeal and then to the House of Lords.

Enforcing the Decision of a Tribunal

Tribunals cannot enforce decisions they make. If it is necessary for a decision to be enforced, then the party wishing to carry out the enforcement must apply to the county court. This is done by producing to the county court the original award and filing a copy of the award with the court, together with an affidavit verifying the amount payable. This application is made without notice, i.e., in the absence of the other party.

ACAS

As mentioned above, when an application has been made to the employment tribunal, the relevant forms are sent to ACAS, which is an independent body whose role is to prevent and resolve employment disputes and to conciliate in complaints to employment tribunals.

ACAS will hold workshops and joint working parties in an attempt to help organisations avoid industrial relations problems. They offer conciliation when disputes occur, where those involved can try to reach agreement through discussion and negotiation. However, ACAS cannot impose or recommend settlements. They may also appoint a mediator to help in disputes if the parties request this. If conciliation does not work, the parties can ask ACAS to act as arbitrator, and then an independent arbitrator or board will be appointed to examine the case and make an award. Before the arbitration is arranged, both parties must agree to accept the arbitrator's decision as binding.

ACAS has many enquiry points throughout the country which give free information and advice on most employment matters.

Other Bodies

There are numerous regulatory bodies and offices, e.g., Broadcasting Complaints Commission; Complaints Adjudicator for Companies House; Data Protection Registrar; Police Complaints Authority; Financial Services Authority (FSA); The Adjudicator, who investigates complaints about the Inland Revenue, Customs & Excise and the Contributions Agency of the Department of Social Security; as well as regulators for the public utilities, such as Office of Gas Supply (Ofgas), Office of Water Services (Ofwat), Office of Electricity Regulation (Offer), Office of Telecommunications (Oftel), and various Ombudsmen.

Ombudsmen are independent investigators appointed to look into complaints of various bodies, when an internal complaints procedure has proved unsatisfactory or unfair. Regulators are independent 'watchdogs' who are appointed to look after the interests of customers of privatised utilities such as gas, water and electricity, as mentioned above. Similar to ombudsmen, they will investigate complaints where internal procedures have failed to satisfy.

The Parliamentary Ombudsman, otherwise known as the Parliamentary Commissioner for Administration, deals with complaints by members of the public about their treatment by Government departments and various other public sector bodies. He can only deal with complaints which have been put to him through a Member of Parliament.

Local Government Ombudsmen, othewise known as Local Government Commissioners, deal with complaints of maladministration by local authorities and certain other bodies. Members of the public may make a complaint direct to a Local Government Ombudsman.

There are various other Ombudsmen who investigate complaints, e.g., the Banking Ombudsman, Building Societies Ombudsman, Health Service Ombudsman, Insurance Ombudsman, Legal Services Ombudsman, Pensions Ombudsman, Personal Investment Authority Ombudsman. Some of these have power to make binding awards or decisions. There is also an Ombudsman who investigates complaints regarding the administration of the institutions and bodies of the European Community: The European Ombudsman.

An Ombudsman or regulator should be contacted as a last resort, after the particular organisation being complained about has been given every opportunity to resolve the matter.

Criminal Injury Compensation Authority

One organisation which you may come across is the Criminal Injury Compensation Authority (CICA), which administers the Criminal Injuries Compensation Scheme — a scheme to compensate victims of crimes of violence. Until April 1996, this was operated by the Criminal Injuries Compensation Board (CICB), which the CICA has replaced. Rules concerning eligibility under the scheme are laid down by the CICA.

Applications for compensation must be made in writing on a form obtainable from the CICA and must be made within two years of the incident causing the injury. However, this time limit may be waived in certain circumstances. Under the old CICB scheme, up to 31 March 1996, the time limit for claiming compensation was three years from the date of the incident.

Applications will be decided by claims officers of the CICA. If an applicant disagrees with a claims officer's decision, he may ask for a review of that decision. Such a review must be requested within 90 days. There is a further right of appeal from a decision made on a review and the time limit for an appeal is 30 days. An appeal will be considered by adjudicators, who are members of the Criminal Injuries Compensation Appeals Panel. There may be an oral hearing on appeal, although there is no right to such a hearing. Under the old CICB system, there was a right to request a hearing.

The amount of compensation payable will be a standard amount based on a tariff formulated by the CICA according to the nature and severity of the injury. There is a maximum amount of compensation payable. Similarly, there is a minimum amount payable and any injury must be serious enough to qualify for the minimum award.

The costs of legal representation will not be paid for by the CICA.

Motor Insurers' Bureau

The Motor Insurers' Bureau (MIB) is an independent body funded by motor insurance companies to settle claims brought by injured persons where a negligent driver is uninsured or cannot be traced. Claims for damage to property can also be made to the MIB but not if the driver of the vehicle causing the damage is unknown. There are various important procedures to be followed when making a claim to the MIB, one of these being that victims must report the accident to the police.

Motor insurers are permitted to operate as such only if they belong to the MIB and pay towards its costs.

Shaw's Directory of Tribunals and Regulatory Bodies is a useful book, giving further details of various tribunals and regulatory bodies.

Arbitration

Arbitration is a means of settling disputes, frequently used in specialised matters. It enables the parties to have their dispute resolved by a person or a group of people they have chosen. Arbitration is often preferred to applying to the courts because it can be quicker, there is no public hearing and the arbitrator usually has knowledge of the subject being disputed. Many commercial contracts contain an arbitration clause specifying that if a dispute arises, the parties to the contract will go to arbitration to settle the matter. There are various arbitral and trade institutions which provide for the needs of a specific trade or area, e.g., London Maritime Arbitrator's Association; International Chamber of Commerce; Institute of Civil Engineers; Joint Contracts Tribunal. See also page 149 on arbitration for commercial landlords and tenants. The conduct of the arbitration in these cases is governed by the rules of the particular arbitral institution which has been chosen by the parties to the dispute. Even where a contract does not provide for arbitration, the parties may prefer arbitration rather than going to court. In an arbitration, the final decision is binding on the parties and can be enforced through the High Court.

If you find that you are preparing documents for an arbitration, these will be set out in the same manner as statements of case are set out (see Chapter 3). The person bringing the matter to arbitration is called the Claimant and the other party is known as the Respondent. Appointments for arbitration are arranged between the parties to suit the arbitrators and it may be one of your duties to arrange this.

The Chartered Institute of Arbitrators, which is based in London, organises trade association arbitration schemes. Many businesses and other organisations, including many household names, are members of a trade association arbitration scheme and if someone has a dispute with that organisation, they may make a complaint to the trade association. The trade association will try to help both parties reach an agreement but if they cannot, the association may offer to arbitrate.

Alternative Dispute Resolution/Mediation

Alternative Dispute Resolution (ADR) is the name given to various methods of resolving disputes without the necessity of going to court or a formal arbitration. One of these alternative options is mediation, which enables an independent third party, who could be a solicitor, to discuss the problem with the parties and hopefully help them to reach an amicable solution. In mediation, if either of the parties does not like the solution, they do not have to accept it. Mediation is entirely voluntary and tries to reach a constructive, non-hostile solution agreeable to both parties which, of course, helps enormously if they wish to preserve any sort of business or other relationship.

Some professional bodies, e.g., the Royal Institute of Surveyors, provide services for disputes which involve their members. One of the principal international organisations which can assist in matters relating to the use of ADR in commercial matters is the Centre for Dispute Resolution (CEDR), based in London.

An important organisation which provides mediation and conciliation services for employment related matters is ACAS, as mentioned earlier. Also mentioned previously are ombudsmen and regulators who can investigate complaints and get matters put right or give satisfactory answers. NHS patients seeking an explanation or apology, if appropriate, can utilise the NHS Complaints Procedure, which has been implemented for that purpose.

The courts are increasingly urging lawyers to refer suitable cases for mediation early on in proceedings and at various stages of proceedings. A voluntary mediation service is available at the Central London County Court for those who have an action proceeding in that court. If someone has an action proceeding in another county court in London, it may be possible for them to have their action transferred if they wish to take part in the Central London County Court's mediation scheme. This particular scheme is available to deal with money claims over £5,000. If agreement is not reached through mediation, the parties may still continue with their court action. Also, if the mediation is unsuccessful, everything that has been said during the mediation is confidential and cannot be mentioned later in court. The mediation is an informal process, taking place in small rooms in the court building.

There are many other mediation and conciliation services available to commercial organisations. With regard to non-commercial matters, there are various organisations offering these services. For example, Mediation UK, based in Bristol, can provide details of local community mediation schemes for matters such as neighbour disputes, e.g., disputes about noise, children's behaviour, etc., and other community matters, even relating to bullying at school.

Court welfare officers provide a large proportion of the mediation service in family matters where children are involved. There are also mediators who operate independently of the courts, such as National Family Mediation, the Family Mediators Association and the British Association of Lawyer Mediators, who provide a service to couples involved in divorce or separation. This involves experienced mediators, who have had suitable training, trying to help both parties to reach agreement regarding the care of children and visiting arrangements, housing, financial matters and any other problems which may arise. Of course, divorcing or separating couples do not have to seek the help of mediators but if agreement can be reached in this way, contested court proceedings can often be avoided, thereby saving a lot of distress and expense.

TRIBUNALS, OTHER BODIES, ARBITRATION

Test yourself on Chapter 4

Test your knowledge by completing this assignment. If you find that you have difficulty with anything, read the chapter again until you are happy with your answers.

1. What sort of employment-related matters might the employment tribunal deal with? If someone is not happy with the decision of an employment tribunal, to whom may an appeal be made?
2. Name half a dozen different regulatory bodies. What are Ombudsmen and Regulators?
3. If someone is a victim of a crime of violence, to whom might he make a claim for compensation?
4. In certain matters, it is often preferred to go to arbitration rather than issuing court proceedings. What are some of the possible advantages of arbitration?
5. What is meant by 'Alternative Dispute Resolution' (ADR)? Write a few sentences on some of the different ways of resolving disputes and when they would be used.
6. Now go through the chapter and if there are any words that are unfamiliar to you or that you cannot spell, write or type them correctly several times until you feel you know them.

5 FAMILY LAW

Family law can include not only divorce, but also nullity, legal separation, matters relating to persons co-habiting and children. Some or all of these matters come under the jurisdiction of the High Court, the county court and the magistrates' court.

The Family Law Act 1996

The Family Law Act 1996 will make a number of changes to the law. At the time of writing, it has not all come into effect and it is anticipated that Part II of the Act, which relates to divorce and separation, will be implemented in the year 2000. One of the main aims of the Act is to encourage people to try to save their marriages, perhaps by counselling or, if the marriage cannot be saved, to dissolve it with as little distress to all concerned, including any children.

As new rules and procedures come into force, some of those mentioned in this chapter will also change. One of the new procedures will be a requirement that anyone contemplating divorce must, three months before commencing proceedings, attend an Information Meeting.

Not only will the person wishing to commence the divorce proceedings have to attend an Information Meeting, but the other party (the husband or wife) will have to attend an Information Meeting if they wish to make or contest any court applications regarding children of the family, or any property or financial matters. The parties do not have to attend together but may do so if they wish. The Information Meetings will give the parties information about matters relating to divorce and separation, including marriage counselling; the importance to be attached to the welfare and wishes of the children, and how to help the children cope with the breakdown of the marriage; they will be told about the sort of financial questions that may arise and be given details of services that are available to help them; how to obtain help if one of the parties is violent; information on legal advice and legal aid; mediation; and what the process of divorce will involve.

If it is desired to go ahead with a divorce, the couple will be encouraged to use mediation to make any arrangements and resolve disputes before the divorce is granted. Mediation will be with a trained mediator who will invite the couple to meet together with him in the hope of identifying any issues they need to sort out and to negotiate to find solutions acceptable to both of them. It is hoped that the informal atmosphere of mediation will work for people, rather than them having to express their views formally through solicitors or at court.

Commencing Proceedings

Divorce proceedings are commenced by petition in either a divorce county court or the Divorce Registry in London which, for this purpose, acts as a county court.

Divorces and ancillary matters are dealt with by a judge in open court or in the judge's room. A District judge will deal with matters related to divorce proceedings, such as those concerning property or finance. (See also Chapter 3 for further information on judges and District judges in the county courts.)

If a divorce becomes defended, it may be transferred to the Family Division of the High Court. This can, of course, be in London or any of the District Registries. There is no restriction as to which divorce county court a petition can be brought in, so proceedings are usually commenced in the court most convenient to the Petitioner.

The Petitioner is the person who starts the divorce proceedings and the person against whom they are brought is known as the Respondent. If proceedings are brought to include another person in those proceedings, he or she is known as the Co-Respondent. Instructions and Briefs to Counsel are set out in the same manner as shown in Chapter 3.

The sole ground for divorce is that the marriage has irretrievably broken down. However, the Petitioner must satisfy the court that this is so, and must prove that one or more of five facts apply which will indeed show that the marriage has irretrievably broken down. If the relevant sections of the 1996 Act come into force, the ground for divorce will be the same, but it will not be necessary to prove this by reference to any of the five facts. The five facts which evidence irretrievable breakdown are:

(a)   The Respondent has committed adultery and the Petitioner finds it intolerable to live with the Respondent.

(b)   The Respondent has behaved in such a way that the Petitioner cannot reasonably be expected to live with the Respondent.

(c)   The Respondent has deserted the Petitioner for a continuous period of at least two years immediately preceding presentation of the divorce petition (i.e., two years immediately preceding the commencement of the divorce proceedings).

(d)   The parties have lived apart for a continuous period of at least two years immediately preceding presentation of the divorce petition and the Respondent consents to a divorce.

(e)   The parties have lived apart for a continuous period of at least five years immediately preceding presentation of the divorce petition.

To commence proceedings the following documents must be filed at court:

(a)   The marriage certificate.

(b)   The petition. When the petition is completed you should make a copy for the file, plus a copy for the court's own records, and a copy for each party the petition is to be served on, i.e., the Respondent and perhaps a Co-Respondent.

(c)   A certificate with regard to reconciliation (see page 177).

(d)   A statement of arrangements regarding children (if any) with a copy for the Respondent (see page 177).

(e)   The court fee or an application for exemption of fees, where appropriate.

The documents, once they are checked and signed by the fee earner, can be posted to the court together with a cheque made payable to HM Paymaster General ('HMPG') for the fee and a stamped, self-addressed envelope. Remember always to keep copies of the documents on the file. Most of these documents have backsheets (see page 61) although these are not shown in the examples.

The Marriage Certificate

A photocopy of the marriage certificate is not sufficient. It must be an official copy. If the Petitioner does not have this, a copy may be applied for by post from The Office for National Statistics in Southport. A fee will be charged: cheques should be made payable to HM Paymaster General. A personal application for a copy marriage certificate may be made to the Office for National Statistics in London. Both addresses are given in the address section of this book under 'Births, Deaths and Marriages'. To obtain a copy of a marriage certificate, the applicant must be able to provide the full names of both parties to the marriage and the date of the marriage. A fee is payable for a certificate.

Petition

This can be a pre-printed form containing blank spaces for completion and shows which of the five facts mentioned above is relied on. The form also shows whether it is the husband or the wife who is the Petitioner. Most divorce forms can be obtained from the court or bought from specialist law stationers and some solicitors have many forms readily available on their computers through special software.

A petition starts off with the heading of the matter (see page 52), i.e., the court where the divorce proceedings have been commenced, and has a place for the number it will be given by the court, and states the names of the parties.

The petition is then completed as follows:

1. The first paragraph must give the particulars shown in the marriage certificate as to the name of the parties, and the date and place of the marriage.
2. The address at which the Petitioner and Respondent last lived together.
3. This paragraph shows that the Petitioner is domiciled in England and Wales and gives the addresses and occupations of both parties. The wording of this paragraph may be altered slightly if the Petitioner has lived in England and Wales for a certain time although is not actually a resident.
4. This shows whether there are any children of the family and if so, gives their details.
5. This states whether any other child, now living, has been born to the wife during the marriage.
6. This states whether or not there have been any other relevant court proceedings in England and Wales.
7. This states whether the Child Support Agency (see page 195) has had any involvement.
8. This states whether there are any other continuing proceedings relating to the marriage outside England and Wales.
9. States the marriage has irretrievably broken down.
10. This shows which of the five facts, mentioned at the beginning of this chapter, applies in this case to prove that the marriage has indeed irretrievably broken down.
11. This gives details of the incidents during the marriage which proves that one of the five facts applies.

Where the fact being relied upon is that the parties have lived apart continuously for five years, there is an additional paragraph in the petition which states whether there is any arrangement or proposed arrangement between the parties for the support of either of them or any child of the family. This paragraph will be inserted before 8 above.

The petition then ends with a 'prayer' which simply sets out what the Petitioner is asking the court to do, e.g., that the marriage be dissolved. It is then signed by the solicitor acting on behalf of the Petitioner or, if counsel settled the petition, his name should appear in this place.

Details are then given of the names and addresses of the persons who are to be served with the petition, the Petitioner's address for service (usually the solicitor's address) and the form is dated (normally the date it is filed at court). The pre-printed form of petition has with it some notes to aid in its completion. It also has a backsheet which must be completed in the usual way (see page 61).

SPECIMEN

FAMILY PROCEEDINGS
RULES

IN THE _____ NORTHTOWN _____ **COUNTY COURT***

~~PRINCIPAL REGISTRY~~ *

Rule 2.3
Appendix 2

No. of Matter

The Notes for
guidance in
drafting the
petition are on
a separate sheet.

The Petition of   JANE BLOGGS

Shows that

Note 1.

1. On the   1st   day of April 1994   the Petitioner

was lawfully

married to   JOHN BLOGGS

(hereinafter called the Respondent) at   St Mary's Church,
Northtown, Hertfordshire

Note 2.

2. The Petitioner and the Respondent last lived together as husband and

wife at   64 Rotten Row, Northtown, Herts EG4 6RB

Note 3.

3. The Petitioner is domiciled in England and Wales and is by occupation a
    clerk

Note 4.

and resides

at 28 Sunny Street, Northtown, Herts. EG7 8NB

and the Respondent is by occupation a   pilot   and

resides at   42 Lark Rise, Northtown, Herts   EG8 3BX

Note 5.

4. There is [are]   one   children of the family now living

namely PETER BLOGGS, born on 6th February 1995

Note 6.

5. No other child now living has been born to the Petitioner during

the marriage

Note 7.

6. There are or have been no other proceedings in any court in England

and Wales or elsewhere with reference to the marriage [or to any children of the

family] or between the Petitioner and the Respondent with reference to any property of either or both of them

SPECIMEN

Note 8.

7. There are or have been no proceedings in the Child Support Agency with reference to the maintenance of any child of the family

Note 9.

8. There are no proceedings continuing in any country outside England and Wales which relate to the marriage or are capable of affecting its validity or subsistence

Note 10.

Note 11.

9. The said marriage has broken down irretrievably.

Note 12.

10. The parties to the marriage have lived apart for a continuous period of at least two years immediately preceding the presentation of this Petition and the Respondent consents to a decree being granted.

11.   On or about 2nd May 1996, the parties agreed that they would live apart and have not lived together since that date.

Note 14.

Note 15.

Note 16.

Note 17.

SPECIMEN

The Petitioner therefore prays:–

Note 18.

(1)   That the said marriage may be dissolved;

Note 19.

(2)   That the Respondent   may be
ordered to pay   the costs of this suit;

Note 20.

(3)   That she may be granted the following ancillary relief:–

(i)   an order for maintenance pending suit

(ii)   a periodical payments order

(iii)   a secured provision order

(iv)   a lump sum order

(v)   a property adjustment order

} for herself

(vi)   a periodical payments order

(vii)   a secured provision order

(viii) a lump sum order

(ix)   a property adjustment order

} for the children of the family

Note 21.

(Signed)   *

Note 22.

The names and addresses of the persons who are to be served with this

Petition are:–

John Bloggs

Note 23.

The Petitioner's address for service is:–   John Smith & Co.,
2 Bank Chambers, High Road, Southtown, Herts. LM4 7XB
(ref: AB/cd/123.   tel: 01438-12345)

Dated this   *   day of   *

Address all communications for the Court to: The Court Manager, County Court*...

....

(or to the Family Proceedings Department, Principal Registry, First Avenue House, 42-49 High Holborn, London WC1V 6NP).

The Court Office is open from 10 a.m. till 4 p.m. (4.30 p.m. at the Principal Registry) on Mondays to Fridays only.

SPECIMEN

In the ___NORTHTOWN___ **County Court***

~~Principal Registry~~*

No. of Matter

IN THE MATTER of the Petition of

JANE BLOGGS

═══════════════════════════

Divorce Petition

(Wife against Husband)

(Separation — 2 years)

═══════════════════════════

Note 23.

John Smith & Co.,
2 Bank Chambers,
High Road,
Southtown,
Herts.
LM4 7XB

ref: AB/cd/123

tel: 01438-12345

Solicitors for the Petitioner

©1998 **OYEZ** The Solicitors' Law Stationery Society Ltd,   *1998 Edition*
Oyez House, 7 Spa Road, London SE16 3QQ 9.98 T00933

5046088
* * * * *

Divorce 4W

Certificate with Regard to Reconciliation

This is a certificate signed by the solicitor acting for the Petitioner, stating whether or not he has discussed with the Petitioner the possibility of reconciliation and/or given to the Petitioner the names and addresses of persons qualified to help with reconciliation (e.g., marriage guidance council, known as Relate). The solicitor is not compelled to discuss reconciliation — it may be inappropriate to do so — but he must state whether or not he has done so and whether he has given suitable names to the Petitioner.

If the petitioner is being advised under the Green Form Scheme (see page 218), this document is not completed by the solicitor because, in these circumstances, the petitioner is deemed to be acting for herself and receiving assistance only to complete the forms.

Statement of Arrangements

This is a form which requires the Petitioner to describe the present and proposed arrangements with regard to children of the family (if any). It is also open to the Respondent to file a Statement of Arrangements with the court if he so wishes.

Certificate with regard
to Reconciliation
(Form M3, Appendix 1,
FPR 1991)
Rule 2.6(3)

SPECIMEN

FAMILY PROCEEDINGS RULES

*Complete
and/or delete
as appropriate.

IN THE————— NORTHTOWN —————— **COUNTY COURT** } *

PRINCIPAL REGISTRY } *

No. of Matter

Between .... JANE BLOGGS .... Petitioner

and .... JOHN BLOGGS .... Respondent

I,   JOHN SMITH

the Solicitor acting for the Petitioner in the above cause do hereby certify that I have [not] discussed

with the Petitioner the possibility of a reconciliation and that I have [not] given to the Petitioner the

names and addresses of persons qualified to help effect a reconciliation.

Dated this   *   day of   *

(Signed) ....

Solicitor for the Petitioner
John Smith & Co.,
2 Bank Chambers, High Road,
Southtown, Herts. LM4 7XB

Ref: AB/cd/123

Address all communications for the Court to: The Court Manager, County Court* ....

(or to the Principal Registry, First Avenue House, 42-49 High Holborn, London WC1V 6NP).
The Court Office is open from 10 a.m. till 4 p.m. (4.30 p.m. in the Principal Registry) on Mondays to Fridays only.

Statement of Arrangements for Children
(Form M4, Appendix 1 FPR 1991)

SPECIMEN

FAMILY PROCEEDINGS RULES
Rule 2.2(2)

In the		NORTHTOWN	County Court
Petitioner	JANE BLOGGS		
Respondent	JOHN BLOGGS		
No. of Matter *(always quote this)*		99 D 789	

To the Petitioner

You must complete this form
if you or the respondent have any children ● under 16

or ● over 16 but under 18 if they are at school
or college or are training for a trade,
profession or vocation.

Please use black ink.

Please complete Parts I, II and III.

Before you issue a petition for divorce try to reach agreement with your husband/wife over the proposals for the children's future. There is space for him/her to sign at the end of this form if agreement is reached.

If your husband/wife does not agree with the proposals he/she will have the opportunity at a later stage to state why he/she does not agree and will be able to make his/her own proposals.

You should take or send the completed form, signed by you (and, if agreement is reached, by your husband/wife) together with a copy to the Court when you issue your petition.

Please refer to the explanatory notes issued regarding completion of the prayer of the petition if you are asking the Court to make any order regarding the children.

The Court will only make an order if it considers that an order will be better for the child(ren) than no order.

If you wish to apply for any of the orders which may be available to you under Part I or II of the Children Act 1989 you are advised to see a solicitor.

You should obtain legal advice from a solicitor or, alternatively, from an advice agency. Addresses of solicitors and advice agencies can be obtained from the Yellow Pages and the Solicitors Regional Directory which can be found at Citizens Advice Bureaux, Law Centres and any local library.

To the Respondent

The petitioner has completed Parts I, II and III of this form
which will be sent to the Court at the same time that the divorce petition is filed.

Please read all parts of the form carefully.

If you agree with the arrangements and proposals for the children you should sign Part IV of the form.

Please use black ink. You should return the form to the petitioner, or his/her solicitor.

If you do not agree with all or some of the arrangements or proposals you will be given the opportunity of saying so when the divorce petition is served on you.

1

SPECIMEN

Part I – Details of the children

Please read the instructions for boxes 1, 2 and 3 before you complete this section

1. Children of both parties

(Give details only of any children born to you and the Respondent or adopted by you both)

	Forenames	Surnames	Date of birth
(i)			
(ii)			
(iii)			
(iv)			
(v)			

2. Other children of the family

(Give details of any other children treated by both of you as children of the family: for example your own or the Respondent's)

	Forenames	Surname	Date of birth	Relationship to Yourself	Respondent
(i)					
(ii)					
(iii)					
(iv)					
(v)					

3. Other children who are not children of the family

(Give details of any children born to you or the Respondent that have not been treated as children of the family or adopted by you both)

	Forenames	Surnames	Date of birth
(i)			
(ii)			
(iii)			
(iv)			
(v)			

2

SPECIMEN

Part II – Arrangements for the children of the family

This part of the form must be completed. Give details for each child if arrangements are different. If necessary, continue on another sheet and attach it to this form

4.	**Home details** *(Please tick the appropriate boxes)*	
	(a) The addresses at which the children now live	
	(b) Give details of the number of living rooms, bedrooms, etc. at the addresses in (a)	
	(c) Is the house rented or owned and by whom? Is the rent or any mortgage being regularly paid?	☐ No ☐ Yes
	(d) Give the names of all other persons living with the children including your husband/wife if he/she lives there. State their relationship to the children.	
	(e) Will there be any change in these arrangements?	☐ No ☐ Yes *(please give details)*

3

SPECIMEN

5.	Education and training details *(Please tick the appropriate boxes)*	
	(a) Give the names of the school, college or place of training attended by each child.	
	(b) Do the children have any special educational needs?	☐ No ☐ Yes *(please give details)*
	(c) Is the school, college or place of training, fee-paying?	☐ No ☐ Yes *(please give details of how much the fees are per term/year)*
	Are fees being regularly paid?	☐ No ☐ Yes *(please give details)*
	(d) Will there be any change in these arrangements?	☐ No ☐ Yes *(please give details)*

4

SPECIMEN

6.	**Childcare details** *(Please tick the appropriate boxes)*	
	(a) Which parent looks after the children from day to day? If responsibility is shared, please give details.	
	(b) Does that parent go out to work?	☐ No ☐ Yes *(please give details of his/her hours of work)*
	(c) Does someone look after the children when the parent is not there?	☐ No ☐ Yes *(please give details)*
	(d) Who looks after the children during school holidays?	
	(e) Will there be any change in these arrangements?	☐ No ☐ Yes *(please give details)*

7.	**Maintenance** *(Please tick the appropriate boxes)*	
	(a) Does your husband/wife pay towards the upkeep of the children? If there is another source of maintenance, please specify.	☐ No ☐ Yes *(please give details of how much)*
	(b) Is the payment made under a court order?	☐ No ☐ Yes *(please give details, including the name of the court and case number)*
	(c) Is the payment following an assessment by the Child Support Agency?	☐ No ☐ Yes *(please give details of how much)*
	(d) Has maintenance for the children been agreed?	☐ No ☐ Yes
	(e) If not, will you be applying for: ● a child maintenance order from the court	☐ No ☐ Yes
	● child support maintenance through the Child Support Agency?	☐ No ☐ Yes

5

SPECIMEN

8.	**Details for contact with the children** *(Please tick the appropriate boxes)*	
(a) Do the children see your husband/wife?	☐ No	☐ Yes *(please give details of how often and where)*
(b) Do the children ever stay with your husband/wife?	☐ No	☐ Yes *(please give details of how much)*
(c) Will there be any change to these arrangements? Please give details of the proposed arrangements for contact and residence.	☐ No	☐ Yes *(please give details of how much)*

6

SPECIMEN

9.	**Details of health** *(Please tick the appropriate boxes)*	
(a) Are the children generally in good health?	☐ Yes	☐ No *(please give details of any serious disability or chronic illness)*
(b) Do the children have any special health needs?	☐ No	☐ Yes *(please give details of the care needed and how it is to be provided)*

10.	**Details of care and other court proceedings** *(Please tick the appropriate boxes)*	
(a) Are the children in the care of a local authority, or under the supervision of a social worker or probation officer?	☐ No	☐ Yes *(please give details including any court proceedings)*
(b) Are any of the children on the Child Protection Register?	☐ No	☐ Yes *(please give details of the local authority and the date of registration)*
(c) Are there or have there been any proceedings in any Court involving the children, for example adoption, custody/residence, access/contact wardship, care, supervision or maintenance? (You need not include any Child Support Agency proceedings here).	☐ No	☐ Yes *(please give details and send a copy of any order to the Court)*

7

SPECIMEN

Part III – To the Petitioner

Conciliation

If you and your husband/wife do not agree about the arrangements for the child(ren), would you agree to discuss the matter with a Conciliator and your husband/wife?

☐ No   ☐ Yes

Declaration

I declare that the information I have given is correct and complete to the best of my knowledge.

Signed   (Petitioner)

Date:

Part IV – To the Respondent

I agree with the arrangements and proposals contained in Part I and II of this form.

Signed   (Respondent)

Date:

8

OYEZ The Solicitors' Law Stationery Society Ltd, Oyez House, 7 Spa Road, London SE16 3QQ

1993 Edition
11.97 F34412
5046127
★★

Action taken by the Court

Once the court receives these documents, it allocates the case a matter number. This begins with the last two digits of the year, followed by D for divorce, and the serial number for each case (e.g., 99 D 1234). The court acknowledges receipt and posts to the Respondent the petition sealed with the court seal, plus the statement of arrangements, if applicable, together with a form of Acknowledgment of Service. This form differs slightly according to which of the five facts is alleged.

The Acknowledgment of Service form asks the Respondent certain questions. He should answer these and return the completed form to the court within eight days. The court will then send a photocopy of this form to the Petitioner's solicitors.

If the Respondent does not return the Acknowledgment of Service, the court will send to the Petitioner's solicitors notification of non-service. The Petitioner may then try another way of effecting service of the petition on the Respondent.

Service of the Petition

Service may be effected in one of the following ways:

(a) In the first instance, by the court by post.

(b) By the court bailiff. In this case a further copy of the petition and appropriate fee must be filed with the court.

(c) Personal service by a solicitor or process server. On no account may the Petitioner personally serve the Respondent with these documents. If personal service is effected, an affidavit of service must then be filed with the court.

(d) Substituted service — in certain circumstances, an order for substituted service may be obtained (e.g., newspaper advertisement).

Answer

If your firm is acting for the Respondent, and he wishes to defend the divorce, he has a specific number of days from the service of the petition to file an Answer. (This is equivalent to a defence in other types of actions: see Chapter 3.) The Answer must be headed with the title of the matter and each paragraph numbered. A backsheet also has to be completed.

The Answer will be sent to the court and the case will proceed to trial either in the county court or will be transferred to the Family Division of the High Court. If it is transferred, it will then be given a new matter number by the High Court. If a Co-Respondent is included in the proceedings, he or she also has a right to file an Answer. Once an Answer is filed, a copy is sent to the Petitioner's solicitors by the court and the case will proceed.

Affidavit in Support of Petition

Before a divorce can be granted, the court will always want evidence. This may be in the form of an affidavit, i.e., a sworn statement by the Petitioner verifying the petition and dealing with certain other matters. The affidavit must contain certain specific information and printed forms are available. The forms vary according to which of the five facts are relied upon (see page 170). The rules provide that the affidavit must be sworn by the Petitioner before a solicitor who is not her own. See also the section on affidavits in Chapter 3. The original affidavit, together with any exhibits, are sent to the court, copies being kept in the file. At the same time, a form of Application for Directions for Trial is sent to the court.

The District judge considers the affidavit and any other documents and, if he is satisfied that the Petitioner is entitled to a divorce, he will issue a certificate which informs the parties of when and where the decree nisi will be pronounced (see page 193). This certificate does not mean that the divorce has been granted.

The District judge will, at the same time, consider the statement of arrangements regarding any children and may make certain directions regarding any children.

Affidavit by Petitioner in support of petition under s. 1(2)(d), M.C. Act 1973.

FAMILY PROCEEDINGS *SPECIMEN*   No. of Matter......9.9...D...7.8.9......
RULES

Rule 2.24(3); Form M7(d)

*Complete
and/or delete as
appropriate.

IN THE ——— NORTHTOWN ——— **COUNTY COURT***

~~**PRINCIPAL REGISTRY***~~

| Between | JANE BLOGGS | Petitioner |
| and | JOHN BLOGGS | Respondent |

QUESTION	ANSWER
About the Divorce Petition 1. Have you read the petition filed in this case?	Yes
2. Do you wish to alter or add to any statement in the petition? If so, state the alterations or additions.	No
3. Subject to these alterations and additions (if any), is everything stated in your petition true? If any statement is not within your own knowledge, indicate this and say whether it is true to the best of your information and belief.	Yes
4. State the date on which you and the respondent separated.	2nd May 1996
5. State briefly the reason or main reason for the separation.	The marriage was unhappy for some time and it was agreed that we should live apart.
6. State the date when and the circumstances in which you came to the conclusion that the marriage was in fact at an end.	2nd May 1996

1

7. State as far as you know the various addresses at which you and the respondent have respectively lived since the last date given in the answer to Question 4, and the periods of residence at each address:

	Petitioner's Address		*Respondent's Address*
From 2.5.96 To present date	28 Sunny Street, Northtown, Herts. EG7 8NB	From 2.5.96 To present date	42 Lark Rise, Northtown, Herts. EG8 3BX

SPECIMEN

8. Since the date given in the answer to Question 4, have you ever lived with the respondent in the same household?

   If so, state the addresses and the period or periods, giving dates.

   No.

About the Children of the Family

9. Have you read the Statement of Arrangements filed in this case?

   Yes.

10. Do you wish to alter anything in the Statement of Arrangements or add to it?

    If so, state the alterations or additions.

    No.

11. Subject to these alterations and addition(s) (if any), is everything stated in your petition [and Statement of Arrangements for the child(ren)] true and correct to the best of your knowledge and belief?

    Yes.

2

I, JANE BLOGGS **SPECIMEN** *(full name)*

of 28 Sunny Street, Northtown, *(full residential*
Herts. EG7 8NB *address)*

clerk *(occupation)*

make oath and say as follows:-

1. I am the petitioner in this cause.

2. **The answers to Questions 1 to 11 are true.**

(1) Insert name of the respondent exactly as it appears on the acknowledgment of service signed by him/her.

3. I identify the signature ....J. BLOGGS.............................(¹)
appearing on the copy acknowledgment of service
now produced to me and marked "A" as the signature of my husband/wife, the
respondent in this cause.

4. I identify the signature ....J. BLOGGS.............................(¹)
appearing at Part IV of the Statement of Arrangements dated ....*.................
now produced to me and marked "B" as the signature of the respondent.

(2) Exhibit any other document on which the petitioner wishes to rely.

5. (²)

(3) If the petitioner seeks a judicial separation, amend accordingly.

(4) Delete if costs are not sought.

6. I ask the Court to grant a decree dissolving my marriage with the respondent(³)
on the grounds
stated in my petition [and to order the respondent
to pay the costs of this suit] (⁴),

SWORN at

in the County of

this   day of   }   ....

Before me

A Commissioner for Oaths.

(5) Delete as the case may be.

Officer of a Court appointed by
the Judge to take affidavits(⁵).

Address all communications for the Court to: The Court Manager, County Court* ....
....

(or to the Principal Registry, First Avenue House, 42-49 High Holborn, London WC1V 6NP) quoting the number in the top right-hand
corner of the first page. The Court Office is open from 10 a.m. till 4 p.m. (4.30 p.m. in the Principal Registry) on Mondays to Fridays
only.

3

191

Application for Directions for Trial (Special Procedure)

FAMILY PROCEEDINGS   **No. of Matter** 99 D 789

RULES (Rule 2.24)   **IN THE**   NORTHTOWN   **COUNTY COURT**

Between   JANE BLOGGS   Petitioner

SPECIMEN

and   JOHN BLOGGS   Respondent

Application for Directions for Trial (Special Procedure)

The Petitioner   JANE BLOGGS   applies to
the District Judge for directions for the trial of this undefended cause by entering it in the Special Procedure
List.

The Petitioner's affidavit of evidence is lodged with this application.

Signed   *   [Solicitor for] the Petitioner

Dated   *

If you write to the Court please address your letters to "The Court Manager"

and quote the **No. of Matter** at the top of this form.

The Court Office is at

and is open from 10am to 4pm on Monday to Friday.

Divorce 51A

Decree Nisi

The certificate which is issued by the District judge gives the date when a judge will pronounce the decree nisi in open court. The decree nisi is an order granted by the judge declaring that unless something comes to light within six weeks to show why a divorce should not be granted, then after that six weeks, an application may be made to the court for a decree absolute, which will be the decree making the divorce final. It is not necessary to attend court to hear the decree nisi being pronounced.

During the six-week period an appeal may be lodged or matters dealing with children can be sorted out. If it is a straightforward divorce with nothing to be sorted out, neither party needs to attend court. If, however, the District judge is not satisfied with proposed arrangements for any children, he may direct that one or both of the parties attend before him, or that a welfare report is prepared, or that further evidence, by way of affidavit, is filed. These directions do not normally hold up the divorce proceedings.

Decree Absolute

Diary notes should be made for six weeks after the decree nisi as after that period has elapsed the final divorce decree — the decree absolute — can be applied for. It is this decree which finally dissolves the marriage. This is not pronounced in open court but is applied for through the post on a prescribed form, together with the appropriate fee. All being well, the court will send the parties a sealed form of Decree Absolute and the divorce is final.

The procedure outlined above for obtaining a divorce is known as the 'special procedure'. However, it is in fact the usual procedure where divorces are straightforward and undefended and there are no children involved.

FAMILY LAW

Notice of Application for Decree Nisi to be made Absolute.
(Form M8, Appendix 1, F.P.R. 1991)

FAMILY PROCEEDINGS RULES

Rule 2.49(1)

*Complete
and/or delete as
appropriate.
If proceeding in a
District Registry,
delete both head-
ings and insert "in
the High Court of
Justice, Family
Division, District
Registry".

IN THE ——— NORTHTOWN ———

SPECIMEN

COUNTY COURT*

~~**PRINCIPAL REGISTRY***~~

No. of Matter   99 D 789

Between .... JANE BLOGGS .... Petitioner

and .... JOHN BLOGGS .... Respondent

TAKE NOTICE that the Petitioner   JANE BLOGGS

applies for the decree nisi pronounced in his (her) favour on the   *

day of   *   , to be made absolute.

Dated this   *   day of   *

Signed ....
Solicitors for Petitioner
John Smith & Co.,
of 2 Bank Chambers,
High Road,
Southtown,
Herts   LM4 7XB

ref: AC/cd/123
tel: 01438-12345

Address all communications for the Court to: The Court Manager, County Court* ....

....

(or to the Principal Registry, First Avenue House, 42-49 High Holborn, London WC2V 6NP) quoting the number in the top right-hand corner of this form.
The Court Office is open from 10 a.m. till 4 p.m. (4.30 p.m. at the Principal Registry) on Mondays to Fridays only.

Applications

As in other court procedures, different applications may be made to the court before the divorce is finalised and sometimes afterwards. The Family Proceedings Rules 1991 specify how each application is to be made, and these can be made either 'on notice' or 'without notice' (see page 117). Applications made without notice normally have to be supported by an affidavit which is filed with the court at the same time as the application. (See Chapter 3 for further information on interlocutory applications and affidavits.)

Orders (see page 120) made in matrimonial proceedings are normally drawn up by the court and sent to the parties.

Examples of types of orders that may be made are those which relate to such things as where any children of the marriage will live, or ancillary relief, which includes certain matters relating to the finances or property of the parties. When the relevant provisions of the Family Law Act 1996 come into force, ancillary relief will be known as financial provision. Where a Respondent receives notice of an application to be made for ancillary relief, he must within the specified time limit file an affidavit of means (i.e., regarding his financial circumstances) with the court and send a copy to the Petitioner or her solicitors. Therefore, if you are acting for the Respondent, make a diary note as to when this affidavit must be filed.

Child Support Agency

With regard to child support maintenance, which is money that absent parents pay as a contribution to the upkeep of their children, it is generally no longer possible for people who do not already have a court order or a written maintenance agreement to make arrangements for child maintenance through the courts. Child maintenance has been dealt with by the Child Support Agency (CSA) since 5 April 1993. However, the CSA will accept applications for child maintenance usually only when everyone involved is habitually resident in Great Britain or Northern Ireland. The courts will continue to deal with cases where one of those concerned lives abroad. The CSA investigates the parents' means and assesses how much maintenance should be paid.

The amount of support to be paid is reviewed every two years, but the CSA can be asked to consider reviewing an assessment whenever there is a change in circumstances. The CSA also provides a collection service. It may collect payments from the absent parent and pass them on to the person who is to receive them. If the absent parent falls into arrears with payments, the CSA may take action to enforce payment.

Notice of Change of Solicitor

If any party wishes to change their solicitor after proceedings have been issued the new solicitor must complete a Notice of Change of Solicitor form. A copy must be served on all the parties and lodged with the court. See also Notice of Change of Solicitor on page 137.

Involvement of Magistrates' Courts

Magistrates courts have various powers in family matters but do not have the power to dissolve a marriage. For the purposes of dealing with family matters, a magistrates' court is known as a family proceedings court.

Part of the business of the family proceedings courts is to make orders for personal protection and exclusion of a spouse from the matrimonial home (usually where violence is involved). They may also make certain orders relating to financial provisions and some contact and residence orders involving children. The family proceedings courts may also deal with adoptions and various other matters involving children, e.g., where an unmarried father wishes to exercise his parental responsibilities, he can apply to the court for an order to be made in this regard. Adoption proceedings are held in private (*in camera*), and the court also has power to exclude various people during certain proceedings.

Test yourself on Chapter 5

Test your knowledge by completing this assignment. If you find that you have difficulty with anything, read the chapter again until you are happy with your answers.

1. Who are the Petitioner, Respondent and Co-Respondent?
2. Before certain parts of the Family Law Act 1996 are implemented, one or more of five facts must be proved to show that a marriage has irretrievably broken down. What are these five facts? What is the sole ground for divorce?
3. Which documents should be filed at court in order to commence divorce proceedings?
4. Complete as far as you can the form included with this assignment for a Wife's Petition (Separation — 2 years), using the following details.

> Your firm, Peter Wolf & Co., of Red Riding Hood Lane, Northtown, Sussex, S21 4PQ (tel: 01646 58903; ref: PW/Smith/23), is acting for Emma Smith of 35 Strawberry Close, Maintown, Sussex. She has lived there since 5 July 1996, the day she separated from her husband. She married Giles Smith on 1 April 1991 at St. Peter's Church, Maintown, Sussex. The address where they lived together was Flat 4, Brighton Court, Maintown. Emma Smith works as an administrator and her husband is a chef, living at 64 Astronomer's Row, Northtown, Sussex. There is one child of the family, John Smith, born on 8 February 1995. They have lived apart for three years, separating on 5 July 1996 because the marriage had been unhappy for a while and they decided to live apart. Emma Smith would like to obtain maintenance for herself and the child. The divorce proceedings will be commenced in the Maintown County Court.

5. Complete as far as possible the form for Petitioner's Affidavit in support of Petition, based on the details given above.
6. What is a Statement of Arrangements for Children?
7. Explain the differences between a decree nisi and decree absolute.
8. What information is needed to complete a Notice of Application for Decree Nisi to be made absolute?
9. What is the function of the Child Support Agency?
10. What sort of family matters might the magistrates' court become involved in?
11. Now go through the chapter and if there are any words that are unfamiliar to you or that you cannot spell, write or type them correctly several times until you feel you know them.

FAMILY LAW

Wife's Petition (Separation —2 years)

FAMILY PROCEEDINGS RULES

Rule 2.3
Appendix 2

The Notes for guidance in drafting the petition are on a separate sheet.

SPECIMEN

IN THE _____ **COUNTY COURT***

PRINCIPAL REGISTRY*

No. of Matter

The Petition of

Shows that

Note 1.

1.   On the   day of   the Petitioner

was lawfully

married to

(hereinafter called the Respondent) at

Note 2.

2.   The Petitioner and the Respondent last lived together as husband and

wife at

Note 3.

3.   The Petitioner is domiciled in England and Wales and is by occupation a

Note 4.

.   and resides

at

.

and the Respondent is by occupation a   and

resides at

Note 5.

4.   There is [are]   children of the family now living

.

.

.

Note 6.

5.   No other child now living has been born to the Petitioner during

the marriage

.

Note 7.

.

6.   There are or have been no other proceedings in any court in England

and Wales or elsewhere with reference to the marriage [or to any children of the

family] or between the Petitioner and the Respondent with reference to any property of either or both of them

SPECIMEN

Note 8.

7. There are or have been no proceedings in the Child Support Agency with reference to the maintenance of any child of the family

Note 9.

8. There are no proceedings continuing in any country outside England and Wales which relate to the marriage or are capable of affecting its validity or subsistence

Note 10.

Note 11.

9. The said marriage has broken down irretrievably.

Note 12.

10. The parties to the marriage have lived apart for a continuous period of at least two years immediately preceding the presentation of this Petition and the Respondent consents to a decree being granted.

11.

Note 14.

Note 15.

Note 16.

Note 17.

SPECIMEN

The Petitioner therefore prays:–

Note 18.

(1) That the said marriage may be dissolved;

Note 19.

(2) That the Respondent   may be

ordered to pay   the costs of this suit;

Note 20.

(3) That she may be granted the following ancillary relief:–

    (i)   an order for maintenance pending suit ⎫

    (ii)   a periodical payments order   ⎪

    (iii) a secured provision order   ⎬ for herself

    (iv) a lump sum order   ⎪

    (v)   a property adjustment order   ⎭

    (vi) a periodical payments order   ⎫

    (vii) a secured provision order   ⎬ for the children

    (viii) a lump sum order   ⎪ of the family

    (ix) a property adjustment order   ⎭

Note 21.

(Signed)

Note 22.

The names and addresses of the persons who are to be served with this Petition are:–

Note 23.

The Petitioner's address for service is:–

Dated this   day of

Address all communications for the Court to: The Court Manager, County Court*..

....

(or to the Family Proceedings Department, Principal Registry, First Avenue House, 42-49 High Holborn, London WC1V 6NP,

The Court Office is open from 10 a.m. till 4 p.m. (4.30 p.m. at the Principal Registry) on Mondays to Fridays only.

SPECIMEN

In the ———————— **County Court***

Principal Registry*

No. of Matter

IN THE MATTER of the Petition of

═══════════════════════════════

Divorce Petition

(Wife against Husband)

(Separation — 2 years)

═══════════════════════════════

Note 23.

©1998 **OYEZ** The Solicitors' Law Stationery Society Ltd, *1998 Edition*
Oyez House, 7 Spa Road, London SE16 3QQ 9.98 T00933
5046088
* * * * *

Divorce 4W

Affidavit by Petitioner in support of petition under s. 1(2)(d), M.C. Act 1973.

FAMILY PROCEEDINGS RULES

Rule 2.24(3); Form M7(d)

*Complete
and/or delete as
appropriate.

SPECIMEN

No. of Matter.............................

IN THE ————————

COUNTY COURT *

PRINCIPAL REGISTRY *

Between

and

Petitioner

Respondent

QUESTION	ANSWER
About the Divorce Petition 1. Have you read the petition filed in this case?	
2. Do you wish to alter or add to any statement in the petition? If so, state the alterations or additions.	
3. Subject to these alterations and additions (if any), is everything stated in your petition true? If any statement is not within your own knowledge, indicate this and say whether it is true to the best of your information and belief.	
4. State the date on which you and the respondent separated.	
5. State briefly the reason or main reason for the separation.	
6. State the date when and the circumstances in which you came to the conclusion that the marriage was in fact at an end.	

1

7. State as far as you know the various addresses at which you and the respondent have respectively lived since the last date given in the answer to Question 4, and the periods of residence at each address:

	Petitioner's Address		*Respondent's Address*
From		From	
To		To	

SPECIMEN

8. Since the date given in the answer to Question 4, have you ever lived with the respondent in the same household?

   If so, state the addresses and the period or periods, giving dates.

About the Children of the Family

9. Have you read the Statement of Arrangements filed in this case?

10. Do you wish to alter anything in the Statement of Arrangements or add to it?

    If so, state the alterations or additions.

11. Subject to these alterations and addition(s) (if any), is everything stated in your petition [and Statement of Arrangements for the child(ren)] true and correct to the best of your knowledge and belief?

2

I, *(full name)*

of *(full residential address)*

(occupation)

make oath and say as follows:-

1. I am the petitioner in this cause.

2. **The answers to Questions 1 to 11 are true.**

SPECIMEN

(1) Insert name of the respondent exactly as it appears on the acknowledgment of service signed by him/her.

3. I identify the signature ....(1) appearing on the copy acknowledgment of service now produced to me and marked "A" as the signature of my husband/wife, the respondent in this cause.

4. I identify the signature ....(1) appearing at Part IV of the Statement of Arrangements dated .... now produced to me and marked "B" as the signature of the respondent.

(2) Exhibit any other document on which the petitioner wishes to rely.

5. (2)

(3) If the petitioner seeks a judicial separation, amend accordingly.

(4) Delete if costs are not sought.

6. I ask the Court to grant a decree dissolving my marriage with the respondent(3) on the grounds stated in my petition [and to order the respondent to pay the costs of this suit] (4),

SWORN at

in the County of

this   day of

}   ....

Before me

A Commissioner for Oaths.

(5) Delete as the case may be.

Officer of a Court appointed by the Judge to take affidavits(5).

Address all communications for the Court to: The Court Manager, County Court* ....

(or to the Principal Registry, First Avenue House, 42-49 High Holborn, London WC1V 6NP) quoting the number in the top right-hand corner of the first page. The Court Office is open from 10 a.m. till 4 p.m. (4.30 p.m. in the Principal Registry) on Mondays to Fridays only.

3

SPECIMEN

Affidavit

By Petitioner in support of petition under section 1(2)(d) of the Matrimonial Causes Act 1973

Date of swearing:

OYEZ The Solicitors' Law Stationery Society Ltd, Oyez House, 7 Spa Road, London SE16 3QQ

1998 Edition
5.98 T00852

5046737

Divorce 89

****

6 CRIMINAL LAW

Criminal law is quite varied and complicated and this chapter tries to give you a broad idea of the sort of things you may encounter.

Once a person has been charged (see page 210) with a criminal offence he will be tried in either a magistrates' court or the Crown Court. The law provides that some offences should be tried in the magistrates' court (triable 'summarily') and other, more serious offences tried in the Crown Court (triable 'on indictment'). There are some offences which may be tried in either court and these are often referred to as 'triable either way'.

The standard of proof in criminal cases is much higher than that required in civil cases; a criminal case must be proved 'beyond reasonable doubt'. Where a jury is involved, the jurors must endeavour to reach a unanimous verdict. If this is not possible, the judge may indicate that he will accept a majority verdict, i.e., at least 10 out of 12 jurors must agree on the verdict.

The Magistrates' Court

A magistrates' court normally consists of not less than two nor more than three Justices of the Peace, who are assisted by a legally qualified clerk, or of one magistrate only who is himself legally qualified (called a 'stipendiary'). In court the clerk does not actually sit with the magistrates, but apart from them, usually in front of them. He is there only to advise on procedural matters and has no say in the outcome of the case. The clerk is also responsible for the administrative side of the court offices and has staff to assist him.

Magistrates may find persons guilty of certain offences and/or send them to the Crown Court for trial and/or sentence. When the magistrates' court deals only with the first stage of a serious offence, i.e., to decide whether there is in fact a case to answer, this is known as 'committal proceedings'. Committal proceedings can be dealt with in one of two ways. One procedure is that the magistrates (also known here as 'examining justices') may hear the relevant evidence from the prosecution. Evidence will be produced by way of documentation and exhibits — witnesses will not be called. The evidence will either be read out or summarised and the magistrates will inspect any exhibits. They will also hear any submissions the accused wishes to make. If the magistrates decide that there is a case to answer, the accused will be sent to the Crown Court for trial at a later date. He may be released on bail (see below) or remanded in custody until the trial date. If the magistrates decide that there is no case to answer, the case will be dismissed.

Alternatively, a committal known as a 'formal' or 'paper' committal is more common. This involves witness statements being served by the prosecution on the defendant who will read the statements. If the defendant agrees that these show there is a case to answer, he may consent to the case being committed for trial without the magistrates having to consider the evidence. This method may be employed only where the defendant is legally represented.

In certain fraud cases and some cases involving offences against children, another procedure may be followed, rather than committal proceedings. This other procedure is known as a notice of transfer and the involvement of the magistrates' court, subject to certain exceptions, ceases in relation to that case. The notice of transfer specifies the proposed place of trial and the relevant charges, together with any additional required information. Serious and complex fraud cases are heard at specially designated Crown Court centres.

Magistrates' courts also have jurisdiction with regard to certain family matters and some administrative matters, such as licensing.

The Crown Court

The best known Crown Court, of course, is the Central Criminal Court or the Old Bailey. There are other Crown Courts throughout England and Wales and these are presided over by a judge who may be assisted by a jury. The different kinds of judge who may sit at the Crown Court are the High Court judge, the Circuit judge, Deputy Circuit judge and the Recorder (and Assistant Recorder). A Recorder is a barrister or solicitor in practice, but sits as a judge at the Crown Court for a certain number of days each year. The Crown Courts deal with more serious offences where an accused person has been sent by a magistrates' court to the Crown Court for trial or sentence. With certain offences there is a right to trial by jury and this must be heard by the Crown Court.

Things you may be Doing

As a secretary, you could find yourself working in a lawyer's office dealing with criminal law or working for the police or the Crown Prosecution Service.

As a criminal offence is, strictly speaking, an offence against the Crown, you will often find that a case is headed something like 'R –v– Smith'. 'R' means *Regina*, the Latin word for Queen. 'R' also stands for *Rex* or King, if appropriate. You will find, however, if the name of the case is spoken in court, it will be said as, for example, 'The Queen against Smith'.

Legal Aid forms (see Chapter 7) are frequently used in criminal work. Instructions and Briefs to Counsel (see page 79) are also quite common. These documents must contain the name of the court and the number of the charge or the summons (see later), together with any other court reference number and are set out as shown in Chapter 3.

It is extremely important to proofread (see page 27) documents in criminal cases. It must always be remembered that a person's liberty may be at stake and therefore accuracy is vital. Confidentiality must always be strictly adhered to. There may be instances where certain material must not reach the jury or there may be an express no-publication order. Never give out any information to the Press or to anyone else. Do not even admit that you are acting for a certain person. Any queries from persons outside the firm must be referred to a fee earner. If you attend court you must not speak to the jurors or witnesses in the box (see also page 36).

Statements

You may find that you have to type many statements, either of witnesses or of an accused person. These are also known as 'proofs of evidence'.

Witness statements should be typed in double spacing. Only one side of the paper should be used, a space larger than normal should be left at the top of the first page for headings to be entered by the clerk of the court, and each page should have a wide margin on the left.

Example Witness Statement

Statement of witness (CJ Act 1967, s. 9; MC Act 1980, ss. 5A(3)(a) and 5B, MC Rules 1981, r. 70)

STATEMENT OF [*name of witness*]

Age of Witness: (*if over 18 enter 'over 18'*)

Occupation of witness:

This statement [, consisting of * pages each signed by me,] is true to the best of my knowledge and belief and I make it knowing that, if it is tendered in evidence, I shall be liable to prosecution if I have wilfully stated in it anything which I know to be false or do not believe to be true.

Dated the   *   day of   *   19**

(Signed)...................

[Additionally, if the person making the statement is unable to read, it would be read to him by someone else who would also sign the statement as follows:

[*Name of person making the statement*] being unable to read the above statement, I [*name and address of person reading the statement to him*], read it to him before he signed it.

Dated the   *   day of   *   19**

(Signed)...................

[*Note*: the content of the statement will be typed in double line spacing.]

How is Someone Brought to Court?

Criminal proceedings are commenced by way of charge, indictment or summons.

Note that there are many strict rules with regard to criminal procedures. Some of these include the fact that the police must caution an accused person at certain times (see page 212), he has a right to contact a solicitor whilst being questioned, and at court an accused person's previous criminal record cannot be disclosed until he is found guilty.

Most prosecutions are brought by the police through the Crown Prosecution Service. This was set up in 1985 and is completely independent of the police. Other authorities, such as HM Customs & Excise, or the Inland Revenue, may sometimes bring prosecutions too. A private individual can also bring criminal proceedings.

Offences are divided into arrestable offences and non-arrestable offences. Arrestable offences include those whose penalty is fixed by law, such as murder, which carries life imprisonment. Other quite serious offences, such as those under the Theft Acts, are also arrestable. In fact, all offences of any seriousness are arrestable. Non-arrestable offences are mainly motoring offences, although under certain circumstances an arrest may be made here. In certain circumstances, an individual other than a police officer may make what is known as a 'citizen's arrest'.

Arrest and Charge

If the police wish to question a person at a police station, they must either arrest him or ask him to attend voluntarily. The Police and Criminal Evidence Act 1984 deals with police powers of arrest.

An arrest may be made either with a warrant or without a warrant. A warrant is an authority signed by a magistrate giving a police officer the power to arrest a person. The procedure for arrest with a warrant is usually that the police officer makes a written statement regarding the alleged offence and swears on oath that it is true before a magistrate who then signs the warrant. This is called 'laying an information'. An Information can be laid by someone else who wishes to bring a case before a magistrates' court when an offence has been committed. An Information is basically information put before the court in order to start proceedings. The most common method of arrest, however, is arrest without a warrant. A police officer may arrest without warrant any person he reasonably suspects of committing, having committed or being about to commit an arrestable offence. Of course, when an Information is laid, this does not always lead to someone's arrest; a summons may be issued.

Example Information

INFORMATION
(MC Act 1980, s.1; MC Rules 1981, r 41)

........................Magistrates' Court [*Code*]

Date:

Accused:

Address:

Alleged offence: [*short particulars and statute*]

The information of:

Address:

Telephone No:

Who [*upon oath*] states that the accused committed the offence of which particulars are given above.

Taken [*and sworn*] before me

Justice of the Peace

[*Justices' Clerk*]

One of the times when a person must be cautioned as to his rights is at the time of his arrest or as soon as practicable thereafter. A caution informs the arrested person that he does not have to say anything unless he wishes to do so, but anything he does say may be given in evidence. An accused person used to have the right to maintain silence without any adverse inferences being drawn, but that right to be free from adverse inferences was removed by the Criminal Justice and Public Order Act 1994, and 'proper' inferences may now be drawn against the accused if he remains silent regarding any facts which he should have mentioned in his defence. The caution he is given by the police reflects this and it must be made clear to the accused the risks he incurs if he fails to mention any relevant facts. A person should also be cautioned when he is informed that he will be reported for an offence and told that he may receive a summons to attend court with regard to that offence.

Once a person is arrested and taken to a police station (a 'designated' police station if he is to be detained for more than six hours), he is handed over to an officer who has the rank of sergeant or above, known as the 'custody officer', who will ensure that a custody record is kept of all procedures and events at the police station involving that person. A designated police station is one which has facilities for detaining arrested persons. The custody officer decides if there is sufficient evidence to charge the arrested person. A charge is a way of formally accusing a person of an offence. The accusation on the charge sheet forms an Information.

A person may not normally be detained for longer than 24 hours unless he is charged, although in certain circumstances and if certain conditions are met, he may be detained for a longer period. Once a person is charged, he may be detained in custody until he first appears before a court. He must be brought before a court as soon as practicable and this should not be later than the first time the court sits after he has been charged with the offence. This is usually the same day that he is charged or perhaps the next day.

If a person is not detained in custody pending his court appearance, he may be released on bail.

Bail

Bail is the release of the defendant from a police station or court subject to his surrendering himself into custody at a later date. A person commits a further offence and can be arrested if he is granted bail and fails to surrender to his bail. Bail is sometimes conditional on a surety, i.e., someone must guarantee that the defendant will turn up on the appointed date. If the person on bail does not turn up on the appointed date the surety may have to pay a sum of money, known as a 'recognisance'. There are often certain other conditions to be complied with before bail will be granted.

Indictment

An indictment is a written accusation of a crime which is triable only by the Crown Court, e.g., very serious offences such as murder, rape and robbery. An indictment is the basis for the trial of an accused person who has been committed for trial at the Crown Court. It states where the trial will take place and gives details of the offence.

Summons

A person may also appear at court by way of summons. The summons will have on it the date the accused person must appear at court and will give details of the offence for which he is being summoned. It is not necessary for separate summonses to be issued against a person for each separate offence where there is more than one offence. However, if different offences are specified in one summons, each offence must be stated separately.

A summons relating to criminal matters is issued by the court and service on a person (not a corporation) may be effected by:

(a)   delivering it to the person to whom it is addressed; or

(b)   by leaving it for him with someone at his last known or usual place of abode; or

(c)   by sending it by post in a letter addressed to him at his last known or usual place of abode. However, service by post is not allowed if the summons requires the attendance of someone to give evidence or to produce a document or thing.

Service of a summons on a corporation may be effected by delivering the summons at, or sending it by post to, the registered office (see Chapter 10) of the corporation if that office is in the United Kingdom, or, if there is no registered office in the United Kingdom, any place in the United Kingdom where the corporation trades or conducts its business. In the case of another document not a summons that is being served on a corporation, where 'United Kingdom' has been mentioned, 'England and Wales' becomes relevant instead.

Mitigation

When a person pleads guilty to an offence he may submit to the court a plea in mitigation. This gives details of any circumstances which may have led to him committing the offence and any other information which may be helpful to the court when considering sentence, for example, the offender may have been under some pressure at home or at work which caused him to commit the offence and if the court knows of this, it may be more lenient when sentencing him.

Offender's Past History

Once a person has been convicted of an offence and before he is sentenced, the court is told of that person's previous criminal record, if any.

The court is also informed of the offender's personal circumstances, such as his salary, savings, whether he has any family, etc. This can assist the court if, for example, a fine is to be imposed. This information is called the offender's 'antecedents'.

Taking Offences into Consideration

An offender can also have other offences taken into consideration. He may ask for other offences he has committed, e.g., a series of burglaries, to be taken into consideration when sentence is passed. If someone does have other offences taken into consideration, this effectively means he cannot be tried for those other offences at another time.

Youth Courts

Where the magistrates' court deals with young offenders under the age of 18 (juveniles), the court is known as a youth court. There are special rules to be adhered to when it comes to dealing with children and young persons, one being that they must normally have a parent or guardian with them when they are being dealt with under the process of the law. A 'child' is a person under the age of 14 years and a 'young person' is a person who has attained the age of 14 years but is under 18. In pre-trial procedures, e.g., the investigation of an offence or remand proceedings, juveniles who have attained the age of 17 are treated in the same manner as adults. No child under the age of 10 years can be guilty of a criminal offence.

It is extremely important to remember that juveniles must not be identified to the public in any way, and you must always bear in mind that confidentiality is of the utmost importance. Any newspaper reports of proceedings in a youth court must not reveal the name, address or any other identifying detail of any juvenile (even those who are witnesses) who is involved in the proceedings unless the court specifically permits this.

Youth courts not only deal with offences committed by children and young persons, but also matters relating to their care and treatment. A youth court is always heard in private (*in camera*) and members of the public are not allowed in.

It is also possible, under certain circumstances, for a juvenile who has committed an offence to be cautioned by the police without having to go to court. This means that the juvenile offender attends at an appointed time, with his parent or guardian, at a police station before a senior police officer who will warn him as to his future behaviour. This is a practice evolved to prevent young people from having criminal records.

Driving Offences

In driving offences, apart from any other punishment the court can impose, it may order the offender's licence to be endorsed. According to what the magistrates decide, a number of penalty points varying from 1-11 are noted on the licence. If the number of penalty points reaches 12 or more within three years, the court will normally disqualify that person from driving for at least six months. Certain offences also require disqualification to be ordered automatically.

In some cases (often less serious driving offences), and under certain circumstances, the defendant may be permitted to plead guilty by post instead of having to attend court.

Dealing with Offenders

Generally, magistrates' courts may fine offenders — the maximum fine is set by legislation — and imprison them for up to six months on one charge, or not more than twelve months if more than one charge. With certain exceptions, there is no statutory limit on the amount of the fine which the Crown Court may impose. With regard to sentencing, the Crown Court's powers are limited only by the maximum sentence prescribed for the offence in question. Some of the other methods of dealing with offenders are:

(a) Absolute discharge. The person has been convicted of an offence but is released immediately without any punishment. This usually happens in trivial or technical cases.

(b) Conditional discharge. The offender may be discharged on condition that, for a specified period of up to three years, he does not commit another offence. If he does commit another offence then he will be sentenced for that and for the original offence.

(c) Deferred sentence. The court may decide not to pass sentence until a period of up to six months has passed. The offender must agree to this. The purpose of doing this is to give the offender an opportunity to show the court that he intends to improve himself and keep out of trouble.

(d) Suspended sentence. A sentence of imprisonment is given but the offender does not have to serve it, provided that during a specified period of between one and two years he does not commit another offence. If he does commit another offence punishable with imprisonment, then he will be sentenced for the new offence and will have to serve the term imposed for the original offence.

(e) Probation. The offender must agree to a probation order being imposed for a period from six months to three years. The offender has to be supervised during the time of the order by a probation officer who tries to help the offender improve himself and keep out of trouble.

(f) Community Service Order. The offender may, with his agreement, be ordered to do a certain number of hours work for the community, e.g., gardening or decorating. This is done under supervision and can be between 40 and 240 hours, spread out over certain days.

(g) Compensation Order. The court may order the offender to pay to his victim a sum by way of compensation for injury or damage caused. An order may also be made to restore goods to their rightful owner.

(h) Deprivation. Where property has been used to commit an offence, e.g., a car or tools for breaking into property, the court may make an order depriving the offender of his rights, if any, in the property.

(i) Binding over to keep the peace and/or be of good behaviour. The defendant must agree to keep the peace (not to cause further trouble) for a certain period of time. He is 'bound over' for that time in a certain sum of money. If he does not keep the peace for that time he can be brought before the court and may have to forfeit that sum of money. The court can in fact bind over anyone appearing before it, e.g., a witness, even though that person is not a defendant.

(j) Curfew order. This requires a convicted person to remain for specified periods at a specified place or places. The order must include the provision for making someone responsible for monitoring the offender's whereabouts during the curfew periods. A curfew order may include electronic monitoring of the offender's whereabouts during the curfew periods.

There are various other orders the courts can make, e.g., combination order, where a probation order and a community service order are combined; disqualification from driving and endorsement of driving licence; deportation of non-citizens for certain offences.

Criminal Cases Review Commission

This is an independent body set up under the Criminal Appeal Act 1995. It investigates suspected miscarriages of criminal justice in England, Wales and Northern Ireland. However, the Commission can normally only review a case if the original case was appealed against or the person was refused permission to appeal.

Although the Commission cannot overturn a conviction or change a sentence, it can refer cases which meet specified criteria to the Court of Appeal, the Crown Court or the relevant court in Northern Ireland. The court will treat a case referred to it by the Commission as an appeal against the original conviction and it is the court that will decide whether to alter the conviction or sentence. In some cases, legal aid (see Chapter 7) is available to apply to the Commission.

Prisoners

It may be helpful to know that prisoners whose whereabouts you do not know can be traced through the Prisoner Location Service, P.O. Box 2152, Birmingham B15 1SD; tel: 0121–626 2773; fax: 0121–626 3474.

Test yourself on Chapter 6

Test your knowledge by completing this assignment. If you find that you have difficulty with anything, read the chapter again until you are happy with your answers.

1. At which courts may a person be tried for a criminal offence?
2. What are committal proceedings?
3. Write out the layout for a witness statement.
4. What is an Information?
5. Explain the meaning of bail.
6. What is the role of the Crown Prosecution Service?
7. Name four ways offenders may be dealt with upon conviction.
8. With relation to driving offences, what are penalty points?
9. What must be remembered when dealing with juveniles in relation to publicity about them?
10. Explain what is meant by someone having other offences 'taken into consideration'.
11. Now go through the chapter and if there are any words that are unfamiliar to you or that you cannot spell, write or type them correctly several times until you feel you know them.

7 LEGAL AID

Legal aid is available to people who need legal assistance but cannot afford to pay for either all or part of it. Anyone may apply for legal aid — whether or not they qualify depends on their financial position. The Legal Aid Board has responsibility for administering legal aid under the Legal Advice and Assistance scheme, which includes Assistance by Way of Representation and legal aid for civil proceedings. The Legal Aid Board's head office is in London and there are 13 area offices throughout the country (see the address section at the back of this book). The area offices will make decisions about granting or refusing legal aid. Legal Aid for criminal matters is the responsibility of the Lord Chancellor's Department.

To obtain legal aid, a solicitor must first be consulted. A legal aid solicitor will display the Legal Aid sign in his firm's window (the sign is shown on the top left-hand corner of the Legal Aid form in this chapter). Many solicitors are franchised by the Legal Aid Board, which means that they are specially approved by the Board, having been checked to ensure that they meet certain standards and provide a quality service. One advantage of being a franchisee is that they can grant certain legal aid applications without reference to the Legal Aid Board, but there are limitations on this.

In some cases, where money or property is obtained with the assistance of legal aid, some or all of the legal costs may have to be repaid to the Legal Aid Board. This repayment is known as the statutory charge. Solicitors must inform clients about this before the application for legal aid is made.

Legal Advice and Assistance (Green Form Scheme)

This Scheme broadly covers aid to be given by way of advice and assistance only. Advice and assistance includes such things as giving general advice, writing letters, negotiating on the client's behalf, drafting documents, interviewing witnesses and assisting the client to complete an application form for full legal aid. It does not cover court proceedings nor conveyancing or drafting wills, except in particular circumstances.

Before someone can obtain aid under this scheme the solicitor must ask him certain questions about his means. The solicitor then has to work out whether that person is eligible for legal aid. He does this by using a 'Key Card' issued by the Legal Aid Board which gives him information necessary to make the calculations. An application form, known as the 'Green Form', must then be completed. There is a limit on the amount of time he can give, which is slightly higher in some matrimonial cases. A solicitor may apply to do more work for the client under this Scheme, if necessary.

Assistance by way of Representation (ABWOR)

This covers the cost of a solicitor preparing a case and representing his client in court. It is available in the majority of civil cases in magistrates' courts (known as family proceedings courts for such matters). These include some adoption proceedings, separation, maintenance (not child maintenance — the Child Support Agency deals with this) and custody. It also includes one or two other types of proceedings. For details of assistance in criminal proceedings, see below.

Preliminary advice may be given under the Green Form Scheme (Legal Advice and Assistance) but the legal aid office must approve any application before Advice by Way of Representation can be given. For approval of work to be done under ABWOR, a form must be completed by the solicitor and submitted to the legal aid office.

Civil Court Proceedings

Civil Legal Aid allows work to be carried out under the Legal Aid scheme by a solicitor or barrister. This will cover all the work leading up to a court case and for the court case itself relating to most civil matters. If a client is eligible for legal aid here, the initial advice will usually be given under the Green Form Scheme.

Full legal aid may be granted after information relating to the client's financial means are submitted to the Legal Aid Board. The granting of full legal aid may also depend on whether the applicant has some prospect of winning his case. Sometimes when legal aid is granted, a contribution may be required from the applicant, depending on his circumstances. If the legally aided person wins his case, the other party will usually have to pay the costs and if the legally aided person had to make a contribution, he will normally recover this. If the legally aided person loses, he may have to contribute to the other party's costs.

The most common types of application forms are:

(a) APP1 — Non-matrimonial proceedings.
(b) APP2 — Matrimonial proceedings.

The application form is sent to the local area office of the Legal Aid Board with another form giving details of the applicant's income. The forms vary, depending on whether or not the applicant is receiving income support or income-based Jobseeker's allowance, or whether his main home is outside the UK. The relevant forms are MEANS 1; MEANS 2 and MEANS 3. There is MEANS 4 for a child applicant aged under 16. If the applicant is earning money, a statement of earnings must be included with the application. L17 is a statement of earnings by present employers, and L18 is for self-employed people.

In cases of extreme urgency, a telephone application for legal aid may be made, followed by a completed postal application within five days. For other urgent applications but which do not have quite the same urgency, an application may be made by fax using the Legal Aid emergency fax application form, but again, a postal application must be made within five days of the grant of the faxed application.

When full legal aid has been granted a Notice of Issue of Legal Aid Certificate must be served on the other party's solicitors and also lodged with the court. Notice of Issue of Legal

Aid Certificate must be included with certain papers in various different types of court proceedings.

Legal Aid in Criminal Court Proceedings

There are various ways in which a person who is accused of committing or being questioned about a criminal offence can obtain legal assistance.

(a) Legal Advice and Assistance Scheme. A person can obtain aid under this Scheme even if he has not been charged with an offence, but this is very limited. Advice given under this Scheme must be given at the solicitor's office, and it does not cover the solicitor to go to court or a police station.

(b) A person being questioned by the police whether at a police station or otherwise, has a right to see a 'duty solicitor'. These are ordinary solicitors who are available on a 24-hour rota basis and are paid from public funds through the Legal Aid Board for any such advice they give. The person in custody may ask to speak to a solicitor and either a duty solicitor will be called or the accused can ask to see his own solicitor. Advice received in this way is free and is not means tested.

Similarly, if an accused person appears in court without having had legal advice, he can, in certain circumstances, ask for an available court duty solicitor to represent him. If the case continues, the solicitor can make an ordinary application on the Defendant's behalf for criminal legal aid (see (c) below).

(c) An application for full legal aid in criminal matters is made to the court — either to the justices' clerk or orally to the court. Financial circumstances are taken into consideration here but this will be assessed by court staff because speed is often of the essence in criminal matters. As with civil legal aid, the merits of the case are also considered and it must be shown that it is in the interests of justice that legal aid is granted: there are certain criteria to be met. Application forms for criminal legal aid are available at court offices.

Advice on appeal is covered by the original legal aid, but for the appeal itself application must be made to the magistrates' court or to the Crown Court.

If a person is denied legal aid by the court, he can appeal to the Criminal Legal Aid Committee.

Legal Aid Board

LEGAL AID ACT 1988

Regulation 50 Civil Legal Aid (General) Regulations 1989

NOTICE OF ISSUE OF [EMERGENCY] CERTIFICATE

No.   99.2487

In the

[NORTHTOWN   [County Court][~~Division~~]]

Between

                                                          Claimant
         JOHN GREEN   [~~Applicant~~][~~Plaintiff~~][~~Petitioner~~]

                          and

         JOHN JONES   [Defendant] [~~Respondent~~]

TAKE notice that [an Emergency] [a Legal Aid] Certificate No. 99/B/64/8764

dated the   *   day of   *   has been issued in

Legal Aid Area No.   3   to   John Green

                          who, since that date has been an assisted person.

The description/scope of legal aid is:

Appeal cases only - the limitation (if any) [costs limitations need not be disclosed] is:

Emergency certificates only - the emergency certificate [has][has not] been granted for a specified period. [It will expire on]:

To:

From:

Signed:

Date:

NOTE TO ASSISTED PERSON'S SOLICITOR.

1. This notice **must** be served in accordance with reg. 50 Civil Legal Aid (General) Regulations 1989.

NOTES TO OPPONENT OR OPPONENT'S SOLICITOR.

1.   An assisted person's solicitor must notify the Legal Aid Area Office which issued the assisted person's legal aid certificate if a legal aid certificate is issued to another party to the proceedings - reg. 70 Civil Legal Aid (General) Regulations 1989.

2. All monies payable to the assisted person must be paid to his/her solicitor or, if he/she is no longer represented by a solicitor, to the Legal Aid Board. This is so even if his/her certificate has been discharged or revoked. Only the solicitor or the Legal Aid Board is capable of giving a good discharge for monies so payable - reg. 87 Civil Legal Aid (General) Regulations 1989.

Application SPECIMEN APP1
for legal aid

Non-Matrimonial cases
(Use APP12 for Clinical Negligence applications)

Please complete in block capitals

Please write the page numbers of the pages you are submitting in the adjoining box.

Your details

Title: _____ Initials: _____

Surname: _____

First name: _____

Surname at birth: _____
(if different)

Date of birth: _____ / _____ / _____ *(if there is a next friend or guardian ad litem fill in page 10).*

National Insurance number: [| | | | | | | | |]

Sex: ☐ Male ☐ Female

Marital status: ☐ Single ☐ Married ☐ Cohabiting

☐ Separated ☐ Divorced ☐ Widowed

Place of birth: _____ Job: _____
(town)

Current address: _____

Town: _____

County: _____ Postcode: _____

Daytime phone: _____

Correspondence address (if different): _____

Town: _____

County: _____ Postcode: _____

Have you applied for any legal aid before?

☐ Yes ☐ No

If known, give the legal aid case reference numbers:

_____

_____

Acting solicitor's details

➤ *Your solicitor should fill in this section.*
➤ *Complete the section on "Your Involvement"*

SPECIMEN

Legal aid supplier number: ⌊⌊⌊⌊⌊⌊⌊⌋   ⌊⌊⌊⌊⌊⌊⌊⌋

Name of firm:_____

Phone:_____ Fax: _____

Name of acting solicitor: _____

➤ *The acting solicitor must have a valid practising certificate. The Board cannot pay for any work done during any period in which the acting solicitor does not have a practising certificate.*

Solicitor's reference:_____

Contact name for enquiries:_____

Which category of work does this application relate to?

☐ Personal injury   ☐ Debt   ☐ Housing   ☐ Mental Health

☐ Welfare benefits   ☐ Immigration   ☐ Employment   ☐ Consumer/ general contract   ☐ Other

Type of case

➤ *You should ask your solicitor which type your application relates to.*

Tell us the type of case this application is for:

Answer the questions on:

☐ Negligence (includes personal injury) — *page 3*

☐ Medical Negligence — *page 3*

☐ Nuisance — *page 3*

☐ Trespass — *page 3*

☐ Interference with goods — *page 3 and 4*

☐ Wrongful arrest, false imprisonment or malicious prosecution — *page 3 and 4*

☐ Partnership — *page 3*

☐ Employment — *page 3 and 4*

☐ Debt — *page 5*

☐ Company Law — *page 3*

Answer the questions on:

☐ Contract — *page 3*

☐ Housing — *page 3 and 4*

☐ Land law (includes section 14 Trusts of Land and Appointment of Trustees Act 1996) — *page 3 and 4*

☐ Trusts — *page 3*

☐ Malicious falsehood — *page 3*

☐ Immigration — *page 5*

☐ Administrative law — *page 5*

☐ Probate and inheritance — *page 5*

☐ Intellectual property — *page 3*

☐ Data protection — *page 3 and 4*

☐ Protection from harassment (without a family element) — *page 3*

➤ *Tell us the details and reasons for the case in the statement of case section on page 8. You must also fill in page 9 onwards.*

Your involvement

SPECIMEN

Are you: ☐ bringing the case   ☐ defending the case   ☐ involved in another way

If involved in another way, say how: _____

Date you first visited the solicitor about **this** case: _____ / _____ / _____

What are you asking the court to do?

If you are appealing against a decision by the court,
tell us the date of that decision: _____ / _____ / _____

Details about your case

➤ *Answer the questions in this section for **all** types of cases **except** for those
about debt, probate and inheritance, administrative law and immigration.*

**If your case is about Negligence, Nuisance, Trespass, or (except where there is a
family element) Harassment, tell us:**

What date, or over what period, did the incident(s) occur?

What injury or loss, if any, was suffered?

If your application is for trespass or harassment tell us exactly what Legal Aid you want
including whether an injunction is required.

If the injury was caused by you tripping over something give the exact height of the obstacle
that tripped you up:

_____ inches or _____ centimetres

Where did the incident(s) take place?

Was any part of the incident your fault?

☐ Yes   ☐ No   ➤ *If yes, give details in your statement on page 8.*

What date did you become aware of any injury or loss?   _____ / _____ / _____

If your case is about an agreement, contract or partnership, tell us:

The date any agreement or contract started: _____ / _____ / _____

The type of any agreement or contract: ☐ written   ☐ oral   ➤ *If written attach a copy*

If there has been a breach, the nature of the breach: _____

The date of dissolution of the partnership: _____ / _____ / _____

APP1   **Page 3**

Details about your case *SPECIMEN*

If your case is about employment, tell us:

The date the employment started: _____ / _____ / _____

How you are, or were, paid: ☐ weekly ☐ monthly ☐ fixed term contract

---

If your case is about housing, property or land, tell us:

The date of any tenancy agreement or lease: _____ / _____ / _____

The date of any notice served by the Landlord relating to either possession or disrepair: _____ / _____ / _____

If property or land is at issue, give a description of what is at issue:

The value of property or land: £ _____ : _____

Your interest in the property or land: _____

If your case is about wrongful arrest, false imprisonment or malicious prosecution, tell us:

Length of time you were detained (if relevant): _____

Were you charged? ☐ Yes ☐ No

If yes, what was the outcome of the case:

_____

_____

If your case is about interference with goods, tell us:

The grounds for this case: ☐ Acts (to have done something to cause the incident) or omissions (to have not carried out an action to prevent the incident)

☐ Damage to property

The second hand value of the goods: £ _____ : _____

➤ *You should give a list of the goods in your statement on page 8.*

If your case is about data protection, tell us:

Is your opponent registered under the Data Protection Act? ☐ Yes ☐ No

If yes, the date of registration: _____ / _____ / _____

and their registration number: _____

Details about your case *SPECIMEN*

If your case is about Debt, tell us

Date of any agreement: _____ / ___ / _____ ➤ *Attach a copy of the agreement*

Date any statutory demand was served or received: _____ / ___ / _____

The amount you are being asked to pay or is owed to you: £ _____ : _____

If your case is about Probate and Inheritance, tell us

What was the date of the grant of probate or letters of administration? _____ / ___ / _____

What was your relationship to the deceased? _____

Were you dependent on the deceased? ☐ Yes   ☐ No

If yes, in what way? _____

_____

Why are you contesting the will? _____

_____

What is the value of the estate?   £ _____ : _____

What is the amount of the claim?   £ _____ : _____

If your case is about Administrative law, tell us

What are the proceedings you propose to take? _____

If you are challenging a decision what date was the original decision made? _____ / ___ / _____

What was the decision? _____

_____

In what way are you challenging the decision? _____

_____

Have you exhausted all other appeal options? ☐ Yes   ☐ No

If your case is about Immigration, tell us

What date did you arrive in the UK? _____ / ___ / _____

What is the date of the application to remain? _____ / ___ / _____

What was your port of entry or name of reception centre where you were held?

_____

Have you exhausted all other appeal options? ☐ Yes   ☐ No

APP1　　　　Page 5

Multi-party action case *SPECIMEN*

➤ *Please ask your solicitor to fill in this section.*
➤ *Use form APP12 where a clinical healthcare provider/prescriber is included as a defendant.*

Do you have any other clients who have applied for or have been granted legal aid for this action?

☐ Yes   ☐ No

If yes, give their legal aid case reference numbers or the reference number of the lead case:

_____

Do you know of any other potential clients for this action?

☐ Yes   ☐ No

If yes, tell us the number:

_____

Are there any private clients involved in this action?

☐ Yes   ☐ No

If yes, tell us the number of private clients involved:

_____

Is it likely there will be a need for generic work?

☐ Yes   ☐ No

Are there any other firms, with clients, involved in this action?

☐ Yes   ☐ No

If yes, give the firm's name:

_____

Tick the box relevant to this action, e.g. if the action involves a drug, tick 'product':

☐ Product   ☐ Disaster   ☐ Disease or condition

Give details of what caused the incident:

What is the common name?

_____

What is the name of the group this action forms a part of (if applicable)?

_____

APP1   Page 6

Costs and merits
➤ *Your solicitor must fill in this section*

SPECIMEN

Which of the following best describes the prospects of achieving the outcome your client wants?

☐ A Very good (80%+) ☐ B Good (60-80%) ☐ C Average (50-60%)

☐ D Below average ☐ E Impossible to say. Seeking a limited certificate.

If you have ticked boxes C, D, or E please say what factors lead you to make this assessment and why legal aid should be granted:

Estimate your likely final costs, assuming the case goes to trial, including disbursements.

☐ Less than £1,500 ☐ £1,500 - £2,500 ☐ £2,500 - £5,000

☐ £5,000 - £7,500 ☐ £7,500 - £10,000 ☐ Over £10,000

If over £10,000 please give an approximate amount £ _____ : ____

Give an estimate of the likely value of any claim £ _____ : ____

If you have selected box E, or are seeking a limited certificate for other reasons, tell us what work needs to be done under a limited certificate and at what cost.

at an estimated cost of: £ _____ : ____

Give details of any properties which are in dispute, e.g. shares, insurance policies, a boat, a house, business, money.

Address
of property in dispute: _____
(if relevant)

Town: _____

County: _____ Postcode: _____

APP1   Page 7

Statement of case

➤ *Please describe the events in the order they occurred.*
If you are bankrupt by an order of the court, give details and information
on how this may affect your case

SPECIMEN

➤ *If you need more space, please attach a separate sheet to this form.*

Court details

SPECIMEN

Has any court action started or is any about to start? ☐ Yes ☐ No

Name of court: _____

Date court action started: _____ / ____ / _____   Date of next hearing: _____ / ____ / _____

Court case number: _____

Your opponent's details

➤ *Please provide as much of the following information as you can.*

Title: _____   Initials: _____   Surname or
organisation name: _____

First name: _____   Date of birth: _____ / ____ / _____

Address: _____

Town: _____

County: _____   Postcode: _____

Job: _____   Your relationship to opponent: _____

Is your opponent insured against your claim?

☐ Yes   ☐ No   ☐ Don't Know

Tell us any information you have about your opponent's financial resources and why you think that they will be able to pay any monies which the court orders to be paid to you.

Has your opponent applied for legal aid for this case?

☐ Yes   ☐ No

If known, tell us the legal aid case reference number:

_____

Other people

➤ *Do not give details of the opponent in this section.*

SPECIMEN

Is anyone else involved directly or indirectly in this case? ☐ Yes ☐ No

Tell us how they are involved:

☐ Former spouse or cohabitee ☐ Next friend or guardian ad litem

☐ Insurers ☐ Trade union ☐ Other (give details)

_____

Fill in the relevant details about the other person:

Title: _____ Initials: _____ Surname or organisation name: _____

Address: _____

Town: _____

County: _____ Postcode: _____

Date of birth: ___ / ___ / ___ Job: _____

If the other person or organisation stands to gain anything if your action is successful, tell us why and how they stand to gain:

Is the other person or organisation willing to help out with any or all of the legal costs?

☐ Yes ☐ No ☐ Don't know

If yes how are they willing to help?

_____

If you have a policy or membership which provides for legal help, please tell us why you do not want to take it up or why it is not available to deal with this case:

APP1 Page 10

Declaration to be signed by the applicant

➤ *This page must be completed.*

I promise to tell the Legal Aid Board straight away if:

SPECIMEN

➤ my financial position changes;
➤ I stop living with my spouse or partner;
➤ I get married or start living with somebody as husband and wife;
➤ I change my address.

I also promise to provide information promptly if the Legal Aid Board asks me for it.

I understand that:

➤ if I do not keep these promises, my legal aid may be stopped or cancelled;
➤ if my legal aid is cancelled, I will have to pay for all my case as if I never had legal aid and, if the court orders me to pay my opponent's solicitor's charges, I will be liable for them as if I never had legal aid;
➤ the Legal Aid Board may use any information about my case to carry out any of its functions under the Legal Aid Act 1988, but my name and other personal details which could identify me will be kept confidential;
➤ I may have to pay for some or all of my case, out of any money or property I recover or protect;
➤ unless my legal aid contribution is NIL, I will be sent an offer of legal aid which sets out the contribution I will have to pay if I accept the offer;
➤ if my financial position changes my legal aid contribution could be changed;
➤ if I no longer qualify financially, my legal aid will be stopped;
➤ if I get emergency legal aid, this will only cover urgent action and will be cancelled if I do not qualify financially or if I do not accept an offer of full legal aid.

My solicitors have given me to keep:

➤ The Legal Aid Board's leaflet explaining what happens next;
➤ The Legal Aid Board's leaflet explaining the statutory charge.

My solicitors have explained the legal aid statutory charge to me.

I authorise the Legal Aid Board to give information about my case to:

_____

As far as I know, all the information I have given is true and I have not withheld any relevant information. I understand that if I knowingly give false information or withhold relevant information my legal aid may be stopped or cancelled and criminal proceedings may be taken against me.

Signed: _____ Date: ____/____/____

Certification

I certify that:

➤ We have explained to the applicant their obligations and the meaning of their declaration.
➤ We have given to the applicant to keep the Legal Aid Board's leaflets referred to in their declaration and have explained the statutory charge to them.
➤ We have provided as accurately as possible the information requested on page 7 of this form.

Signed: _____ Date: ____/____/____
(A Solicitor or a Fellow of the Institute of Legal Executives)

Name: _____

Emergency details

➤ *Your solicitor should fill in this section.*

SPECIMEN

Has a full application already been submitted? ☐ Yes ☐ No

➤ *If yes, you should only complete the sections of this form where the information will be different from the full application.*

Has the area office already granted emergency legal aid? ☐ Yes ☐ No

Give the legal aid case reference number: _____

Is the applicant in receipt of Income Support or
Income Based Job Seeker's Allowance: ☐ Yes ☐ No

Why is this case considered to be urgent?

Has the court action already begun? ☐ Yes ☐ No

Tell us the name of the Court: _____

Tell us what emergency legal aid is needed for:

If granted under devolved powers:

Tell us the date you granted emergency legal aid to your client: ___ / ___ / ___

Give us a brief description of the proceedings and tell us the wording code(s) you used for them:

Give us a brief description of the limitation(s)/condition(s) and tell us the wording code(s) you used for them: ➤ *Please note the standard cost limitation will apply unless a higher figure is provided and can be justified.*

Enclosures

➤ *Your solicitor should fill in this section.*

➤ *Any enclosures should NOT be the originals, except the means assessment and L17 forms.*

The enclosures sent in support of this application are:

☐ pleadings ☐ affidavit(s) ☐ court order(s) ☐ expert report(s)

☐ contract(s)/ agreement(s) ☐ MEANS 1 ☐ MEANS 2 ☐ MEANS 3

☐ MEANS 4 ☐ L17 ☐ L18

☐ other *(give details)*: _____

(c) Legal Aid Board 1998
V.6 January 1999

LEGAL AID

Test yourself on Chapter 7

Test your knowledge by completing this assignment. If you find that you have difficulty with anything, read the chapter again until you are happy with your answers.

1. What is legal aid, and who is responsible for administering legal aid?
2. What is the Green Form Scheme?
3. In civil court proceedings, what procedure would be followed to apply for full legal aid? How might an application be made in cases of extreme urgency?
4. In what circumstances might someone make use of the services of a duty solicitor?
5. In criminal matters, to whom would an application be made for full legal aid?
6. Read through the Legal Aid Form APP1 and consider how it might be completed.
7. Now go through the chapter and if there are any words that are unfamiliar to you or that you cannot spell, write or type them correctly several times until you feel you know them.

8 LICENSING

Licences can include such matters as applying for a liquor licence (i.e., a licence to sell alcoholic drinks) which could be for a restaurant, a club, an off-licence or a public house. This could be applying for a new licence, renewing or transferring an existing licence and many other matters. You may also find yourself typing applications for a Betting Office Licence, Bookmaker's Permit or for a club that wishes to have gaming on its premises. The procedures outlined in this chapter are brief and if you wish to know more about licensing, it is best to consult a specialist book.

Liquor Licences

Applications for liquor licences are made to the licensing justices who sit at magistrates' courts during licensing sessions. Licensing justices are ordinary justices of the peace who deal with licensing matters. Licensing sessions consist of a general annual licensing meeting held in the first fortnight of February, and a number of Transfer Sessions throughout the year. For the purposes of applying for a new licence or transfer, there is little difference in the different types of licensing sessions. A licensing application must be made at one of the appointed licensing sessions. In some instances, the clerk to the licensing justices has power to grant certain transfers, e.g., where an application is being made by someone who already holds a justices' licence.

When dates have been settled on to hold licensing sessions, the clerk to the licensing justices must advertise in a local newspaper, and send to certain persons such as those already holding a licence and to the Chief Officer of Police, a notice stating when and where the licensing sessions will be held. The clerk to the licensing justices keeps details of all the licences granted in his area.

Liquor licences may authorise the sale of all types of intoxicating liquor or put a limit on the type of liquor that is sold, e.g., wine only. Various conditions have to be satisfied before a licence is granted.

The following are some of the different types of liquor licence:

   (a)   An on-licence which normally allows intoxicating liquor to be consumed both on and off the premises.
   (b)   An off-licence allowing consumption off the premises only.
   (c)   Restaurant licence which allows for the sale of liquor with meals.
   (d)   Residential licences are granted to places such as boarding houses.
   (e)   Club licence.

Generally, a licence is granted for three years and has to be renewed at the end of the next three-year licensing period unless it was granted within the last three months of the three-year licensing period, in which case, it will last to the end of the next three-year period. Anyone may oppose an application for a licence.

Occasional licences authorise the holder of an on-licence to sell intoxicating liquor at a place other than his ordinary licensed premises. Provisional licences may also be applied for. These relate to buildings which have not yet been completed or constructed and, in these cases, the owner of the property will want to be fairly sure, before going to the expense of constructing or altering a building, that he is likely to be granted a licence to sell intoxicating liquor. He can, therefore, apply for a provisional licence. Applications for a provisional licence must be accompanied by plans of the building.

An appeal from the decision of licensing justices may be made to the Crown Court.

How to Apply for a Liquor Licence

The procedure for applying for a new justices' licence is as follows. The applicant prepares Notice of Application for Grant of Licence. This must be signed by the applicant or his authorised agent. It must contain:

(a) The applicant's name and address.
(b) His trade during the six months preceding the notice.
(c) The situation of the premises.
(d) The type of licence applied for.
(e) A plan of the premises.
(f) A radius map, usually of either a half a mile or a quarter of a mile, showing either all licensed premises of a certain type (e.g., all off-licences) or all licensed premises within the specified radius of the particular premises. However, the requirements for a radius map may differ from area to area.

Notice of this application must be given to the clerk to the licensing justices, the Chief Officer of Police, the local authority, the local fire authority and, if the premises are situated where there is a community council, to the proper officer of that council. The Notice of Application must be displayed near the premises in a public place for a period of seven days not more than 28 days before the licensing sessions. The Notice is also advertised in a local newspaper. This Notice of Application must be submitted to the clerk to the licensing justices not less than 21 days before the licensing sessions.

An application to renew a liquor licence is more simple and the application to renew may or may not be made on a form, depending upon local procedures.

Structural alterations at licensed premises

Where alterations are proposed to be made to on-licensed premies, these alterations will, in certain circumstances, require the consent of the licensing justices before the alterations can be carried out. An example of such circumstances would be where the alterations will give increased drinking facilities in a public part of the premises.

Application for Club Registration

This is made to the magistrates' court in the area where the club is based. The procedure is as follows.

The application for registration of a club must be lodged with the clerk to the justices, with at least four copies. Copies of the application are sent by the clerk to the justices to the Chief Officer of Police, the fire authority and the local authority.

The application must be either displayed on or near the premises in a public place for seven days beginning with the date of application, or by advertising on at least one of those days in a local newspaper.

Gaming Clubs

Applications regarding betting and gaming licences are the responsibility of the betting licensing committee for a particular area. This committee is made up of justices of the peace for each area.

Notices are served on the clerk to the betting licensing committee (together with a certificate of consent from the Gaming Board). The notice must also be sent to:

  (a) The Gaming Board for Great Britain at Berkshire House, 168–173 High Holborn, London WC1V 7AA (tel: 0171–306 6200);

  (b) the appropriate Chief Officer of Police;

  (c) the appropriate fire authority;

  (d) the local authority;

  (e) the Customs & Excise office for the relevant area. The address for the relevant Customs & Excise office may be obtained from Customs & Excise Department, New King's Beam House, 22 Upper Ground, London SE1 9PJ (tel: 0171–620 1313).

Notice of making the application must be published in a local newspaper and be displayed outside the entrance to the premises. A copy of the newspaper advertisement must be sent to the clerk to the justices.

Music and Dancing

Application to use premises for public dancing or other public entertainment should be made to the relevant London borough council in London or the relevant district council outside London. However, in the case of licensed premises, there is no need to make any such application provided the entertainment is by television or radio, or by way of music and singing only which is provided solely by the reproduction of recorded sound, or by not more than two performers.

If it is desired to play copyright music in public, the performance of that music must be licensed by the owner of the copyright. Applications for such licences should normally be made to The Performing Right Society, 29-33 Berners Street, London W1P 4AA (tel: 0171-580 5544).

If it is desired to play a copyright record or tape in public, e.g., in a bar or restaurant, application for such a licence should normally be made to Phonographic Performance Ltd, 1–3 Upper James Street, London W1R 3HG (tel: 0171-437 0311).

LICENSING

Test your knowledge by completing this assignment. If you find that you have difficulty with anything, read the chapter again until you are happy with your answers.

1. Who deals with applications for liquor licences?
2. What are licensing sessions?
3. Name four different types of liquor licences.
4. What is the procedure for applying for a liquor licence?
5. Who deals with applications for betting and gaming licences?
6. Now go through the chapter and if there are any words that are unfamiliar to you or that you cannot spell, write or type them correctly several times until you feel you know them.

9 APPEALS, JUDICIAL REVIEW, CASE STATED

You will understand this chapter better if you read it in conjunction with other relevant chapters in this book so that you are familiar with the terms used. It is not appropriate, in a book of this nature, to deal too deeply with appeals, and this chapter is meant to give you only a brief insight into the subject. The appeals mentioned in this chapter are a broad outline only and procedures can vary according to the type of matter being dealt with. Further information on appeals may be obtained from the relevant rules governing each type of proceeding.

If someone is not happy with the decision of a court they may, in certain circumstances, appeal against it to a higher court. The court from which the appeal is made is known as the court of first instance. The party who appeals is the appellant and the other party is the respondent. Where an appeal is made and the decision on the appeal has been reached, the appeal is said to be either dismissed or allowed. If it is allowed, then the decision of the lower court is reversed or varied. In criminal cases when an appeal against a conviction is successful, the conviction is quashed. The Court of Appeal may also order a new trial to take place.

Currently, there are proposals for some changes to be made to civil appeal procedures.

Civil Matters

Small Claims

An appeal may be brought against an order made in a county court where there was either a serious irregularity affecting the proceedings or where the court made a mistake of law. If the decision appealed against was made by a District judge, the appeal will be made to a Circuit judge.

If an appeal is to be made, the party wishing to appeal must file, within the specified time limit, a notice of appeal with the court which made the order being appealed against. The court will serve a copy of the notice on all parties to the action.

Fast Track and Multi-track cases

Appeal may be made to a circuit judge against decisions of a District judge. Notice of appeal must be issued within a specified time of the decision being appealed against and must be served on all parties to the proceedings.

An appeal against a circuit judge is made to the Court of Appeal. Permission to appeal to the Court of Appeal is required in practically every case.

Appeals to the Court of Appeal

As stated in the previous paragraph, permission to appeal to the Court of Appeal is nearly always necessary. Permission will normally be obtained from the circuit judge but if it is refused, permission to appeal may be sought from the Court of Appeal itself. Notice of appeal must be served within four weeks of the date on which the order or judgment which is being appealed against was sealed. The Civil Procedure Rules contain a specimen form for permission to appeal.

Skeleton arguments

In applications for permission to appeal and in appeals to the Civil Division of the Court of Appeal, except those heard with exceptional urgency, skeleton arguments must normally be lodged with the court and with the other party.

A skeleton argument is a document outlining and summarising the points to be relied upon at certain hearings. It is submitted to the court prior to the hearing to assist the judge. When making an application for permission to appeal, two copies of the skeleton argument must accompany the bundle of relevant documents lodged with the Civil Appeals Office by the applicant's solicitors. Although the skeleton arguments are lodged with the bundle of documents, they do not form part of the bundle and should, therefore, not be bound in with the bundle. The skeleton arguments must be lodged with the court and served on other parties within a specified time limit. A chronology of events outlining significant dates may also be served with the skeleton argument.

Where permission to appeal has been granted by the Court of Appeal, the same skeleton arguments may be used that were used in the application for permission to appeal, with any necessary minor amendments being made, or fresh skeleton arguments may be prepared if preferred. The Appellant's solicitors must submit with the appeal bundle of relevant documents four copies of their skeleton argument — again — this is submitted with, but not bound in, the appeal bundle. At the same time, a copy of the skeleton argument and bundle of relevant documents must also be served on the Respondent's solicitors. The Respondent's solicitors must lodge with the Civil Appeals Office four copies of their skeleton argument within the specified time limit. Once skeleton arguments have been lodged, they may not be added to or revised without the permission of the court. Do not forget to keep copies on your file.

House of Lords

Appeals to the House of Lords are rare. It is unlikely in any event that you will type the final documents for the appeal as they have to be set out in a certain way and these are often sent to specialists to be typed or printed. However, an appeal may be made from the Court of Appeal to the House of Lords. Permission to appeal must be obtained from either the Court of Appeal or the House of Lords. If permission from the House of Lords is sought, the petition and a copy of the order appealed against must be lodged with the House of Lords within one month. In some circumstances, an appeal may be made direct from the High Court to the House of Lords.

Appeals from Licensing Justices

Appeals against decisions of licensing justices may be made to the Crown Court. Notice of appeal must be given to the clerk to the licensing justices within the specified time. If appropriate, notice must also be given to the person who opposed the grant of the licence. If the appeal is against the grant of a licence, notice of appeal must be given to the person who applied for the licence.

Family Proceedings from Magistrates' Courts

In the majority of cases, appeal is made to a High Court judge of the Family Division.

Criminal Matters

Appeal to the Crown Court

An appeal may be made to the Crown Court against the decision of a magistrates' court either against sentence if the appellant pleaded guilty at the magistrates' court, or against sentence or conviction if he pleaded not guilty. The notice of appeal must be given within 21 days of the decision appealed against and must be served on the clerk to the magistrates and on the prosecution. An appeal may also be made to the Crown Court against a magistrates' court's binding over or contempt of court order.

Court of Appeal

An appeal may be made in certain cases to the Court of Appeal (Criminal Division) by a person who has been convicted and/or sentenced by the Crown Court. Permissions to appeal must sometimes be obtained from the Court of Appeal before the appeal can proceed. Notice of appeal, or application for permission to appeal, must be given within the specified time from the date of conviction or sentence and must be served on the Registrar of Criminal Appeals. See also page 215 regarding the Criminal Cases Review Commission.

House of Lords

Before an appeal can be made to the House of Lords, permission is required. Either the convicted person or the prosecutor may apply and is only granted permission if the court from which the appeal is made certifies that a point of law of general public importance is involved and that the court thinks the House of Lords should consider the point. Application to the lower court for permission to appeal to the House of Lords must be made within 14 days of the decision being appealed against. If permission is refused, application to appeal may be made by petition to the House of Lords within 14 days of the refusal.

Judicial Review/Case Stated

In certain circumstances, in both civil and criminal matters, decisions of courts, tribunals and certain other bodies may be questioned by application to the Divisional Court of the High Court for judicial review or by way of case stated. In such applications the parties are called the applicant and the respondent.

Very briefly, an application for judicial review is made as follows:

(a) An application without notice (see page 117) for permission to apply for judicial review must be made within the relevant time. This is done by lodging at the Crown Office a statement and an affidavit in support.

(b) The case is listed for hearing and if permission is given, the applicant must serve a notice of motion and a supporting affidavit on all parties, including any court registrar or clerk, or judge, where appropriate.

Other parties may wish to serve affidavits in reply, and this is usually in civil matters. The case is then heard and an order is either granted or refused.

On judicial review, some of the orders the court may make are as follows:

(a) *Certiorari* — to quash a decision where an error of law has been made or where an order, conviction, etc., has been made without jurisdiction, or where the rules of natural justice have not been observed.

(b) Prohibition — to prevent an unlawful decision from taking effect.

(c) *Mandamus* — to compel a tribunal, court or public body to perform a certain duty.

(d) Injunction — normally, on judicial review, an injunction is used to provide interim relief.

(e) Declaration — this is normally used to challenge the reasoning behind a certain decision or to state the court's view of a decision without actually quashing that decision.

(f) Damages may be awarded.

An appeal by way of case stated may be made from certain decisions of magistrates' courts or the Crown Court to the Divisional Court of the High Court. If a party to proceedings wishes to appeal by way of case stated, they may apply to the court which made the decision to state a case for the opinion of the High Court. A magistrates' court will prepare a statement of the matters which are relevant to the point being appealed. Where the Crown Court is asked to state a case, the appellant drafts a case which is put before the judge who presided over the relevant proceedings. The respondent may also draft a case and submit it to the Crown Court judge for consideration. The judge will read the draft(s) and then state and sign a case. If the application to state a case is refused, the refusing court will provide the applicant with a certificate stating that the application has been refused. The applicant may then apply to the Divisional Court for an order of *mandamus* compelling the court to state a case.

Of course, the High Court also has jurisdiction to hear a case stated by others, e.g., tribunals, government departments, a Minister of the Crown, etc.

Appeals from Tribunals and Arbitrations

Depending on the type of tribunal, etc., an appeal may be made in certain circumstances either to the courts or to another specific body, e.g., Employment Appeal Tribunal. The right of appeal from a tribunal decision is specified in the statute or regulation which set up that particular tribunal. The appellant has a specified time limit after the date of the order, decision or award against which he is appealing to file a request for the entry of the appeal, together with the appropriate number of copies, plus a copy of the order, decision or award he is appealing against.

Appeal from an employment tribunal may be made as follows:

(a) In certain specified circumstances, application for a review of the case may be made by either party at the hearing or within 14 days. If the application is granted, there is a re-hearing.

(b) On a point of law, appeal may be made to the Employment Appeal Tribunal. This is presided over by a High Court judge with two lay members assisting him.

Appeal on a point of law from the Employment Appeal Tribunal may be made, with permission, to the Court of Appeal and then on to the House of Lords.

There is only a limited right of appeal with regard to arbitration, and this is on a question of law, to the High Court. Further appeal is allowed to the Court of Appeal only if there are special grounds and the court grants permission. This is usually given only if the matter is of general public importance.

Test yourself on Chapter 9

Test your knowledge by completing this assignment. If you find that you have difficulty with anything, read the chapter again until you are happy with your answers.

1. Explain what is meant by allowing or dismissing an appeal.
2. What is the 'court of first instance'?
3. To whom should appeals be made against decisions of the following:

    (a) a District judge in the county court?
    (b) licensing justices?
    (c) magistrates' courts?

4. What is meant by judicial review and case stated?
5. When may an appeal be made against the decision of an employment tribunal?
6. Now go through the chapter and if there are any words that are unfamiliar to you or that you cannot spell, write or type them correctly several times until you feel you know them.

10   COMPANIES AND BUSINESSES

There are several ways to carry on a business or trade:

(a)   A sole trader, or sole proprietor, being a person carrying on business on his own. Although being a sole trader is possibly the simplest way for a person to set up in business on his own account, the law does require him to comply with certain requirements, e.g., keeping employment documents, and certain other obligations. The sole trader will be entirely liable for any debts he may incur in his business and he can be sued personally for his business debts.

(b)   A partnership, where two or more persons carry on business together, with a view to profit. The Partnership Act 1890 defines exactly what makes a partnership. There does not have to be a written formal agreement between partners but a great deal of partnerships do in fact have formal partnership agreements. Partners are liable personally for debts incurred by the partnership, except in certain circumstances where the partnership is registered as a limited partnership. We need not go into detail about this here. A partnership deed will be engrossed onto good quality paper. It should normally be typed on both sides of the paper and have a backsheet and/or frontsheet (see pages 319 and 20).

(c)   A company. Basically, companies fall into one of four categories: a public limited company (plc); a private company limited by shares; a private company limited by guarantee and a private unlimited company. The first two are the most common. If a company is limited, it means that the liability of the members of the company is limited to the amount, if any, unpaid on the shares they hold or the amount they have already undertaken to contribute if the company is wound up. Companies are regulated by several Companies Acts. A company is a 'legal person'. This means that all transactions are carried out in the name of the company and not in that of its shareholders. The company itself owns property and is sued for any debt incurred. Once a company is 'born' or comes into existence it is 'incorporated'.

Information about Companies

Companies are registered (details of the company are lodged) with the Registrar of Companies at Companies House and are given a registered number. As well as lodging registration documents with Companies House, there are legal requirements to lodge various other documents. The original documents are kept by Companies House who photograph them to produce a microfilm. Because Companies House produces microfilm records, the documents submitted to them must be easy to photograph for their purposes. They can, in fact, reject documents if they cannot copy them clearly. Companies House requires documents to show in a prominent position the registered number of the company.

COMPANIES AND BUSINESSES

This should be on the first page of any document and preferably at the top right corner. Documents should be on plain white, A4 size paper and the text should be in black and legible. Carbon copies should not be used and it should be borne in mind that even photocopies can be dark and, therefore, unsuitable because dark pages will not photograph well. Paper with a matt finish, rather than glossy, should be used. In addition, pages must have a margin all round not less than 10mm wide, and if the document is bound, the bound edge should have a margin not less than 20mm.

Companies House will accept documents in other formats and for guidance on print requirements and comfiche formats, contact 01222 380306; for guidance on magnetic tape systems and formats, contact 01222 380242.

Information on a company can be obtained, on payment of a fee, by post, fax, courier or by a personal search at one of Companies House Information Centres. These are at the main offices in Cardiff, London and Edinburgh, or at regional centres in Birmingham, Manchester, Leeds and Glasgow. Documents can be delivered to the Registrar at any of these offices, but companies with registered offices in Scotland should deliver documents to Scottish offices. It is possible, however, to order records of Scottish companies from the English and Welsh offices and records of English and Welsh companies from the Scottish offices. Documents relating to Northern Ireland companies may be ordered from any of the Companies House offices. When you receive any documents you have ordered depends on which office you have ordered them from and the time you ordered them, but it is useful to know that urgent and same-day requests can be made through certain offices, depending on where the company is registered.

Company documents may be requested to be in hard copy or microfiche. The microfiche can be viewed on special viewers at Companies House or some firms have their own viewing equipment.

It is also possible to obtain information about a company by subscribing to Companies House on-line service called Companies House Direct. Information can be viewed directly on your firm's PC, images of accounts can be downloaded, and copies of documents on fiche or hard copy can be ordered via the computer.

Companies House Monitor is a service for anyone wishing to monitor a company and wishes to receive particular documentation about that company as soon as it is registered at Companies House. The documents specified will be sent to you by fax. If you are monitoring more than 3,000 companies, the information may be delivered on a special tape. It is necessary to have an account with Companies House to take advantage of this service.

Another service offered is the Companies House CD-ROM Directory which contains basic information on all live registered and recently dissolved companies. It is updated monthly and the customer has the choice of buying just one disk or taking out an annual subscription for 12 disks.

Many firms requiring information on companies employ agencies who specialise in company searches.

Companies House has a Call Centre at 01222 380801 which can deal with most queries, and their web site is very informative.

Starting a Company

Some specialist firms will sell 'off the shelf' ready-made companies with appropriate documents already drawn up. However, your firm may have to draw up the documents themselves and some of these are briefly explained below.

Memorandum of Association

A limited company must have a Memorandum of Association. You may come across the term 'Table B' when reference is made to a Memorandum of Association. This is a form of Memorandum set out in Table B of Companies (Tables A to F) Regulations 1985 (as amended). Any Memorandum of Association must comply as nearly as possible with the form set out in Table B.

A Memorandum of Association must contain the following:

(a)   The name of the company.

(b)   Whether the registered office of the company is in England and Wales, or in Scotland. The registered office is the address where it is known that communications will be received by the company, e.g., where documents can be served on the company. This address is lodged with the Companies Registrar at Companies House on Companies Form 10. A change of address of registered office must be notified to Companies House within 14 days and this is done on Companies Form 287. The registered office does not have to be the address from which the company carries on business. Quite a few solicitors' offices are registered offices for companies. Court proceedings relating to companies should be served at their registered office unless, of course, a solicitor has been instructed to accept service on behalf of that company. (See Chapter 3 for further information regarding 'service'.)

(c)   An Objects Clause. This is a statement of the company's objects and powers. It will usually include what a company may wish to do in the future as well as at the present, e.g., it may state that the object of the company is to carry on business as a general commercial company. The Objects Clause can be changed by a special resolution being passed by the members of the company.

(d)   A clause stating that the company has limited liability.

(e)   A statement showing the amount of nominal capital held by the company and declaring how it is divided into shares.

(f)   The subscribers sign the Memorandum stating they wish to form a company and the number of shares they will have. This is known as the Association Clause.

Articles of Association

This states the rules governing the internal management of the company. When reference is being made to the Articles of Association you may come across the term 'Table A'. This is a standard form of Articles of Association set out in Table A of Companies (Tables A to F) Regulations 1985. By statute, if no other articles apply, then Table A is adopted.

Other Documents

(a)   Declaration of Compliance on Application for Registration (Companies Form 12). This is a declaration made by either a solicitor engaged in the formation of the company or a secretary or director named on Form 10 (see below) stating that the Companies Acts have been complied with. It must be witnessed by someone who has the power to administer oaths (see page 121).

247

(b)   First Directors and Secretary and Intended Situation of Registered Office (Companies Form 10). This gives details of the first directors and secretary and also states where it is intended that the registered office should be situated. It must be signed by those who signed the Memorandum of Association.

These forms are all sent to the appropriate Companies House together with the registration fee.

One additional document must be filed if the company being formed is going to be a public limited company. This is Companies Form 117: application by a public company for certificate to commence business.

The Registrar of Companies issues a Certificate of Incorporation, all being well, and issues a plc with a Certificate of Compliance (also called a Trading Certificate) as well as the Certificate of Incorporation.

Many other forms may need to be completed and sent to the Registrar of Companies. Most of them have a large number on them at the top as can be seen from the example Form 10, and consist mainly of completing appropriate boxes.

Once a company has been incorporated it may have a 'company seal'. A company seal is the 'mark' of the company, in other words, a type of signature. It is a circular impression or stamp showing the name of the company and is often used when a company signs a document which binds the company. It is usually stamped over a red wafer seal, i.e., a thin red circular 'star' about an inch or so in diameter. (This replaces the old usage of red wax for seals.) The seal on a document is usually accompanied by a signature of one or more officers of the company, e.g., a director and/or secretary of the company. The company 'secretary' here does not mean a secretary such as yourself: it means an officer of the company with certain duties and powers within that company.

There is generally no longer a legal requirement for a company to have a seal although, for various reasons, many companies will still have one and use it. (See also page 271 on deeds.) It should be borne in mind that certain corporations which have not been incorporated under the Companies Acts still generally have to execute deeds under seal.

SPECIMEN

10

First Directors and Secretary and Intended Situation of Registered Office

Please complete in typescript, or in bold black capitals.

Notes on completion appear on final page.

F0100C10

Company Name in full	BLOGGS AND BLACK LIMITED

Proposed Registered Office
(PO Box numbers only, are not acceptable)

	2 MILKY WAY
Post town	BARNET
County/Region	HERTS

Postcode | EN4 6PP

If the memorandum is delivered by an agent for the subscriber(s) of the memorandum mark the box opposite and give the agent's name and address.

X

Agent's Name	ANGEL GABRIEL & CO
Address	2 MILKY WAY
Post town	BARNET
County/Region	HERTS

Postcode | EN4 6PP

Number of continuation sheets attached.

Please give the name, address, telephone number, and if available, a DX number and Exchange of the person Companies House should contact if there is any query.

MR A STAR (ref: AS/468)
ANGEL GABRIEL & CO, 2 MILKY WAY
BARNET, HERTS. Tel 01638-1234
DX number 123   DX exchange   BARNET

When you have completed and signed the form please send it to the Registrar of Companies at:

Companies House, Crown Way, Cardiff, CF4 3UZ
for companies registered in England and Wales **DX 33050 Cardiff**
or
Companies House, 37 Castle Terrace, Edinburgh, EH1 2EB
for companies registered in Scotland   **DX 235 Edinburgh**

[P.T.O.

COMPANIES AND BUSINESSES

Company Secretary (see notes 1-5)

SPECIMEN

Company Name | BLOGGS AND BLACK LIMITED

*Voluntary details. **NAME***

| *Style/Title | | *Honours etc. | |

Forename(s) | JOHN

Surname | BLACK

Previous forename(s) |

Previous surname(s) |

Address | 34 NORTH STREET

Usual residential address
For a corporation, give the registered or principal office address.

Post town | SOUTHTOWN

County/Region | HERTFORDSHIRE | **Postcode** | EN5 2PP

Country | ENGLAND

I consent to act as secretary of the company named on page 1

Consent signature | | **Date** |

Directors (see notes 1-5)
Please list directors in alphabetical order.

NAME

| *Style/Title | | *Honours etc. | |

Forename(s) | JOHN

Surname | BLACK

Previous forename(s) |

Previous surname(s) |

Address | 34 NORTH STREET

Usual residential address
For a corporation, give the registered or principal office address.

Post town | SOUTHTOWN

County/Region | HERTFORDSHIRE | **Postcode** | EN5 2PP

Country | ENGLAND

	Day	Month	Year		
Date of birth	7	7	49	**Nationality**	BRITISH

Business occupation | SALESMAN

Other directorships | NONE

I consent to act as director of the company named on page 1

Consent signature | | **Date** |

Directors (continued) (see notes 1-5)

SPECIMEN

NAME

*Voluntary details.

*Style/Title	
*Honours etc.	
Forename(s)	PETER
Surname	BLOGGS
Previous forename(s)	
Previous surname(s)	

Address

Usual residential address
For a corporation, give the registered or principal office address.

Address	81 GREEN STREET
Post town	SOUTHTOWN
County/Region	HERTFORDSHIRE
Postcode	EN3 6PP
Country	

	Day	Month	Year		
Date of birth	29	12	47	Nationality	BRITISH

Business occupation	SALESMAN
Other directorships	NONE

I consent to act as director of the company named on page 1

Consent signature		Date	

This section must be signed by

Either an agent on behalf of all subscribers	Signed		Date	
Or the subscribers (i.e. those who signed as members on the memorandum of association).	Signed		Date	
	Signed		Date	
	Signed		Date	
	Signed		Date	
	Signed		Date	
	Signed		Date	

251

Shares

Normally shares in a company are equal. There are different classes of shares:

(a) Ordinary shares: often also called equity shares. Persons who own ordinary shares normally take the most risk in the business but also normally receive most of the profit. These shares usually carry full voting rights.

(b) Preference shares: these give preference in some stated way over other shares, e.g., holders of preference shares may receive their dividend payments first.

(c) Deferred shares: usually, other shares take priority over these. They are often held by first members who originally formed the company, in order to give confidence to other new members.

(d) Debentures: these are not really shares but a type of secured loan to the company.

The officers of a limited company are directors, the managing director and company secretary. Auditors to the company must also be appointed.

Meetings

The Annual General Meeting (AGM)

These are held each calendar year and must not be more than 15 months apart. A newly incorporated company must hold its first AGM within 18 months of incorporation. When an AGM is called, the notification of it to members of the company must specify that it is the AGM and not any other meeting.

Extra-Ordinary General Meeting

This is a specially called meeting of the members of the company and may be called by shareholders holding a certain amount of shares in the company. All members of the company are entitled to attend these meetings unless they are specifically excluded by the company's Articles of Association.

There are certain other meetings which may be held by members of a company. If a member of the company wishes to vote on a matter being discussed at a meeting of the company and he cannot attend, he can give someone else his right to vote. This is known as his 'proxy'.

Decisions made at general meetings of a company are known as resolutions. There are certain formalities relating to resolutions. Rules governing company meetings are laid down in the Companies Acts.

Annual Return and Accounts

Every year a company must deliver its Annual Return to the Registrar of Companies. This is done by updating the previous year's Annual Return and must be made up to the date which is the company's 'return date', which is either the anniversary of the company's incorporation or, if the company's last return was delivered on a different date in accordance with the Companies Acts, the anniversary of that date. This must be filed with the Registrar within 28 days after the date to which it is made up. The Annual Return must state the date to which it is made up and must contain certain information relating to the company including, among other things, the address of its registered office, details of directors and secretary, the address where the register of members of the company is kept, principal business activities and details of issued share capital to the return date. The annual return is made on Form 363a and must be sent to Companies House, together with a fee.

Companies must also prepare annual accounts and submit these to the Registrar of Companies. Annual accounts report on the company's financial activities during the previous year, and this period of accounting is called the financial year. The financial year starts on the day after the previous financial year ends or, if it is a new company, it starts on the day the company was incorporated. The day on which a company's financial year ends is its accounting reference date and there are certain rules which apply to this.

Companies House will accept a company's accounts drawn up in the euro for accounting periods ending on or after 1 January 1999, if the directors and auditors of the company consider that by using that currency a true and fair view of the company's affairs will be given.

Dissolution of a Company

When a company is no longer going to exist it is 'wound up' or 'goes into liquidation'. This can be voluntary or it can be compulsory. The court may order a company to be wound up under certain circumstances when it is petitioned to do so by creditors of the company. When a company is wound up, a liquidator may be appointed to sort out the company's financial affairs. Sometimes the Official Receiver is appointed as liquidator. If a company cannot pay its debts it is said to be 'insolvent'.

Other Matters Involving Companies and Businesses

Companies and businesses can, of course, just like individuals, become involved in a variety of court actions. One type of court action is a 'passing off' action which occurs where one company or business tries to pass off its product as though it has been manufactured by another company, usually a larger, better known company.

You may come across the term 'intellectual property' or 'industrial property'. This type of property refers to rights over such things as patents, copyright, trade marks, designs and goodwill. Such property can be transferred from one person to another in the same manner as other property.

You may encounter references to the Director General of Fair Trading, who performs the functions assigned to him by the Fair Trading Act 1973. The Director General is appointed by the Secretary of State and is head of the Office of Fair Trading. He has responsibilities regarding consumer protection and competition law enforcement. Competition law is the law that governs the processes of competitiveness in trade.

You may also hear of the Competition Commission (called the Monopolies and Mergers Commission until April 1999). This body will continue to deal with aspects of the work carried out by the Monopolies and Mergers Commission regarding monopolies and mergers. It will also be the body to whom appeals may be made against decisions of the Director General under the Competition Act.

COMPANIES AND BUSINESSES

As with all matters relating to a lawyer's office, confidentiality is of the utmost importance. It must also be remembered that information gained inside the lawyer's office cannot be used for other purposes, for example, you may have access to information not known to the public which could assist someone in deciding to buy or sell certain shares in a particular company. This information must not be divulged or used in any way. If it is so used, this could amount to a criminal offence being committed, known as 'insider dealing'.

The law relating to companies and businesses is extensive and it is inappropriate to go any further into this subject in this type of book.

Test yourself on Chapter 10

Test your knowledge by completing this assignment. If you find that you have difficulty with anything, read the chapter again until you are happy with your answers.

1. A company is a 'legal person'. What does this mean?
2. What is the registered office of a company?
3. How might you obtain information about a limited company registered at Companies House?
4. What sort of information does a Memorandum of Association contain?
5. What are Articles of Association?
6. Complete as far as possible the Form 10 included with this assignment, using the following information:
    > You are employed by a firm called John Smith & Co., of 2 Bank Chambers, High Road, Westbourne, Suffolk (tel: 01876 9342; ref: JL/Orange/43), and you are working for Jane Lawman, a solicitor in that firm. Jane is acting for Peter Green and Ann Brown who wish to form a limited company called The Orange Company Limited. The registered office will be at 64 Hillside View, Westbourne, Suffolk WA3 2AB. Peter Green lives at 87 Summer Road, Westbourne, Suffolk WA3 8LB; his date of birth is 11.3.1970; his occupation is landscape gardener. Ann Brown lives at 69 Spring Hill, Westbourne, Suffolk, WA3 4PQ; her date of birth is 15.8.1965 and she is also a landscape gardener. They are both British. Peter Green will also be the company secretary.
7. Explain the difference between an Annual General Meeting and an Extra-Ordinary General Meeting.
8. What is meant by a company's 'financial year'?
9. Explain the term 'intellectual property'.
10. What is the process called whereby a company ceases to exist?
11. Now go through the chapter and if there are any words that are unfamiliar to you or that you cannot spell, write or type them correctly several times until you feel you know them.

COMPANIES AND BUSINESSES

OYEZ

Please complete in
typescript, or in
bold black capitals.

Notes on completion appear on final page.

F0100C10

10

First Directors and Secretary and Intended Situation of Registered Office

Company
Name in full

Proposed Registered Office
(PO Box numbers only, are not acceptable)

Post town

County/Region   Postcode

If the memorandum is delivered by an agent for
the subscriber(s) of the memorandum mark the
box opposite and give the agent's name and
address.

Agent's Name

Address

Post town

County/Region   Postcode

Number of continuation sheets attached.

Please give the name, address, telephone
number, and if available, a DX number and
Exchange of the person Companies House should
contact if there is any query.

Tel

DX number   DX exchange

When you have completed and signed the form please send it to
the Registrar of Companies at:

Companies House, Crown Way, Cardiff, CF4 3UZ
for companies registered in England and Wales **DX 33050 Cardiff**
or
Companies House, 37 Castle Terrace, Edinburgh, EH1 2EB
for companies registered in Scotland   **DX 235 Edinburgh**

[P.T.O.

256

Company Secretary (see notes 1-5)

Company Name

*Voluntary details. **NAME**   *Style/Title   *Honours etc.

Forename(s)

Surname

Previous forename(s)

Previous surname(s)

Address

Usual residential address
For a corporation, give the
registered or principal office
address.

Post town

County/Region   Postcode

Country

I consent to act as secretary of the company named on page 1

Consent signature   Date

Directors (see notes 1-5)
Please list directors in alphabetical order.

NAME   *Style/Title   *Honours etc.

Forename(s)

Surname

Previous forename(s)

Previous surname(s)

Address

Usual residential address
For a corporation, give the
registered or principal office
address.

Post town

County/Region   Postcode

Country

Day   Month   Year

Date of birth   **Nationality**

Business occupation

Other directorships

I consent to act as director of the company named on page 1

Consent signature   Date

257

COMPANIES AND BUSINESSES

Directors (continued) (see notes 1-5)

NAME	*Style/Title		*Honours etc.
*Voluntary details.	Forename(s)		
	Surname		
	Previous forename(s)		
	Previous surname(s)		
Address			
Usual residential address			
For a corporation, give the registered or principal office address.	Post town		
	County/Region		Postcode
	Country		

	Day	Month	Year	
Date of birth				**Nationality**

Business occupation

Other directorships

I consent to act as director of the company named on page 1

Consent signature   Date

This section must be signed by

Either
an agent on behalf
of all subscribers   Signed   Date

Or the subscribers
(i.e. those who signed
as members on the
memorandum of
association).

Signed   Date

Signed   Date

Signed   Date

Signed   Date

Signed   Date

Signed   Date

Notes

1. Show for an individual the full forename(s) NOT INITIALS and surname together with any previous forename(s) or surname(s).

If the director or secretary is a corporation or Scottish firm — show the corporate or firm name on the surname line.

Give previous forename(s) or surname(s) except that:

— for a married woman, the name by which she was known before marriage need not be given,

— names not used since the age of 18 or for at least 20 years need not be given.

A peer, or an individual known by a title, may state the title instead of or in addition to the forename(s) and surname and need not give the name by which that person was known before he or she adopted the title or succeeded to it.

Address:

Give the usual residential address.

In the case of a corporation or Scottish firm give the registered or principal office.

Subscribers:

The form must be signed personally either by the subscriber(s) or by a person or persons authorised to sign on behalf of the subscriber(s).

2. Directors known by another description:

—A director includes any person who occupies that position even if called by a different name, for example, governor, member of council.

3. Director's details:

Show for each individual director the director's date of birth, business occupation and nationality.

The date of birth must be given for every individual director.

4. Other directorships:

—Give the name of every company of which the person concerned is a director or has been a director at any time in the past 5 years. You may exclude a company which either is or at **all times during the past 5 years**, when the person was a director, **was:**

—dormant,

—a parent company which wholly owned the company making the return,

—a wholly owned subsidiary of the company making the return, or

—another wholly owned subsidiary of the same parent company.

If there is insufficient space on the form for other directorships you may use a separate sheet of paper, which should include the company's number and the full name of the director.

5. Use Form 10 continuation sheets or photocopies of page 2 to provide details of joint secretaries or additional directors and include the company's number.

OYEZ The Solicitors' Law Stationery Society Ltd, Oyez House, 7 Spa Road, London SE16 3QQ

1999 Edition
2.99 T01299
5017288

Companies 10

11 PROBATE

Probate departments usually deal with such things as advice on inheritance tax, Wills and other related matters including those where people have died without making a Will.

Wills

A Will is a document which states the wishes of a person as to how he or she would like their property dealt with after their death. If a person dies without making a Will, he dies 'intestate'. There are certain legal conditions to be met before a Will can be made. These are not all dealt with here because it is the responsibility of the fee earner to ensure these conditions are met.

A Will must normally be in writing, be signed by the testator (the person making it), or by someone else in his presence and at his direction, e.g., where the testator is unable for some reason to sign it himself. At the signing of a Will it is dated and the signature must be written or acknowledged in the presence of two or more witnesses who must both be present at the same time. The normal procedure for witnesses is that they also sign the Will, or acknowledge their signatures, in the presence of each other and in the presence of the testator, all being present at the same time. The clauses at the end of the Will which show that the Will has been signed and witnessed in this way are called the 'testimonium' and the 'attestation clause' (see also page 25). It may be that as a secretary you will often be asked to witness a Will. If you are lucky enough to be a beneficiary of a Will, you should not witness it, as this may bar you from obtaining your inheritance!

The basic contents of a Will can be explained as follows:

(a)   The name, address and occupation of the testator, followed by a declaration that this is his last Will.

(b)   The appointment of executors (also known as personal representatives). Broadly speaking, an executor (a female executor is called an executrix) is someone who will ensure that the wishes of the person who made the Will are carried out. Executors are sometimes beneficiaries under the Will and/or often professional people, such as bank managers and solicitors. If an executor is a professional person there is usually a clause in the Will stating that such a person may charge a fee for his service.

(c)   The main body of the Will then contains details of any gifts or legacies and powers and obligations of the trustees in the Will.

(d)   Finally, the Will is executed, i.e., dated and signed, as explained earlier, by the testator and witnesses. It should also have a typed backsheet (see page 263) as shown.

Any new Will cancels out (revokes) a previous Will. If amendments are to be made to an existing Will, a Codicil (see page 264) should be drawn up.

The Will should be typed on good quality paper. Some firms have special 'Will paper' which is rather thick and has the first few words printed in black writing, the paper having black edging. However, in these days of word processors, it is usual to use a good quality plain paper of A4 size. It should not have any unnecessary spaces or blank pages in it and should be typed on both sides of the paper. There should not be any alterations or erasures to a Will but if any are made you must bring these to the attention of the fee earner before the Will is signed. If the alterations are acceptable, they must be initialled by both the testator and the witnesses, otherwise the Will must be re-typed. If there are any figures showing sums of money in the Will these are often typed both in words and then in figures in brackets, e.g., ONE HUNDRED POUNDS (£100).

Paragraphs in the Will should be numbered and, as you will see from the example, the first word at the beginning of each paragraph and certain other words are usually typed in capitals and underlined. (This layout is not essential — it is simply traditional.) You will come across certain much used words in Wills such as 'devise' and 'bequeath'. These are explained in the glossary of this book.

On no account should you staple or attach anything by paperclips, etc. to a Will. This is because at some later stage, if the Will is in dispute and it bears a mark of something having been attached to it, then those disputing it may argue that part of the Will is missing. If a Will consists of more than one sheet of paper, it is usually sewn together in the top left-hand corner (see page 32) but remember, do not hold the sheets of paper together with a paperclip. The Will may also be bound together in a different fashion — find out what your own firm does.

Clients sometimes retain their Will or ask the firm of solicitors to keep it for them. In any event, it is normal to keep a photocopy of it in the file. If the original is kept by the firm it must be kept in the firm's safe.

PROBATE

Example Will

I JANE BLOGGS of 123 North Road Southtown Essex Waitress <u>HEREBY REVOKE</u> all Wills and testamentary dispositions heretofore made by me and declare this to be my last Will

1.   <u>I APPOINT</u> my sister <u>DOREEN BLOGGS</u> of 234 South Road Northtown Essex to be the Executor and Trustee of this my Will or any Codicil hereto (hereinafter called 'my Trustee')

2.   <u>I DIRECT</u> that all my just debts funeral and testamentary expenses shall be paid as soon as possible after my death

3.   <u>I GIVE</u> the sum of <u>ONE THOUSAND POUNDS</u> (£1000) to <u>SOUTHTOWN DOGS HOME</u> of 4 Barking Road Southtown aforesaid and <u>I DECLARE</u> that the receipt of the proper officer for the time being of the said charity shall be sufficient discharge to my Trustee

4.   <u>I DEVISE AND BEQUEATH</u> the residue of my estate both real and personal to my said sister <u>DOREEN BLOGGS</u>

IN WITNESS whereof I have hereunto set my hand this   *   day of   *   199*

SIGNED by the said JANE BLOGGS)
as her last Will in the presence   )
of us both present at the same   )
time and who in her presence and)
in the presence of each other have)
hereunto subscribed our names as)
witnesses   )

[or perhaps, more simply:]

SIGNED by the testator   )
JANE BOGGS in our joint presence)
and then by us in hers   )

DATED   199*

_____

WILL

of

JANE BLOGGS

Angel Gabriel & Co.,
2 Milky Way,
Barnet,
Herts.

tel: 01638 1234
ref: ABC/123

Codicils

You may also be asked to type a codicil to a Will. This is a document adding to or altering a previous Will and is set out in the same manner as a Will but states that it is a codicil to a Will dated whatever, by whoever. It has to be executed in the same manner as a Will. As with Wills, nothing should be stapled or attached to a codicil.

Grants

Persons who are named as executors in a Will or Codicil may apply for a Grant to the deceased's estate. This enables them to call in the estate, i.e., collect monies from banks, sell property, etc., and pay out accordingly. The main types of Grants are Grant of Probate and Letters of Administration with or without the Will annexed (see below).

Applications for a Grant are made to the Family Division of the High Court, either to a district probate registry or to the Principal Registry of the Family Division in London. In some cases, it is not necessary to obtain a Grant.

When applying for a Grant, the Oath for Executors must be completed. This is an affidavit (see page 121) containing evidence which establishes the executor's right to administer the estate. As with other affidavits, it must not be sworn before a solicitor whose firm is dealing with the matter. A pre-printed form is available and it must be typed carefully. If there are any alterations or erasures, they must be initialled by the solicitor administering the oath, as well as by the person swearing it. There are notes in the margin of the form to help with its completion.

Grant of Probate

This is granted where the validity of the Will has been proved. The Grant is issued to the executors of the Will. To obtain the Grant of Probate, the following must be lodged with the court:

(a) Oath for Executors.
(b) Original Will and any Codicils. These are signed by the executors and by the person administering the oath. The Will is then said to be 'marked'. Typed copies or drafts may be accepted if the original is lost. You should always keep a copy of any documents before sending them anywhere.
(c) Any other relevant affidavit evidence.
(d) The receipted account for inheritance tax purposes (see below) unless no tax is payable. If tax is to be paid, this must be done before applying for the Grant.
(e) The appropriate fee. Fees are on a sliding scale according to the value of the estate.

If the court is satisfied that everything is in order, they will issue the Grant. They will send to the solicitor the original Grant which will be bound to a copy of the Will, and any office copies required, i.e., further copies of the grant bearing the seal of the court, will be provided but without a further copy of the Will.

Letters of Administration

There are two types of Letters of Administration:

(i) A Grant of Letters of Administration (with Will annexed), which is issued to a person, other than an executor, for various reasons, e.g., there is no executor appointed by the Will or where the appointed executor has died without proving the Will.

(ii) A Grant of Letters of Administration, which is issued where a person has died intestate and the Grant is necessary to administer the estate. When the value of the estate is small, it is not always necessary to obtain a Grant, but this depends on the circumstances.

Applications for Grants of Letters of Administration may be made to the appropriate probate registry and must be supported by:

(a) An Oath for Administrators.
(b) An Inland Revenue Account, if appropriate (see (d) above).
(c) A fee.

If the court is satisfied, they will send the solicitor the Grant of Letters of Administration together with any office copies requested.

Receipt of the Grant of Probate or Grant of Letters of Administration is proof that the executor is entitled to act in the matter. Solicitors acting for executors may have to send office copies of the Grant to certain persons to enable the executor to gather in all the money belonging to the estate (i.e., the property of the deceased person). This could be, for example, sending a copy of the Grant to a building society where the deceased person had a savings account. On receipt of the Grant, the building society would close the account and send the money to the executor or his solicitors so that it could be dealt with properly. All this administration of the deceased person's property (known as his 'estate') is called 'winding-up the estate'.

SPECIMEN

Oath for Executors

IN THE HIGH COURT OF JUSTICE
Family Division

Extracting Solicitor ...Angel..Gabriel..&..Co............

Address ....2 Milky Way, Barnet,
...............Herts...(ref.:.ABC./.123.)...........

† "Principal" or "District Probate". If "District Probate" add "at...................".

The†   District   Registry at Southtown

* If necessary to include alias of deceased in grant add "otherwise (alias name)" and state below which is true name and reason for requiring alias.

(1) "I" or "We". Insert the full name, place of residence and occupation, or, if none, description of the deponent(s) adding "Mrs", "Miss", as appropriate, for a female deponent.

IN the Estate of*   JANE BLOGGS   deceased.

(1)   I, DOREEN BLOGGS of 234 South Road, Northtown, Essex
School Teacher

(2) Or "do solemnly and sincerely affirm".

(3) Each testamentary paper must be marked by each deponent, and by the person administering the oath.

(4) "with one, two (or more) Codicils", as the case may be.

make Oath and say (2)   that
(1)   I   believe the paper writing now produced to and marked by (3) me
to contain the true and original last Will and Testament (4)

of* JANE BLOGGS
of   123 North Road, Southtown, Essex

formerly of

                              deceased,

(5) If exact age is unknown, give best estimate.

(6) Where there are separate legal divisions in one country, the state, province, etc., should be specified.

(7) Delete "no", if there was land vested in deceased which remained settled land notwithstanding his or her death.

(8) Settled land may be included in the scope of the grant provided the executors are also the special executors as to the settled land; in that case the settlement must be identified.

who was born on the   1st   day of   June 1900   and
who died on the   2nd   day of   July 1999
aged   99   years (5) domiciled in (6)   England
and that to the best of   my   knowledge, information and belief there was (7) [no]
land vested in the said deceased which was settled previously to her   death (and
not by her Will (4)   )
and which remained settled land notwithstanding her   death (8)

~~And (1) further make oath and say (2)~~
~~that notice of this application has been given to~~

(9) Delete or amend as appropriate. Notice of this application must be served on all executors to whom power is to be reserved unless dispensed with by a Registrar under Rule 27 (3).

~~the executor(s) to whom power is to be reserved, (save~~

                                          ]. (9)

And (1)   I further make Oath and say (2)
           that (10) (11) I am the lawful daughter of the
said deceased,

(10) "I am" or "we are". Insert relationship of the executors to the deceased only if necessary to establish title or identification.

(11) "The sole", or "the surviving", or "one of the", or "are the", or "two of the", etc.

named in the said   Will   Executrix

(12) If there was settled land and the grant is to include it, insert "including settled land" but, if the grant is to exclude the settled land, insert "save and except settled land".

and that (¹)　I　will (i) collect, get in and administer according to the law the real and personal estate (¹²)　　　　　　　　　　　　　　　　　　　　　　　　　of the said deceased; (ii) when required to do so by the Court, exhibit on oath in the Court a full inventory of the said estate (¹²)
and when so required render an account of the administration of the said estate to the Court; and (iii) when required to do so by the High Court, deliver up the grant of probate to that Court; and that to the best of　　　　　　　knowledge, information and belief

(13) Complete this paragraph only if the deceased died on or after 1 April 1981 and an Inland Revenue Account is not required; the next paragraph should be deleted.

(¹³) [the gross estate passing under the grant does not exceed (¹⁴) £　　　　　, and the net estate does not exceed (¹⁵) £　　　　　, and that this is not a case in which an Inland Revenue Account is required to be delivered]

(14) The amount to be inserted here should be in accordance with the relevant figure shown in paragraph 1 of the PEP List.

(¹⁶) [the gross estate passing under the grant amounts to £ 125,000 and the net estate amounts to £ 100,000　　　　　].
*

(15) The amount to be inserted here should be in accordance with the relevant figure shown in paragraph 2 of the PEP List.

(16) Complete this paragraph only if an Inland Revenue Account is required and delete the previous paragraph.

N.B. The names of all executors to whom power is to be reserved must be included in the Oath.

SPECIMEN

SWORN by　DOREEN BLOGGS　　the above-named
Deponent

at　　　　*

this　　*　day of　　　　*

Before me,

A Commissioner for Oaths/Solicitor.

1999 Edition
1.99　F36105
5073580
★★★★★

Probate 4

Other Grants

There are certain other grants you may come across and very briefly, some of these are as follows:

(a)   Double probate: when an original Grant of Probate is made, power may be reserved to another executor. When this executor later applies for probate he will be issued a Grant of Probate known as double probate.

(b)   A Grant of Administration *de bonis non administratis*: issued where a sole personal representative dies or becomes incapacitated without having completed the administration of the estate.

(c)   Limited probate: the executor's appointment may be limited e.g., he may deal with only certain matters relating to the estate.

(d)   Administration *durante absentia*: this is a limited grant given to an interested party when the executor is out of the jurisdiction of the High Court.

(e)   A *cessate* grant: when a grant which is limited in its duration is terminated, e.g., because of its time limit, a further grant may be issued and this is the *cessate* grant.

(f)   Administration *ad colligenda bona*: this is to preserve the assets of the estate until a general grant can be taken out.

(g)   Administration *pendente lite*: an interested party in a probate action at court may request a person not connected with the action to apply for the grant to deal with the estate until the action is settled.

(h)   A Grant of Administration for the use and benefit of a minor: if someone under 18 is an executor then until he reaches the age of majority, the grant will usually be issued to his parent or guardian.

(i)   During mental or physical incapacity: if a person named as executor is incapacitated in this way then the grant will normally be issued to another person for the period of the incapacity.

These grants are rare but it is always useful to know what they relate to (or at least how to spell them!) when you do meet them.

Copies of Wills and Grants

If a copy of a Will or grant is required, postal applications should be made to the York Probate Sub-Registry, Duncombe Place, York YO1 2EA (DX 61543 York), accompanied by the appropriate fee — cheques should be made payable to HM Paymaster General. Any known relevant information should be quoted in the application, e.g., grant type, issuing Registry and grant issue date, and if a photocopy of the grant is available, so much the better. Personal applications for copies may be made to the Principal Registry of the Family Division in London.

Inheritance Tax

Depending on the value of the estate, Inheritance Tax may be payable, in which case certain Inland Revenue forms must be completed. These are IHT 202 and IHT 200. Which form to be used is determined by the total net value of the estate and certain other conditions. IHT 40 is used to list all stocks, shares and securities owned by the deceased. These are printed forms and the information to complete them will be given to you by the fee earner. When

Inheritance Tax has been assessed, the assessed account and payment should be sent to the Capital Taxes Office, Ferrers House, PO Box 38, Castle Meadow Road, Nottingham NG2 1BB (DX 701205 Nottingham 4). Cheques should be made payable to 'Inland Revenue only' and they should show the deceased's full name and date of death on the reverse.

Possible Disputes

If anyone is disputing a Will or wishes something to do with it to be decided at court, such proceedings are usually commenced in the Chancery Division of the High Court. Some county courts have jurisdiction provided the net estate does not exceed a certain amount.

Executors, before disposing of property under the Will, must advertise in the London Gazette and locally giving at least two months' notice of distribution of the estate so that any creditors or would-be claimants under the Will can come forward.

Caveats

A *caveat* is a written notice given by someone to (in this instance) the Principal Registry or a district registry not to issue a Grant without first giving notice to that person. A fee is payable to the court when entering a *caveat*. These are sometimes entered by a person who, for various reasons, has an interest in the estate of a deceased person. Where a *caveat* has been entered and an application is subsequently made for a Grant, various procedures must be followed. A *caveat* is effective only for six months, although extensions may be applied for. An application may be made to find out whether there is a *caveat* against the issue of a Grant. Such application may be made to any registry, as they all hold a computerised index.

Standing search

If someone simply wants to know whether a Grant has been issued, they may make an application to the Principal Registry or to a district probate registry accompanied by the appropriate fee. They will be sent an office copy of any Grant made within 12 months before, or six months after, receipt of the application. The application can be renewed at the end of six months.

Other Deeds

During the course of working in a probate department, you will come across deeds (see page 271) of trust and of gift, among many other things. If these are not typed onto a printed form they are typed in the same way as other deeds, i.e., usually no blank pages and with a backsheet. If there is more than one page, the deed is normally sewn up with green tape as shown on page 29 or bound in some other way. It is best to check your firm's requirements on this point.

Test yourself on Chapter 11

Test your knowledge by completing this assignment. If you find that you have difficulty with anything, read the chapter again until you are happy with your answers.

1. Explain the basic contents of a Will.
2. Type out a draft Will basing the clauses and layout on the example given in this chapter. Use the following information to do this. The Will is for Valerie Simmons of 19 Astronomer's Row, Northtown, Sussex SE4 2LQ. She has appointed her son, Andrew Simmons of the same address to be the executor. She wishes to include suitable clauses stating that: any debts should be paid off; she is leaving £750 to a cats' home called Pussies Galore of Cat Hill, Felixstowe, Suffolk FG3 5PQ; the remainder of her estate will be left to her son, Andrew.
3. What sort of information must be included in an Oath for Executors?
4. What is inheritance tax?
5. What is the purpose of applying for a Grant to a deceased person's estate? Explain the procedures involved.
6. Explain the following terms:

    (a) codicil;
    (b) caveat.

7. How might you obtain a copy of a Will or Grant?
8. How would you find out whether a Grant had already been issued to someone?
9. Now go through the chapter and if there are any words that are unfamiliar to you or that you cannot spell, write or type them correctly several times until you feel you know them.

12   CONVEYANCING

Conveyancing includes matters relating to the transfer of ownership of land, rights and usage over land and buildings on that land. Such property is either 'freehold' or 'leasehold' (see below). The person selling property is called the 'Vendor' or 'Seller' and the person buying it is the 'Purchaser' or 'Buyer'.

Freehold

Freehold land can be inherited without restriction after the owner dies, is owned immediately the transaction transferring possession of it has taken place and is free from conditions, e.g., it is not held for a specified period of time. You may come across the term 'fee simple absolute in possession' which means that the property is freehold. You will find that most houses are freehold.

Leasehold

A lease gives exclusive possession to the person holding the lease. It sets out the rights and obligations of the landlord and tenant to each other, states the rent payable and the period of time the lease is to be held for. Leasehold property is owned for a definite period of time, e.g., 99 years. A tenancy is usually a much shorter period of time. You may come across the term 'term of years absolute' which means that the property is leasehold. Most flats are leasehold.

A Deed

Most transactions involving leasehold and freehold property must be made by deed, except in cases involving leasehold property where the term does not exceed three years, although in those cases, there are certain conditions to be fulfilled. A deed is a document which passes something, for example, property, a right or an obligation, from one person to another. A deed must be in writing and it must be clear from the deed that it is intended to be a deed by the person making it. This can be done either by describing itself as a deed or expressing itself to be executed or signed as a deed. You will see in old documents that a deed bore the words at the end 'SIGNED, SEALED and DELIVERED by ... in the presence of' and it was signed by the parties to the deed. Alongside their signatures was a little red wafer seal (a red circular 'star' about half an inch in diameter). There is no longer a requirement for an individual to seal a deed or for all companies to have a seal, and you will now encounter words at the end such as 'SIGNED and DELIVERED as a deed by . . . in the presence of' or 'SIGNED as a deed by . . . in the presence of'. (See also Chapter 10 regarding company seals and page 25 regarding attestation clauses and general information regarding deeds and other documents.) This signing of a deed is known as 'executing' it and it must be done in the correct manner. How this is done varies as to whether it is to be executed by an individual or a company. Before a deed becomes effective, it has to be 'delivered'. 'Delivery' occurs when the person executing the deed (or someone authorised to act on his behalf) does something to show that he intends the deed to be effective, e.g., handing over the deed to the other party; or confirming that it has been sent through the post.

Registration of Land

A great deal of land in England and Wales is registered with the Land Registry. The purpose of registration is to enable a record of ownership and any mortgages (see page 320) and certain other interests in that land to be recorded, which greatly simplifies transactions involving that land. All land is now subject to compulsory registration. This means that if it has not been previously registered, then once there is a dealing (see below) in that land, e.g., sale/purchase, the land must be registered with the Land Registry. All applications to register charges or other interests in land must be made on the appropriate form. The Land Registry has local district registries to cover particular areas (not always the one nearest the property) and owners of land in each particular area must register details of transactions concerning the land with the relevant district registry. It is important that all applications to the Land Registry are made to the correct district registry.

Registered property is given a Title Number. This is the number given to it by the Land Registry and is shown on all documents relating to that land. All correspondence and forms sent to the Land Registry should bear the Title Number. The Title Number has two letters first and then a figure, e.g., HD 123456. The letters show the area in which the land was registered.

The owner of registered property is called the 'registered proprietor' by the Land Registry and a transfer of property such as by a Transfer or Conveyance (a type of deed) is often referred to as a 'dealing'.

Addresses and details of the relevant District Land Registry relating to a particular area can be obtained from any district land registry or from the *Directory of Local Authorities* (Sweet & Maxwell). Land Registry addresses are also included at the back of this book. All cheques for the Land Registry should be made payable to 'HM Land Registry'.

Where land is unregistered, the process of buying and selling varies slightly, and this is dealt with briefly on page 308.

Sale/Purchase of a Freehold Property which has been Registered

Usually the first steps in the sale and/or purchase of a house are done through an estate agent. In any event, the parties to the transaction agree to sell or buy the house at a certain price 'subject to contract' (see page 274). This means that the terms they have agreed between them are not legally binding until contracts are exchanged (see page 290). Quite often the property will include the sale of curtains, carpets, etc. at an agreed price for these items. The steps to be taken shown here may be varied at certain stages and some of the forms used may differ slighty with regard to domestic conveyancing if the firm you are working for is implementing the National Conveyancing Protocol (see page 326).

The Deeds

The solicitor acting on behalf of the person selling the house ('the Vendor') must obtain the deeds to the property ('the title deeds'), i.e., the documents which prove ownership of the property. To obtain the deeds where the property is mortgaged, the solicitor will need to know from the Vendor the full name(s) of the borrrower(s), the full address of the property, including the postcode, the mortgage account number (also known as the 'roll number') and the name and address of the lender. The Vendor's solicitor will then write to the building society or other lender, because they will hold the deeds if the property is mortgaged to them, and ask them to send the deeds to him so that he can proceed with the sale of the property. The solicitor will undertake to hold the deeds on behalf of the building society (hold them 'to their order'). Such a letter would be in the following form:

Dear Sirs,

Roll No: 12,345
Mortgagor: Albert Francis Brown
Property: 76 Burnt Oak Road, Moreland, EN6 8LB

We act on behalf of the above named mortgagor in connection with the proposed sale of this property. Please accept this letter as notice of our client's intention to redeem his present mortgage.

In order that we may proceed with the sale, we would be obliged if you would send us the deeds to the property on our undertaking to hold them to your order pending completion.

We will notify you as soon as contracts are exchanged.

Yours faithfully,

If the property is not mortgaged, the Vendor will arrange to provide the deeds to his solicitor.

Deeds to a house will contain the Land Certificate or Charge Certificate (see below) and various other documents.

The Land Certificate

The Land Certificate shows details of the property which are registered at the Land Registry. It shows the last time it was returned to the Land Registry, usually when some transaction takes place, e.g., a sale, purchase or mortgage. The Certificate will also normally contain a plan of the property. A Charge Certificate is similar to a Land Certificate and is issued when the property is mortgaged.

A Land Certificate has in it copies of the entries on the Register held by the Land Registry which relate to a particular property:

(a)   The Property Register. This describes the land, i.e., gives the address or location of the property and refers to a filed plan (or 'title plan') showing the boundaries of the property.

(b)   The Proprietorship Register gives details of the registered proprietor or owner. It also shows whether, for example, the land is freehold or leasehold.

(c)   The Charges Register consists of entries adverse to the land, for example, a mortgage (see page 320), and also gives notice of rights and interests to which the property may be subject, for example, a right of way over the property.

The 'Register' consists of the above registers and is bound up by the Land Registry inside a thick paper cover. When applying for office copy entries (see page 279) or reference is made to entries on the Register, it is this Register or office copies of the entries on it which are usually referred to in property matters.

Subject to Contract

The Purchaser's solicitor will write to the solicitor acting for the Vendor to confirm that he is acting in the matter. Correspondence between the parties up to exchange of contracts is normally headed 'Subject to Contract' or it is stated in the correspondence that everything is subject to contract. This confirms that everything agreed at this stage is not legally binding until signed contracts have been exchanged. However, although this is the usual procedure, it is unlikely that a contract would be entered into just because 'subject to contract' was accidentally omitted from the correspondence. Section 2 of the Law of Property (Miscellaneous Provisions) Act 1989 requires the contract not only to be in writing, but it must also be signed by both parties. An example of this type of letter is shown below.

Dear Sirs,

re: Green from Brown   SUBJECT TO CONTRACT
76 Burnt Oak Road, Moreland, EN6 8LB

We are acting on behalf of Miss Elizabeth Mary Green who, we understand, has agreed to purchase the above property from your client, Mr Albert Francis Brown, at the price of £96,000, subject to contract.

We look forward to receiving the draft contract from you as soon as possible.

Yours faithfully,

Enquiries of the Local Authority

Before contracts can be exchanged, certain enquiries have to be made by the Purchaser's solicitors of the local authority where the property is situated. The enquiries are made by requesting the local authority to carry out searches relating to the property in question. The procedure is known as 'making local searches'. These searches are made to ensure that there are no adverse entries in the register of charges kept by the local authority which might affect the land, e.g., there could be some financial charge or restriction on the property, and also to ascertain whether there is anything else affecting the property that the local authority may know about. The searches are made irrespective of whether or not the land is registered.

Addresses of local authorities can be found in the *Directory of Local Authorities* (Sweet & Maxwell). This directory lists the local authorities in England, Wales and Scotland and also contains information relating to conveyancing and land registration fees and charges. To find details relating to a particular authority, if the district is known, it can be looked up under its name, but if the district is not known, the relevant authority can be found by looking up the place name in another part of the book which lists by name thousands of towns, cities, villages, etc. The *Directory* also contains names and addresses of other useful organisations. You may find the *Directory* useful when you have to provide details of the administrative area of a property. This information is often required to be entered on Land Registry forms. An administrative area is the county, county and district, county borough or London borough. If you are not sure whether you should enter two area names, e.g., the county and the district, then enter both. If you are dealing with registered property, you should find the administrative area on the land or charge certificate; office copies of the register; or the title plan.

Two forms are used when making local searches. One is the Requisition for Search in the Register of Local Land Charges, which requests the local authority to search their register and to certify either that there are no entries affecting that property, or to give details of any entries. This form is LLC1. The form must be completed in duplicate and has a copy attached for this purpose. However, it is not self-carbonating and therefore you will have to use carbon paper with this form.

The other form, to accompany LLC1, is the form of Enquiries of Local Authority, Form Con 29 (1994). Again, this must be submitted in duplicate. A copy is not attached to Con 29 (1994) and therefore you must send two forms: a carbon copy will suffice. This form enquires about matters not in the Register of Local Land Charges, but over which the local authority has control, e.g., various planning matters, compulsory purchase orders, etc. Con 29 (1994) is in two parts. The enquiries in Part I will be answered by the local authority on payment of a fee. The actual enquiries are listed inside the form. However, a separate fee is payable for each optional enquiry listed in Part II. These optional enquiries are referred to on the front of the form under 'G' and where answers are required for any, a tick should be placed in the appropriate box on the front of the form. Any further additional enquiries must be attached on a separate sheet of paper in duplicate, and an additional fee will be charged for any which the council is willing to answer. The local authority's answers to any additional enquiries will be given on a separate sheet of paper which will then be attached to the form and returned to the enquirer. Where optional or additional enquiries are being made, this should also be indicated in the box at 'D' on the front of the form.

If a plan is necessary to identify the property being searched against, this should be submitted in duplicate.

The searches will reveal only matters relevant to the particular property in question and not to any neighbouring property, even if something on neighbouring property could affect the property being searched, e.g., planning permission may have been granted to build on adjoining land, but this will not be revealed on the search — a search would also have to be made relating to the adjoining land.

If a search is urgent, you should write clearly, in red, on the forms 'Urgent: please expedite'. You should also telephone the local authority to see if they can do the search quickly. However, they are not obliged to do your search any quicker than anyone else's.

The forms are signed and dated and then sent off to the local authority where the land is situated with the cheque for the fee. The cheque should be made payable to the authority. A covering letter is not required. The fee would be for a single parcel of land if it is just one property that is concerned, plus the fee for any Part II and additional enquiries. Property is often referred to as a 'parcel of land'. Simply, a parcel is one particular property or piece of land and has one Title Number (see page 272). The fees payable for these searches may vary with each local authority so you should check with them by telephone as to what their fees are before sending the forms to them. A note should be made on the file that the search has been sent off (or a copy of the search kept on the file), the date it was sent, and how much the fee was.

If local searches have been made and have become more than two months old before contracts are exchanged (see later), fresh searches will normally be carried out so that the information is up to date.

There are other search forms which you may occasionally have to type, such as a Coal Mining Search (Con 29M), which is used to ascertain whether a property is or may be affected by any previous, current or proposed coal mining activity in a particular area. A Coal Mining Search would be sent to The Coal Authority. Further information on coal mining searches may be obtained by telephoning the Mining Searches Recorded Information Helpline on 0845-601 2608. Another search that you may occasionally make is a Commons Registration Search (CR Form 21) which is made to find out whether land is registered as a village green or common land, which would give members of the public certain rights over it, e.g., such as allowing animals to graze on it. This type of search would usually be carried out where a building company is buying undeveloped land to build on, especially if the land is already near a village green.

Form LLC1. (*Local Land Charges Rules 1977 Schedule 1. Form C*)

The duplicate of this form must also be completed:
a carbon copy will suffice.

For directions, notes and fees see overleaf.

Insert name and address of registering authority in space below

> Land Charges Department
> Moreland District Council
> 56 Green Street
> Moreland
> Herts
> EN3 2NL

SPECIMEN

Register of local land

charges

Requisition for search

and official certificate

of search

fold

Requisition for search

(*A separate requisition must be made in respect of each parcel of land except as explained overleaf*)

An official search is required in ~~PART~~ _____ ~~of~~[1]
the register of local land charges kept by the above-named registering authority for subsisting registrations against the land [defined in the attached plan and][2] described below.

Description of land sufficient to enable it to be identified

> 76 Burnt Oak Road, Moreland,
> EN7 8CB

Name and address to which certificate is to be sent

> Peter Wolf & Co
> Red Riding Hood Lane
> Northtown
> Essex
> 1CD 3LA

Signature of applicant (*or his solicitor*)

*

Date

1st June 1999

Telephone number

01234-5678

Reference

PW/74

Enclosure
Cheque/Money Order/Postal Order/Giro

Official certificate of search

It is hereby certified that the search requested above reveals no subsisting registrations[3]

or the_____registrations described in the Schedule hereto[3] up to and including the date of this certificate.

Signed ....

On behalf of ....

Date

1 Delete if inappropriate. Otherwise insert Part(s) in which search is required.

2 Delete if inappropriate. (A plan should be furnished in duplicate if it is desired that a copy should be returned.)

3 Delete inapplicable words. (The Parts of the Schedule should be securely attached to the certificate and the number of registrations disclosed should be inserted in the space provided. Only Parts which disclose subsisting registrations should be sent.)

4 Insert name of registering authority.

CON. 29 (1994)
To be submitted in duplicate *SPECIMEN*

ENQUIRIES OF LOCAL AUTHORITY
(1994 EDITION)

Please type or use BLOCK LETTERS

Search No...

The Replies are given on the attached sheet(s)

Signed ....
                                              Proper Officer

Date...

A.

To

LAND CHARGES DEPARTMENT
MORELAND DISTRICT COUNCIL
56 GREEN STREET
MORELAND
HERTS
EN3 2NL

A. Enter name and address of District or Borough Council for the area. If the property is near a Local Authority boundary, consider raising certain Enquiries (e.g. road schemes) with the adjoining Council.

B. Enter address and description of the property. A plan in duplicate must be attached if possible and is insisted upon by some Councils. Without a plan, replies may be inaccurate or incomplete. A plan is essential for Optional Enquiries 18, 37 and 38.

B.

Property

76 BURNT OAK ROAD
MORELAND
EN7 8CB

C. Enter name and/or location of (and mark on plan, if possible) any other roadways, footpaths and footways (in addition to those entered in Box B) for Enquiry 3 and (if raised) Enquiries 19 and 20.

D. Answer every question. Any additional Enquiries must be attached on a separate sheet in duplicate and an additional fee will be charged for any which the Council is willing to answer.

E. Details of fees can be obtained from the Council or The Law Society.

F. Enter name and address of the person or firm lodging this form.

G. Tick which Optional Enquiries are to be answered.

PLEASE READ THE NOTES ON PAGE 4.

C.

Other roadways, footpaths and footways

G.

	Optional Enquiries
	17. Road proposals by private bodies
	18. Public paths or byways
✓	19. Permanent road closure
	20. Traffic schemes
	21. Advertisements
	22. Completion notices
	23. Parks and countryside
	24. Pipelines
	25. Houses in multiple occupation
	26. Noise abatement
✓	27. Urban development areas
	28. Enterprise zones
	29. Inner urban improvement areas
	30. Simplified planning zones
	31. Land maintenance notices
	32. Mineral consultation areas
	33. Hazardous substance consents
	34. Environmental and pollution notices
	35. Food safety notices
	36. Radon gas precautions
	37. Sewers within the property
	38. Nearby sewers

D.

A plan in duplicate is attached   YES/NO

Optional Enquiries are to be answered (see Box G)   YES/NO

Additional Enquiries are attached in duplicate on a separate sheet   YES/NO

E.

Fees of £   *   are enclosed.

Signed :   *

Date :   1st June 1999

Reference :   PW/74

Tel. No. :   01234-5678

F.

Reply to

PETER WOLF & CO
RED RIDING HOOD LANE
NORTHTOWN
ESSEX
1CD 3LA

OYEZ The Solicitors' Law Stationery Society Limited, Oyez House, 7 Spa Road, London SE16 3QQ
Conveyancing 29(1994)

LAW SOCIETY COPYRIGHT
9.97   F34273   5033379

Office Copy Entries

The Vendor's solicitor will obtain as soon as possible, from the appropriate district registry of the Land Registry, office copies of any entries in the Register (see page 274) at the Land Registry and a copy of the filed plan. These are copies of the entries in the Register and are marked with the date of issue so that anyone looking at them may know how up to date they are. Once these office copies are received, they are sent to the Purchaser's solicitors, a copy having been kept for your file. The Purchaser's solicitors will also later apply for up-to-date office copy entries. One of the reasons for obtaining office copy entries is to see whether anything new has been registered against the land. Application for office copy entries is made on Form 109 (Forms 110 and 110A are used in certain circumstances), together with the appropriate fee. No covering letter is required, but the file should be marked or a copy of the form kept to indicate when the application was sent.

If the title number of the property is unknown, the application on Form 109 can still be made and the words 'Please supply the title number' should be printed in bold lettering at the top of the form. An additional fee may be payable in this instance.

See also below regarding applications to the Land Registry by fax, telephone and direct computer access, and key numbers.

Search of the Index Map

The Index Maps are large-scale Ordnance Survey maps held by the Land Registry, and which cover all of England and Wales. The maps show whether or not a piece of land is registered and, if so, its title number and whether it is freehold or leasehold.

An application for a search of the Index Map may be made on Land Registry Form 96. This search will be required to ascertain whether land is registered, or to find out an unknown title number of land. It will also ascertain whether there is a pending application to register the land for the first time, or whether there is any caution against first registration of the land, or whether there are any priority notices affecting the land.

This application will frequently be accompanied by a plan showing the property boundaries (usually edged in red), so remember to ensure that any copy plan is correctly coloured and marked to be the same as the original. See also page 18 regarding copying documents.

Application for **Office
Copies of Register/Title Plan;
a certificate in Form 102**

HM Land Registry

Form

SPECIMEN

109

(Rule 2 Land Registration (Open Register) Rules 1991)

STEVENAGE ——— District Land Registry
BRICKDALE HOUSE
SWINGATE
STEVENAGE
HERTS
SG1 1XG

**Please complete the numbered panels on this form in
typescript or BLOCK LETTERS.
No covering letter is necessary.
Applications for office copies of specified documents
must be made on Form 110.
Use one form per title.**

1
Title Number
(if known)

| H | D | 1 | 2 | 3 | 4 | 5 | | | |

(Use one character per box)

2
Flat No., if
applicable

Property Description

Postal number
or description | 76

Name of road | BURNT OAK ROAD

Name of locality |

Town | MORELAND

Administrative
area (including
district or
borough if any) | MORELAND, HERTFORDSHIRE

Post code | EN7 8CB

3 Application

I ___ PETER WOLF & CO
(enter here name and address of person or firm making the application)
of ___ RED RIDING HOOD LANE

___ NORTHTOWN, ESSEX

___ 1CD 3LA

apply for

[X] office copy(ies) of the **register** of the above mentioned property;

[ ] office copy(ies) of the **title plan** of the above mentioned property;

[ ] a certificate in Form 102 in which case, either:–

    [ ] an Estate Plan has been approved and the Plot Number is [ ]
    or
    [ ] no Estate Plan has been approved and a certificate is to be
    issued in respect of the land shown _____
    _____ on the attached plan and copy.

For official use only | Record of
Fees paid

Fee
Debited | £ | | |

4   **PAYMENT OF FEE**

Please enter X in the appropriate box:–

[X] the Land Registry fee of £ [*] accompanies this application,
    or
[ ] please debit the Credit Account mentioned below with the
appropriate fee payable under the current Land Registration
Fees Order.

**FOR COMPLETION
BY APPLICANTS
WHO ARE CREDIT
ACCOUNT
HOLDERS**

YOUR KEY NUMBER:–

| | | | | | |

YOUR REFERENCE:– (See over)

5 Please enter X in the appropriate box:–

[X] I am, or act for, either the registered proprietor, or an
intending purchaser or mortgagee.

[ ] The above does not apply.

Note: This information is requested for statistical purposes only.

6 Where the title number is NOT quoted in Panel 1 please enter X in
the appropriate box(es):–
As regards this property, I am interested in the

[ ] Freehold estate.

[ ] Leasehold estate.

7 In case there is an application for registration pending against the
title, please enter X in the appropriate box:–

[X] I require an office copy back dated to the day prior to the
receipt of that application,
    or
[ ] I require an office copy on completion of that application.

Signature
of applicant:–   *   Date   *   Daytime telephone No:–   01234-5678

8 Reference ___ PW/74

PETER WOLF & CO
RED RIDING HOOD LANE
NORTHTOWN
ESSEX
1CD 3LA

Where you have requested that the fee be paid
by Credit Account the appropriate fee has been
debited.

Please enter above using BLOCK LETTERS the name and either
address (including postcode) OR (if applicable) the DX number of the
person to whom the office copies are to be sent.

Application for an
**Official Search
of the Index Map**   (Note 1)

HM Land Registry

SPECIMEN

Form
96

(Rule 9 Land Registration (Open Register)
Rules 1991)

FOR EXPLANATORY NOTES SEE OVERLEAF
Please complete in typescript or in BLACK BLOCK LETTERS all details
within the thick black lines.

To___STEVENAGE___District Land Registry
BRICKDALE HOUSE
SWINGATE
STEVENAGE
HERTS
SG1 1XG

(Note 2)

For official use only	
Description	Date

Fees Debited £			Record of Fees paid

(Note 5)

Please enter X in the appropriate box:–

☐ the Land Registry fee of £ _____ accompanies this application,

or

☒ please debit the Credit Account mentioned below with the
appropriate fee payable under the current Land Registration
Fees Order.

I   PETER WOLF & CO

of   RED RIDING HOOD LANE
NORTHTOWN
ESSEX
1CD 3LA

(enter name and address of person or firm making the application)

apply for an official search of the Index Map or General Map
and Parcels Index, and the list of pending applications for
first registration, in respect of the land referred to below and
shown [   ] on the attached plan.

NOTE – Any attached plan must contain sufficient details of the
surrounding roads and other features to enable the land to be identified
satisfactorily on the Ordnance Survey Map. However, a plan may be
unnecessary if the land can be identified by postal description. Nevertheless,
the Chief Land Registrar reserves the right to ask for a plan to be supplied
where he considers it necessary.

YOUR KEY NUMBER:–

1	2	3	4	5		

YOUR REFERENCE:– (Note 6)

PW/74

Signed   *
Date   *
Telephone No.   01234-5678
Reference   PW/74

HM Land Registry

Property

Postal number or description	76
Name of road	BURNT OAK ROAD
Name of locality	
Town	MORELAND
Postcode	EN7 8CB
Administrative area (Note 3) (including district or borough if any)	MORELAND HERTFORDSHIRE
Ordnance Survey Map Reference (Note 4)	
Known Title Number(s)	HD 12345

Enter Name and either address including postcode OR (if applicable)
DX number of the person to whom the official certificate of result of
search is to be sent.

PETER WOLF & CO
RED RIDING HOOD LANE
NORTHTOWN
ESSEX
1CD 3LA

Reference	PW/74

**CERTIFICATE OF RESULT OF OFFICIAL SEARCH OF
THE INDEX MAP**   (Form 96 Result)

It is certified that the official search applied for has been made with the
following result:– **(Only the statements opposite the boxes marked X apply.)**

☐ The land_____
is not registered. (Note 7)

☐ The land_____
is not affected by any caution against first registration
or any priority notice.

☐ The land_____
is affected by a pending application for first registration
under the following reference _____

☐ The land_____
is registered freehold under Title No._____

☐ The land_____
is registered leasehold under Title No._____

☐ The land_____
is affected by a rentcharge under Title No._____

☐ The land_____
is affected by a caution against first registration/
priority notice under Title No._____

Official stamp

When applying for first
registration of the above
property or writing in
relation to it, please
enclose this result of
search and any plan
annexed thereto.

Key Numbers and Credit Accounts

When completing Land Registry forms, you will see there is a place for a 'key number'. This is the firm's account number with the Land Registry and it should be quoted on all forms, etc. Some firms have a rubber stamp bearing their key number to avoid mistakes being made. If your firm has a credit account with the Land Registry a cheque does not have to be sent immediately for the fee, if one is payable — the firm will be billed later.

A great advantage of having a credit account with the Land Registry is that many applications and searches may be made by telephone, fax, telex and direct computer access by those with a credit account. Of course, where telephone applications are made, there is no need even to complete a form. However, these methods are acceptable only where the firm concerned has a credit account. Further information about credit accounts with the Land Registry may be obtained by telephoning the Credit Accounts Section on 01752 635600.

If it is desired to make payment through a credit account, then you must place a 'X' in the appropriate box at the top of the form. Cheques must be made payable to 'HM Land Registry'. Land Registry forms do not require a covering letter to go with them but the file must be noted to show that the form has been sent or a copy of the form retained on the file. See also page 313 dealing with Land Charges Searches.

Land Registry Application by Telephone

Credit account holders may make application by telephone for searches of the index map, office copies and searches of whole with priority (see later), provided the property can be identified without a plan (otherwise the operator will not be able to identify the particular property over the telephone). Telephone enquiries are made through the Land Registry Telephone Services facility to one central number which deals with requests wherever the land is situated. The number is 0845 308 4545.

The service is available as follows: for searches of the index map and office copies, Monday to Friday, from 9.30 am to 5.00 pm; for official searches of whole with priority — Monday to Friday, from 11.00 am to 5.00 pm. Facilities are closed during public holidays.

There is also a Telephone Services Centre which specialises in Welsh place names and offers a Welsh speaking service. This Centre will also accept Land Charges Searches. The Swansea number is 0845 307 4535.

The Telephone Services numbers should not be used for general enquiries, in which case the relevant District Land Registry should be contacted.

Before making an application by telephone to the Land Registry, you should ensure you have all the relevant information to hand so that the operator can process your application. This will include:

(a)   your key number;
(b)   the name, address and telephone number of your firm, as well as your reference, and the name and address of anyone different, if applicable, that the certificate should be sent to by the Land Registry;
(c)   the title number of the property. If you do not know the title number, you should provide the operator with the postal address of the property, including the postcode, if

possible, together with the name of the relevant administrative area (see page 275) and any Ordnance Survey map reference, if known. You should also be able to tell the operator whether you are interested in the leasehold or freehold of the property.

Plus any other information the fee earner may give to you.

Where appropriate, applicants will be given the results of their telephone search immediately. Following every telephone search, a guaranteed paper result will be sent to the applicant by post or by DX, usually on the same or next working day.

If you wish to make a telephone search without priority, the relevant Land Registry serving the area in question must be contacted, and not the telephone number above.

Land Registry Application by Fax

Certain applications may be made to the Land Registry by fax by credit account holders only. Although the application may be made by fax, the Land Registry will not, at present, return information by fax. Any office copies or search results will be sent by post or through the DX to the applicant. Several types of application may be made by fax and these must be made to specific fax numbers at the relevant Land Registry. Details of such applications and the fax numbers are available from the Land Registry. Fax applications should be completed in black ink or black type.

The fax facility for applications is available between 10.00 am and 4.00 pm Monday to Friday. Applications cannot be made on public holidays or after 4.00 pm on the day before a public holiday. The fax facility may also be used for correspondence to the Land Registry, provided there is no accompanying documentation.

Computerised Searches

Land Registry credit account customers are able to conduct searches via their own computer provided, of course, that they are registered to do so with the Land Registry. This on-line access has been named 'Direct Access'. As long as the user has the title number or postal address, they can gain access to a computerised register of a particular property. Hard copies for internal office use can be printed out from the screen. The user may order office copies directly through the computer and these will normally be posted on the same day by the Land Registry. It is also possible to send correspondence electronically to any district Land Registry via Direct Access.

Lines are open Monday to Friday from 8.30 am to 5.30 pm; the official search (Form 94A) facility is provided from 11.00 am to 5.00 pm.

Draft Contract

The Vendor's solicitor prepares a draft contract for sale. A contract must incorporate all the terms which have been expressly agreed by the parties and includes details of the parties to the transaction, describes the property, including the Title Number if it is registered, the agreed price of the property (the 'consideration'), whether any deposit is to be paid and the completion date (see page 302). It will also provide for any payment for 'chattels' which, in this type of matter, means other property included in the sale, e.g., carpets, etc. Where the National Conveyancing Protocol has been adopted (see page 326), any such items included in the sale will be listed on a Prop 6 (Fixture, Fittings and Contents) Form which must be attached securely to each part of the contract. Once contracts are exchanged (see page 290), the parties to it are bound by it.

The contract may be typed on A4 size paper but usually a standard printed form is used. This is the Law Society's Agreement (Incorporating the Standard Conditions of Sale (Third Edition)) and only the outer pages are to be completed. The inner pages contain general conditions of sale which apply to all contracts drawn up on that form unless expressly varied or excluded. The printed conditions must not be actually physically amended. Any alteration to the conditions must be by a Special Condition on the back of the form. The contract should be prepared in duplicate. Contracts are dated with the date they are exchanged, so do not date the contract unless you are asked to do so by the fee earner — just leave the space for the date blank.

The contract may refer to an attached plan, in which case, you must ensure that the plan is correctly coloured and marked (see page 18). Each copy of the contract would have a copy of any plan securely attached to it. Once the draft contract is agreed by the parties, final copies or 'engrossments' can be prepared for signature.

AGREEMENT
(Incorporating the Standard Conditions of Sale (Third Edition))

Agreement date	:	
Seller	:	ALBERT FRANCIS BROWN of 76 BURNT OAK ROAD MORELAND HERTS EN7 8CB
Buyer	:	ELIZABETH MARY GREEN of 46 OLD ROAD NORTHTOWN HERTS EN4 7AB
Property **(freehold/~~leasehold~~)**	:	76 BURNT OAK ROAD, MORELAND HERTFORDSHIRE registered at H.M. Land Registry under Title No. HD 12345.
~~Root of title~~/Title Number	:	The Seller's title is registered with absolute title under Title No. HD 12345 at the Stevenage District Land Registry.
Incumbrances on the Property	:	None
Title Guarantee **(full/~~limited~~)**	:	Full title guarantee
Completion date	:	*
Contract rate	:	2% per annum above the base rate from time to time of the Greenback Bank plc.
Purchase price	:	£96,000
Deposit	:	£9,600
Amount payable for chattels	:	£500
Balance	:	£86,900

SPECIMEN

The Seller will sell and the Buyer will buy the Property for the Purchase price.
The Agreement continues on the back page.

WARNING This is a formal document, designed to create legal rights and legal obligations. Take advice before using it.	**Signed** Seller/Buyer

SPECIAL CONDITIONS

1. (a) This Agreement incorporates the Standard Conditions of Sale (Third Edition). Where there is a conflict between those Conditions and this Agreement, this Agreement prevails.

   (b) Terms used or defined in this Agreement have the same meaning when used in the Conditions.

2. The Property is sold subject to the Incumbrances on the Property and the Buyer will raise no requisitions on them.

3. Subject to the terms of this Agreement and to the Standard Conditions of Sale, the Seller is to transfer the property with the title guarantee specified on the front page.

4. The chattels on the Property and set out on any attached list are included in the sale.

5. The Property is sold with vacant possession on completion.

(or) 5. The Property is sold subject to the following leases or tenancies:

SPECIMEN

Seller's Solicitors : Angel Gabriel & Co., 2 Milky Way, Barnet, Herts. EN5 6AX

Ref: ABC/612   Tel: 01638-1234

Buyer's Solicitors : Peter Wolf & Co., Red Riding Hood Lane, Northtown, Essex 1CD 3LA

Ref: PW/74   Tel: 01234-5678

Standard Conditions of Sale

Enquiries before Contract

Before the Purchaser's solicitors can approve any contract, they must have all details of the registered title and of any unregistered rights or obligations affecting the property. They will also want any other relevant information, such as guarantees for any work done to the property; details of any disputes with neighbours, etc. They will ask certain questions of the Vendor's solicitor in a form of preliminary enquiries or Enquiries Before Contract (Con 29). There is a printed form available with standard enquiries on it or the solicitor can prepare his own form. This form is typed and sent out in duplicate so that when the other solicitors answer the queries, they can keep a copy of the questions and answers.

The questions are posed on the left-hand side of the page, so that the answers can be given alongside the questions. Extra questions may be added if this is desired. When the Vendor's solicitors receive these enquiries, a copy is sent to the Vendor for him to answer as best he can. When they receive his replies back they complete the form in duplicate, with the answers on the right-hand side of the page and return one copy to the Purchaser's solicitors. The form should be signed and dated before it is sent out.

Where the Conveyancing Protocol (see later in this chapter) is adopted for a transaction, the Seller's Property Information Form would replace Con 29. Part II of the Seller's Property Information Form is prepared by the Seller's solicitors and a copy is sent to the Buyer's solicitors with a copy of Part I of the Seller's Property Information Form, which has been completed by the Seller himself. Accompanying these would be another form giving details of fixtures, fittings and contents. Copies should be kept in the file.

Any relevant documents, such as guarantees, etc., should be kept in the file or with the deeds and copies only should be sent to the other party.

Short description of the property re 76 Burnt Oak Road, Moreland

Parties BROWN

to GREEN

SPECIMEN

OYEZ
ENQUIRIES
BEFORE CONTRACT

Please strike out enquiries which are not applicable

Replies are requested to the following enquiries.

*

Proposed Buyer's solicitors.

*

Date *

ENQUIRIES

The replies are as follows.

*

Proposed Seller's solicitors.

Date *

REPLIES

These replies, except in the case of any enquiry expressly requiring a reply from the Seller's solicitors, are given on behalf of the proposed Seller and without responsibility on the part of his solicitors, their partners or employees. They are believed to be correct but the accuracy is not guaranteed and they do not obviate the need to make appropriate searches, enquiries and inspections.

1. Boundaries

(A) To whom do all the boundary walls, fences, hedges and ditches belong?

(B) If no definite indications exist, which has the Seller maintained or regarded as his responsibility?

1. All fences belong to the property.

2. Disputes

Is the Seller aware of any past or current disputes regarding boundaries or other matters relating to the property or its use, or relating to any neighbouring property?

2. None so far as the vendor is aware.

3. Notices

Please give particulars of all notices relating to the property, or to matters likely to affect its use or enjoyment, that the Seller (or, to his knowledge, any predecessor) has given or received.

3. None so far as the vendor is aware.

4. Guarantees etc.

(A) Please supply a copy of any of the following of which the Buyer is to have the benefit:

agreement, covenant, guarantee, warranty, bond, certificate, indemnity and insurance policy,

relating to any of the following matters, and affecting the property, any part of it, or any building of which it forms part:

construction, repair, replacement, treatment or improvement of the fabric; maintenance of any accessway; construction costs of any road (including lighting, drainage and crossovers) to which the property fronts, and adoption charges for such a road; defective title; breach of restrictive covenant.

(B) What has become apparent, which might give rise to a claim under any document mentioned in (A), and what claims have third parties made, and has notice of such a claim been given?

4.
(A) There are none with the title deeds and the vendor believes there are none.

(B) Nothing so far as the vendor is aware. The purchaser must rely on inspection and survey.

5. Services and Facilities

(A) Does the property have drainage, water, electricity and gas services and are they all connected to the mains?

(B) Are any of the following facilities either shared, or enjoyed by exercising rights over other property?

access for light and air; access for pedestrians and vehicles; emergency escape routes; access and facilities for repair, maintenance and replacement; pipes and wires for services not mentioned in (A).

If so, please give particulars (including copies of relevant documents; liabilities for carrying out work and for making payment; work proposed, in hand, and completed but not paid for).

5.
(A) Yes

(B) No

SPECIMEN

6. Adverse Rights

(A) Please give details of any rights of facilities over the property to which anyone other than the owner is entitled, or which any such person currently enjoys.

(B) (i) Please give the full names, and ages if under 18, of all persons in actual occupation of the property.

(ii) What legal or equitable interest in the property has each of those persons?

(C) Is the Seller aware of any other overriding interests as defined by the Land Registration Act 1925, s. 70(1)?

7. Restrictions

Have all restrictions affecting the property or its use been observed up to the date hereof? If not, please give details.

8. Planning

(A) When did the present use of the property commence?

(B) Please supply a copy of any planning permission authorising or imposing conditions upon this use, and authorising the erection or retention of the buildings now on the property.

(C) Please supply a copy of any bye-law approval or building regulations consent relating to the buildings now on the property.

9. Fixtures, Fittings etc.

(A) Does the sale include all of the following items now on the property, and attached to or growing in it?

Trees, shrubs, plants, flowers, and garden produce. Greenhouses, garden sheds and garden ornaments. Aerials. Fitted furniture and shelves. Electric switches, points and wall and ceiling fittings.

(B) What fixtures to the property are not included in the sale?

(C) If any central heating or other oil is to be sold to the Buyer, what arrangements are proposed?

10. Outgoings

What periodic charges affect the property or its occupier, apart from council tax and water services charge?

11. Completion

(A) How long after exchange of contracts will the Seller be able to give vacant possession of the whole of the property?

(B) The Buyer's solicitors wish to complete by adopting the Law Society's Code for Completion by Post (1984 edition). Do the Seller's solicitors agree?

© 1998 **OYEZ** The Solicitors' Law Stationery Society Ltd, Oyez House, 7 Spa Road, London SE16 3QQ

10.98 F35632

5033028

Conveyancing 29 (Short)

CONVEYANCING

Exchanging Contracts

Once the Purchaser's solicitor receives the replies to Enquiries Before Contract, the searches back from the local authority, the office copy entries and is satisfied that all is clear, he can go ahead and approve the draft contract.

The parties will agree on a completion date, i.e., the day the purchase money is handed over in exchange for the title deeds and other formalities are completed to finalise the transaction. This completion date will be inserted into the contract.

If the draft contract is unaltered it can be used for signature, otherwise a fresh one may need to be re-typed. A copy has to be sent to the other solicitor for his client's signature. Clients either call in to the office to sign their contract or do this through the post. The contract must not yet be dated at this stage. It will be dated the day it is exchanged.

The contracts signed by all parties are then exchanged between solicitors so that each party holds the copy of the contract signed by the other. Even if it has been signed, it is not yet binding until it has been exchanged. It is normal for solicitors to agree by telephone that contracts are exchanged at a certain day and time and then put them in the post to the other solicitors. This telephone agreement assists greatly especially where there is a 'chain' of Purchasers and Vendors. *Never* agree to exchange contracts without first having explicit permission from a fee earner. When contracts are exchanged you may hear of reference being made to Formula A, B or C. These are procedures for exchange of contracts laid down by the Law Society and are the responsibility of the fee earner. Once contracts have been exchanged, the Purchaser normally insures the property and this is something his solicitor may help him with.

Once contracts are exchanged, a deposit may be paid by the Purchaser to the Vendor. This is normally 10% of the purchase price and the sum paid will be deducted from the final price at completion. If the Purchaser does not complete the purchase, the Vendor can keep the deposit, unless there is a very good reason for not proceeding. In some cases, instead of paying a deposit, the Purchaser may take out an insurance policy whereby the insurance company will pay the money if he does not proceed with the purchase after exchange of contracts. This type of insurance is known as a deposit guarantee scheme.

The Purchaser's solicitor also has to ensure that the balance of the purchase money — 'completion monies' — will be available. This usually entails correspondence with the Purchaser's building society. (See the section on Mortgages below.)

Requisitions on Title

The Purchaser's solicitor puts final questions to the Vendor's solicitors to ensure nothing has altered since the Enquiries before Contract were answered and also puts any additional queries he may have. These are called Requisitions on Title. There are a couple of different types of this Form; Con 28B is shown here. They are typed and sent out in duplicate in the same format as Enquiries Before Contract. The printed forms available can be for either freehold or leasehold property, or both. Requisitions are signed and dated by each party's solicitors as they are sent out and returned. The answers to the requisitions include details about water rates, service charges, etc. If these have been paid in advance, they will have to be apportioned, i.e., the Purchaser will have to pay for the share for the period of time the Vendor has already paid in advance, for example, the Vendor has paid a charge up to August but the completion date is in the middle of June. The Purchaser will get the benefit from the date of completion to August so he must pay to the Vendor the amount of that charge from completion date to August.

Where the National Conveyancing Protocol (see later) has been adopted, Form Prop 7, Completion Information and Requisitions on Title, will be used.

These requisitions are copyright and may not be reproduced

Short description of the property *re* ..... 76 Burnt Oak Road, Moreland .....

Parties ..... BROWN .....

to ..... GREEN .....

SPECIMEN

—— *OYEZ* ——
REQUISITIONS
ON TITLE
(For use where Enquiries before Contract have already been answered)

Please strike out any requisitions not applicable.

---

1. PREVIOUS ENQUIRIES

If the enquiries before contract replied to on behalf of the Seller were repeated here, would the replies now be the same as those previously given? If not, please give full particulars of any variation.

1. These are confirmed unless varied by correspondence.

---

2. OUTGOINGS AND APPORTIONMENTS

(A) On completion the Seller must produce receipts for the last payments of outgoings, of which either he claims reimbursement of an advance payment or arrears could be recovered from the Buyer.

(B) (i) In the case of a leasehold property or property subject to a legal rentcharge, the receipt for rent due on the last rent day before the day of completion, as well as the receipt for the last fire insurance premium, must be produced on completion.

(ii) Does the former receipt contain any reference to a breach of any of the covenants and conditions contained in the lease or grant?

(C) Please send a completion statement.

2.
(A) Confirmed

(B) N/A

(C) Herewith

---

3. TITLE DEEDS

A. *Unregistered land*

(i) Which abstracted documents of title will be delivered to the Buyer on completion?

(ii) Who will give to the Buyer the statutory acknowledgment and undertaking for the production and safe custody of those not handed over?

(iii) Why will any documents not handed over be retained?

B. *Registered land*

(i) If the Land Registry has approved an estate lay-out plan for use with official searches of part of the land in the title, on what date was it approved?

(ii) If the Seller's land certificate is on deposit at the Land Registry, what is the deposit number?

3.
(A) N/A

(B)
(i) N/A

(ii) N/A

---

4. MORTGAGES

(A) Please specify those mortgages or charges which will be discharged on or before completion.

(B) In respect of each subsisting mortgage or charge:

(i) Will a vacating receipt, discharge of registered charge or consent to dealing, entitling the Buyer to take the property freed from it, be handed over on completion?

(ii) If not, will the Seller's solicitor give a written undertaking on completion to hand one over later?

(iii) If an undertaking is proposed, what are the suggested terms of it?

4.
(A) Mortgage dated 7th July 1994 between Givemore Building Society and Albert Francis Brown.

(B) Yes.

SPECIMEN

5. POSSESSION

(A) (i) Vacant possession of the whole of the property must be given on completion.

   (ii) Has every person in occupation of all or any part of the property agreed to vacate on or before completion?

   (iii) What arrangements will be made to deliver the keys to the Buyer?

Or

(B) The Seller must on completion hand over written authorities for future rents to be paid to the Buyer or his agents.

5.

(A) (i) Confirmed

   (ii) Yes

   (iii) The Vendor and Purchaser have made their own arrangements.

6. NOTICES

Please give the name and address of any solicitor, residential tenant or other person to whom notice of any dealing with the property must be given.

6. None that the Vendor knows of.

7. COMPLETION ARRANGEMENTS

Please answer any of the following requisitions against which X has been placed in the box.

7.

☐ (A) Where will completion take place?

☒ (B) We should like to remit the completion monies direct to your bank account. If you agree, please give the name and branch of your bank, its sort code, and the title and number of the account to be credited.

☐ (C) In whose favour and for what amounts will banker's drafts be required on completion?

☐ (D) Please confirm that you will comply with the Law Society's Code for Completion by Post (1998 edition).

(B) Greenback Bank plc
62 Southside Avenue
Moreland, Herts.
SG4 2AP

Sort Code: 46 00 21

Account: Angel Gabriel & Co
(No.1 A/c) No. 123456000.

The right is reserved to make further requisitions which may arise on the replies to the above, the usual searches and enquiries before completion, or otherwise.

Note. — Requisitions founded on the title or contract must be added to the above.

DATED   *   DATED   *

       *   *Buyer's Solicitor.*   *   *Seller's Solicitor.*

1998 Edition
7.98 F35399
5032056
★ ★ ★ ★

Conveyancing 28B

Transfer

The document which actually transfers ownership of freehold registered land is a deed called a Transfer. This is prepared by the Purchaser's solicitors on a TR or TP form. Here we are using Form TR1 (transfer of whole). A different form is used for certain other matters, such as where the property is part of a larger registered title, e.g., a new house on an estate which is registered under one title number and it has been divided into plots. The cost of the property (the consideration) is shown on the form and this is given in both words and figures. The Transfer form has numbered panels. Do not alter these numbers even if there is nothing to go in a particular numbered panel. Stamp duty is payable on certain documents, such as a Transfer, and such documents contain a certificate of value. This states that the consideration or purchase price does not exceed a certain amount, or that the transaction does not form part of a series of transactions whereby the consideration or purchase price exceeds a certain amount. These amounts are divided into certain bands and stamp duty will be payable according to the relevant band. It could also be that the value is below a specified amount where no stamp duty is payable. (See also page 302 regarding stamp duty.)

If there is not enough room on the printed form, a continuation sheet in Land Registry Form CS must be used and then stapled to the form of which it has become a continuation. Form CS is for use with several Land Registry forms where the panel on a form does not allow enough room for the information to be provided. Form CS is self-explanatory, asking you to type on it the number of the form which you are continuing from, e.g., TR1. Also to be included are the title number of the property, the panel number to be continued, i.e., if you need to expand on the information for panel number 12, you would state this on the Form CS. Finally, Form CS asks you to provide the sheet number you are now working on and the total number of sheets.

Once the draft Transfer form is approved by the Vendor's solicitors, the top copy is returned to the Purchaser's solicitors. If necessary, a fresh copy will be typed or 'engrossed' for signature but if no amendments have been made, it is quite usual to use the draft. Do not type a date on to the Transfer. This must be done only when completion of the transaction is to take place and must be authorised by the person who is dealing with the matter.

Only the Vendor has to sign the Transfer, which is a deed (see page 271), unless it contains any covenants by the Purchaser or where there are joint Purchasers, when it must be signed by all parties. Once the Transfer has been signed by the Purchaser(s) if necessary, it is then sent to the Vendor's solicitors for their client's signature.

If you are typing a particular type of transfer where it is permitted not to use a TR or TP Form, or another similar deed which may be typed on to A4 paper, it would be typed 'back to back', i.e., without any blank pages, but you must check your firm's requirements here. Again, whether the document is in single or double line spacing is something for you to check with your firm.

A Transfer on the printed form will not require a backsheet or a frontsheet (see pages 319 and 20) but other longer deeds, such as a Conveyance (see section on Unregistered Land) or Lease (see later), do usually need one or the other. The backsheet shows the date of the document, the parties, the address of the property and describes what the document is, e.g., 'Lease', and it gives the details of the firm of solicitors preparing the document.

If you have to type a sum of money, it is normal to set this out in words first and then in figures in brackets, e.g., TWENTY THOUSAND POUNDS (£20,000). Some firms like this written in capitals as shown. Dates are also sometimes written in words instead of figures, e.g., 10 September 1999 would be written as 'the tenth day of September One thousand nine hundred and ninety-nine'. In longer documents (see example of Lease) each numbered paragraph often has the first word of each paragraph and certain other key words, typed in capitals and perhaps underlined. For further information on preparation and presentation of documents, see Chapter 1. Drafts of these documents (not the printed forms) are normally typed on one side of the paper only in one and a half or double line spacing, and the pages should be numbered.

Remember, when you have engrossed a document which has involved any re-typing, such as amendments being made to the draft, you should proofread it, i.e., read it out aloud with someone else checking the draft. This helps to eliminate any typing errors. Firms also differ in their ideas about sewing up documents. Engrossments may be sewn up with green tape or bound by machines. (See the sections in Chapter 1 on Tips on Proofreading and Sewing up Documents.)

Completion Statement

The Purchaser's solicitors prepare a completion statement (see example) for their client, to show exactly what money will be needed for completion day. This usually includes the firm's bill.

**Transfer of whole
of registered title(s)** *SPECIMEN* HM Land Registry **TR1**

(if you need more room than is provided for in a panel, use continuation sheet CS and staple to this form)

1. Stamp Duty

Place "X" in the box that applies and complete the box in the appropriate certificate.

☐ I/We hereby certify that this instrument falls within category ☐ in the Schedule to the Stamp Duty (Exempt Instruments) Regulations 1987

☒ It is certified that the transaction effected does not form part of a larger transaction or of a series of transactions in respect of which the amount or value or the aggregate amount or value of the consideration exceeds the sum of

£ 250,000

2. Title Number(s) of the Property *(leave blank if not yet registered)*

HD 12345

3. Property   76 Burnt Oak Road, Moreland, Herts. EN7 8CB

If this transfer is made under section 37 of the Land Registration Act 1925 following a not-yet-registered dealing with part only of the land in a title, or is made under rule 72 of the Land Registration Rules 1925, include a reference to the last preceding document of title containing a description of the property.

4. Date   *

5. Transferor *(give full names and Company's Registered Number if any)*

Albert Francis Brown

6. Transferee for entry on the register *(Give full names and Company's Registered Number if any; for Scottish Co. Reg. Nos., use an SC prefix. For foreign companies give territory in which incorporated.)*

Elizabeth Mary Green

Unless otherwise arranged with Land Registry headquarters, a certified copy of the transferee's constitution (in English or Welsh) will be required if it is a body corporate but is not a company registered in England and Wales or Scotland under the Companies Acts.

7. Transferee's intended address(es) for service in the U.K. *(including postcode)* **for entry on the register**

76 Burnt Oak Road, Moreland, Herts. EN7 8CB

8. The Transferor transfers the property to the Transferee.

9. Consideration *(Place "X" in the box that applies. State clearly the currency unit if other than sterling. If none of the boxes applies, insert an appropriate memorandum in the additional provisions panel.)*

☒ The Transferor has received from the Transferee for the property the sum of *(in words and figures)*

ninety-six thousand pounds (£96,000)

☐ *(insert other receipt as appropriate)*

☐ The Transfer is not for money or anything which has a monetary value

P.T.O.

10. The Transferor transfers with *(place "X" in the box which applies and add any modifications)*

[x] full title guarantee   [ ] limited title guarantee

SPECIMEN

11. Declaration of trust *Where there is more than one transferee, place "X" in the appropriate box.*

[ ] The transferees are to hold the property on trust for themselves as joint tenants.

[ ] The transferees are to hold the property on trust for themselves as tenants in common in equal shares.

[ ] The transferees are to hold the property *(complete as necessary)*

12. Additional Provision(s) *Insert here any required or permitted statement, certificate or application and any agreed covenants, declarations, etc.*

13. *The Transferors and all other necessary parties should execute this transfer as a deed using the space below. Forms of execution are given in Schedule 3 to the Land Registration Rules 1925. If the transfer contains transferees' covenants or declarations or contains an application by them (e.g. for a restriction), it must also be executed by the Transferees.*

Signed as a deed by   Sign here
ALBERT FRANCIS BROWN
in the presence of:

Signature of witness....................
Name (in BLOCK CAPITALS) ....
Address ....

Signed as a deed by   Sign here
ELIZABETH MARY GREEN
in the presence of:

Signature of witness ....
Name (in BLOCK CAPITALS) ....
Address ....

[Note: The Transfer only has to be signed by the transferee under certain circumstances, e.g., if the transferee is entering into a covenant or making a declaration.]

OYEZ The Solicitors' Law Stationery Society Ltd, Oyez House, 7 Spa Road, London SE16 3QQ   1.98 F34697
5061088

**Continuation sheet
for use with
application and
disposition forms**

HM Land Registry

SPECIMEN

CS

---

1. Continued from Form [   ]   Title number(s) [   ]

---

2. *Before each continuation, state panel to be continued, e.g. "Panel 12 continued".*

Continuation sheet [   ] of [   ]

*(insert sheet number and total number of continuation sheets
e.g. "sheet 1 of 3")*

P.T.O.

Example

COMPLETION STATEMENT

Sale of 2 Railway Cuttings

Sale price			£65,000.00
Less:	Mortgage redemption	30,000.00	
	Deeds redemption fee	10.00	
	Legal fees, etc. (as per attached bill)	250.00	30,260.00
	Due to you:		34,740.00

Purchase of 76 Burnt Oak Road

Purchase price			£96,000.00
Less:	Mortgage	35,000.00	
	Sale proceeds from 2 Railway Cuttings	34,740.00	
	Bank loan	2,000.00	71,740.00
			24,260.00
Plus:	Chattels	500.00	
	Search fees, etc.	40.00	
	Apportionment of outgoings	200.00	
	Legal fees, etc.	750.00	1,490.00
	Balance due to complete		£25,750.00

E. & O.E.

Land Registry search with 'Priority'

About ten days before completion, the Purchaser's solicitors will make an application for an official search with priority (Form 94A) to the Land Registry either by first class post or by another permitted method (see below). Form 94B (search of part) is used where the property is part of a larger property registered under one title number, such as a new house on a building estate where the whole estate is divided into plots. The official search will ascertain whether any further entries have been registered with the Land Registry since office copy entries were last received. See also page 282 regarding searches made by telephone, fax and computerised on-line access. The certificate received back from the Land Registry shows the 'priority date', i.e., the date by which the Purchaser must lodge at the Land Registry the Transfer and any supporting papers for registration as the new owner. The priority date gives a period of 30 working days. Up until this date the Land Registry guarantees that no other entries will be registered ahead of the new owner. The relevant documents must be lodged with the Land Registry by 9.30 am on the date given as the priority date.

Application by Purchaser[a] for Official Search with priority of the whole of the land in either a registered title or a pending first registration application

HM Land Registry

SPECIMEN

Form **94A**

Land Registration (Official Searches) Rules 1993

STEVENAGE	District Land Registry [b]
BRICKDALE HOUSE	
SWINGATE	
STEVENAGE, HERTS	
SG1 1XG	
DX 6099 Stevenage (2)	

Small **raised letters in bold** type refer to explanatory notes overleaf.

Please complete the numbered panels

1 Title number (one only per form) - enter the title number of the registered land or that allotted to the pending first registration.

HD 12345

2 Registered proprietor(s) / Applicant(s) for first registration[c] - enter FULL name(s) either of the registered proprietor(s) of the land in the above title **or** of the person(s) applying for first registration of the land specified in panel 8.

SURNAME / ~~COMPANY NAME~~   BROWN

FORENAME(S):   ALBERT FRANCIS

SURNAME / COMPANY NAME:

FORENAME(S):

3 Search from date - for a search of a **registered title** enter in the box a date falling within (a) of the definition of search from date in rule 2(1).[d] Note: If the date entered is not such a date the application may be rejected. In the case of a **pending first registration** search, enter the letters 'FR'.

*

4 Applicant(s) - enter FULL name of each purchaser, **or** lessee **or** chargee.

ELIZABETH MARY GREEN

5 Reason for application - I certify that the applicant(s) intend(s) to:- (enter X in the appropriate box)

| X | P | purchase | | L | take a lease of | | C | take a registered charge on |

(enter X in the appropriate box)

| X | the **whole** of the land in the above registered title **or** |

| | the **whole** of the land in the pending first registration application referred to above. |

6 Enter the key number[e] (if any) and the name and (DX) address of the person lodging the application (use **BLOCK LETTERS**).

Key number: | 1 | 2 | 3 | 4 | 5 | | |

Name: PETER WOLF & CO

DX No: 7749   DX Exchange: NORTHTOWN

Address including postcode (if DX not used):

Reference: [f]   PW/74

7 Enter, using BLOCK LETTERS, the name and either address (including postcode) OR (if applicable) the DX No and exchange of the person to whom the result is to be sent. (**Leave blank if result is to be sent to the address in panel 6.**)

Reference: [f]

8 Property details
Administrative area [g]

MORELAND, HERTFORDSHIRE
Address (including postcode) or short description:

76 BURNT OAK ROAD
MORELAND
EN7 8CB

9 Type of search (enter X in the appropriate box)

| X | **Registered land search** Application is made to ascertain whether any adverse entry[b] has been made in the register or day list since the date shown in panel 3 above. |

| | **Pending first registration search** Application is made to ascertain whether any adverse entry has been made in the day list since the date of the pending first registration application referred to above. |

10   **PAYMENT OF FEE** [i]

Please enter X in the appropriate box.

| | The Land Registry fee of £ _____ accompanies this application; **or** |

| X | Please debit the Credit Account mentioned in panel 6 with the appropriate fee payable under the current Land Registration Fees Order. |

Note: **If the fee is not paid by either of the above methods the application may be rejected.**

Signature

Date   *   Telephone   01234-5678

Completion

Completion monies (the balance due to complete the purchase) can be paid by way of a banker's draft or building society cheque. More usually, the money is electronically transferred by the Purchaser's solicitors' bank to the Vendor's solicitors' bank account. The other formalities then normally take place through the post or DX in accordance with the code laid down by the Law Society. However, completion can be carried out personally by the Purchaser's solicitor attending at the offices of the Vendor's solicitors. Arrangements are made for the collection of the keys to the property once completion has taken place. The keys are often held by estate agents and are handed over by the estate agent to the Purchaser once it has been confirmed that completion has taken place. Once you are experienced in conveyancing matters, you might be asked to attend a completion yourself. You will have to ensure that you take all the correct documents with you and receive back the correct documents. The fee earner will tell you exactly what is required. If you encounter any problems at all on completion then you must telephone back to your office straight away before completing.

Paying Stamp Duty

Stamp duty is payable to the Inland Revenue on certain property transactions, including those where the value of the property exceeds a certain amount, or where the transaction is part of a larger transaction where the total value exceeds that amount. The stamp duty is calculated according to which band the value of the property falls into, i.e., if the value of the property is under a certain amount, then no stamp duty is payable; if it falls into the next category, stamp duty is payable at a certain percentage of the purchase price; the next category incurs a higher percentage and the next is higher still. The band within which the property falls is certified on the deed transferring the property, for example, if the property has been sold for £185,000, this falls within the band having a value of between £60,000 and £250,000 and it would be certified that the value of the transaction did not exceed £250,000, rather than merely certifying the actual purchase price. This certificate of value on the deed has specific wording as follows:

It is certified that the transaction effected does not form part of a larger transaction or of a series of transactions in respect of which the amount or value or the aggregate amount or value of the consideration exceeds the sum of £*******

This means that not only does the particular property not exceed the stated value, but also that the property does not form part of another transaction which exceeds that value.

After completion, the Purchaser's solicitors complete a Particulars Delivered form (STAMPS L(A) 451) known as a 'PD' form. 'Particulars Delivered' means that details of the transaction have been notified to the Inland Revenue so that they can update their records of land transactions. The form has to be taken or sent, together with the Transfer (or other document transferring title) and stamp duty payable, to the Inland Revenue Stamp Office. Most solicitors' firms are registered with the Inland Revenue and are given a registered number. This is written on their cheques to the Inland Revenue when paying stamp duty. By doing this, the Inland Revenue will not wait until the cheque has been cleared and this therefore helps to speed matters up. Cheques should be made payable to 'Inland Revenue only — Stamp Duties'. The document will be stamped by the Inland Revenue at the top to show that the stamp duty has been paid.

If there is no stamp duty payable to the Inland Revenue, the PD form is sent to the Land Registry with the application for registration (see below).

Inland Revenue

PARTICULARS OF INSTRUMENTS TRANSFERRING OR LEASING LAND

SPECIMEN

SECTION 28 FINANCE ACT 1931
as amended by the Land Commission Act 1967
and Section 89 Finance Act 1985

FOR OFFICIAL USE

VO No. ....

PD No. ....

ANALYSIS CODE ....

DESC ....

GV/NAV ....

DW CODE ....

....

RETURN ....

O.S. No. ....

OTHER ....

1. Description of Instrument   **TRANSFER**

2. Date of Instrument   **22 July 1999**

3. Name and address of Transferor or Lessor *(Block Letters)*

ALBERT FRANCIS BROWN
76 BURNT OAK ROAD
MORELAND
HERTS
EN9 7HP

4. Name and address of Transferee or Lessee *(Block Letters)*

ELIZABETH MARY GREEN
46 OLD ROAD
NORTHTOWN
HERTS
WN4 7AB

5. Situation of the land. Sufficient information must be given to enable the land to be identified accurately, e.g., by including any dimensions stated in the instrument and by attaching a plan to this form or by describing the boundaries in full. For premises the full postal address including the post code is required   Please indicate whether a plan is provided in the appropriate box.

76 BURNT OAK ROAD, MORELAND, EN7 8CB

Plan Attached Yes ☐
Plan Attached No ☒

COUNTY ...... HERTFORDSHIRE ......   RATING AUTHORITY ...... MORELAND DISTRICT COUNCIL ......

6. Estate or Interest Transferred. Where the transaction is the assignment or grant of a lease, or the transfer of a fee simple subject to a lease, the terms of the lease, the date of commencement of the term and the rent reserved must be stated.

FREEHOLD

7. Consideration   State separately:

(a) any capital payment, with the date when due if otherwise than the execution of instrument: **£96,000**

(b) does the consideration stated include a charge to VAT

~~Yes~~/No

If Yes please state the amount paid:

(c) any debt released, covenanted to be paid or to which the transaction is made subject:

(d) any periodical payment (including any charge) covenanted to be paid:

(e) any terms surrendered:

(f) any land exchanged:

(g) any other thing representing money or money's worth:

8. Any Minerals, Mineral Rights, Sporting Rights, Timber or Easements reserved: (on a separate sheet if necessary)

9. Any Restrictions, Covenants or Conditions affecting the value of the estate or interest transferred or granted: (on a separate sheet if necessary)

10. Signature of Transferee or Lessees or person on his behalf:

.... Date .... *

11. Name and Address of the Transferor's or Lessor's Solicitor: *(Block Letters)*

ANGEL GABRIEL & CO
2 MILKY WAY
BARNET
HERTS   EN5 6AX

12. Name, Address and Telephone Number of Signatory if other than Transferee or Lessee: *(Block Letters)*

PETER WOLF & CO
RED RIDING HOOD LANE
NORTHTOWN
ESSEX 1CD 3LA

STAMPS L(A) 451   (3/95)

CONVEYANCING

Registering the New Owner

After completion, the documents have to be submitted promptly to the Land Registry so that the Register may be updated and a Land Certificate prepared showing the new Purchaser as the registered proprietor. The documents are usually submitted with Land Registry Application to Change the Register, Form AP1. This form is currently being amended by the Land Registry so that just the one form can be used for applications concerning dealings relating to the whole of titles or for dealings relating to part of a title. The example AP1 shown here is the version current at the time of writing, and it is very similar to the anticipated new form. A 'dealing' is a term for something that affects the registered title to land, such as the sale of the land.

The documents being sent to the Land Registry will be listed on the form. Besides sending original documents, it is sometimes a requirement that certified copies (see below) must be sent as well. If a copy is sent, this must be listed separately as such on the form. The documents that will be sent to the Land Registry are documents such as the Transfer; the new mortgage (or 'charge') and a copy of the charge; and the form of discharge of the Vendor's mortgage (Form DS1) or certified copy (see below). A fee is payable to the Land Registry for this application. The fee will normally be based upon the value of the transaction. Reference cards to assist in the calculation of fees are obtainable from district land registries. Cheques should be made payable to HM Land Registry and you should write the title number or address of the property on the reverse of the cheque. Credit accounts cannot be used for making this application. Because this application contains original deeds and other important documents, it should normally be sent by registered post or by DX (see page 16).

When sending the application to the Land Registry, you should also include a completed acknowledgment form (C4B) so that the Land Registry can return this to you on receipt of the application, so that you will know they have received the application. They will also usually mark on the C4B the likely date that the application will be processed. Ensure that you have kept a copy of your application and Form C4B for your file before sending them to the Land Registry.

Form AP1, together with the relevant documents, must be lodged with the Land Registry within a certain time limit (the time when the 'priority' period expires — see above). The form of discharge of the Vendor's mortgage (Form DS1) may not be available within that time limit because it has to be signed by his lender showing that the mortgage has been repaid. In this case, the Vendor's solicitors will supply an undertaking to the Purchaser's solicitors that they will forward to them the signed DS1 as soon as they receive it. A certified copy of this undertaking will be sent to the Land Registry and DS1 will be sent on to them when it becomes available. However, it is preferable for the DS1 to be sent wherever possible with the other documents, so as to save time and expense, and there is usually plenty of time within which to do this. See also page 321 on Paying off the Mortgage.

A certified copy is a photocopy of the original document, marked and signed to the effect that it is a true copy. You should ensure that all copies are legible and any plans, etc. are coloured and marked the same as the original. See page 18 regarding copying documents. On the copy of the document, usually at the top, words in the following format are typed certifying the document as a true copy:

We hereby certify this to be a true copy of the original.
Dated this   *   day of   *   2000

This is signed by the solicitor dealing with the matter and the firm's name and address are also given.

Registration can take many weeks, depending on how busy the Land Registry is. Once the registration is complete, the Land Registry will send the Land Certificate or Charge Certificate to the solicitors registering the property. If the property is mortgaged, the solicitors will then send the Charge Certificate and other documents on to the building society. If it is not mortgaged, the new owner may wish to keep the deeds himself or ask for them to be placed in the firm's safe.

Application to change the register *SPECIMEN* HM Land Registry

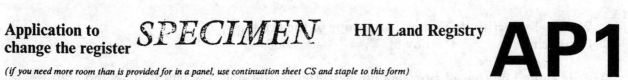

AP1

(if you need more room than is provided for in a panel, use continuation sheet CS and staple to this form)

1. Administrative area(s) and postcode *(if known)*	Moreland – Hertfordshire EN3 2NL

2. Title Number(s) HD 12345	**Deposit No.** *(if any)*

3. Application, Priority and Fees

Nature of applications in priority order	Value £	Fees paid £
1. Discharge		
2. Transfer	96,000	*
3. Charge	35,000	*
4.		
5.		
6.		
TOTAL £		

FOR OFFICIAL USE ONLY
Record of fees paid

Particulars of under/over payments

Accompanying cheques or postal orders should be made payable to "HM Land Registry".

4. Documents lodged with this form

1. Charge Certificate	2. Form DS1	3. Transfer
4. Charge	5. Copy Charge	6.
7.	8.	9.
10.	11.	12.
13.	14.	15.

5. Application lodged by

Land Registry Key No.   12345
Name   Peter Wolf & Co
~~Address~~/DX No.   7749 NORTHTOWN

Reference   PW/74

Telephone No. 01234-5678	Fax No. 01234-8904

FOR OFFICIAL USE ONLY
Codes
Dealing

Status

6. Where the Registry is to deal with someone else

The Registry will send any land/charge certificate to the person named in panel 5 above and will, if necessary, contact that person.
You can change this by placing "X" against one or more of the statements and completing the details below.

[X] Please send any land/charge certificate to the person shown below

[ ] Please raise any requisitions or queries with the person shown below

[ ] Please issue to the person shown below the following document(s)

If you have placed "X" against any statement above, complete the following name and address details:

Name   The Deeds Administrator

Address/DX No.   Givemore Building Society
Peartree House, 1 Little Road
Southtown, Herts   EN3 8LX

Reference 86403	Telephone No. 01876-2389

P.T.O.

7. Address for service *place "X" in the appropriate box*

[X] Enter the proprietors' address(es) for service from the transfer/assent

[ ] Enter the proprietors' address(es) for service in the U.K., *including postcode*, as follows:

SPECIMEN

8. Information in respect of a chargee or mortgagee
Do not give this information if a Land Registry MD reference is printed on the charge, unless the charge has been transferred. Full name and address within the U.K. (including postcode) for service of notices and correspondence of the present proprietor of each charge or mortgage to be registered. *Where the owner is a company include Company's Registered Number if any; for Scottish Co. Reg. Nos., use an SC prefix. For foreign companies give territory in which incorporated.*

```
Givemore Building Society
Peartree House
1 Little Road
Southtown
Herts  EN3 8LX
```

Unless otherwise arranged with Land Registry headquarters, the following documents are required:
(i) the original and a certified copy of any incorporated documents as defined in r.139, Land Registration Rules 1925;
(ii) a certified copy of the chargee's constitution (in English or Welsh) if it is a body corporate but is not a company registered in England and Wales or Scotland under the Companies Acts.

9. Signature(s) of person(s)
lodging this form _____ * _____ Date _____ *
(A form lodged by solicitors/licensed conveyancers must be signed in the firm's name)

This form is not part of the statutory form. Its completion is voluntary. No individual property or person will be identifiable from the information collected. The information will be used to improve the Registry's forecasting and its published Price Reports and may be supplied to the Office of National Statistics.

The property is
[X] a single residential property with vacant possession

It is a [X] secondhand [ ] new [ ] newly converted

[ ] flat/maisonette [X] terraced house [ ] semi-detached house [ ] detached house

with [ ] no more than one [X] two [ ] three [ ] four [ ] five or more bedrooms

[ ] other residential

[ ] non-residential

OYEZ The Solicitors' Law Stationery Society Ltd, Oyez House, 7 Spa Road, London SE16 3QQ

1.98 F34699
5061589

Unregistered Land

Land in all areas is now subject to compulsory registration and where the property has not been previously registered there are some additional procedures to be dealt with.

Proof of Title to Unregistered Land

Because transactions relating to unregistered land have not been registered with the Land Registry, the person owning the land must be able to produce all old deeds and documents to prove he has good title (or ownership) to that land. Usually, he has to be able to prove good title back through the last 15 years. The transaction chosen to begin proving title is known as the 'root of title'.

Abstract of Title

It is sometimes necessary to refer to an earlier deed which may be mentioned in the documents and this document may be 'abstracted'. Abstracting is a very specialised procedure and would normally be done by a fee earner. It used to be prepared on brief paper (A3 size). It is headed 'Abstract of Title' and gives the address of the property and the names of the parties to each document. If you see an Abstract you will notice that everything is written in the past tense and is in an abbreviated form, e.g., 'Witnessed in the presence of' becomes 'Witned in psce of', 'The Vendor hereby acknowledges' becomes 'Vdr thby acknd', and so on. In the margin it shows the date of the original document and states that it has been examined with the original, e.g., '1 May 1999. exd. with orig. at the offices of Smith & Jones, 1 High Street, Barnet'. It must also show details of the stamp duty (see page 302) that was paid on the original deed, e.g., 'Stp. £10'. Thus, an Abstract is an abbreviated form of an original document. If you do speedwriting you will get the idea very fast!

Epitome of Title

Alternatively, and this is the preferred method these days, photocopies of all deeds and documents constituting proof of title are provided, together with an 'epitome of title'. This is really a schedule listing the deeds of which copies are supplied.

The schedule will show the year that it is being prepared, with details of the property concerned. The name and date of each document will be typed in date order, with the oldest first and the most recent last, also giving the names of the parties to the document (if any), such as the names of any Purchaser and Vendor. Each document should be numbered consecutively in the schedule. It should also state whether the original document or a photocopy will accompany the schedule. The schedule may even include details of documents that will not be supplied, such as death and marriage certificates, because they may show that ownership in the property has passed to someone else.

[Insert the year of typing the epitome]

Epitome of Title

Relating to freehold/leasehold property *[delete as appropriate]*

Known as: *[insert the description (address) of the property]*

Date of document	Number of document	Details of document	Parties	Whether photocopy or abstract	Whether original to be handed over

The typed schedule should be attached securely to the documents, often by sewing them together in the top left-hand corner (see page 32), or by using some other form of fastening, such as a treasury tag. Before land was registered, the document most commonly used to transfer the land was called a Conveyance. It is the equivalent of a Transfer (see above) but is a longer document. A Conveyance may still be used for the transfer of unregistered land only, although a Transfer may be used instead. Remember, when photocopying deeds, check that the copies are legible and if there is a plan in the original document, you must colour the photocopy to look the same as the original (see Chapter 1 regarding deeds and documents).

Registration

After completion of the purchase of unregistered freehold land, the solicitor for the Purchaser has two months in which to lodge the deeds with the Land Registry, together with the application for first registration on Form FR1. This form must be accompanied by the deeds and certain other documents listed on form DL (in duplicate). Where you have to send a copy of a deed, rather than an original, you must indicate this on the form by typing, e.g., 'Copy Conveyance' or 'Certified copy Conveyance', whatever is appropriate. Before sending the deeds to the Land Registry, ensure that you have kept photocopies on the file. The appropriate fee must also be sent to the Land Registry. In due course, the Land Registry will send the Land Certificate to the Purchaser's solicitors.

If you run out of space when typing form DL, you should type on the back of the form and if you need more space than that, you should type a continuation sheet using the same layout. However, you must not use another Form DL or Form CS.

CONVEYANCING

First Registration Application	*SPECIMEN*	HM Land Registry	**FR1**

(if you need more room than is provided for in a panel, use continuation sheet CS and staple to this form)

---

1. Administrative area   Moreland – Hertfordshire

---

2. Superior title *(if any)*   **Deposit No.**

---

3. Address (including postcode) or other description of the property to be registered

76 BURNT OAK ROAD, MORELAND, HERTFORDSHIRE, EN7 8CB

On registering a rentcharge, show the address as follows:– "Rentcharge over 2 The Grove, Anytown, Northshire NE2 900".

---

4. Extent to be registered *(place "X" in the appropriate box)*

[x] The property is fully identified on the plan to the ___Conveyance 27.4.99___ *(enter nature and date of deed)*

[ ] The property is fully identified on the attached plan and shown _____ *(enter reference e.g. "edged red")*

[ ] The description in panel 3 is sufficient to enable the property to be fully identified on the O.S. map.

---

5. Application, Priority and Fees

Nature of applications **in priority order**	Value/premium £	Fees paid £
1. **First Registration** of the property	96,000	*
2. Charge	50,000	–
3.		
4.		

TOTAL £ *

Accompanying cheques or postal orders should be made payable to "HM Land Registry".

FOR OFFICIAL USE ONLY
Record of fees paid

Particulars of under/over payments

---

6. The title applied for is *(place "X" in the appropriate box)*

[x] absolute freehold   [ ] absolute leasehold   [ ] good leasehold   [ ] possessory freehold   [ ] possessory leasehold

---

7. Application lodged by

Land Registry Key No.   12345
Name   Peter Wolf & Co
Address/DX No.   DX 7749 NORTHTOWN

Reference   PW/74

Telephone No. 01234-5678	Fax No. 01234-8904

FOR OFFICIAL USE ONLY
Status codes

---

8. Where the Registry is to deal with someone else

The Registry will send any land/charge certificate to the person named in panel 7 above and will, if necessary, contact that person.
You can change this by placing "X" against one or more of the statements and completing the details on Form DL.

[x] Please send any land/charge certificate to the person shown in panel 2 on Form DL

[ ] Please raise any requisitions or queries with the person shown in panel 2 on Form DL

[ ] Please send the document(s) listed in panel 3 on Form DL to the person shown in panel 2

---

9. Full name(s) and address(es) within the U.K. (including postcode) for service of notices and correspondence **of every owner of the land**

Where the owner is a company include Company's Registered Number if any; for Scottish Co. Reg. Nos., use an SC prefix. For foreign company give territory in which incorporated.

Elizabeth Mary Green, 76 Burnt Oak Road, Moreland,
Herts. EN7 8CB

Unless otherwise arranged with Land Registry headquarters, a certified copy of the owner's constitution (in English or Welsh) will be required if it is a body corporate but is not a company registered in England and Wales or Scotland under the Companies Acts.

P.T.O.

10. *Where the owners are joint proprietors, place "X" in the appropriate box.*

☐ The owners are holding the property on trust for themselves as joint tenants.

☐ The owners are holding the property on trust for themselves as tenants in common in equal shares.

☐ The owners are holding the property *(complete as necessary)*

SPECIMEN

---

11. The title is based on the title documents listed on Form DL which are all those which the applicant holds or has control of.
Place "X" in the appropriate box. If applicable complete the second statement; include any interests disclosed only by searches. Any interests disclosed by searches which do not affect the land being registered should be certified.

☒ All rights, interests and claims affecting the property known to the applicant are disclosed in the title documents. There is no-one in adverse possession of the property or any part of it.

☐ In addition to the rights, interests and claims affecting the property disclosed in the title documents, the applicant only knows of the following:

---

12. Information in respect of a chargee or mortgagee
Do not give this information if a Land Registry MD reference is printed on the charge, unless the charge has been transferred.
Full name and address within the U.K. (including postcode) for service of notices and correspondence of the present proprietor of each charge or mortgage to be registered. *Where the proprietor is a company include Company's Registered Number (if any); for Scottish Co. Reg. Nos., use an SC prefix. For foreign companies give territory in which incorporated.*

```
Givemore Building Society
Peartree House
1 Little Road
Southtown
Herts   EN3 8LX
```

Unless otherwise arranged with Land Registry headquarters, the following documents are required:
(i) the original and a certified copy of any incorporated documents as defined in r. 139, Land Registration Rules 1925;
(ii) a certified copy of the chargee's constitution (in English or Welsh) if it is a body corporate but is not a company registered in England and Wales or Scotland under the Companies Acts.

---

13. *Place "X" in this box if you are NOT able to give this certificate* ☐
I/We have investigated or caused to be investigated the title in the usual way on the applicant's behalf on a transaction for value.

---

14. I/We confirm that we have authority to lodge this application and request the Registrar to complete the registration.

Signature of person
lodging this form _____ * _____ Date _____ * _____

(A form lodged by solicitors/licensed conveyancers must be signed in the firm's name)

N.B. Failure to complete the form honestly and with proper care may deprive the applicant of protection under the Land Registration Acts if, as a result, a mistake is made in the register. Any dealing with the land not lodged with this form must be lodged with the appropriate application form and will take priority from the day it is deemed to be delivered.

This form is not part of the statutory form. Its completion is voluntary. No individual property or person will be identifiable from the information collected. The information will be used to improve the Registry's forecasting and its published Price Reports and may be supplied to the Office of National Statistics.

The property is
☒ a single residential property with vacant possession

It is a ☐ secondhand ☐ new ☐ newly converted

☐ flat/maisonette ☒ terraced house ☐ semi-detached house ☐ detached house

with ☐ no more than one ☒ two ☐ three ☐ four ☐ five or more bedrooms

☐ other residential

☐ non-residential

List of Documents

For use with FR1 only
Please complete in duplicate.

HM Land Registry

SPECIMEN

1. Property
76 Burnt Oak Road, Moreland, Herts EN7 8CB

2. Where the Registry is to deal with someone else

Give below the details of the person with whom the Registry should deal as directed in panel 8 of Form FR1.

Name The Deeds Administrator, Givemore Building Society

Address Peartree House, 1 Little Road,
Southtown, Herts
EN3 8LX

Telephone No. 01876-2389	Fax No. 01876-2468

3. As directed in panel 8 of Form FR1, the following documents are to be issued to the person named in panel 2 above *(for ease of completion, reference can be made to the item number only)*

Charge Certificate

4. Documents lodged

Notes   (i)   Number the documents in sequence; copies should also be numbered and listed as separate documents.
         (ii)   The "retain" column is for official use only. If the Land Registry places an asterisk "*" in this column, it shows that they have kept that document.

Item No(i)	Date	Document	Parties	Retain(ii)
1.	1968	Abstract of Title		
2.	27.4.99	Conveyance	(1) Albert Francis Brown (2) Elizabeth Mary Green	
3.	27.4.99	Copy Conveyance		
4.	27.4.99	Charge	(1) Elizabeth Mary Green (2) Givemore Building Society	
5.	27.4.99	Copy Charge		

Land Charges Searches

It is essential to carry out a search of the Land Charges Register at Plymouth if land is not registered with the Land Registry. The Land Charges Register is computerised and has records of charges and interests which may be registered against a particular owner of land. The Land Charges search is normally carried out within 15 days before completion. A solicitor acting for a building society or other lender must carry out a bankruptcy only search in the Land Charges Register to check that the purchaser is solvent, whether the land is registered or not.

Form K15 is completed to make a full search. The form must specify the precise name of the person being searched against, the district and the period of years to be covered. Where the form mentions 'former county', this is to be completed if the name of the county has been changed, or if the property is now in a different county, e.g., where county boundaries may have been changed. The fee earner will provide you with any necessary information. A search is usually made against present owners and sometimes previous owners. Make sure you enter the names to be searched against exactly as requested on the form, taking care that the surname is entered on the correct line of the form. This is extremely important. You should use the names as shown on the title documents or however the fee earner specifies, always ensuring that they are correctly typed: the name entered on the form is the name that will be searched against. If there is any doubt about how a person's name is set out, for example, whether double barrelled or not, then an extra search should be applied for, covering each possibility. This applies to all variations of names, such as abbreviations or change of name. Each name must be entered separately on the form and should be in capital letters. If a person is titled, or the name being searched against is a company or other organisation, the form must be completed in accordance with the instructions laid down by the Land Registry. These instructions can be found in a booklet which is available from the Land Charges Department, and gives full instructions on all aspects of completing the form.

Search forms are normally sent through the post and do not need an accompanying covering letter, but a note must be made on the file to show that the search has been done. It is best to keep a photocopy on your file. See below for information on making Land Charges searches in person or by fax, telephone, or telex. A fee per name searched against is payable. Postal or hand delivered searches may be paid for by cheque (payable to HM Land Registry), postal order, money order or credit account. See also page 282 regarding key numbers and credit accounts.

If the result of a search shows an entry, the Purchaser's solicitor will send it to the Vendor's solicitor, asking if the entry does in fact relate to the property in question. Often it will not, and the Vendor's solicitor will certify on the search result form that the entries do not relate to that property. If further information is required relating to an entry which has been revealed, an application may be made on Form K19.

Bankruptcy only Searches

A solicitor acting for a building society or other lender may carry out a bankruptcy only search in the Land Charges Register to check that the potential borrower is solvent. This application is made on Form K16 and is similar to K15, except that it requires only the names to be searched to be inserted on the form. However, if a full search on form K15 is made, a bankruptcy only search is not necessary because a full search includes a bankruptcy search.

The Land Charges Department will return the result of the search on a form which will reveal any subsisting entries or will state that there are none.

Form K15

SPECIMEN

Land Charges Act 1972

APPLICATION FOR AN OFFICIAL SEARCH

NOT APPLICABLE TO REGISTERED LAND

Application is hereby made for an official search in the index to the registers kept pursuant to the Land Charges Act 1972 for any subsisting entries in respect of the under-mentioned particulars.

Payment of fee

Insert a cross (X) in this box if the fee is to be paid through a credit account (see Note 3 overleaf)

[X]

IMPORTANT: Please read the notes overleaf before completing this form

For Official Use only		NAMES TO BE SEARCHED (Please use block letters and see Note 4 overleaf)		PERIOD OF YEARS (see Note 5 overleaf)	
STX				From	To
	Forename(s)	ALBERT FRANCIS		1994	1999
	SURNAME	BROWN			
	Forename(s)	MARY		1994	1999
	SURNAME	BROWN			
	Forename(s)	MARY		1994	1999
	SURNAME	WHITE			
	Forename(s)				
	SURNAME				
	Forename(s)				
	SURNAME				
	Forename(s)				
	SURNAME				

COUNTY (see Note 6 overleaf)	HERTFORDSHIRE
FORMER COUNTY	
DESCRIPTION OF LAND (see Note 7 overleaf)	76 BURNT OAK ROAD MORELAND, EN7 8CB
FORMER DESCRIPTION	

Particulars of Applicant (see Notes 8, 9 and 10 overleaf)		Name and Address (including postcode) for despatch of certificate (Leave blank if certificate is to be returned to applicant's address)
KEY NUMBER	Name and address (including postcode)	
12345	PETER WOLF & CO RED RIDING HOOD LANE NORTHTOWN ESSEX 1CD 3LA	

Applicant's reference: PW/74	Date *	FOR OFFICIAL USE ONLY

Land Charges Searches in Person

Personal applications for full searches may be made to the Land Charges Department during the hours of 11.00 am to 3.00 pm. The applicant will be able to see the result of the search on the Land Charges operator's computer terminal screen, up to a maximum of 25 entries against one name. However, if a personal application is made, no certificate is issued by the Land Charges Registry at the time of the search — it will be posted in Form K17 or K18 to the address supplied by the applicant. Personal applications must be paid for by cash or credit account.

Telephone, telex and fax searches and those by direct computer access can only be made where solicitors have a credit account with the Land Charges Registry. The solicitor has a reference number to quote, known as a 'key number' (see page 282). If you make a search other than by post, do *not* write to confirm it.

The Land Charges Department is at Drake's Hill Court, Burrington Way, Plymouth, Devon, PL5 3LP (General enquiries, tel: (01752) 635600) and applications may be made only on weekdays.

Land Charges Searches by Fax

Certain applications may be made by fax and these are as follows:

(a) Application for a full or bankruptcy only search on Form K15 or K16.
(b) Application for an office copy of an entry in a register on Form K19.

Applications by fax may be made between 9.00 am and 5.00 pm on Mondays to Fridays on fax number Plymouth (01752) 766666 and must be paid by credit account.

The result of the search or office copy will be sent to the applicant by post.

Land Charges Searches by Telephone

Telephone applications for full searches or bankruptcy only searches may be made from 10 am to 4 pm by telephoning Plymouth (01752) 635635. Applications for office copies may only be made by telephone if it transpires that there is an entry whilst a search is being conducted by telephone. The procedure is as follows:

(a) Dial the correct number
(b) When the operator answers, give your key number, together with the name and address of the firm.
(c) Give your firm's reference — the maximum number of digits allowed is 10, including punctuation. This will be printed on the certificate.
(d) The operator will ask if you require a full search or a bankruptcy only search.

If a full search is required, give particulars of the first search to be done, in the following order:

(i) County (and any former county).
(ii) Name to be searched — forename and then surname.
(iii) Period in whole years to be covered by the search.

If a bankruptcy only search is required, the only particulars needed are the names to be searched.

If there are 10 or less entries, the operator will read them out over the telephone. If there are more than 10, the operator will state this but will not read them out. If there are more than 100 entries the operator will ask for a short description of the land (and any former description). If an entry is disclosed you can ask for an office copy of that entry.

The Land Charges Registry will post the certificate (on Form K17 or K18) and any office copies. They will be sent only to the firm making the application. Form K17 shows that there is no entry on the Register. Form K18 shows details of any entry.

Land Charges Searches by Telex

Telex applications for full searches may be made during the hours of 9 am to 5 pm. The fee must be paid through a credit account. The telex number for such applications is 45545 (Answer back LANDCHG). There will be no telex reply — the certificate in Form K17 or K18 will be sent by post to the applicant.

A telex message should take the following form (each item must be on a separate line in double spacing in the order given below):

(a)   Your firm's answer back code and telex No. — show the date in brackets.
(b)   The word 'SEARCH'.
(c)   The first name to be searched. Forenames should be shown first and be separated from the surname by an oblique stroke.
(d)   Type the letters 'PD' followed by the period to be searched for the first name. The years should be typed in numbers for the inclusive period to be covered by the search and should be separated by the word 'TO'.
(e)   Items (c) and (d) above should be repeated on separate lines for each additional name to be searched.
(f)   The letters 'CO' followed by the county. If there is a former county it should be typed on the same line and be put in brackets.
(g)   If you are giving a short description of the land the letters 'DES' should be typed on the next line followed by the description. If there is a former description it should be typed on the next line in brackets.
(h)   On the next line type the letters 'KN' followed by your firm's key number.
(i)   Type the letters 'REF' followed by your firm's reference. The maximum number of digits allowed is 10, including punctuation, and this will be shown on the certificate of the result of search. It is important to include the reference otherwise there may be difficulty in finding who is dealing with the matter when the certificate is sent to your firm.

Example

TO: LANDCH PLYM

FROM: SMITH JON   12345   (27/04/99)

           SEARCH

           PETER SAMUEL/JONES

PD.   1991 TO 1999

CO.   GREATER LONDON (HERTFORDSHIRE)

DES.   2 RAILWAY CUTTINGS, BARNET

           (PLOT 17 RAILWAY ESTATE, BARNET)

KN.   1786542

REF: ABC/123/TY

Application for office copy entries may also be made by telex in a similar format to that shown above, but for the exact layout and further details on all Land Charges Department searches, you should consult their booklet called 'Computerised Land Charges Department — A Practical Guide for Solicitors'.

Leases

In some transactions, the deed must be engrossed in duplicate, so that when the transaction has been completed, each party holds a copy executed by the other. A Lease, which is a document granting occupancy of property for a specified time in exchange for a sum of money or rent, is normally dealt with in this way, the documents being known as the 'original' and 'counterpart'. A Lease is often a long document and the layout of one page only is shown in the example here. You will see each paragraph is numbered and normally the first word of each paragraph, along with certain other key words, are typed in capital letters and perhaps underlined. For further information on the layout of documents and attestation clauses, see Chapter 1.

The owner of the property is the Landlord or Lessor, and the person to whom he grants the occupancy of the property is the Tenant or the Lessee. A person holding a Lease may wish to sell his rights in it to another person. This is called 'assigning the lease' and the document is called an Assignment. The original landlord is then called Head Lessor or Superior Landlord and the document he holds is the Head Lease or Superior Lease. The person who is assigning the Lease is the Assignor, Vendor or Seller, and the person taking it is the Assignee or Purchaser.

Payment of rent under a lease is usually made on the 'usual quarter days'. These are 25 March, 24 June, 29 September and 25 December.

CONVEYANCING

Example lease

THIS LEASE is made the   day of   2000 B E T W E E N JOSEPH BLOGGS of 123 North Road Southtown in the County of Essex Salesman (hereinafter called the 'Lessor' which expression where the context so admits includes the owner or owners for the time being of the reversion immediately expectant on the term hereby granted) of the one part and JEAN SMITH of 234 South Road Northtown in the County of Essex Waitress (hereinafter called the 'Lessee' which expression shall where the context so admits include her successors in title) of the other part

NOW THIS DEED WITNESSES as follows:

1.   THE Lessor hereby demises unto the Lessee ALL THAT ground floor flat known as 22A Seventeen Street Northtown aforesaid (hereinafter called the 'property') TO HOLD the same unto the Lessee for the term of eighteen years from the   day of   2000 YIELDING AND PAYING therefor during the said term the yearly rent of FIVE THOU-SAND THREE HUNDRED POUNDS (£5300) free of all deductions by equal quarterly payments on the usual quarter days in every year the first of such payments to be made on the   day of   2000

2.   THE Lessee hereby covenants with the Lessor as follows

(1)   TO PAY the said rent free of all deductions at the times and in the manner aforesaid

(2)   TO PAY all rates taxes assessments charges and outgoings which are now or shall during the said term become payable in respect of the property

IN WITNESS of which this deed has been executed on the first date before written

Signed as a deed by   )
JOSEPH BLOGGS in the   )
presence of:)

Signature of witness ....
Name (in BLOCK CAPITALS) ....
Address ....

....

Signed as a deed by   )
JEAN SMITH in the   )
presence of:)

Signature of witness ....
Name (in BLOCK CAPITALS) ....
Address ....

....

DATED   2000

JOSEPH BLOGGS

to

JEAN SMITH

LEASE

of

Flat 22A Seventeen Street
Northtown Essex

Peter Wolf & Co.,
Red Riding Hood Lane,
Northtown,
Essex

tel: 01234 5678
ref: PW/89

NHBC Agreement

This is another document you may come across in a conveyancing transaction. A body called the National House Building Council (NHBC) was set up some years ago to protect house Purchasers from, among other things, bad workmanship of builders who subsequently became insolvent. Most reputable building firms are now registered members of the NHBC and in fact building societies will not normally lend money on a new property unless the builder is registered as a member of the NHBC.

The NHBC Scheme gives a ten-year warranty to Purchasers and the newest scheme is called the Buildmark Scheme. If the first Purchaser sells his property then subsequent Purchasers are still covered by the scheme until its cover ends. Any documents relating to the NHBC should be kept with the deeds to the property.

Enfranchisement

This is a term you may come across. It applies mainly to houses (rather than flats) which are leasehold. It is not appropriate to go into this too deeply here, except to say that, broadly speaking, to 'enfranchise' land means that a lessee may, under certain circumstances, have the right to buy the freehold of the land or renew the lease for an extra 50 years on advantageous terms.

Public Sector Housing

You may also meet the expression 'public sector housing'. This relates to housing where, for example, the landlord is a local authority, a housing corporation or certain other specified public body. Under certain circumstances, persons renting such housing have the right to buy their house or flat at a discounted price.

Business Premises

Leasing of business premises varies in some instances from the way in which matters relating to dwellinghouses are dealt with.

Business leases, i.e., for factories, shops, offices, etc., are usually for relatively short terms. There is often no purchase price as the property is let out at a full market rent for a set period of years. There is often no contract. The parties agree on the rent and terms of the tenancy — known as 'heads of agreement'. If the tenant has to carry out all the maintenance on the property, this is known as a 'full repairing lease'.

Business tenancies can be terminated under the Landlord and Tenant Act 1954 (see section on Landlord and Tenant in Chapter 3).

Mortgages

Most people buying property take out a loan or 'mortgage' with a building society, bank or other financial institution. In some cases, a local authority will lend money, especially if the property in question belongs to the council and is being sold to the tenant. A mortgage is also known as a 'legal charge'.

There are several types of mortgage available, e.g., repayment mortgage, endowment mortgage, pension mortgage, and often the terms of individual mortgages will vary depending on any special incentives offered by the lender or other factors taken into consideration.

Building Society's Panel of Solicitors

Solicitors acting for a Purchaser will also often act for the building society which is providing the mortgage. The solicitor must normally be on the building society's 'panel'. This means that the building society has approved that firm of solicitors to act for it in dealing with mortgages. Most firms dealing in conveyancing are on most national building societies' panels.

Offer of Advance

The building society will usually carry out its own survey on the property to be purchased. Once the building society (the 'mortgagee') is happy that the property is suitable to lend money on, and its enquiries about the person to whom it is lending money (the 'mortgagor') are satisfactory, it will make an 'offer of advance' to the mortgagor, i.e., an offer to lend him an amount of money using the property in question as security. This offer of advance is sent to the mortgagor and to his solicitors.

Once contracts have been exchanged, the building societies (both those of the Vendor and the Purchaser) are informed by their respective solicitors of the completion date.

Building Society Forms

After exchange of contracts, the Vendor's solicitors will request a redemption statement from the building society, i.e., a statement showing how much money is required to pay off the outstanding mortgage on the completion date. Then when the completion monies are received from the Purchaser's solicitors, the Vendor can account to the building society for outstanding monies and thus redeem his mortgage. The building society's redemption statement will also show the daily rate of interest due in case there is a delay in completion. Also, after exchange of contracts, the Purchaser's solicitors report to the building society on a form provided by the building society, known as the Report on Title. This is to assure the building society that title to the property is satisfactory and that there are no adverse obligations or covenants affecting the property.

The building society reference relating to the mortgage is also called a roll number and must be quoted in all correspondence with the building society. The mortgage deed also has to be completed and signed by the mortgagor. This, with the title deeds, once it has been returned by the Land Registry bound inside the Charge Certificate, will be held by the building society until the mortgage has been repaid.

Paying off the Mortgage

When someone wishes to sell his property, he must pay off any mortgage or 'redeem' or 'discharge' it. The solicitors acting for the borrower will complete the appropriate form, usually Land Registry Form DS1, and send it, together with the cheque if the money has not already been remitted, to the lender to sign or seal the form by way of receipt. You should ensure that a copy is kept on the file before it is posted. The form will then be returned to the borrower's solicitors and this is proof that the mortgage has in fact been settled. However, the form cannot be signed by the lender until it knows that the money has been paid (usually this will be after the sale has been completed). Therefore, the Vendor's solicitors will undertake to the Purchaser's solicitors to obtain this form duly executed (signed and/or sealed) from the lender and then forward it on to the Purchaser's solicitors.

Where the only transaction taking place is the paying off of a mortgage, and there is no sale or purchase to consider nor anything else that would normally be required to be registered with the Land Registry, Form DS2 (application to cancel entries relating to a registered charge) will be completed and sent to the Land Registry.

**Cancellation of entries
relating to a
registered charge**

*This form should be accompanied
by either Form AP1 or Form DS2.*

HM Land Registry

DS1

SPECIMEN

(if you need more room than is provided for in a panel, use continuation sheet CS and staple to this form)

1. Title Number(s) of the Property	HD 12345
2. Property	76 Burnt Oak Road, Moreland, Hertfordshire EN7 8CB
3. Date	*
4. Date of charge	7th July 1994
5. Lender	Givemore Building Society

6. The Lender acknowledges that the property is no longer charged as security for the payment of sums due under the charge.

7. Date of Land Registry facility letter *(if any)*

8. *To be executed as a deed by the lender or in accordance with the above facility letter.*

```
[The appropriate attestation clause will
 be inserted here, and a large red seal
 will be stuck on the right-hand side of
 the page, where appropriate.]
```

OYEZ The Solicitors' Law Stationery Society Ltd, Oyez House, 7 Spa Road, London SE16 3QQ   1.98 F34687
5061291

DS1/DS2

CONVEYANCING

Sending the Deeds to the Building Society

After completion has taken place, the mortgage deed is lodged with the Land Registry for registration at the same time as the other title deeds are lodged (see page 304). The Land Registry will return it bound inside the Charge Certificate.

Once this is received by the Purchaser's solicitors, they must send all the deeds to the building society, usually listed on a printed schedule form provided by the building society with copies (one copy being kept in the file). A schedule can also be typed on plain A4 paper. The deeds are listed on the schedule in date order starting with the oldest date first, giving details of what the document is and the parties to it (see example). The building society will receipt and date a copy and send it back to the solicitors. Each firm has its own way of posting deeds — some are insured when sent through the post. It is best to check the system used in your own firm.

Where there is a Land or Charge Certificate, this would be listed last on the schedule, giving the title number of the property. If the purchase deed, e.g., a Transfer, is dated the same date as a mortgage deed, the purchase deed would be listed before the mortgage deed. Where an insurance policy document is included in the schedule, the policy number should be quoted. If one of the documents listed in the schedule is a copy, this should be stated, otherwise it will be assumed that the document is an original. Three copies of the schedule are normally prepared: two would be sent to the building society or other lender with the deeds and one would be kept on your file. As well as including the building society's reference (the roll number) on the schedule, you should ensure that your own firm's reference is on the schedule, so that when the receipted schedule is returned to your office, it will not get lost.

Example

Schedule of Deeds and Documents

relating to

2 Railway Cuttings, Barnet, Herts.

1.	7th July 1949	Conveyance	J. Bloggs and P. Smith (1) A. Plodd (2)
2.	7th July 1949	Mortgage	Southtown Building Society Ltd (1) A. Plodd (2)
3.	1999	Abstract of Title	
4.	29th December 1999	Conveyance	A. Plodd (1) B. Gunn (2)
5.	5th May 2000	Transfer	B. Gunn (1) B. Ware (2)
6.		Various search forms	

Received the above documents the   *   day of   *   2000

(Signed).....................

MIRAS

You may come across the initials 'MIRAS'. Mortgages up to a certain amount are eligible for some tax relief on the interest. Repayments of mortgages at that rate are paid to the lender net of basic tax rate. This system is known as MIRAS — Mortgage Interest Relief At Source. Any tax relief due on a higher mortgage is given through the mortgagor's tax office by tax codings or notice of assessment. However, over the last few years MIRAS has gradually been phased out and will be abolished in April 2001.

Second Mortgage

You may often come across people taking out a second mortgage on their property. This is to obtain a further loan since taking out the first mortgage.

Insurance Policies

Insurance policies are often taken out at the same time as a mortgage. This is to protect the building society or other lender (the 'mortgagee') in case the mortgagor dies before the mortgage has been repaid. If this unfortunate event does not occur and once the mortgage is finally repaid, the insurance policy will often provide for a lump sum to be paid to the insured person. This type of insurance policy is different from the insurance policies taken out to cover the property itself.

National Conveyancing Protocol

This is a scheme which may be used on a voluntary basis by solicitors when dealing with domestic conveyancing matters. It is designed to speed up conveyancing procedures and make those procedures easier for clients to understand. Although the scheme, which is known as TransAction, is not compulsory, most solicitors are registered with the Law Society as potential users of it. The scheme uses the terms 'Buyer' and 'Seller', rather than 'Purchaser' and 'Vendor'.

Solicitors involved in domestic conveyancing must notify the solicitors acting for the other party whether they will be using the Protocol and, if so, whether the whole transaction will be carried out under the Protocol, or just part of it. Once the Protocol is in use for a particular transaction, any departure from it must be notified in writing to the other party.

For those firms who are users of the scheme, some of the forms and documents used are different from those mentioned earlier. The idea of TransAction is to do away with lengthy questions and answers between the Buyer and Seller — this system uses questionnaires and information forms where, in many cases, all that is required is the ticking of a box. Part II of a Seller's Information Form is shown here to give you an idea as to what the TransAction forms look like. Part I of the Seller's Property Information Form is sent to the Seller by his solicitors. It asks the Seller to give information affecting the property, such as information on the property boundaries, disputes, guarantees for work carried out, any jointly shared costs and other relevant information which may affect the property. This completed form is sent to the Buyer's solicitors.

Briefly, if the Protocol is to be adopted, the Seller's solicitor puts together as much information about the property as possible so that as soon as a buyer is found, the solicitor can send a prepared package of information to the Buyer's solicitor. This package will contain such documents as a draft contract, office copy entries, the Seller's Property Information Form (Part I and Part II), the relevant form giving details of fixtures and fittings which are included in the sale and, if the property concerned is leasehold, a copy of the lease, together with details of insurance, maintenance charges, etc. Notification should also be given of the Seller's anticipated date for completion. The Seller's solicitor should also supply details about the Seller's own sale, provided he has consent to divulge this information. At the same time, the Buyer's solicitor should be asked whether the Buyer will be paying a 10% deposit. The sale will continue to completion using, where appropriate, the TransAction forms.

If you do find you are working under this scheme, you will easily get used to a few things being done at different stages and the different forms being used. Forms for local searches, etc. are still the same.

Further information on the Protocol scheme is available from the Law Society.

SPECIMEN

SELLER'S PROPERTY INFORMATION FORM

Part II – to be completed by the seller's solicitor and to be sent with Part I

Address of the Property:

A | Boundaries

Does the information in the deeds agree with the seller's reply to 1.1 in Part I?

Please tick the right answer

YES	NO (PLEASE GIVE DETAILS)

B | Relevant Documents

Are you aware of any correspondence, notices, consents or other documents other than those disclosed in Questions 3 or 4 of Part I?

YES	NO

C | Guarantees

If appropriate, have guarantees been assigned to the seller and notice of an assignment given?

YES	NO	NOT KNOWN

If "Yes", please supply copies, including copies of all guarantees not enclosed with Part I of this Form.

D | Services

Please give full details of all legal rights enjoyed to ensure the benefit of uninterrupted services, e.g. easements, wayleaves, licences, etc.

Prop 2/1

CONVEYANCING

SPECIMEN

E | Adverse Interests

Please give full details of all overriding interests
affecting the property as defined by the Land
Registration Act 1925, s.70(1).

F | Restrictions

Who has the benefit of any restrictive covenants?
If known, please provide the name and address of
the person or company having such benefit or the
name and address of his or its solicitors.

G | Mechanics of Sale

Please tick the right answer

(a) Is this sale dependent on the seller buying
another property?

YES	NO

(b) If "Yes", what stage have the negotiations
reached?

(c) Does the seller require a mortgage?

YES	NO

(d) If "Yes, has an offer been received and/or
accepted or a mortgage certificate obtained?

YES	NO

H | Deposit

Will the whole or part of the deposit be used on a
related transaction?

NO	YES (PLEASE GIVE DETAILS)

If so, please state to whom it will be paid and in
what capacity it will be held by them.

Seller's Solicitor ....

Date...

Reminder
1. The Fixtures, Fittings and Contents Form should be supplied in addition to the information above.
2. Copies of all planning permissions, buildings regulations consents, guarantees, assignments and notices should
   be supplied with this form.
3. If the property is leasehold, also complete the Seller's Leasehold Information Form.

Prop 2/2

THE LAW SOCIETY

This form is part of The Law Society's TransAction scheme © The Law Society 1994.
The Law Society is the professional body for solicitors in England and Wales.
The Solicitors' Law Stationery Society Ltd, Oyez House, 7 Spa Road, London SE16 3QQ

OYEZ   3.98   F34963
         5065063
         ★ ★

Prop 2

Forms

Forms are often sent without a covering letter. In these cases, you must note your file in some way to show exactly what form went out and when, together with a note of any fee paid. Some people make a note on the file and others keep a photocopy of the form. It is worth remembering that the Land Registry uses the DX system (see page 16) and therefore if your firm is on the DX you should give your DX number in the address box on the Land Registry forms. It is essential that forms go to the correct district Land Registry.

Many forms are now electronically produced within firms either by using software they have purchased or their own forms which have been approved by the Land Registry, rather than completing forms which have been individually purchased. Where Land Registry forms have been produced electronically, the plural may be used instead of the singular and the singular instead of the plural. A considerable number of forms are used in conveyancing — more than can be mentioned here — but once you have the ability to complete those which have been mentioned here and you have grasped conveyancing terminology, you have more than won the battle. Also, there are often helpful notes on forms to assist with their completion. The Land Registry is currently in the process of revising its forms and the new forms are being introduced in phases. You will, therefore, encounter them as and when it becomes necessary to use them.

Test yourself on Chapter 12

Test your knowledge by completing this assignment. If you find that you have difficulty with anything, read the chapter again until you are happy with your answers. There are several forms for you to complete with this assignment. Use the following information to complete the forms.

Assume that the land is registered freehold property unless otherwise stated. If a date is required on a form and you would normally insert the date before posting it, insert the date you are actually completing the form. No plan of the property is necessary for questions in this assignment.

Michael Peterson lives at 77 Copenhagen Hill, Ashton, Hertfordshire P38 6PQ. He is selling this house to Miss Joanne Howard. His solicitors are: Ryan Loganberry & Co., of 13 High Road, Ashton, Hertfordshire (tel: 01834 5863; ref: RL/MP/266). Their DX number is 3821 Ashton. The property is mortgaged to the Greenback Building Society, Moneypenny Road, Farthingdale, Suffolk FG4 38H, the roll number with the building society being 27/3864-474. The Title Number of the property is LB 1234. It has been agreed that the purchase price of the property will be £190,000. Additionally, carpets and curtains will be sold for a total of £500.

The local authority is the Ashton District Council. Their DX number is 434 Ashton.

Miss Joanne Howard is buying Mr Peterson's house. She lives at 54 Leamington Road, Ashton, Hertfordshire, AH3 5PQ. Her solicitors are: Greg Pottersbury & Co., of 15 Sticklepath Row, Ashton, Hertfordshire, AH5 6PQ (tel: 01834 555789; ref: GP/JH). Their DX number is 5986 Ashton and their key number for their credit account with the Land Registry is 67417.

Assume that after all the formalities have been completed, completion of the sale/purchase takes place by a deed of Transfer (for purposes of this assignment, choose any date about a month ahead of when you are answering the relevant question).

1. The first pages only of the forms necessary for making local searches are reproduced here. Complete these using the details given above. How many copies of these forms would you send to the local authority and how would you find out how much any fee payable to the local authority might be? Why would you be making local searches?
2. What is a Land Certificate and what does it contain?
3. What is the purpose of writing on certain correspondence the words 'Subject to Contract'?
4. Prepare, as far as you are able, the draft contract for this transaction.
5. Complete as far as possible the form TR1, including the attestation clause.
6. Complete form 94A (making sure you know why you are doing it).
7. How is it decided how much stamp duty is payable on a particular transaction? Complete the PD form.
8. If you have to make a Land Charges search by telephone, what is the procedure?
9. Complete the application for an Official Search relating to unregistered land (Form K15). What differences are there between this form and the form for an application for a bankruptcy only search?

10. Form DS1 will have to be signed by Michael Peterson's solicitors to prove that he has paid off his mortgage on the property he is selling. Complete the appropriate form as far as you can.
11. Explain what is the National Conveyancing Protocol.
12. Now go through the chapter and if there are any words that are unfamiliar to you or that you cannot spell, write or type them correctly several times until you feel you know them.

Form LLCl. (*Local Land Charges Rules 1977 Schedule 1, Form C*)

**The duplicate of this form must also be completed:
a carbon copy will suffice.**

For directions, notes and fees see overleaf.

Insert name and address of registering authority in space below

Official Number_____
(*To be completed by the registering authority*)

SPECIMEN

Register of local land

charges

Requisition for search

and official certificate

of search

Requisition for search

(*A separate requisition must be made in respect of each parcel of
land except as explained overleaf*)

fold

An official search is required in *Part(s)*_____*of* [1]
the register of local land charges kept by the above-named
registering authority for subsisting registrations against the land
[defined in the attached plan and] [2] described below.

Description of land sufficient to enable it to be identified

Name and address to which certificate is to be sent

Signature of applicant (*or his solicitor*)

Date

Telephone number

Reference

Enclosure
Cheque/Money Order/Postal Order/Giro

Official certificate of search

To be completed by authorised officer

It is hereby certified that the search requested above reveals
no subsisting registrations [3]

or the_____registrations described in the Schedule
hereto [3] up to and including the date of this certificate.

Signed..

On behalf of...[4]

Date

---

1 Delete if inappropriate. Otherwise insert Part(s) in which
search is required.

2 Delete if inappropriate. (A plan should be furnished
in duplicate if it is desired that a copy should be returned.)

3 Delete inapplicable words. (The Parts of the Schedule should
be securely attached to the certificate and the number of
registrations disclosed should be inserted in the space provided.
Only Parts which disclose subsisting registrations should be sent.)

4 Insert name of registering authority.

CON. 29 (1994)
To be submitted in duplicate

SPECIMEN

ENQUIRIES OF LOCAL AUTHORITY
(1994 EDITION)

Please type or use BLOCK LETTERS

Search No.................................
The Replies are given on the attached sheet(s)

Signed ....
Proper Officer

Date...

A.
To

B.
Property

C.
Other roadways, footpaths and footways

D.
A plan in duplicate is attached   YES/NO

Optional Enquiries are to be answered (see Box G)   YES/NO

Additional Enquiries are attached in duplicate on a
separate sheet   YES/NO

E.
Fees of £   are enclosed.

Signed :

Date :

Reference :

Tel. No. :

F.
Reply to

A. Enter name and address of District or Borough Council for the area. If the property is near a Local Authority boundary, consider raising certain Enquiries (e.g. road schemes) with the adjoining Council.

B. Enter address and description of the property. A plan in duplicate must be attached if possible and is insisted upon by some Councils. Without a plan, replies may be inaccurate or incomplete. A plan is essential for Optional Enquiries 18, 37 and 38.

C. Enter name and/or location of (and mark on plan, if possible) any other roadways, footpaths and footways (in addition to those entered in Box B) for Enquiry 3 and (if raised) Enquiries 19 and 20.

D. Answer every question. Any additional Enquiries must be attached on a separate sheet in duplicate and an additional fee will be charged for any which the Council is willing to answer.

E. Details of fees can be obtained from the Council or The Law Society.

F. Enter name and address of the person or firm lodging this form.

G. Tick which Optional Enquiries are to be answered.

PLEASE READ THE NOTES ON PAGE 4.

G.
Optional Enquiries

17.	Road proposals by private bodies
18.	Public paths or byways
19.	Permanent road closure
20.	Traffic schemes
21.	Advertisements
22.	Completion notices
23.	Parks and countryside
24.	Pipelines
25.	Houses in multiple occupation
26.	Noise abatement
27.	Urban development areas
28.	Enterprise zones
29.	Inner urban improvement areas
30.	Simplified planning zones
31.	Land maintenance notices
32.	Mineral consultation areas
33.	Hazardous substance consents
34.	Environmental and pollution notices
35.	Food safety notices
36.	Radon gas precautions
37.	Sewers within the property
38.	Nearby sewers

AGREEMENT
(Incorporating the Standard Conditions of Sale (Third Edition))

Agreement date :

Seller :

Buyer :

Property
(freehold/leasehold) :

Root of title/Title Number :

Incumbrances on the Property :

Title Guarantee
(full/limited) :

Completion date :

Contract rate :

Purchase price :

Deposit :

Amount payable for chattels :

Balance :

The Seller will sell and the Buyer will buy the Property for the Purchase price.
The Agreement continues on the back page.

WARNING	Signed
This is a formal document, designed to create legal rights and legal obligations. Take advice before using it.	*SPECIMEN* Seller/Buyer

SPECIAL CONDITIONS

1. (a) This Agreement incorporates the Standard Conditions of Sale (Third Edition). Where there is a conflict between those Conditions and this Agreement, this Agreement prevails.

    (b) Terms used or defined in this Agreement have the same meaning when used in the Conditions.

2. The Property is sold subject to the Incumbrances on the Property and the Buyer will raise no requisitions on them.

3. Subject to the terms of this Agreement and to the Standard Conditions of Sale, the Seller is to transfer the property with the title guarantee specified on the front page.

4. The chattels on the Property and set out on any attached list are included in the sale.

5. The Property is sold with vacant possession on completion.

(or) 5. The Property is sold subject to the following leases or tenancies:

SPECIMEN

Seller's Solicitors   :

Buyer's Solicitors   :

©1995 **OYEZ**   The Solicitors' Law Stationery Society Ltd,
Oyez House, 7 Spa Road, London SE16 3QQ

© 1995 **THE LAW SOCIETY**

1.97 F33188
5065046
3rd Edition

Standard Conditions of Sale

Transfer of whole
of registered title(s)

HM Land Registry

TR1

(if you need more room than is provided for in a panel, use continuation sheet CS and staple to this form)

SPECIMEN

---

1. Stamp Duty

Place "X" in the box that applies and complete the box in the appropriate certificate.

☐ I/We hereby certify that this instrument falls within category ☐ in the Schedule to the Stamp Duty (Exempt Instruments) Regulations 1987

☐ It is certified that the transaction effected does not form part of a larger transaction or of a series of transactions in respect of which the amount or value or the aggregate amount or value of the consideration exceeds the sum of

£

---

2. Title Number(s) of the Property *(leave blank if not yet registered)*

---

3. Property

If this transfer is made under section 37 of the Land Registration Act 1925 following a not-yet-registered dealing with part only of the land in a title, or is made under rule 72 of the Land Registration Rules 1925, include a reference to the last preceding document of title containing a description of the property.

---

4. Date

---

5. Transferor *(give full names and Company's Registered Number if any)*

---

6. Transferee **for entry on the register** *(Give full names and Company's Registered Number if any; for Scottish Co. Reg. Nos., use an SC prefix. For foreign companies give territory in which incorporated.)*

Unless otherwise arranged with Land Registry headquarters, a certified copy of the transferee's constitution (in English or Welsh) will be required if it is a body corporate but is not a company registered in England and Wales or Scotland under the Companies Acts.

---

7. Transferee's intended **address(es) for service in the U.K.** *(including postcode)* **for entry on the register**

---

8. The Transferor transfers the property to the Transferee.

---

9. Consideration *(Place "X" in the box that applies. State clearly the currency unit if other than sterling. If none of the boxes applies, insert an appropriate memorandum in the additional provisions panel.)*

☐ The Transferor has received from the Transferee for the property the sum of *(in words and figures)*

☐ *(insert other receipt as appropriate)*

☐ The Transfer is not for money or anything which has a monetary value

P.T.O.

10. The Transferor transfers with *(place "X" in the box which applies and add any modifications)*

☐ full title guarantee ☐ limited title guarantee

11. Declaration of trust *Where there is more than one transferee, place "X" in the appropriate box.*

☐ The transferees are to hold the property on trust for themselves as joint tenants.

☐ The transferees are to hold the property on trust for themselves as tenants in common in equal shares.

☐ The transferees are to hold the property *(complete as necessary)*

12. Additional Provision(s) *Insert here any required or permitted statement, certificate or application and any agreed covenants, declarations, etc.*

13. *The Transferors and all other necessary parties should execute this transfer as a deed using the space below. Forms of execution are given in Schedule 3 to the Land Registration Rules 1925. If the transfer contains transferees' covenants or declarations or contains an application by them (e.g. for a restriction), it must also be executed by the Transferees.*

SPECIMEN

OYEZ The Solicitors' Law Stationery Society Ltd, Oyez House, 7 Spa Road, London SE16 3QQ

1.99 F35917
5061088
★ ★ ★ ★ ★

CONVEYANCING

Application by **Purchaser**[(a)] for **Official Search with priority of the whole of the land in either a registered title or a pending first registration application**

HM Land Registry

SPECIMEN

Form

94A

Land Registration (Official Searches) Rules 1993

District Land Registry [(b)]

Small raised letters in **bold** type refer to explanatory notes overleaf.

Please complete the numbered panels

1 **Title number** (one only per form) - enter the title number of the registered land or that allotted to the pending first registration.

2 **Registered proprietor(s) / Applicant(s) for first registration**[(c)] - enter FULL name(s) either of the registered proprietor(s) of the land in the above title **or** of the person(s) applying for first registration of the land specified in panel 8.

SURNAME / COMPANY NAME:

FORENAME(S):

SURNAME / COMPANY NAME:

FORENAME(S):

3 **Search from date** - for a search of a **registered title** enter in the box a date falling within (a) of the definition of search from date in rule 2(1).[(d)]
Note: If the date entered is not such a date the application may be rejected. In the case of a **pending first registration** search, enter the letters 'FR'.

4 **Applicant(s)** - enter FULL name of each purchaser, **or** lessee **or** chargee.

5 **Reason for application** - I certify that the applicant(s) intend(s) to:- (enter X in the appropriate box)

| P | purchase | L | take a lease of | C | take a registered charge on |

(enter X in the appropriate box)

☐ the **whole** of the land in the above registered title **or**

☐ the **whole** of the land in the pending first registration application referred to above.

6 Enter the key number[(e)] (if any) and the name and (DX) address of the person lodging the application (use **BLOCK LETTERS**).

Key number: ☐☐☐☐☐☐☐

Name:

DX No: DX Exchange:

Address including postcode (if DX not used):

Reference: [(f)]

7 Enter, using BLOCK LETTERS, the name and either address (including postcode) OR (if applicable) the DX No and exchange of the person to whom the result is to be sent. (**Leave blank if result is to be sent to the address in panel 6.**)

Reference: [(f)]

8 **Property details**
Administrative area [(g)]

Address (including postcode) or short description:

9 **Type of search** (enter X in the appropriate box)

☐ **Registered land search**
Application is made to ascertain whether any adverse entry[(h)] has been made in the register or day list since the date shown in panel 3 above.

☐ **Pending first registration search**
Application is made to ascertain whether any adverse entry has been made in the day list since the date of the pending first registration application referred to above.

10 **PAYMENT OF FEE** [(i)]

Please enter X in the appropriate box.

☐ The Land Registry fee of £ [   ] accompanies this application; **or**

☐ Please debit the Credit Account mentioned in panel 6 with the appropriate fee payable under the current Land Registration Fees Order.

Note: If the fee is not paid by either of the above methods the application may be rejected.

Signature

Date   Telephone

338

**PARTICULARS OF INSTRUMENTS
TRANSFERRING OR LEASING LAND**

SPECIMEN

SECTION 28 FINANCE ACT 1931
as amended by the Land Commission Act 1967
and Section 89 Finance Act 1985

1. Description of Instrument

2. Date of Instrument

3. Name and address of Transferor or Lessor *(Block Letters)*

4. Name and address of Transferee or Lessee *(Block Letters)*

5. Situation of the land. Sufficient information must be given to enable the land to be identified accurately, e.g., by including any dimensions stated in the instrument and by attaching a plan to this form or by describing the boundaries in full. For premises the full postal address including the post code is required   Please indicate whether a plan is provided in the appropriate box.

Plan Attached Yes ☐

Plan Attached   No ☐

COUNTY .... RATING AUTHORITY ....

6. Estate or Interest Transferred. Where the transaction is the assignment or grant of a lease, or the transfer of a fee simple subject to a lease, the terms of the lease, the date of commencement of the term and the rent reserved must be stated.

7. Consideration   State separately:

(a) any capital payment, with the date when due if otherwise than the execution of instrument:

(b) does the consideration stated include a charge to VAT

Yes/No

If Yes please state the amount paid:

(c) any debt released, covenanted to be paid or to which the transaction is made subject:

(d) any periodical payment (including any charge) covenanted to be paid:

(e) any terms surrendered:

(f) any land exchanged:

(g) any other thing representing money or money's worth:

8. Any Minerals, Mineral Rights, Sporting Rights, Timber or Easements reserved: (on a separate sheet if necessary)

9. Any Restrictions, Covenants or Conditions affecting the value of the estate or interest transferred or granted: (on a separate sheet if necessary)

10. Signature of Transferee or Lessees or person on his behalf:

.... Date ....

11. Name and Address of the Transferor's or Lessor's Solicitor: *(Block Letters)*

12. Name, Address and Telephone Number of Signatory if other than Transferee or Lessee: *(Block Letters)*

STAMPS L(A) 451   (3/95)

Form K15

Land Charges Act 1972

Payment of fee

Insert a cross (X)
in this box
if the fee is
to be paid through a
credit account
(see Note 3 overleaf)

APPLICATION FOR AN OFFICIAL SEARCH

NOT APPLICABLE TO REGISTERED LAND

Application is hereby made for an official search in the index to the registers kept pursuant to the Land Charges Act 1972 for any subsisting entries in respect of the under-mentioned particulars.

SPECIMEN

IMPORTANT: Please read the notes overleaf before completing this form

For Official Use only			NAMES TO BE SEARCHED (Please use block letters and see Note 4 overleaf)	PERIOD OF YEARS (see Note 5 overleaf)	
				From	To
STX					
		Forename(s)			
		SURNAME			
		Forename(s)			
		SURNAME			
		Forename(s)			
		SURNAME			
		Forename(s)			
		SURNAME			
		Forename(s)			
		SURNAME			
		Forename(s)			
		SURNAME			

COUNTY (see Note 6 overleaf)

FORMER COUNTY

DESCRIPTION OF LAND (see Note 7 overleaf)

FORMER DESCRIPTION

Particulars of Applicant (see Notes 8, 9 and 10 overleaf)		Name and Address (including postcode) for despatch of certificate (Leave blank if certificate is to be returned to applicant's address)
KEY NUMBER	Name and address (including postcode)	

Applicant's reference:	Date	FOR OFFICIAL USE ONLY

Cancellation of entries relating to a registered charge

This form should be accompanied by either Form AP1 or Form DS2.

HM Land Registry **DS1**

SPECIMEN

(if you need more room than is provided for in a panel, use continuation sheet CS and staple to this form)

1. Title Number(s) of the Property
2. Property
3. Date
4. Date of charge
5. Lender
6. The Lender acknowledges that the property is no longer charged as security for the payment of sums due under the charge.
7. Date of Land Registry facility letter *(if any)*
8. *To be executed as a deed by the lender or in accordance with the above facility letter.*

DS1/DS2

13 FORMS OF ADDRESS

Secretaries may have to write letters to people of title or rank and this chapter deals with forms of address for members of the judiciary, e.g., a High Court judge. Everyone mentioned in this chapter is not necessarily mentioned otherwise in the book. For more information and other forms of address there are a number of books on etiquette.

How to end a letter is not shown below because nowadays the form of 'Yours faithfully' or 'Yours sincerely' is nearly always used for those mentioned here, according to whether it is a formal or social matter and this is perfectly acceptable. However, for those wishing to stick to the older rules of etiquette for peers, etc., there are other ways of ending a letter to such persons but these are not gone into here as it is not essential. When addressing correspondence to a peer it is best to check whether he is, for example, 'Lord Bloggs' or 'Lord Bloggs of Northshire'. His correct title should be used and if you are not sure about this, a glance in *Who's Who* should help you. If there is further doubt about this or any other matter relating to the form of address to be used, you should telephone the appropriate clerk or secretary, usually to be found at the Royal Courts of Justice in London when it concerns a member of the judiciary.

Lord Chancellor

His proper title is the Lord High Chancellor of Great Britain and he is the chief judicial officer.

Address the envelope to: The Rt. Hon. the Lord Chancellor

Letter:
    Salutation (instead of
    'Dear Sir'):   Formal matters: My Lord
                              Social matters: Dear Lord Chancellor

If he holds a different rank in the peerage, he will be addressed accordingly. Do not put the letters QC after his name. The Lord Chancellor's Department is at the House of Lords.

Lord Chief Justice of England

He is head of the judges in the Queen's Bench Division and also presides over the Court of Appeal (Criminal Division).

Address the envelope to: The Rt. Hon. the Lord Chief Justice of
                                                                England

Letter:
    Salutation: Formal matters: My Lord
                                       Social matters: Dear Lord Chief Justice

If he holds a different rank in the peerage, he will be addressed accordingly. Do not put the letters QC after his name.

Master of the Rolls

He presides over the Court of Appeal (Civil Division). As with some other appointments (President of the Family Division and Vice-Chancellor; see below), he is usually a knight on appointment and is often created a peer after appointment. He should be addressed according to his rank. If you are not sure about this, telephone the Royal Courts of Justice in London who should be able to assist.

President of the Family Division

He presides over the Family Division of the High Court. See under 'Master of the Rolls' above for further information.

Vice-Chancellor

He presides over the Chancery Division of the High Court. See under 'Master of the Rolls' above for further information.

Lords of Appeal in Ordinary

They preside over appeals relating to judicial matters in the House of Lords. They are created peers for life. Do not use the letters QC after their name.

Lords Justice of the Court of Appeal

They sit in the Court of Appeal with the Master of the Rolls. Do not put the letters QC after their name.

Address the envelope to: The Rt. Hon. Lord Justice Bloggs

Salutation: Formal matters: My Lord
                                      Social matters: Dear Lord Justice

A retired Lord Justice is addressed as, for example, 'The Rt. Hon. Sir John Bloggs'.

High Court judge

Address the envelope to:

Formal and
judicial matters: The Hon. Mr Justice Bloggs
Social matters: Sir John Bloggs

Salutation:

Formal matters: Dear Sir, or Sir
Judicial matters: My Lord
Social matters: Dear Judge (do not use his name)

Do not use the letters QC after his name.

Female High Court judge

Address the envelope to:

Formal matters: The Hon. Mrs Justice Bloggs
Social matters: Dame Jane Bloggs

Salutation:

Formal matters: Dear Madam, or Madam
Social matters: Dear Dame Jane

Do not use the letters QC after her name.

Retired High Court judge

Address the envelope to:

All matters: Sir John Bloggs

Salutation:

Formal matters: Dear Sir, or Sir
Social matters: Dear Judge (do not use his name)
If slightly
acquainted: Dear Sir John Bloggs

Circuit judge

In this instance the letters QC should be used after the name in correspondence, if appropriate.

Address the envelope: All matters: His (or Her) Honour Judge Bloggs

If there is more than one Circuit judge of the same name at the same address, the forename may be added in brackets.

If he has been knighted
Address the envelope to:

Formal matters: His Honour Judge Sir John Bloggs
Social matters: Sir John Bloggs

Salutation:

Formal matters: Dear Sir, or Sir or Dear Madam, or Madam
Social matters: Dear Judge

Retired Circuit judge

Address the envelope:	All matters:	His Honour John Bloggs, or Her Honour Jane Bloggs
If knighted:		His Honour Sir John Bloggs
Salutation:	Formal matters: Social matters:	Dear Sir, Sir, or Madam Dear Mr Bloggs or Dear Mrs Bloggs or Dear Judge

Recorders

Address the envelope:	All matters:	J. Bloggs, Esq.
Salutation:	Formal matters: Official matters: Social:	Dear Sir, or Sir Dear Mr Recorder Ordinary form of address or according to his rank.

Senior District judge of the Principal Registry of the Family Division

Address the envelope:	Senior District Judge, Principal Registry of the Family Division
Salutation:	Dear Judge

District judge

Address the envelope:	District Judge Bloggs
Salutation:	Dear Judge

Barristers

If a barrister is a QC, the letters QC are placed after his name whilst he is still at the Bar. A barrister is no longer referred to as a 'barrister-at-law' but simply a 'barrister'. See also page 79 as to instructing barristers.

Other

Most other legal persons, such as magistrates and coroners, are addressed in the ordinary way. A Justice of the Peace may have the letters 'JP' after his name.

References to Judges

The correct way of referring to a judge in a document intended to be read by lawyers is shown in the following examples:

(a)	The Lord Chancellor	Lord Irvine of Lairg LC
(b)	The Lord Chief Justice	Lord Bingham of Cornhill CJ
(c)	The Master of the Rolls	Lord Woolf MR
(d)	The President of the Family Division	Sir Stephen Brown P
(e)	The Vice-Chancellor	Sir Richard Scott V-C
(f)	Two or more Court of Appeal judges	Bloggs and Jones LJJ
(g)	Court of Appeal judge	Bloggs LJ
(h)	Two or more High Court judges	Bloggs and Jones JJ
(i)	High Court Judge (i.e., those from the Queen's Bench, Chancery and Family Divisions)	Bloggs J
(j)	Circuit and County Court judge	Judge Bloggs

When two or more judges have the same surname, they should be referred to by their first name and their surname, e.g., Joseph Bloggs LJ, Peter Bloggs LJ. If a Deputy Judge is being referred to, the name and position held are used, e.g., Mr Joseph Bloggs QC (sitting as a Deputy High Court Judge). A retired Court of Appeal judge is referred to by name, e.g., Sir Joseph Bloggs. If the judge is a peer, he is referred to as such, e.g., Lord Woolf.

When judges are referred to in a document drafted for non-lawyers to read, abbreviations of position should not be used; the document should say, e.g., Mr Justice Bloggs.

With regard to members of the House of Lords, if the member is, for example, Lord Bloggs of Northshire, this is his correct name and he should (at least the first time he is mentioned) be referred to as such, and not just as Lord Bloggs.

See also page 36 on addressing judges in court.

Legal Documents

When a person of a certain rank is a party to a legal document he or she should be described in the document in such a way as to show his or her rank or title, e.g., 'The Most Noble John Joseph Duke of . . . . .'. At the end of the document where their name is typed for signature, their rank or title should also be shown. *Butterworth's Encyclopaedia of Forms and Precedents* is very helpful in this and it sets out how certain ranks and titles should be described in legal documents. Similarly, *Atkin's Court Forms* (Butterworths (2nd edn)) gives the correct titles of parties to an action, i.e., the correct way to describe certain parties when they become involved in a court action, e.g., Bank of England, a building society, local authority, peers of the realm, police forces and many more. Both of these publications consist of several volumes and to find which volume contains a particular topic, look in the Index volume under, e.g., 'PARTY', 'PARTIES' or 'PARTY TO ACTION'. This will then refer you to the appropriate part of the volume you need.

ADDRESSES AND TELEPHONE NUMBERS

ACAS (Advisory Conciliation and Arbitration Service).
There are various local and regional offices where telephone numbers can be found in local telephone directories.

AC Legal Secretarial Training
e-mail: aclegalsec@yahoo.com   07930-273641
(For details of legal secretarial courses run by the author)

Accountant General of the Supreme Court,
(See under Royal Courts of Justice Funds Office)

Births, Deaths and Marriages (certificates)
General Register Office

Postal applications:
Office for National Statistics,
Postal Applications Section,
Smedley Hydro,
Trafalgar Road,
Southport PR8 2HH   01704-563563

Personal applications:
Office for National Statistics,
Family Records Centre,
1 Myddleton Street,
London EC1 1RU

British Association of Lawyer Mediators,
The Shooting Lodge,
Guildford Road,
Sutton Green,
Guildford GU4 7PZ   01483-235000

Capital Taxes Office,
Ferrer's House,
P. O. Box 38,
Castle Meadow Road,
Nottingham NG2 1BB   0115-9742400
DX 701201 Nottingham 4

ADDRESSES AND TELEPHONE NUMBERS

Capital Taxes Office,
16 Picardy Place,
Edinburgh EH1 3NB   0131-524 3000

Capital Taxes Office,
Level 3,
Dorchester House,
52–58 Great Victoria Street,
Belfast BT2 7QL   01232-505353

Central London County Court,
13-14 Park Crescent,
London W1N 4HT
DX 97325 Regents Park 2   0171-917 7920

Centre for Dispute Resolution,
Princes House,
95 Gresham Street,
London EC2V 7NA   0171-600 0500

Charity Commission,
Harmas House,
13–15 Bouverie Street,
London EC4Y 8DP   0870–3330123

Chartered Institute of Arbitrators,
International Arbitration Centre,
24 Angel Gate,
City Road,
London EC1V 2RS   0171-837 4483

Child Support Agency,
(There are various offices
throughout the country.)   0345-133 133 (National Enquiry Line)

Companies House

Companies House,
Crown Way,
Cardiff CF4 3UZ   01222-388588

Companies House,
37 Castle Terrace,
Edinburgh EH1 2EB   0131-535 5800

Companies House,
21 Bloomsbury Street,
London WC1B 3XD   01222-380801

There are also Companies House regional centres in Birmingham, Manchester, Leeds and Glasgow.

Court of Protection,
Stewart House,
24 Kingsway,
London WC2B 6JX   0171-664 7000

Criminal Cases Review Commission,
Alpha Tower,
Suffolk Street Queensway,
Birmingham,
West Midlands B1 1TT   0121-633 1800

Criminal Injury Compensation Authority,
Tay House,
300 Bath Street,
Glasgow G2 4JR
DX GW 379 Glasgow   0141-331 2726

Crown Prosecution Service,
50 Ludgate Hill,
London EC4M 7EX   0171-273 3000

Delia Venables,
10 Southway,
Lewes,
E. Sussex BN7 1LU
e-mail: delia@venables.co.uk   01273-472424

DVLA,
Customer Enquiries (Drivers),
Swansea
SA6 7JL   01792-772151

DVLA
Customer Enquiries (Vehicles)
Swansea
SA99 1BL   01792-772134

Employment Appeal Tribunal,
Audit House,
58 Victoria Embankment,
London EC4Y 0DS   0171-273 1041

Employment Tribunals
There are various regional offices throughout the country.
Enquiry line: 0345-959775

ADDRESSES AND TELEPHONE NUMBERS

Equal Opportunities Commission,
Overseas House,
Quay Street,
Manchester M3 3HN   0161-833 9244

Fair Trading, Office of
Field House,
15-25 Bream's Buildings,
London EC4A 1PR   0171-211 8000

Financial Services Authority,
25 The North Colonnade,
London E14 5HS   0171-676 1000

Home Office,
50 Queen Anne's Gate,
London SW1H 9AT   0171-273 3000

Inland Revenue,
Stamps & Adjudication Office,
Room 35, Ground Floor,
East Block,
Barrington Road,
Worthing,
West Sussex BN12 4XJ
DX 3799 Worthing 1   01903-700222

Land Charges Department,
HM Land Registry,
Drake's Hill Court,
Burrington Way,
Plymouth PL5 3LP   01752-635600
DX 8249 Plymouth 3

District Land Registries

Birkenhead (Rosebrae) District Land Registry,
Rosebrae Court,
Woodside Ferry Approach,
Birkenhead,
Merseyside L41 6DU
DX 24270 Birkenhead 4   0151-472 6666

Birkenhead (Old Market) District Land Registry,
Old Market House,
Hamilton Street,
Birkenhead,
Merseyside L41 5FL
DX 14300 Birkenhead 3   0151-473 1110

Coventry District Land Registry,
Leigh Court,
Torrington Avenue,
Tile Hill,
Coventry CV4 9XZ   01203-860864 (Enquiries)
DX 18900 Coventry 3   01203-860860

Croydon District Land Registry
Sunley House,
Bedford Park,
Croydon CR9 3LE   0181-781 9103 (Enquiries)
DX 2699 Croydon 3   0181-781 9100

Durham (Boldon House) District Land Registry,
Boldon House,
Wheatlands Way,
Pity Me,
Durham DH1 5GJ
DX 60860 Durham 6   0191-301 2345

Durham (Southfield House) District Land Registry,
Southfield House,
Southfield Way,
Durham DH1 5TR
DX 60200 Durham 3   0191-301 3500

Gloucester District Land Registry,
Twyver House,
Bruton Way,
Gloucester GL1 1DQ
DX 7599 Gloucester 3   01452-511111

Harrow District Land Registry,
Lyon House,
Lyon Road,
Harrow,
Middx. HA1 2EU
DX 4299 Harrow 4   0181-235 1181

Kingston-upon-Hull District Land Registry,
Earle House,
Portland Street,
Hull HU2 8JN
DX 26700 Hull 4   01482-223244

Lancashire District Land Registry,
Birkenhead House, East Beach,
Lytham St Annes,
Lancs FY8 5AB
DX 14500 Lytham St Annes 3   01253-849849

ADDRESSES AND TELEPHONE NUMBERS

Leicester District Land Registry,
Westbridge Place,
Leicester LE3 5DR
DX 11900 Leicester 5

0116-265 4001 (Enquiries)
0116-265 4000

Lytham District Land Registry,
Birkenhead House,
East Beach,
Lytham St Annes,
Lancs. FY8 5AB
DX 14500 Lytham St Annes 3

01253-849849

Nottingham (East) District Land Registry,
Robins Wood Road,
Nottingham NG8 3RQ
DX 716126 Nottingham 26

0115-906 5353

Nottingham (West) District Land Registry,
Chalfont Drive,
Nottingham NG8 3RN
DX 10298 Nottingham 3

0115-935 1166

Peterborough District Land Registry,
Touthill Close,
City Road,
Peterborough PE1 1XN
DX 12598 Peterborough 4

01733-288288

Plymouth District Land Registry,
Plumer House,
Tailyour Road,
Crownhill,
Plymouth PL6 5HY
DX 8299 Plymouth 4

01752-636123 (Enquiries)
01752-636000

Portsmouth District Land Registry,
St Andrew's Court,
St Michael's Road,
Portsmouth,
Hants. PO1 2JH
DX 83550 Portsmouth 2

01705-768888

Stevenage District Land Registry,
Brickdale House,
Swingate,
Stevenage,
Herts. SG1 1XG
DX 6099 Stevenage 2

01438-788889 (Enquiries)
01438-788888

Swansea District Land Registry,
Tŷ Bryn Glas,
High Street,
Swansea SA1 1PW
DX 33700 Swansea 2   01792-458877

Telford District Land Registry,
Parkside Court
Hall Park Way,
Telford TF3 4LR
DX 28100 Telford 2   01952-290355

Tunbridge Wells District Land Registry,
Forest Court,
Forest Road,
Tunbridge Wells,
Kent TN2 5AQ
DX 3999 Tunbridge Wells 2   01892-510015

Weymouth District Land Registry,
Melcombe Court,
1 Cumberland Drive,
Weymouth,
Dorset DT4 9TT
DX 8799 Weymouth 2   01305-363636

York District Land Registry,
James House,
James Street,
York YO10 3YZ
DX 61599 York 2   01904-450000

Wales The District Land Registry for Wales,
Tŷ Cwm Tawe,
Phoenix Way,
Llansamlet,
Swansea SA7 9FQ   01792 355095 (Enquiries)
DX 82800 Swansea 2   01792-355000

Land Registry Headquarters
H.M. Land Registry,
Lincoln's Inn Fields,
London WC2A 3PH
DX 1098 London/Chancery Lane   0171-917 8888

Law Society,
113 Chancery Lane,
London WC2A 1PL
DX 56 Lon/Ch'ry Ln WC2   0171-242 1222

ADDRESSES AND TELEPHONE NUMBERS

Legal Aid Offices

Legal Aid Board Head Office,
85 Gray's Inn Road,
London WC1X 8AA
DX 450 London   0171-813 1000

London/Brighton Group

London
29-37 Red Lion Street,
London WC1R 4PP
DX 170/Chancery Lane   0171-813 5300

Brighton
3rd & 4th Floors,
Invicta House,
Trafalgar Place,
Brighton BN1 4FR
DX 2752 Brighton   01273-699622

North East Group

Newcastle
Eagle Star House,
Fenkle Street,
Newcastle-upon-Tyne NE1 5RU
DX 61005 Newcastle-u-Tyne   0191-2323461

Leeds
City House,
New Station Street,
Leeds LS1 4JS
DX 12068 Leeds 1   0113-2442851

North West Group

Manchester
2nd Floor,
Elisabeth House,
16 St Peter's Square,
Manchester M2 3DA
DX 14343 Manchester 2   0161-228 1200

Chester
2nd Floor,
Pepper House,
Pepper Row,
Chester CH1 1DW
DX 19981 Chester   01244-315455

Liverpool
Cavern Court,
8 Matthew Street,
Liverpool L2 6RE
DX 14208 Liverpool   0151-236 8371

Midlands Group

Birmingham
Centre City Podium,
5 Hill Street,
Birmingham B5 4UD
DX 13041 Birmingham 1   0121-632 6541

Nottingham
1st Floor,
Fothergill House,
16 King Street,
Nottingham NG1 2AS
DX 10035 Nottingham 1   0115-9559600

Cambridge
Kett House,
Station Road,
Cambridge CB1 2JT
DX 5803 Cambridge   01223-366511

Wales and the West Group

Bristol
33–35 Queen Square,
Bristol BS1 4LU
DX 7852 Bristol   01179-214801

Cardiff
Marland House,
Central Square
Cardiff CF1 1PF
DX 33006 Cardiff   01222 388971

Reading
80 Kings Road,
Reading RG1 4LT
DX 4050 Reading 1   01189 589696

Lloyd's of London,
One Lime Street,
London EC3M 7HA   0171-327 1000

ADDRESSES AND TELEPHONE NUMBERS

Lloyd's Register of Shipping,
100 Leadenhall Street,
London EC3A 3BP   0171-709 9166

Mediation UK,
Alexander House,
Telephone Avenue,
Bristol BS1 4BS   0117-904 6661

Metropolitan Police Office,
New Scotland Yard,
Broadway,
London SW1H 0BG   0171-230 1212

Monopolies & Mergers Commission,
New Court,
48 Carey Street,
London WC2A 2JT   0171-324 1407

Motor Insurers Bureau,
152 Silbury Boulevard,
Central Milton Keynes MK9 1NB   01908-240000

Official Receiver,
21 Bloomsbury Street,
London WC1B 3SS   0171-637 1110

Official Solicitor,
81 Chancery Lane,
London WC2A 1DD
DX 0012 Lon/Ch'ry Ln WC2   0171-911 7127

Office for Supervision of Solicitors,
Victoria Court,
8 Dormer Place,
Royal Leamington Spa CV32 5AE
DX 292320 Leamington Spa 4   01926-822082

Ombudsman Association, British and Irish
70 Gray's Inn Road
London WC1X 8NB   0171-242 5713

Principal Registry of the Family Division,
First Avenue,
42-49 High Holborn,
London WC1V 6NP   0171-936 6000

Public Record Office,
Ruskin Avenue,
Kew,
Richmond TW9 4DU   0181-876 3444

Racial Equality, Commission for
Elliot House,
10/12 Allington Street,
London SW1E 5EH   0171-828 7022

The Registry Trust Ltd, (also known as The Registry of County Court Judgments)
173/175 Cleveland Street,
London W1P 5PE   0171-380 0133

Royal Courts of Justice,
Strand,
London WC2A 2LL
DX 44450 Strand WC2   0171-936 6000

Royal Courts of Justice,
Court Funds Office,
22 Kingsway,
London WC2B 6LE
DX 37965 Kingsway   0171-936 6000

Social Security, Department of
Richmond House,
79 Whitehall,
London SW1A 2NS   0171-238 0800 (General enquiries)

Stock Exchange, Council of the
Old Broad Street,
London EC2N 1HP   0171-588 2355

Summons Production Centre,
County Court Bulk Centre,
St Katherine's House,
21/27 St Katharine's Street,
Northampton NN1 2LH
DX 702886 Northampton 7   01604-601636

Treasury Solicitor,
Queen Anne's Chambers,
28 Broadway,
London SW1H 9JX
DX 123242 St James Park   0171-210 3000

USEFUL WEB ADDRESSES

ACAS   http://www.acas.org.uk/home__m.htm
Arbitrators, Chartered
  Institute of   http://www.arbitrators.org
Bank of England   http://www.bankofengland.co.uk
Bar Council   http://www.barcouncil.org.uk
BBC News   http://news.bbc.co.uk
Blackstone Press Limited   http://www.blackstonepress.com
Legal publishers
(and publishers of this
book)
Business Information
  Sources on the Internet   http://www.dis.strath.ac.uk/business
Business Information Zone   http://www.the biz.co.uk/default.htm
Links to UK relevant business
information.
CCTA Government
  Information Service   http://www.open.gov.uk
A good starting point for
anything Government related.
Numerous links through the
indexes maintained on this
site.
Chamber of Commerce,
  International   http://www.iccwbo.org
Charity Commission   http://www.open.gov.uk/charity/ccintro.htm
Child Support Agency   http://www.dss.gov.uk/csa
Companies House   http://www.companieshouse.gov.uk
Court Service   http://www.courtservice.gov.uk
Gives links to certain
judgments, Practice
Directions, and daily
lists. Many court forms
in an interactive format
can also be downloaded
from here.
Criminal Cases Review
  Commission   http://www.ccrc.gov.uk
Crown Prosecution Service   http://www.cps.gov.uk

Currency Converter   http://www.oanda.com/converter/classic
The OANDA site gives a quick
currency converter, as well as
currency rates on a daily basis
going back to 1990.

Data Protection Registrar   http://www.open.gov.uk/dpr/dprhome.htm

Date and Time Gateway   http://www.bsdi.com/date
Gives international time zones
so that you can tell what day
or time it is practically
anywhere in the world.

Delia Venables   http://www.venables.co.uk/legal
Extremely useful site with
links to all sorts of legal
resources.

Driver and Vehicle
   Licensing Agency
   (DVLA)   http://www.open.gov.uk/dvla/dvla.htm

Euro   http://www.euro.gov.uk
This is an official UK
Government site containing
information for businesses
about the euro. Includes links
to other sites where you can
download the euro symbol.

Euronews   http://www.euronews.net

Europa   http://www.europa.eu.int
Provides information and
links on European
institutions.

Evening Standard   http://www.standard.co.uk

Fair Trading (Office of)   http://www.oft.gov.uk

Financial Services
   Authority   http://www.sib.co.uk

Financial Times   http://www.ft.com

Health & Safety
   Executive   http://www.open.gov.uk/hse/hsehome.htm
Practical advice for employers
on safety at work.

HM Stationery Office
   (HMSO)   http://www.hmso.gov.uk

Home Office   http://www.homeoffice.gov.uk

Inland Revenue   http://www.inlandrevenue.gov.uk

ITN   http://www.itn.co.uk
News, weather, etc.

Land Registry   http://www.landreg.gov.uk

Law Society   http://www.lawsoc.org.uk

Legal Aid Board   http://www.open.gov.uk/lab/legal.htm

LLP (formerly Lloyd's of
   London Press)   http://www.llplimited.com

Lloyd's of London   http://www.lloydsoflondon.co.uk

USEFUL WEB ADDRESSES

Local Governments   http://www.gwydir.demon.co.uk/uklocalgov

London Underground   http://www.londontransport.co.uk

Here you can download and print out a tube map, plus lots of other useful information.

Lord Chancellor's Department   http://www.open.gov.uk/lcd/index.htm

As well as other information, you can download the CPR (see Chapter 3).

Marriage Support Agencies   http://www.open.gov.uk/lcd/family/marsup/famtxt.htm

Links to a variety of these.

Met Office   http://www.meto.govt.uk

The latest UK weather.

Metropolitan Police   http://www.met.police.uk/metfront.htm

Multi Media Mapping   http://uk.multimap.com

An interactive atlas of Great Britain where you can get a detailed map; as well as street names for the London area.

Newslink   http://ajr.newslink.org/news.html

Links to thousands of newspapers around the world.

Office of Fair Trading   http://www.oft.gov.uk

Official Solicitor   http://www.offsol.demon.co.uk

Ombudsman (British & Irish Ombudsman Association)   http://www.intervid.co.uk/bioa

Information and directory.

Oyez Straker   http://www.oyez.co.uk

Legal forms suppliers, business services, office supplies.

Parliament   http://www.parliament.uk

The UK Parliament site includes links to the House of Lords and House of Commons pages, and from these to legislation before Parliament, as well as other useful links and information.

Patent Office   http://www.patent.gov.uk

Public Record Office   http://www.pro.gov.uk

RAC   http://www.rac.co.uk

Provides the latest travel news, has a route planner, plus lots of other interesting information.

Racial Equality, Commission for   http://www.cre.gov.uk

Railtrack
Travel information on the
trains.

http://www.railtrack.co.uk

Royal Mail
Has a postcode finder and an
address finder as well as other
useful information.

http://www.royalmail.co.uk

Search engines
A selection of search engines
to help you find things on the
Internet.

http://www.altavista.digital.com
http://www.excite.com
http://www.infoseek.com
http://www.lycos.com
http://www.ukplus.com
http://www.yahoo.com

Searching
A couple of helpful sites
full of useful tips.

http://daphne.palomar.edu/TGSEARCH
http://www.monash.com/spidap.html

Social Security,
 Department of

http://www.dss.gov.uk

Stock Exchange, London

http://www.londonstockex.co.uk

Ticketmaster UK Ltd
Book tickets, search for
events.

http://www.ticketmaster.co.uk

The Times

http://www.the-times.co.uk

Treasury, HM

http://www.hm-treasury.gov.uk

United Nations
Links and news about the UN.

http://www.un.org

US House of
 Representatives
Access to their Internet law
library plus other links.

http://www.house.gov

World Trade Organisation

http://www.wto.org